Routledge Revivals

A History of Spain

Originally published in 1958, this was the first scholarly anglophone history of Spain. It covers the whole story from Spanish pre-history onwards and includes a full treatment of the various states until their fusion as a modern nation, and on through the Civil War until the late 20th Century. The book explains the origins and development of Spanish society and the special commitments which determined Spanish policies.

A History of Spain

Harold Livermore

First published in 1958 by George Allen & Unwin Ltd.

This edition first published in 2024 by Routledge
4 Park Square, Milton Park, Abingdon, Oxon, OX14 4RN

and by Routledge
605 Third Avenue, New York, NY 10158.

Routledge is an imprint of the Taylor & Francis Group, an informa business

© 1958 George Allen & Unwin Ltd.

The right of Harold Livermore to be identified as the author of this work has been asserted by him in accordance with sections 77 and 78 of the Copyright, Designs and Patents Act 1988.

All rights reserved. No part of this book may be reprinted or reproduced or utilised in any form or by any electronic, mechanical, or other means, now known or hereafter invented, including photocopying and recording, or in any information storage or retrieval system, without permission in writing from the publishers.

ISBN 13: 978-1-032-91395-7 (hbk)
ISBN 13: 978-1-003-56309-9 (ebk)
ISBN 13: 978-1-032-91400-8 (pbk)
Book DOI 10.4324/9781003563099

A HISTORY OF
SPAIN

BY

HAROLD LIVERMORE

Ruskin House
GEORGE ALLEN & UNWIN LTD
MUSEUM STREET LONDON

First Published in 1958

© *George Allen and Unwin Ltd.*, 1958

*Printed in Great Britain
in* 12 *pt. Aldine Bembo Type
by C. Tinling & Co. Ltd.,
Liverpool, London and Prescot*

CONTENTS

PART ONE

I.	ANTIQUITY	page	13
	1. Physical Spain		13
	2. The Formation of the Spanish Races		16
	3. 'Almerians' and Indo-Europeans		21
	4. 'Tartessian' and Semitic Spain		28
	5. Roman Spain		35
II.	VISIGOTHIC SPAIN		51
III.	THE MUSLIM ASCENDANCY		64
	1. The Conquest		64
	2. Asturias		69
	3. The Emirate		70
	4. The Resettlement		79
	5. The Western Caliphate		84
	6. The Leonese Empire		91
IV.	THE GREAT RECONQUEST		101
	1. The Formation of the Five Kingdoms		101
	2. Al-Andalus and Africa		118
	3. The Completion of the Reconquest		126
V.	MEDIAEVAL SPAIN—PART ONE		132
	1. Castile and Leon 1254-1368		132
	2. Aragon 1272-1412		147
	3. Navarre and the Basque Provinces		156
	4. Naṣrid Granada		158
VI.	MEDIAEVAL SPAIN—PART TWO		162
	1. Castile 1368-1474		162
	2. The Trastámaras in Aragon 1412-1479		176
VII.	FERDINAND AND ISABELLA		183

PART TWO

VIII.	THE HAPSBURGS—PART ONE page	207
	1. Charles I	207
	2. Philip II	230
	3. The New World	255
	4. Spain in the Sixteenth Century	265
IX.	THE LATER HAPSBURGS	285
X.	THE BOURBON RÉGIME	319
XI.	LIBERALISM	352
XII.	SPAIN AND THE SOCIAL AGE	402
	AFTERWORD	451
	INDEX	453

MAPS

1. Pre-Roman Spain	29
2. Roman Spain	36
3. The Reconquest	102
3a. Spain in the Middle of the 11th Century (inset)	102
4. Spain in the Middle of the 12th Century: The Five Kingdoms	127
5. The Struggle for the Straits and the Wars of Granada	184
6. Spain in the Hapsburg Age	266
7. Hapsburg Europe	304–305
8. Political Divisions of Modern Spain	403

PART ONE

I

ANTIQUITY

1. PHYSICAL SPAIN

THE general structure of physical Spain was already decided by the end of the Tertiary epoch. Long before the appearance of the higher animals, the Balearic islands were separated from the mainland; and its few volcanic areas, near Ciudad Real on the central meseta and Olot in the Catalan Pyrenees, had subsided into passivity. One fundamental change remained to be made. In the earliest shaping of things Europe and Africa were linked by a land-bridge uniting the two Pillars of Hercules. It lasted long enough for plants and animals to cross between the two land masses, and its breaching took place much before the last glaciation. When this, the first fact of Spanish history, had occurred, Spain had become a peninsula, and its evolution was for many millennia exclusively European.

Its limits were now perfectly distinct. The Pyrenees rose like a wall to mark it off from the rest of the continent, and its coast was clear and economical. In early times men were struck by the sharpness of its outline: Strabo compared it to a stretched ox-hide, and the metaphor of a rough, tawny surface lying taut and dry in the strong sun is an apt one. The Peninsula is in appearance self-contained and seems to stand aloof from the main mass of Europe. It stretches further south than Greece and as far west as all but the Atlantic fringe of Ireland. Only a minor part of its surface belongs to the Mediterranean, for excepting the deep incision of the Ebro valley, the watershed between sea and ocean lies far over to the east, and the vast tablelands of its interior are tilted gently towards the Atlantic, into which four of its five great rivers find their way. It is these semi-continental mesetas that rise like a breast of stone to distinguish the Peninsula from the rest of Europe. Their distant horizons and widely separated ranges with saw-edged silhouettes, the sierras, form a strong, uncompromising landscape full of austere beauty.

The rest of the Peninsula is at once more varied and less distinctive. The Atlantic north with its rounded forms and regular rainfall belongs to the same world as the extremities of Brittany or western Ireland, while the worn crests and cloudless skies of the Mediterranean south recall North Africa. The physical affinities of the two 'Pillars of Hercules' or 'Algarves'[1] are indeed striking. But Dumas' much-repeated phrase that 'Africa begins at the Pyrenees' is less than a half-truth. Even southern Spain bears no resemblance to the true ' green Africa', but only to its Mediterranean outskirt. The peninsula is indeed a potential zone of transition, and in this sense it recalls Syria: to Muslim visitors, Granada was the Spanish Damascus. But while in the east the Mediterranean ends in a complex interlocking of three landmasses, its western terminus is a simple channel now nine miles wide and of great depth, joining the central sea with the outer ocean, and making Europe begin at the northernmost of the twin Pillars.

The surface of Spain has continued to change. During the long ages of the Pleistocene it underwent successive waves of heat and cold, but because of its southerly latitude it escaped the more violent ordeals of continental Europe and its heights were covered with ice only during the final glaciation, while the interglacial periods of heat were correspondingly intense. During the last of these the coastal region of northern Spain enjoyed a climate not much different from that of modern Andalusia, which in turn was scorched by a tropical sun. The central mesetas suffered alternations of humidity and aridity: the highlands of Soria (now bitterly cold in winter) sheltered the European elephant from the sweltering heat of the south. Below this stretched a sub-tropical

[1] i.e. the 'two wests'.

vegetation of palms, and the hippopotamus survived in the rivers of Andalusia.

During the last glaciation the climate came to resemble that of central and northern Europe to-day. The northern Atlantic seaboard was as cold as the Scottish highlands, while the central meseta resembled Poland, with its short summer and long, severe winter. But nothing comparable with the ice-sheets of Scandinavia was known: there are few traces of glaciation outside the peaks of the Pyrenees and Cantabrians, the central ranges and the Sierra Nevada, and the glaciers of the latter range are comparatively undeveloped. The northern forests pushed their way southward, and the semi-tropical vegetation retreated to the Mediterranean coast where a milder climate resembling that of modern Provence or the Dalmatian seaboard persisted. Most of the tropical flora was eliminated, leaving only a few degenerate survivals in the south. The hippopotamus and southern elephant disappeared, while the woolly mammoth wandered over central Spain, and the northern reindeer advanced as far south as Catalonia.

The peak of the last glacial period probably occurred about twenty millennia ago, and its fauna, the mammoth, bison and moose, are depicted in cave-dwellings of the Magdalenian period. There followed a swing of the cosmic pendulum, and it seems probable that in historic times the climate of Spain has grown progressively warmer and drier. The gradual desiccation of North Africa, which converted a rolling parkland into a vast desert, became general only in late prehistoric or early historic times, and the northern migration of peoples from the Sahara contributed to the Berberisation of Roman Africa. A similar process of desiccation has occurred in south-eastern Spain, where within the last four millennia the temperate forest has receded northward, leaving only such plants as the dwarf-palm, sole survivors of a primitive tropical vegetation, to take its place. Much of the Sierra Nevada, now bare, was wooded in Roman times, and traces of ancient forests are still found in northern Granada. Not far away, in Almería, one of the most ancient cities in Spain, Los Millares, now stands on a bare and almost soilless hillside, which four thousand years ago must have yielded ample harvests and pasture for flocks. When this denudation took place it is still hard to say. Man has destroyed the primitive forest for agriculture, for mining and for domestic and industrial fuel, and the face of Spain has been further disfigured by deliberate devastation in time of war. But because of its attachment to the European continent northern Spain has altered less in historical times than the south and east. There the topographical setting of ancient civilisations has been largely modified: the gates of Los Millares still survive, but the capital of Tartessian civilisation appears to have been drowned in sand or water as the Guadalquivir has changed its estuary, while the Roman metal-port of Urci, still a flourishing pirates' nest a thousand years ago, is now far inland, and the anchorages where ancient ships rode are covered with dense groves of orange-trees. These, like the fig and wild-olive and the American agave and prickly-pear, are Man's contribution to a new landscape.

2. THE FORMATION OF THE SPANISH RACES

While physical Spain is thus the product of great changes in the Pleistocene, again modified in the Holocene, the indigenous peoples of the Peninsula find their remote origin in the middle Palaeolithic. In the immensity of the lower Palaeolithic Spain was sparsely populated by groups of Neanderthaloid hunters and food-gatherers. The earliest traces of these primitive stocks are in the Tagus valley in Portugal. In Spain itself the first known human groups are the elephant-hunters of Torralba (Soria), whose hand-axes belong to the Abbevillian culture extending over western Europe and North Africa. Not far away, the Madrid terraces show crude core-implements, the work of other pre-sapiens peoples, side by side with more refined blades and graving-tools devised by creatures much closer to modern man. The two races may have had a long parallel existence before the Neanderthaloid became extinct in the early stages of the last glaciation.

The new-comers, identified by the discovery of their remains at Crô-Magnon in the Dordogne, originated in Asia, spreading westwards round the Mediterranean. It seems improbable that they knew even the simplest type of raft or coracle which would have permitted them to enter Spain from Africa; and the first ancestors of modern man probably arrived, with the Aurignacian blade-culture, in both Spain and North Africa from a common origin.

Of the various Aurignacian stages, the first (Chatelperron) may not have reached the Peninsula; but the second passed through southern France and found its way into Spain at both ends of the Pyrenees, spreading as far afield as Santander in the north, and to Parpalló (Valencia) in the east. The third wave (Gravettian), taking its rise in south Russia, spread across Europe in the wake of its predecessor, and appears again at Santander and Parpalló and also at Burgos. These blade-cultures attained their highest development with the delicate Solutréan 'laurel-leaf', first achieved in Central Europe, and conveyed thence westwards into France and Spain. A centre of innovation had now moved into Europe, corresponding perhaps to the appearance of recognisably 'European' conditions. The perfected Solutréan blade seems to belong to a middle phase of the last glaciation and to have been the work of a broad-headed people accustomed to a cold steppe-like climate and skilled in hunting reindeer and the wild horse. From the intermingling of this stock with the existing Gravettian there arose the Magdalenian culture of southern France and northern Spain, with which Palaeolithic civilisation reached its climax, and the centre of innovation was transferred for the first time to western Europe.

Magdalenian culture is the earliest with which we can form any sort of contact, for it has left behind something more than the highly limited range of durable artefacts which alone permit its predecessors to be distinguished by their greater or less manual skill. The Magdalenians possessed efficient blades and scrapers and also bone needles with which they could make clothing of skins and wind-breaks to protect the mouths of their caves. They fed their fires with the bones of food-animals and stored their fuel apart from the cave-spaces in which they lived and from the recesses reserved for their magic. Testimony of a crude expression of abstract thought is found in upper Palaeolithic burials with daubings of ochre to simulate blood and thus recall the fluid warmth of life, and in gross female statuettes, the evidence of perplexity at the mysterious origin of existence. Already the Chatelperronians had made sketches alluding to their main activity, the chase. These had usually been outlines of animals, often with the heart drawn in and with weapons pointing at it, and sometimes with outspread hands clutching towards the victim. But the lasting achievement of the Magdalenians was to perfect these representations in the great cave-paintings of central France and northern Spain. In the most famous of the Spanish caves, Altamira (Santander), the animals are shown in an attitude of repose or death, and are drawn from dead models in soft reds, greys and blacks. The naturalism of the conception is enriched by a deft stylisation of details, and it is evident that the hand of the maker has attained complete control of its medium and that it is guided by a clear intelligence. The paintings are found in inner recesses set apart for magical ceremonies; and although in Spain the human figure is absent, an extraordinary drawing from Les Trois Frères in France shows the wizard identified with a stag and performing a weird dance, evidently a rite of hunting-magic. The Magdalenian has apprehended the force of wishful thinking which is the seed of faith and basis of religion: his hand, eye and mind are essentially those of modern man, and in the capering figure of Les Trois Frères we can already discern our own barbaric selves.

But Magdalenian man depended directly on glacial conditions. As the climate grew warmer the animals on which he lived went north or perished, and the successors of the people of Altamira were reduced to a more primitive way of life. In the Azilian culture the great hunting-magic has lost its effectiveness and given way to symbolic marks on small pebbles; and this in turn is replaced by a poor culture of food-gatherers in Asturias and Santander, whose middens are composed of limpets and cockles drawn from a warm sea, and whose implements are reduced to simple axes, scrapers and small picks for prising shellfish from rocks.

The 'capital' of Spanish Magdalenian civilisation is in Santander, though there are also sites in the centre and east, and one as far south as Benaoján, near Ronda. But this last is an outpost; Magdalenian culture is essentially temperate and northern. It has been boldly argued that the withdrawal of the Magdalenians at the end of the glacial period accounts for the scattering of pre-Indo-European races such as the Basques, Hungarians and Finns, whose languages appear to obey common, but otherwise forgotten, principles. It is indeed tempting to bridge the gap of a dozen millennia in this way, but all that can be said with confidence is that the Magdalenian gives a point of departure for a primitive pre-racial area uniting central France and northern Spain.

The origins of civilisation in southern Spain offer no comparable point of departure. The caves and rock-shelters of the south-east contain pictures of another type which suggest a different vision of life. These are not objective portraits of single dead animals, but whole scenes in which human shadow-figures are shown busily engaged in joint activities. There are crowded hunting-scenes, festive or ceremonial dances, the performance of feats such as tree-climbing in search of honey, and many others. The whole emphasis is social and extrovert, in contrast to the brooding introspection of Magdalenian art. Both styles appear to have their roots in magic, but the former points towards an individual and the latter towards a social view of religion.

South-eastern rock-paintings occur as far south as Tarifa, near Gibraltar, throughout the Sierra Morena and up the east coast, passing from Catalonia a little into France. They are not found elsewhere in Europe, but they bear a resemblance to the paintings of Palaeolithic Africa, as far away as Rhodesia and the Bushman country. These resemblances have suggested that the ancient culture of eastern Spain may be derived from Africa rather than from Europe. Rock-paintings in the Sahara appear to provide a link, but in Morocco and Algeria the only traces of similar work have been shown to belong not to the Palaeolithic, but to the Neolithic age. Nor is it easy to assign dates to Spanish south-eastern art, which occurs not in fully equipped caves, but often in shallow, empty shelters. Its very diversity indicates that it was produced over a long period of time, while other archaeological evidence suggests that there were no new influences in the south-east in Palaeolithic times, but that the old Abbevillian culture continued to reproduce itself with only small modifications caused by contact with Solutréan and Magdalenian peoples. These contacts may well have brought the northern hunting-magic to southern Spain; but the peoples of the south were not dependent on the northern bison. Their principal quarry was the more temperate deer, and as the cold climate receded they seem to have stood their ground. It would appear that the southern and eastern rock-paintings cover the slow evolution over several millennia of the primitive Palaeolithic peoples of the Peninsula, and that they therefore imply the growth of a distinctly Spanish society in a way which the Magdalenian, with its centre in France, scarcely does. These primitive 'Spaniards' depict themselves naked, or nearly so, but plumed, and they often carry a straight deer-spear. Large groups join in the hunt, and deploy in guerrilla style to drive or ambush their quarry. The women wear long bell-shaped skirts, which, if made of skins, point to some skill in cutting and sewing. Both sexes take part in ceremonial dances or rites. But apart from some inconclusive suggestions of the domestication of animals, there is no evidence of the attainment of any of the great advances of civilisation.

The flowering of Magdalenian culture coincides with the final period of the last glaciation, some sixteen millennia before Christ, and its heavy gravers and blades had given way to the small tools of the Spanish microlithic cultures by the thirteenth or soon after. As the ice-sheets retreated northwards and the warm phase came in, the Saharan area, hitherto a great grass plain, lost its rainfall and became gradually desiccated. This age of drought was probably relieved in the eighth or seventh millennia and only reached its extreme much nearer our own times. Nevertheless, the Mesolithic drought rendered much of the Sahara and of Arabia uninhabitable and confined the peoples of North Africa to the coastal region. In Spain itself survival was less difficult, but the cultures of the south and east tended now to migrate northwards, taking the 'Capsian' microlithic technique and traces of schematic art to the Pyrenees and the caves of the Cantabrian coast. But there is no new advance, and in Mesolithic times Spanish culture seems subdued, as if awaiting the great discoveries of the domestication of animals and farming which would liberate man from his original dependence on the benevolence of Nature. It was an age when peoples mingled and pooled their meagre skills, for amongst the Mesolithic middens of the Tagus estuary broad-headed and long-headed skulls lie side by side, buried under mounds of discarded shells. The life these people lived could have differed little from that of the peoples of the south-east. Both manufactured similar microliths, both stored their shell-fish in small pits, cooked them on hearths of beaten earth, and made similar implements and ornaments of shell and bone.

3. 'ALMERIANS' AND INDO-EUROPEANS

In contrast with the exceedingly slow development of Palaeolithic and Mesolithic man, the peoples of the Neolithic acquired within the space of some three millennia the crafts of basketwork and pottery (first discovered in the Mesolithic), the domestication of animals, the principles of agriculture, the building of houses and boats, the fabrication of cloth, the working of soft metals and finally the founding of bronze. The age of drought brought men and animals together in the fertile river valleys, where the lack of natural pasture caused men to sow primitive cereals, the forerunners of wheat and barley. Baskets lined with clay were used for carrying water, and the firing of the clay gave rise to the art of ceramics. The growth of small farming communities led to the development of building and the invention of new tools of stone and metal, while the perfection of basketry suggested the weaving of wool and eventually the spinning of flax to make cloth. Most of these discoveries were achieved in the sixth or fifth millennia in the 'fertile crescent' of the Near East, the original home of the sheep and of the earliest cereals. By the year 4000 the foundations of pre-dynastic civilisation had been laid in Egypt; and during the succeeding millennium the modern state emerged, with its specialists skilled in working wood and copper or in shipbuilding, its accumulation of resources and its medium for exchange, its formalisation of customs as laws, its ruler and its priesthood.

These extraordinary changes were too complex to be assimilated at once, and while they irradiated outward from the Near-Eastern focus where the three continental land-masses converge, there was a long period during which the simpler peoples of the west seemed to lag far behind. By 3000 Troy had been settled, and even earlier the first sea-power had been founded on the island of Crete. Yet in Europe agriculture had hardly begun to spread westwards from the Danube, and in North Africa the primitive inhabitants continued to pursue their traditional hunting life. But although they had no agriculture and probably no domesticated animals, they were ready to adopt the new stone axes and to acquire the technique of pottery. Thus by way of North Africa and by way of the Mediterranean, the periphery of Nilotic civilisation spread outwards until it finally touched the shores of south-eastern Spain, bringing a new life to the ancient cave-cultures of the west.

The first Neolithic axes and jars appear on the Almerían coast beside the native shell-middens. This region is the natural landfall for navigators arriving in the Peninsula from North Africa. It is possible that the African peoples or the marine gatherers of Spain itself had already developed a simple form of sea-faring that would enable the first-fruits of ancient civilisation to cross the Mediterranean as they came filtering through the primitive cultures of Algeria and Morocco. Whether or not this was so, the impact by which Spain was finally drawn into the orbit of Near Eastern civilisation was as dramatic as the arrival of the Spaniards themselves in Mexico. The people of El Gárcel, the earliest Almerían site, with their grain-pits, their swelling plainware jars and polished stone axes, were colonists and traders. By what course they came or where they started is still uncertain. Even if they arrived from North Africa they must have departed from somewhere in more direct contact with ancient Egypt. Eastern Sicily has a somewhat similar culture of colonists from the east, which is related to the final stages of early Cretan civilisation. If not Crete, some other offshoot of Nilotic culture must have given birth to the Aeneas who made this first conquest in Spain.

Almost certainly these new peoples were attracted to the Peninsula by the presence there of copper. The oldest Almerían sites (El Gárcel and Cabezos), reveal a purely Neolithic economy in which the use of copper is already known. The products of this industry are mingled with the microliths of the indigenous Spaniards, and the new-comers were evidently conquerors. They built villages on hill-tops and defended them with stone walls. Near them they laid out their necropolises, at first a mere trench as at Palaces, or a slab-cist under which a few bodies were deposited; but as the cists were extended they were covered with cairns, forming vaults in which the dead were buried with their ornaments and other possessions. These new funeral practices spread gradually northward up the Mediterranean coast, and by the middle of the third millennium Almerían plainware and graves with their furniture of shell-trinkets are found as far north as Catalonia and are beginning to enter France.

By now Almerían Spain was closely associated with the civilisation of the eastern Mediterranean. The 'new cities' of Los Millares and Almizaraque cover extensive areas, are stoutly walled, and possess strongly buttressed gateways. Around them spread slopes covered with wheat or barley, and flocks were kept in enclosures under the town walls. Also outside the walls lay impressive cemeteries of corbelled chambers covered with cairns and entered from a pit by a passage leading into an ante-chamber or portal of stone-slabs. These 'beehive huts' are the early Minoan tholoi, springing from a civilisation that has already diverged from the Egyptian, with its exaggeration of royal state, and is tending towards the collective or 'democratic' cultures of Greece. But while the group-burials of Los Millares, no less than the simple Almerían idols, are related to an Aegean mode of life, there is also evidence of contact with the Near East in objects of hippopotamus-tusk and beads of ostrich-egg shells, doubtless obtained in exchange for copper, gold and silver. Copper was commonly used for tools, and the site of Almizaraque shows that silver was separated from an argentiferous copper ore.

The indigenous peoples of the Peninsula now took over the heritage of Almerían civilisation or adapted it to their own resources. Leaving their caves and shelters, the peoples of the south and west began to clear such areas as the plains of the lower Guadalquivir for agriculture and stock-raising.

These changes do not necessarily imply any fundamental alteration of the existing human stock. The new-comers could not at first have been numerous, and their blood may soon have fused with that of the native peoples they ruled. The merchant-lords of Los Millares were probably already of mixed descent. Nor did the old cultures fail to make their contribution to the new civilisation. The pottery of Carmona and Palmela owes its fineness and variety to new influences, yet it derives also from the first plainware made by the peoples of the caves. The 'stab-and-drag' technique of Boquique which had spread outwards over much of the Peninsula gave rise to new forms of decoration by finger-printing, and these native wares were now perfected to produce the characteristic form of the bell-beaker, at first a high-waisted and round-bottomed pot decorated with rough zig-zag lines, but later evolving into a variety of open-necked vases and bowls skilfully adorned with patterned bands. By the end of the third millennium the bell-beaker had found its way to the western recesses of Galicia and was mingling with older forms in western Catalonia.

The spread of Almerían culture and of pastoral and agricultural modes of life led to the replacement of the old hunting-magic by new concepts of religion. The burial of seed and its annual resurrection suggested a similar revival of human life, and the dead were carefully supplied with what they might need for the hereafter. Hence the desire for funereal splendour which finds expression in the tombs of Antequera, and which extends westwards by the Sierra Morena, through Portugal and into Galicia. As Almerían culture spread, the corbelled vault made by laying convergent circles of stones and covering the top with a keystone, gave way to chambers built entirely of slabs. In the many tombs at Gor and Guadix (Granada) there are only about eight tholoi to 150 slab-tombs. Here the slab-tombs are smaller and poorer, but a little to the west at Antequera the slab-chambers attain megalithic proportions in the vast caves of Romeral and La Menga. Such massive constructions with heavy slab vaulting borne on monolithic columns could only be produced where a powerful social group devoted unusual skill and energy to the task. In southern Portugal there are still fairly large passage-tombs of the same type, but further north corbelling disappears entirely and large slab-tombs are rare. In this relatively poor and backward region the tombs are small and the entrance-passage tends to be reduced to a simple covered threshold. By the close of the third millennium this burial architecture, slab-cist and megalithic passage-grave, had reached northern Europe, passing through France to Brittany and the British Isles, where the monolithic graves of the Orkneys recall directly those of Antequera.

One final result of the Almerían expansion seems to have been the colonisation of Majorca, hitherto uninhabited.

As the second millennium opened, the civilisation of Los Millares was already in decline, and megalithic burial-places went out as the age of bronze came in. Long before, with the growth of new centres of trade and industry in central Europe, the Aegean had ceased to rely directly on Spain for supplies of copper, and the Peninsula again fell into relative isolation and impoverishment. The old civilisation, with its once-prosperous merchant-towns and its preoccupation with the niceties of burial, may have gone down in strife and anarchy. It was overthrown by peoples who dwelt in fortified hill-villages and who had acquired the military skill of mixing copper with tin to produce weapons harder and more efficient than any used before. By about 1700 the beginnings of this new culture, at first employing only a small quantity of bronze, were established at El Argar and other villages such as El Oficio and Fuente Alamo, still in the Almerían area; and within two centuries the new Almerían culture had spread over most of Spain.

While the first Almerían civilisation implies an active colonisation by a more advanced people, that of El Argar has a more autochthonous character. It corresponds to Bronze Age evolution in other parts of Europe, yet it existed in something approaching isolation. In contrast to the relative peace of megalithic societies, the peoples of El Argar seem to have been pitted against one another from their fortified settlements. Their pottery consisted mainly of simple bowls and round-bottomed beakers, and for their burials they returned to a cist of a few slabs or used a jar placed in an open pit. There were now no necropolises: the leaders alone were given individual burial, and their rank was marked by diadems of silver in addition to beads of shell and stone.

During the whole of the second millennium there was little external interference and the civilisation of El Argar seems to have maintained a surprising stability. By 1600 it had reached its full development, and its characteristic bronze halberd is found side by side with the now archaic stone axe and flint saw-edge. At about the same period it extended to the hills of Upper Andalusia and to the Balearics, and after this expansion Almería ceased to be the centre of civilisation in the Peninsula. Its place was taken by the valley of the Guadalquivir, which not only exceeded it in agricultural resources, but linked the main sources of copper in the Sierra Morena with those of tin in Portugal and Galicia.

This displacement prepares the Peninsular stage for the raising of the curtain on historic times. As Almería itself sinks into obscurity, the basis of the civilisation of 'Tartessos' is laid in the Guadalquivir valley, while a northward extension to the valley of the Ebro paves the way for the 'Iberian' cultures with which the Romans first came in contact soon after the middle of the first millennium. The area of post-Almerían civilisation extended westwards into southern Portugal and embraced the edge of the southern meseta, but all the northern part of the Peninsula from Galicia to Catalonia had only a simple pastoral and agricultural economy, and the rude cave-cultures of southern France still straddled the Pyrenees. The mesetas of central Spain had apparently remained very thinly populated, and perhaps suffered from desiccation during the whole of the second millennium. Possibly primitive cereals could not withstand these conditions, and the peoples of the centre either confined themselves to the mountain regions or moved westwards into Portugal and Galicia, where the greater humidity of the Atlantic coast permitted a much higher density of population. The relative emptiness and unattractiveness of life in the meseta explains the bifurcation of southern civilisation along the line of the Sierra Morena into Portugal and up the Mediterranean coast.

But by the beginning of the first millennium either these conditions were mitigated, as seems probable, or at least new races were driven by inexorable destiny to accept them. These northern invaders had departed from Asia and wandered in successive waves across Europe. They first reached Spain early in the first millennium before Christ, and their last invasions occurred in the fifth century of our own era. These Indo-Europeans consisted of many tribes, broadly divisible into Celts and Germans; and in the course of their movements they divided, fused, and even brought with them smaller groups of non-Indo-Europeans.

The first Indo-European invasions occurred in about 900, when the Celtic urnfield people arrived in Catalonia, crossing the western Pyrenees and establishing themselves in the Llanos de Urgel, the coastal region of Catalonia and parts of lower Aragon. Their settlements were military ones, but they seem to have been too few to maintain a separate existence: most were wiped out or absorbed by the natives before the middle of the millennium. Meanwhile, the first Germanic impulse had reached the lower Rhine, dislocated the Celtic peoples between it and the Elbe, and forced part of them into Holland, France and finally Spain. The first of these retreating peoples was the Pelendones, followed by the Cempsi, the already Germanised Eburones and the Belgae, who also brought with them groups of Germanic peoples. On arriving in the Peninsula these groups spread out over the meseta, each new impulse modifying the effect of the last. Thus the Cempsi were pressed south-westwards through Extremadura and came into contact with Tartessian civilisation in Andalusia, while the Turones resorted to the mountains of the Iberian system; and the Pelendones, long settled on the meseta near Soria, were conquered and subjected by the Belgae. The last arrivals occupied Navarre and part of the Basque country (Suessiones and

Autrigones), part of the Cantabrian coast (Velegienses), and the Leonese meseta (Vaccei and Arevaci), while some Germanic groups who came with them, the Nervii and Tungri, settled in Biscay (on the river Nervión) and in Portugal.

All these were of Indo-European stock, but they were of different linguistic and racial groups, and they settled among peoples almost as diverse as themselves. For a long period the Indo-European invasions appear to have been sporadic infiltrations which developed slowly in intensity and disrupted the life of the more primitive north. A number of Celtic pockets were established in the south and east, but these areas of relatively high civilisation never lost their 'post-Almerían' character. Conversely parts of the northern meseta now occupied had hitherto been almost uninhabited. Others found their way into the more densely populated areas of central Portugal and Galicia, where they mingled their own cultures with those of more primitive natives: hence the persisting 'Celticness' of Galicia in combination with racial characteristics that appear purely 'Mediterranean'. But the area in which Indo-European influences remained most vital was that of Soria in the north-eastern meseta, where the Belgae absorbed the Pelendones and planted themselves firmly on an older Iberian substratum to form the federation of Celtiberia.

4. 'TARTESSIAN' AND SEMITIC SPAIN

The primitive civilisation of Andalusia was linked, or reunited, with the ancient world by the founding of the Phoenician colony of Gadir, or Cádiz, which is generally supposed to be the oldest continuously occupied city in western Europe and was probably founded in the ninth century[1]. The name, meaning 'enclosed space', 'fortress' suggests at once a storehouse for stocks of metal

[1] The date 1100 is often given: but it seems improbable that Gadir was founded much before Utica (c. 820-13). The earliest datable object of Egyptian manufacture yet found in the Peninsula is the scarab of Psammeticus I (7th c.) from Aliseda.

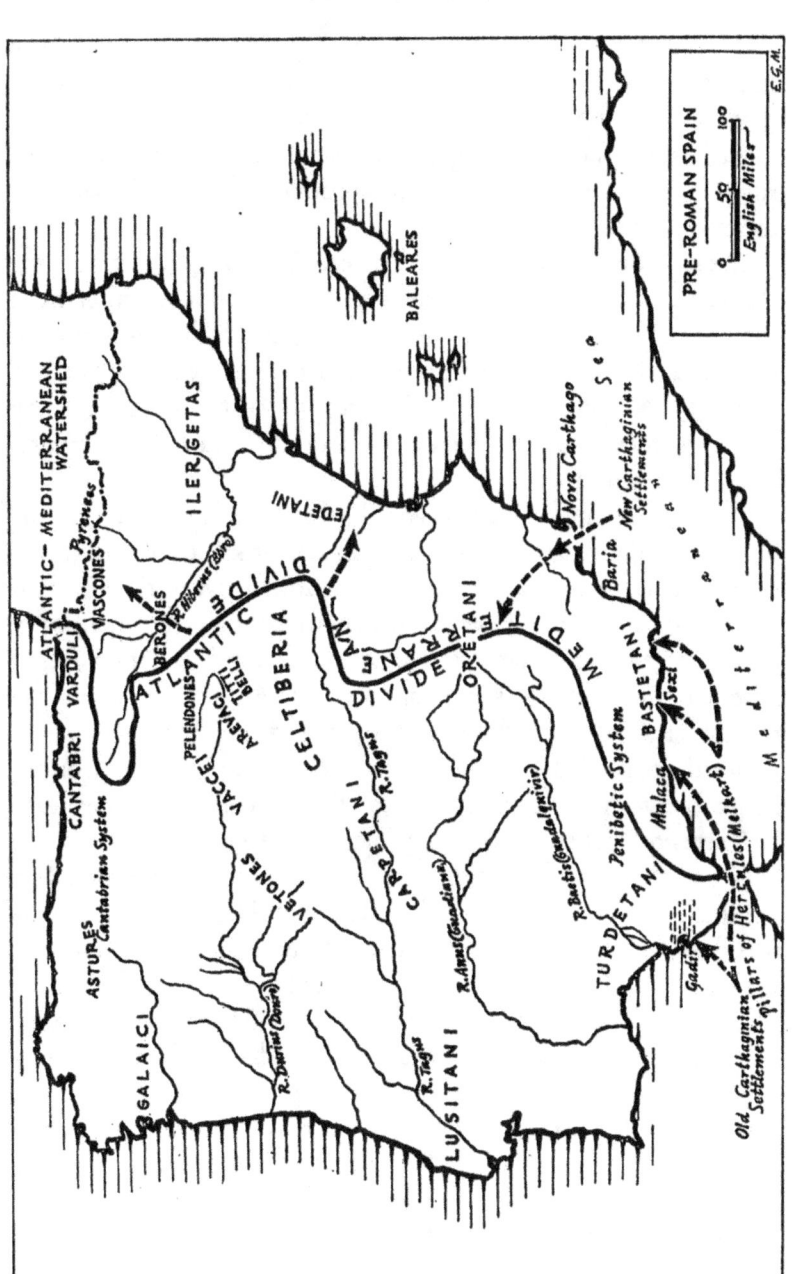

and a stronghold, and this western outpost and emporium was linked with Utica and Tyre by a series of subsidiary ports, Malaca, Sexi and Abdera (Adra), each a small fort on a fertile patch of coastal plain where coasting galleys put in at night and obtained supplies of water and salt fish, the product of local salt-pans and tunny-fisheries.

Gadir was probably severed from Tyre in 680, when the Babylonians overran the mother-city and its colonies either freed themselves or were captured by their neighbours, but their ancient trade may have continued until Nebuchadnezzar laid Tyre low (586–73). At that time the native peoples of the mainland may have regained their independence and the 'Tartessian empire' reached its zenith.

The area of this civilisation was the fertile valley of the Guadalquivir and the metal-bearing hills on its flanks, a region known to the Greeks as Tartessos, and identified with the Biblical Tharshish. There is no certainty that its people were politically united when the Phoenicians arrived. The Bible does not say whether Tharshish was a country, a state or a city; but the earliest classical texts show that by the sixth century it was a political area ruled by a monarch and having its capital on an island between the two mouths of the Guadalquivir, the 'river of Tartessos', where stood the palace of the king.

Herodotus records that the first Greek to visit Tartessos was a Samiot blown off his course, but that the Phocaeans first equipped ships for the journey. He tells how the King of Tartessos invited them to settle, and when they refused, gave them gifts to assist them in their war against the Persians. This ruler was Argantonios, 'the man of silver', said to have lived a hundred and twenty years and to have reigned eighty. His name appears to be Celtic, and the period of Tartessian independence may coincide with Indo-European infiltrations into the south. The reign of this patriarch may lie between 620 and 540, for the Phocaeans phase must fall between 550 and 535, after which the sea-battle of Alalia enabled Carthage to close the south-western Mediterranean to the Greeks and take over the protectorate created by her mother, Tyre.

During the period of open navigation the Greeks had founded

settlements at Hemeroskopeion, the 'watch-tower of the dawn' (Ifach), Odysseia (near Abdera) and Mainaké (Vélez-Málaga?), but after Alalia the last two places passed under Carthaginian control and Mainaké was destroyed. The Greeks were then confined to the east coast, whence they continued to draw on the mineral wealth of the Sierra Morena by a land-route: the discovery of Corinthian helmets (c. 550–500) at Huelva and in the Guadalete and of bronze statuettes in the Sierra Morena bears witness to native trade, possibly indirect, with the Greeks.

In the south, the Greek interlude was followed by three centuries of uncontested Carthaginian influence. Polybius speaks of an early treaty with Rome by which the area west of Cape Farina was recognised as exclusively Carthaginian, but this may be a confusion with the treaty of 349 which established the same frontier with the Graeco-Roman zone. In any case, this Andalusian protectorate remains wrapped in mystery until the two decades between the first Punic war and the second, which brought the final fall of Carthaginian rule. The two Carthaginian ages, colonial and imperial, have left few distinguishable relics. During the first Gadir was governed by two suffetes and a treasurer who safeguarded the interests of the fisc at Carthage. It probably enjoyed a high degree of autonomy. On the mainland the only Carthaginian settlements were the villages in its immediate vicinity and the way-stations on the Andalusian coast, where some Libyans may have been settled. So long as supplies of metals continued to flow into the store-houses of Gadir its masters were apparently content.

But their first war with Rome and the subsequent revolt of the slaves in Carthage turned a trading-state into an empire. Deprived of Sicily and forced to pay a large indemnity in silver, Carthage turned to Spain for men and treasure. Thus in 238 Hamilcar arrived at Gadir with his son-in-law Hasdrubal, his son the boy Hannibal, and an army of Libyans, with which he occupied the valley of the Guadalquivir. The 'post-Tartessians' or Turdetanians, as the Romans called them, and the Celtiberians sought to resist; but, aided by his formidable elephants, Hamilcar broke up their armies and tortured their leaders, Istolatius (the first known hero of Spanish independence) and Indortes. Enlisting the Celtiberians as mercenaries, he subdued the peoples of eastern Spain as far as Cape Palos and took the native capital of the Mastieni, advancing to the very frontier of the Roman-Massiliot zone and founding the city of Akra Leuké, near Alicante. In 231 Rome sent an embassy to protest against this expansion, and Hamilcar justified himself by the need to find silver for the indemnity imposed on Carthage. He remained active on the frontier until his death in battle against the Oretani two or three years later. His successor Hasdrubal brought in new Libyan contingents, completed the occupation of Oretanian territory, married a Spanish princess, and set up his capital near the native Mastia, which he called New Carthage (Cartagena).

The Carthaginian empire in Spain now consisted of two zones. Gadir, with its group of settlements on the mainland[1], was still the centre of trade for the valley of the Guadalquivir and the emporium for the Tin Islands. Its influence extended into southern Portugal where Mago had his winter-quarters, and between this Tartessian area and the new conquests at Cartagena lay the old colonial ports, surrounded by peoples long subjected to Carthaginian influence and known as Phenobastuli, or 'Punic Bastuli'. There were also Punic garrisons in the Guadalquivir valley which may have linked Gadir with the mines.

Under Carthage the old Tartessian monarchy may have lost its unity and split into smaller kingships resembling the taifas of the eleventh century. Some of the Turdetanian kings possessed extensive territories and large towns: their nobles were divided into several classes and were great landowners, whose estates were tilled in part by slaves. Some of the kings and towns employed Celtic or Celtiberian mercenaries for their defence.

The classical authors agree that the early civilisation of Andalusia was much more highly developed than that of the rest of Spain, even including the Iberian east. It embraced more than two hundred 'cities'. If often only their name survives, this is because, unlike the hill-top fortresses of the north and centre, which were conquered and destroyed, most of the southern towns

[1] Belo, Asido (Medina Sidonia), Lascuta (near Jerez), Turris Regina (on the Guadalete), Iptucci (Prado del Rey).

capitulated and survived into Roman times, and in many cases to the present day, being continuously rebuilt.

The cities of Andalusia which impressed the Romans by their appearance consisted of clusters of small dwellings of whitened adobe. Pliny describes how the houses of Spain and Africa were built by filling the space between two planks with clay, which was thus moulded to form walls: a stone foundation might be laid, and the walls were strengthened with wood. The houses thus formed consisted of a single windowless compartment, perhaps subdivided into partitions, and obeyed no fixed design, but included obtuse and acute angles. Arranged in steep streets, they often flowed down a hillside, separated by steps; there is a single reference to a public square, at Astepa.

Native Turdetania possessed few monuments. Its towns had drystone fortifications, and there were numerous forts, which Pliny calls *turres Hannibalis*, isolated watchtowers or strongpoints on coasts and main roads, dating from remote times and designed to defend convoys of metals from the raids of bandits. The sober patterned ware of the southern potters expresses a refined taste and was exported to North Africa and even further afield. But the wealthier magnates of southern Spain acquired through Carthage a taste for the arts of the middle and eastern Mediterranean, and their tombs contain small amphoras of coloured glass, alabaster statuettes and large craters brought from the Greek colonies of Sicily and southern Italy or from North Africa. So too the statuary of the Turdetanians consisted of large figures of winged sphinxes, gryphons and other fantastic creatures either imported from Greece or copied by native craftsmen: the Greek models go back to the sixth and fifth centuries, and their Spanish imitations cover the period from the sixth to the third. These objects may have cramped the growth of a native style, but the limitations of the indigenous imagination are shown by the few remnants of Turdetanian architecture: Spanish craftsmen who had never seen Greek originals erected columns with no understanding of orders and with no apparent reference to a native tradition.

It is not easy to discover the extent of Carthaginian influence in southern Spain. The long Punic protectorates cannot be dismissed lightly merely for want of the material evidences. The art of writing was perhaps introduced from Carthage[1], and the Phoenician religion appears to have spread from Gadir to the native peoples. From their original nature-gods the Phoenicians had evolved a small pantheon of deities with special attributes. Their Baals were 'lords' or owners of places: the baal of Tyre was Melkart, 'the king of the city', who was also worshipped in Carthage and Gadir[2]. Baal-Melkart is also the masculine principle of strength, whence his identification with Hercules; the masculine principle was identified with the tutelary of the place, and any failure in loyalty to him was savagely avenged. The corresponding female principle was modesty or shame, and the sacred object in the temple of the virgin goddess Tanith was a veil: she answered petitions and her temple in Carthage contained a vast number of tablets inscribed to her by grateful votaries. Southern Spain (but not the Indo-European north) is noteworthy also for its lack of nature gods and even of named divinities. As at Carthage, each town appears to have possessed its temple, and some of these shrines were extremely popular as places of pilgrimage and their sites are marked by a profusion of votive statuettes, sometimes showing the donor in an attitude of supplication. It is difficult to avoid seeing here some of the special characteristics of Andalusian religion, the expression of localised and intense fervour, the emotional attachment to the Virgin, and the love of pilgrimages to places of special efficacy.

It is also possible to infer Punic influences in the political and social character of southern Spain. In Phoenicia the balance between kings of royal descent and the wealthy mercantile families who controlled the senate was apparently held by the priest of Melkart, who as minister to the god of the city, had a special responsibility for its safety. Independent Carthage was a plutocratic

---

[1] Early Greek accounts refer to the metrified laws of the Tartessians; as verse was an aid to memory, it may be inferred that writing was still unknown. 'Post-Tartessian' inscriptions contain archaisms such as spiral writing or boustrophedon. Iberian writing is less archaic and probably of Greek inspiration.

[2] A Roman general is found worshipping the Melkart or Punic Hercules of Gadir, presumably to conciliate the Punicized natives.

republic where, as Polybius says, 'no one is blamed however he may have acquired his wealth'. The counterpoise to the oligarchical senate was an alliance between a small number of aristocratic families and the people. The two suffetes who held supreme power were appointed by the senate and ratified by popular assembly: there was no bar to re-election, and Hannibal, a member of the popular-aristocratic Barcidae, was suffete for twenty-two years. These patterns are not unfamiliar in Andalusia.

The brief imperialism of the Barcas soon came to an end. Hasdrubal's work was cut short by his murder at the hands of a Celtic slave, and the command passed to Hannibal, then aged twenty-one. Even if he himself had desired to avoid war with Rome, it seems probable that the rise of Celtiberian power so near the accepted frontier would sooner or later have embroiled the rival colonial powers. In 220 Hannibal marched far into the interior and sacked the towns of the Vaccei, returning to New Carthage without opposition from the peoples of the southern meseta. But his enemies (or those of his allies) made themselves strong in Saguntum under Roman protection. He demanded their surrender, and when it was refused, laid siege to the city. Its fall, after a desperate resistance, made the intervention of Rome inevitable.

5. ROMAN SPAIN

From Spain Hannibal prepared his invasion of Italy, and as he entered it, a Roman army landed at the Massiliot seaport of Emporion and defeated Hanno. As soon as reinforcements arrived, the general, P. Cornelius Scipio, crossed the Ebro and reached Saguntum (214). The oppressed miners of the upper Guadalquivir turned against Carthage, and the Romans entered the metal-towns of Castulo (Cazlona) and Iliturgi, wintering as far south as Urso (Osuna). But on the arrival of Hasdrubal from Africa, these easy successes were soon cancelled out, and the Romans were driven back north of the Ebro. Only in 210, with the decline of Hannibal's fortunes in Italy, were they able to bring new armies to Emporion.

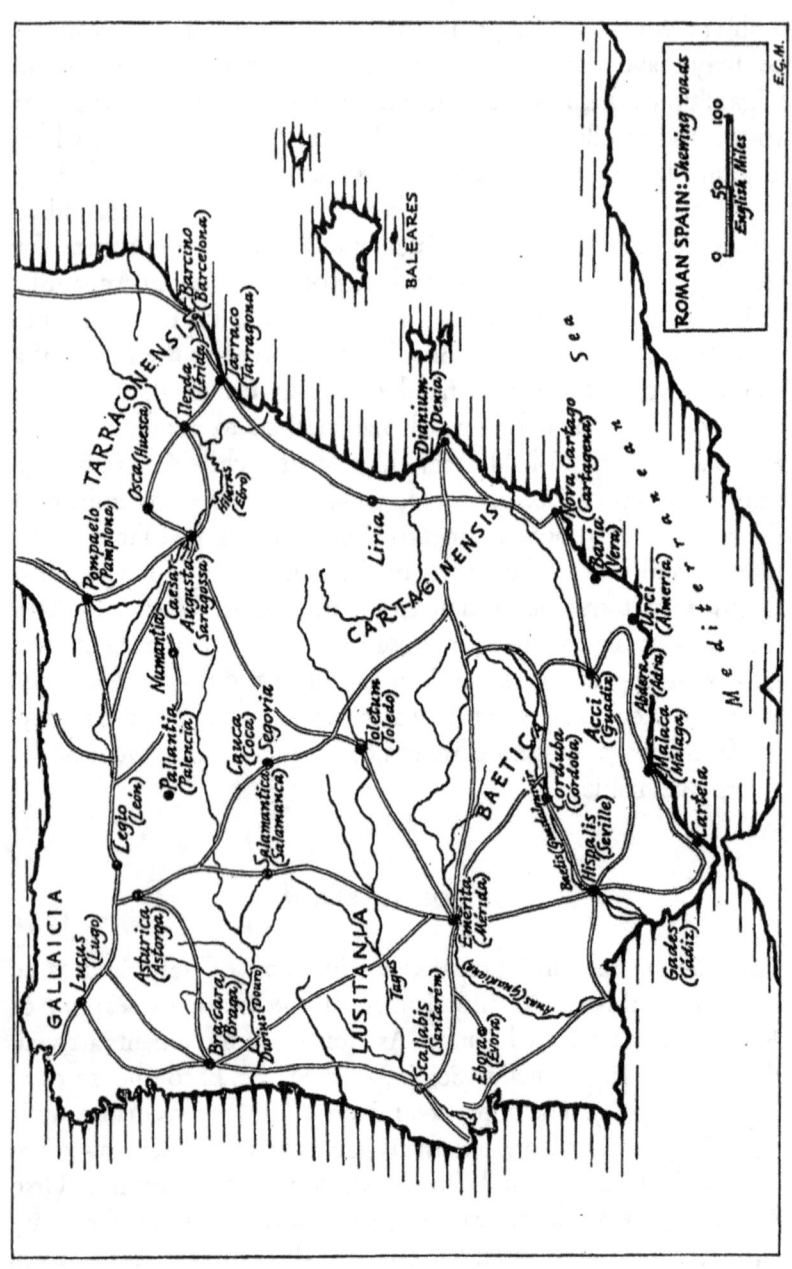

Although the Carthaginians had three armies in the field, New Carthage fell to a sudden attack, and Scipio forced his way into the Guadalquivir valley with the victory of Baecula (Bailén). Ilipa (Alcalá del Río), fought soon after, decided the fate of all Spain, and within little more than a year all that remained of Carthaginian power was Gadir itself, whose merchant community soon accepted favourable terms.

Immediately after Ilipa, the Roman Senate empowered Scipio to establish an administration in the Carthaginian domains. The old Roman-Massiliot zone of influence, the east coast, was now constituted into Hispania Citerior, and the Turdetanian south into Hispania Ulterior. The first two praetors were commissioned to demarcate the provinces, and the boundary was fixed at Baria (Vera): to its north lay Citerior, the coastal strip running to the Pyrenees, with an indentation into the lower Ebro valley; to its south and west, Ulterior, comprising the future province of Baetica, approximately corresponding to modern Andalusia.

Behind each stretched the interior: seventy years were to pass before Roman arms reached the furthest corner of the Peninsula, and even a century later the still unconquered Cantabrians could arouse the neighbouring tribes of the north coast to a long and bitter resistance. Their Basque neighbours, though defeated, were never Romanised.

The Romanisation of Spain was thus both slow and incomplete. In general it varied in intensity in direct proportion to the existing level of civilisation. Throughout the whole Roman period there was no doubt of the supremacy of Baetica. This was the region that supplied metals and wine to Rome, and was the first to receive Roman colonists (not far from the old Carthaginian settlements). After the establishment of the colonies of Roman veterans, its native cities also acquired fora and monuments. In Strabo's time the native languages were already forgotten, and Roman dress was general. Later this was to be the first of all the provinces to give Rome a consul and an emperor, and it was the birth-place of half a dozen great writers of the Silver Age.

The Iberian east coast had had no political unity and it gave the Romans little trouble. Cato reduced the Iacetani and carried

Roman rule beyond Salduba (Saragossa) in 193; such disturbances as occurred after this were probably the work of Celtiberian marauders. The peoples of the Iberian area had long been under the influence of the Massiliot Greeks. Their civilisation was newer, less unified and more vigorous than that of the Punic south. In general the population was sparser. The towns were fewer, but Ibero-Roman coins, often inscribed in Iberian and Latin, illustrate the relatively large number of separate city-states or tribal capitals. There is no certain evidence of hereditary monarchy in this area, and many of the cities were probably governed, like Saguntum, by councils of elders. Some were stoutly defended by 'cyclopean' fortifications, though these are probably of late date: the most famous are at Tarragona, and traces of similar work exist at Gerona, Saguntum and in the Balearics and Murcia.

But Iberian society has been most vividly preserved by its pottery, and particularly by that of San Miguel de Liria, Azaila and Archena. Less graceful in form than the work of the south, it seizes the attention by its ebullient decoration. The ware of Liria especially portrays Iberian society of the second and first centuries in hunting-scenes, elaborate rituals, festive dances in which men and women take hands as if for the *sardana*, battles, duels and pastimes. There is a baroque horror of the void, and a natural effusiveness causes every space to be filled, sometimes with formal patterns of birds and flowers. These features recall the ancient rock-paintings of the Levant and point forward to the Hispano-Moresque pottery of the late Middle Ages. But in contrast with these native productions may be set examples of classical style, of which the finest is the famous Lady of Elche, now in the Prado. This is probably a late work from the hand of an Iberian sculptor trained in the Greek tradition: its elaborate head-dress, of a type frequently found in Iberian statuettes, was probably still worn after the opening of the Christian era.

The Roman conquests in the east and south were linked by a narrow coastal strip which ran under the territory of the Celtiberians. These people, Indo-Europeans who had assimilated the native Iberians, were the most warlike and best armed of the Peninsular races, and at the moment of the Roman impact they were in a state of vigorous ferment. They had apparently attempted ed to force their way into the area of the mines jealously guarded by Hannibal, who diverted them against Saguntum. When the Romans occupied the coast, they turned their energies northwards, pressing back the Basques towards the Pyrenees and occupying the capital of the Vaccei. After these displacements, Rome opened a campaign against them in 182, which was concluded by T. Sempronius Gracchus, the founder of the city of Gracchuris. The Celtiberians now agreed to pay tribute and to build no new walled towns. But in 154 the greed of the Roman tax-collectors caused them to fortify themselves, and when Q. Fulvius Nobilior attacked their capital of Numantia his troops were defeated and his base at Ocilis (Medinaceli) captured. After successive phases of peace and war, and many defeats, the Romans finally conquered Numantia in the great siege of 133. Reduced to the last extremity of hunger, many of its defenders committed suicide rather than surrender, and the city suffered the fate of Carthage.

The Celtiberian territory, the headwaters of the Douro[1], was well peopled, and remains of fifty-four native towns and metropolises have survived. The area supplied Rome with twenty thousand mercenaries at a time, and in 181 it put an army of twenty-five thousand into the field against Rome. The power of the Celtiberians derived partly from their superior numbers and partly from their superior weapons. The first of these they owed to their intermarriage with the Iberians, and the second to their Celtic ancestors. Northern Celtiberia, a region of forest or poor pasture, was occupied by the Pelendones. The rest, high ground suitable for cereals or cultivable river valley, was held by Indo-Europeans who had adopted an Iberian material culture (Lusones, Arevaci, Belli and Titti). The extensive ruins of Numantia still show the importance of their capital, and their secondary city of Termantia is perhaps even more striking. Perched on an escarpment, it was approached by a steep slope cut deep into the earth and flanked by complex underground dwellings. Houses were built irregularly following the curve of the wall, while the escarp-

[1] Between the modern provinces of Burgos and Saragossa from east to west, and Logroño and Guadalajara from north to south.

ment itself was terraced for meetings and for watching spectacles. The general effect is 'Iberian', not northern, and the pottery, though not elegant, is more varied than that of the Indo-Europeans. Like the Iberians, the Celtiberians apparently had their council of elders, though their military leaders are referred to as 'reges'. If Iberians in the arts of peace, they were Indo-Europeans in the practice of arms. Their weapon was a short stubby thrusting sword quite distinct from the sweeping Iberian scimitar or *falcata*. They wore the *sagum*, a rough black tunic of coarse natural wool, in contrast to the fringed red tunics of the Iberians, and were shod with a hemp-soled sandal bound round the ankle, not with the high soft Iberian shoe. They had the unknown god of the south and celebrated his festival at the new moon with long dances, but they also worshipped the stars, hills and other natural objects. They ate much meat, cooked with lard, not oil, and drank wine like the Iberians and brewed a fermented wheat-drink like Celtic beer: their habits were cleanly and they washed their teeth in urine.

To their west dwelt other tribes probably of similar Indo-European stock, but who had settled among simpler people or failed to achieve a similar fusion with them. These were the Vettones, Vaccei and Carpetani,[1] whose tribal area is approximately that of the so-called 'culture of the *berracos*', stone-carvings of boars and bulls. Many of these figures are so crude that the craftsman seems to have neither eye for his subject nor control over his medium: as long as his creations could be recognised, they apparently served their turn as tutelary deities. The 'berracos' have no counterpart in Celtic countries and refer back to the vastly superior zoomorphous statues of the south or even to the votive art of Murcia. But once more, the weapons of the region, notably its swords and daggers, are of northern origin.

The western counterparts of the Celtiberians were the Lusitanians, dwelling mainly in central Portugal. In 150 the praetor of further Spain promised them land and so disarmed them, only to massacre them or sell them into slavery; and the memory of this perfidy fired the survivors to defeat a string of Roman

[1] Occupying the area of the modern provinces of Avila, Cáceres, Salamanca and Zamora.

generals. One defeated consul offered their leader Viriatus recognition as 'rex' and the friendship of the Roman people, but the treaty was rejected in Rome, and in 139 Viriatus was killed in his bed by treachery. Thereafter the resistance of the Lusitanians was soon overcome.

Viriatus' wars were linked with the resistance of the Celtiberians in central Spain and his campaigns were fought over a wide area from Salamanca to Cuenca, with frequent irruptions into Andalusia, but almost never on the soil of his native Lusitania. Viriatus himself was probably an Indo-European, and his people may have arrived in Portugal as a result of Carthaginian and Roman pressure on the central tribes. In central Portugal there seems to have been little integration between the earlier inhabitants and the northerners. The rich open fields of the Tagus valley were probably tilled by farmers of the same stock as the Turdetanians of the Guadalquivir, while the Indo-Europeans remained a pastoral people occupying the higher and poorer soil of the *serras*. Viriatus himself was famous for his frugality and sobriety, and like many of his followers, he had lived by raiding the wealth of Andalusia.

In an approximate gradation of the native Spanish cultures the Lusitanian area would occupy a middle place. After its conquest the Romans faced more primitive peoples who had scarcely felt the effects of Turdetanian or Iberian civilisation. Immediately after the Lusitanian war, in 137, Decius Brutus reduced northern Portugal and Galicia with little serious resistance. The Lusitanians had recently annexed territory north of the Douro, but the whole of the north-west belonged properly to a distinct culture, and this was later recognised by the creation of the province of Galaecia (Calaicia: Galicia) beginning at or near Oporto, the original Portugal (Portus Cale, the entry to the Calaeci). This was a territory peopled with Celts, but where the pre-Indo-European understratum was no longer at a higher level of culture. The remains of native townships, and especially the large *citânias* of northern Portugal, are huddles of cottages of clay or clayed stone which were perhaps interspersed with wooden or mud cabins. These *citânias* are distinguished from the Indo-European *castros* of northern Spain by the survival of the pre-Celtic bee-hive hut. The native world on which the Celts impinged was thus a remote reproduction of that of Almería a millennium earlier. To this archaic culture the Celts gave hard metals, superior arms and a new political structure.[1] In such art as has survived Celtic design predominates: monolithic door-jambs are sometimes decorated with Celtic knotting, while the curious funereal stones, such as the Pedra Formosa of Citânia de Briteiros, seem remotely descended from the sacred plaques of Los Millares, but bear basket-weave designs.

The establishment of a Roman garrison at Asturica Augusta (Astorga) sufficed to hold these peoples in subjection and only the north coast now remained free. Nevertheless, a spirit of opposition to Rome still survived. In 80 the Sabine Q. Sertorius, a former praetor of Citerior who had opposed Sulla in the Roman class-war, set up an independent government in Spain, and the native peoples rallied to him with enthusiasm. By 77 he commanded most of the interior, and only the south remained loyal to his rivals. But in 75 Pompey marched through Celtiberia and founded Pompaelo (Pamplona), and by the following year Sertorius' power was in full decline. Abandoned by his followers, he was murdered at a banquet at Osca (Huesca).

Although the Spaniards were so ready to follow Sertorius, the effect of his rebellion was to hasten rather than delay the process of Romanisation. He brought with him Roman refugees, founded a Roman senate in Spain and set up a Roman college for the sons of native chiefs at Osca. Twenty-four years later, when Pompey fought Caesar in Spain, the Spanish peoples rallied to their former conqueror, less out of love for him than from hatred of Caesar and his exactions. They had again chosen the losing side, and in 45 Caesar won the Baetican south with the victory of Munda (Montilla).

The tribes of the far north were finally reduced in the Cantabrian war of 29–19, after a desperate and bloody resistance. Strabo says that all the peoples of the north had the same customs; this

---

[1] While the peoples of central Spain were called 'gentilitates' or tribes, those of Galicia are distinguished as 'centuries'.

may mean only that they were equally primitive. Three distinct areas are now recognised: Asturias, Cantabria and the Basque Provinces. The Galician-Asturian frontier is an ancient one, and appears to mark the limit of Indo-European ascendancy, though there were still Celtic and Germanic groups further east. The Astures occupied both sides of the western Cantabrian ranges and the Romans distinguished those on the meseta, the first to be conquered, from those on the coast. Cantabria, which particularly impressed the Romans by its wildness and by the primitiveness of the inhabitants, was in part Celtic-dominated, perhaps by warriors who had retired before the Roman advance: personal and place-names show that the resistance to Rome was conducted by Indo-Europeans.

To the east of the Cantabrians dwelt the Basques, who alone in western Europe even to-day possess a pre-Indo-European tongue. It belongs to the same family as pre-Celtic Aquitanian and perhaps to other tongues of the Peninsula now lost. In Roman times its area extended south of the Ebro and eastwards into the central Pyrenees, but this original territory was reduced by the northward pressure of the Celtiberians and by the Romanisation of Navarre after Pompey's conquest, and has been further restricted in modern times: modern Basque carries a strong admixture of both Celtic and Latin. But the linguistic and racial problems of Basque do not necessarily coincide. Despite the existence of a 'Basque type', the race has received many infiltrations and its power lies in its great capacity of absorption. This peculiar natural tenacity, an enduring social relationship, appears to be the special contribution of the pre-Indo-European north to the formation of modern Spain.

Roman power was now secure in the valleys of the Guadalquivir, Ebro and Guadiana; and the old division of two provinces, each with its unconquered hinterland, had ceased to be valid. When Augustus partitioned the empire with the Senate, he retained for himself Citerior and the still-militarised frontiers of the north and north-west. Senatorial Spain was divided into two parts, the old Turdetanian area of Baetica, administered from Corduba, and the valley of the Guadiana and central Portugal, with its capital at Emerita (Mérida). The precaution was also taken of adjusting the ancient frontier from Baria so as to transfer Almería and part of northern Granada to the imperial area, probably with the object of reserving to the emperor the product of the mines and its outlet to the sea.

This dyarchy persisted until the third century, when Caracalla abolished the distinction. Baetica and Lusitania now became independent of one another; and the whole imperial area was divided into three provinces. In the far west Galicia, the land of the 'centuries' and *citânias*, was separated, while the Ebro valley and north coast became Tarraconensis, and the rest, the eastern meseta, the Iberian mountains and the Valencian, Murcian and Almerían seaboard formed Cartaginensis, thus preserving, however inexactly, the name of Hamilcar's 'Carthage'.

A network of roads now linked these provinces together. Entering the Peninsula at the eastern Pyrenees, the legionary marched down the Mediterranean coast and thence across country to the mines and down the valley of the Guadalquivir to Corduba and Gades. From Hispalis (Seville) and Emerita this great route forked northwards through modern Portugal to Bracara (Braga), or across Extremadura to Salmantica, and so to Asturica. From Tarraco (Tarragona) a branch led up the valley of the Ebro to Caesar Augusta (Saragossa), and linked the old Celtiberian area with Legio (León). In addition to this outer framework, military roads crossed the more sparsely settled central mesetas, and local systems joined the clusters of towns in Baetica, the Ebro-Celtiberian region, and the settlements in the northwest and in southern Portugal.

It was along these paths that Roman civilisation travelled outwards. By Augustus' time the populous south was already fully Romanised. Ten of the native cities of Baetica had reached the status of Roman, and twenty-seven that of Latin, *municipia*, and the whole province was divided into four *conventus* for the administration of justice. Corduba was the head of Roman Andalusia; but Gades remained the chief port of all Spain, and Strabo speaks of its enterprising merchants and their fleet of ships, large and small, called 'sea-horses', which ranged the Mediterranean.

Much of their trade was in oil, cereals, dried-fruit, wine, wool, wax, fish and metals for Rome itself, but the existence of a college of Syrian merchants in Malaca (Málaga) shows that the ancient contact with the east had not been lost.

The adjoining province of Lusitania was less urban, though its capital of Emerita had become one of the great cities of Roman Spain. Its main wealth was drawn from the irrigable valleys of the Guadiana and Tagus and the extensive stock-raising of the Portuguese Alemtejo, famous for its horses. In the east the valley of the Ebro and Catalonia formed a similar area of intense rural exploitation, but its inland towns were exceeded in importance by the military and administrative capital of Tarragona on the coast.

The great period of Roman building in Spain was in the first and second centuries of our era, when the chief towns were enhanced with works of practical value, bridges, aqueducts and fora, and also with centres of Roman social life, baths, circuses and theatres. The vast arenas of Italica and Emerita were among the largest in the Roman world, and the presence of great theatres like that of Emerita suggests an intenser colonisation and possibly a general adoption of the Latin language. But in the centre, north and north-west the surviving monuments are largely of the practical sort, bridges spanning rivers on roads to outlying garrison towns such as Asturica and Legio, and aqueducts such as that of Segovia: 'cultural' monuments are relatively few, and inscriptions prove the survival of tribal life. In the northern meseta this was preserved by communal agricultural practices, while on the north coast Celtic culture was probably refreshed by contact with Brittany and the British Isles.

Already in Pliny's day Baetica was recognised as the most Roman province outside Italy, and its sons were the first provincials to achieve office in Rome—L. C. Balbus, a Romanised native of Gades, fought against Sertorius, the Hispanised Roman, and was the first provincial to receive a triumph (−32). In 98 Trajan, a Spaniard from Italica, became the first provincial emperor: his successor, Hadrian, born in Italica of Italian parents, earned the title of 'restitutor hispaniae' for his zeal in public works.

The Baetican colonies and native cities possessed their own senates and elected their own magistrates; and in cities with Latin rights all those who had held office (or from Hadrian's day, all senators), became Roman citizens. Although Romans exercised supreme command as governors, proconsuls or propraetors, subject only to the emperor's intervention, the cities of each province acquired limited rights of self-government through annual provincial councils, which, though originally held to organise the worship of the emperor, delivered an eulogy on the work of the outgoing governor which could also be a censure. Thus Baetica denounced the proconsul Cecilius Classicus to Trajan for his abuses. But even this power was not perhaps attained in other parts of Spain, and there was no inter-provincial organisation.

In the second century the election of magistrates by the inhabitants, the *populus* or pueblo, already ceased, and appointments were made by the municipal authority: only the *flamines* were elected to represent the populace at the provincial council. Possibly the Baeticans, with their traditionally hierarchical municipal life, relinquished Roman democracy without much resistance. The imperial peace had been broken as early as 170 or 171 when the Berbers, pressing against Mauretania, crossed the straits and captured Malaca and besieged the inland capital of Singilis (old Antequera): it was necessary to bring up a fleet and call troops from Lusitania before the intruders could be expelled. But it was the wearing away of the northern frontiers of the empire that brought militarism, autocracy and impoverishment. In the third century the tranquillity of Spanish provincial life was disturbed by the encroachments of the Franks, a series of little-documented infiltrations which link the earlier Indo-European invasions with those of the Germans in the fifth century. The Emperor's omnipotence was completed by Diocletian and his fellow-Illyrians, and the imperial bourgeoisie compensated itself for the loss of rights by closing its ranks and converting itself into an official class, excluding entry from below. The towns ceased to be centres of justice and culture, and became citadels of officialdom and privilege. As the imperial demands for men and treasure grew more urgent, the Seventh Legion, long quartered in northern Spain, was withdrawn, and its place taken by impressed peasants or merely by personal guards formed by magnates and landowners. In the towns the curiae became instruments for raising taxation, and their members were made collectively responsible for providing a stipulated tribute.

These changes developed in the late third century, and when in 301 Diocletian attempted to fix prices throughout the empire, there was no going back. The intervention of the state in local economic life completed the decadence of municipal institutions. *Curatores*, once auditors appointed only when there was evidence of corruption, came to exist everywhere, and judges or *defensores* were appointed to protect the plebeians from abuses. The guilds had already become instruments of control, and craftsmen were bound to their callings. In the countryside, the peasants, even if not slaves, were not allowed to leave the land of the magnates whose protection they had accepted; if they did, it was to take to the hills and live as brigands. As the towns declined, the state was dominated by landowners governing vast estates, and often commanding private armies composed of clients and dependants.

In these circumstances men readily turned from their distant and never-seen earthly ruler, who demanded only tribute and worship, and gave not even justice or protection in return, and joined the ranks of a new religion, which enjoined a better conduct and a higher morality and so offered the vision of a more blessed kingdom. The origins of Spanish Christianity are undocumented. The ports of the south had never lost touch with the eastern Mediterranean, and may have had colonies of Jews as well as Syrians. The fact that the Apostle Paul should have intended to go to Spain (Romans xv, 24, 28), even if he never did so, suggests the presence there of the eastern settlers among whom he worked: however, the earliest known Jewish epigraph in Spain, the tombstone of a child from the old Punic seaport of Adra, goes back no further than the third century.

The most acceptable tradition of the evangelisation of Spain is that of the Seven Holy Men preserved in Mozarabic calendars.

They are said to have founded sees in Almería and Andalusia, and the holding of the first council of the Spanish church at Elvira (Granada) seems to confirm that this was the seeding-ground of the gospel.[1] These Christian origins are attributed to the first century. In 180 St. Irenaeus mentions the churches of Iberia, and twenty years later Tertullian lists 'all parts of Spain' as Christianised, but this is certainly premature. Christianity may have been carried to the north by men serving in the army, and it was they who suffered the first persecutions, attributed to the prefect Decius (c. 250). During the following half-century martyrdoms are recorded from Lusitania and Tarraconensis. A letter from St. Cyprian throws light on the communities of Leon and Astorga, whose bishops had committed apostasy by obtaining false certificates that they had sacrificed to the imperial gods, and had been deposed. The apostates took their tale to Rome and were reinstated, while the faithful appealed to the African theologian, who upheld their action.

Fifty years later Christianity ceased to be a semi-clandestine anti-imperialism and became instead the ally of the secular power. It is in the context of Constantine's change of policy, formally proclaimed in the Edict of Milan of 313, that the first surviving pronouncements of the Spanish church must be placed. The Council of Elvira (?300–314) may have preceded Constantine's decision, but it gave much of its attention to the situation of Christians holding civil power and contains little evidence of a state of persecution. If it discussed questions of theology, its main preoccupation was with the abolition of pre-Christian practices and the establishment of social and doctrinal conformity with a view to the setting up of a Christian society.[2] The canons of Elvira lay emphasis on the need for Christians to distinguish themselves from Jews as from gentiles, and show that religious

---

[1] The sees are: Acci (Guadix), Iliberris (Elvira, Granada), Iliturgis (near Bailén), Urci (Almería), Vergi (Berja), Carcesa (Cazorla? Carchel?) and Abula (Abla).

[2] The council was attended by thirteen bishops from Baetica and single representatives from six other regions. All but one of the twenty-four priests who attended were Baeticans.

discipline, not race or language, marked the faithful off from their neighbours.

Like all the west except Africa, Spain contributed little to the theological controversies of the fourth century. One of the bishops at Elvira, Hosius of Córdoba, was later summoned to attend Constantine in the great dispute with the Arians which threatened to split Christendom, and represented the west at the first universal Council of Nicaea (325). He stood firmly for orthodoxy until his extreme old age; but when at the Council of Alexandria in 362 he finally supported the readmission of penitent Arians, his church, now led by Gregory of Elvira, took the rigid Luciferian view that no compromise should be offered: doctrinal conservatism was thus already persistent among the Andalusian Christians. Meanwhile, Arianism was spreading far and wide in the eastern world, reaching the Goths and Vandals on the Danube and in Pannonia: it was to enter Spain with these peoples at the beginning of the following century.

As Christianity became an official faith of the empire and its leaders 'inherited the earth', the question of uniformity assumed a new importance. In the churches of the east theologians drew on the metaphysical resources of Greek thought to universalise Mosaic monotheism, relegating the inconvenient Christian promise to another sphere. Where the Roman imperial cult had already neutralised local beliefs, official Christianity made its entry without difficulty, but in parts of western Europe a simpler faith was preferred. The spirit of asceticism which led Pope Damasus to forbid the marriage of the clergy in 370 and produced St. Ambrose's and St. Jerome's discourses on the merits of widows and virgins was in some sense an aspiration for primitive Christianity; and in Galicia (where for most of the inhabitants the fourth century was the first of Christianity) the religious leader Priscillian taught that only those who had practised celibacy and asceticism voluntarily should qualify for the priesthood. Priscillianism, with its fasting, retreats and Gospel-readings, spread into Lusitania, and its leader was elected bishop of Avila. A Council held at Saragossa in 380 failed to check it; and although its leader was tried and executed at Treves, and his teaching was made unlawful in 407, it continued to flourish until the latter part of the sixth century. While Galicia thus produced its own faith, other parts of northern Spain were Christianised after a lengthy persecution of the pagans. In 385 the Pope, writing to the Bishop of Tarragona, refers to 'innumerable people seeking baptism', but in 399 the civil authority, the *vicarius*, was forced to suspend the destruction of pagan temples, and later to permit it only when it could be achieved without provoking tumults. Thus in the fifth, sixth and seventh centuries many of the country districts continued obstinately pagan; the rural Basques remained independent of the spiritual empire of Rome, as they had of the temporal, until the eleventh century.

II

VISIGOTHIC SPAIN

WHILE Priscillian and his followers resisted spiritual Romanism, Celtiberia had furnished Rome with a military leader who strove manfully to save the old empire. This was Theodosius, born of a pagan family at Cauca (Coca, Segovia), created Augustus for his victories in Gaul, and set up by his patron Gratian as Emperor of the east. Only then baptised, he attempted to achieve the Constantinian ideal of an earthly empire whose subjects were united by a double allegiance to a single ruler and a single church. At this time the Arian Visigoths were menacing Byzantium, and having defeated them, Theodosius sought to force religious conformity on all his peoples, closing the pagan temples and persecuting the eastern apostates. In 394 he conquered western Rome and attempted to overthrow its pagan gods. He died a year later, and the empire was again divided, this time between his two young sons, Arcadius and Honorius.

His defeat of the Visigoths had been only a temporary check, and his successors were unable to repeat it. Emerging from the Thracian territories assigned to them, they now pressed into Italy and entered Rome itself in 410. Already other, though less powerful, peoples had burst across the imperial threshold from the north. Four groups were to find their way to Spain, the Alans, the two branches of the Vandals, and the Suevi. The first of these were an Iranian folk who had attached themselves to the Asdingian Vandals in Austria in 401. The other branch of the Vandals, the Silingians, had settled for a time on the Main, but entered Gaul in 400. The Suevi, Germans from the area of the Spree, crossed the Rhine into Gaul in 407. These wanderers, numbering many thousands with their wives and children, exhausted the grain supplies of much of Gaul, and the imperial authorities then opened the way for them to cross the Pyrenees. Spanish landowners, by no means complaisant, brought their private armies of peasants from the great estates of the Ebro valley to the Pyrenean passes, but the barbarians were too numerous to be turned back. Diverted from the Hispano-Roman states of Tarraconensis, they repaired to the region of Pallantia (Palencia) where the peaceable Vaccei practised an extensive agriculture under a collective system, dividing the land annually and sharing out the crops. After two years their depredations produced famine and plague, and they appropriated more land. The Silingian Vandals entered Baetica; the Asdingians, southern Galicia; the Alans, Lusitania and Cartaginensis; and the Suevi, the furthermost part of Galicia: Tarraconensis thus still remained in Hispano-Roman hands.

In the following year, 412, the Visigoths left Italy for Gaul, attracted by an offer from the usurper Jovinus, with whom they promptly quarrelled. The Emperor Honorius then came to terms with them and sent them into Tarraconensis, to hold it as allies of Rome against other marauders. On their arrival in Barcelona they quarrelled among themselves, and having murdered two successive kings, elected Walia to lead them. He tried to convey them by sea to the granary of North Africa, but failed to obtain shipping, and being without corn, accepted the task of quelling the earlier intruders in return for pay and food. Marching into Baetica, he defeated the Alans and Silingians so thoroughly that they ceased to exist as separate peoples, and their remnants merged with the Suevi and Asdingians in Galicia. This done, Walia and his people left Spain and settled in south-western France, where the Roman *vicarius* was also the commander for the Peninsula. By 418 therefore Spain was again in Roman hands except that the Suevi and Vandals still shared the north-west with the Galicians.

But these peoples soon fell out. The Vandals first besieged the Suevi and then broke away, pushing aside the Roman general

Castinus and forcing their way into the south, where they took Seville and Cartagena. From these ports they sent expeditions to the Balearic islands and Mauretania, and finally embarked to found a German kingdom in Africa. Meanwhile, the Suevi again plundered Galicia, and although peace was made through the agency of Hydatius, Bishop of Braga, it was not long before they too took the road for the south.

At this time the Visigoths were still serving the Romans as allies or mercenaries. The ravages that had occurred had disrupted the economy of the Peninsula, as of Gaul. In both regions fugitive serfs, preferring the roving life of the German warriors to the unremitting toil of the great estates, had formed their own plundering bands: these *bagaudae* were numerous in Tarraconensis, and overran much of the Ebro valley. The Suevi, after sweeping through the south and east, now took advantage of the disturbed state of Tarraconensis to sack it, and retired with their captives and plunder to their fastness in Galicia. The Roman commander had failed to contain them and had been put to death; and his superior in Gaul therefore sent the Visigoths back into the Peninsula to restore order. In 456 their king Theodoric II led a campaign into Galicia, while his brother Frederic subdued the *bagaudae*. The king of the Suevi was defeated near Braga and died in prison, and once more Theodoric returned to Gaul.

Despite this punishment it was not long before the Suevi again invaded Lusitania and sacked Lisbon: Hydatius, whose duty it was to negotiate with them, complains bitterly of their bad faith. It is probable that the Catholic bishop fought a losing battle in an area still strongly Priscillianist and dominated by the Arians. After Hydatius' chronicle comes to an end, nothing is heard of catholicism in the north-west until the arrival of St. Martin of Dume to reconvert the area in about 550: at that time the Suevi still maintained political and religious independence.

After 461 it became clear that the Roman rulers could no longer maintain their authority in the Peninsula. In that year the Emperor Majorianus visited it with the intention of organising an expedition to overthrow the Vandal kingdom in Africa, but he failed even to set sail and was soon deposed. The Hispano-Romans were now at the mercy of the Visigoths. In 468 Euric killed his brother Theodoric, sent an army to repress the Suevi, occupied Lusitania and established a chain of settlements or garrisons across northern Spain, at Saragossa, Pamplona and Clunia (Coruña del Conde). No new functionaries or commanders were sent from Rome, and Euric was in fact an independent ruler. In 475 he drew up a code of Visigothic laws, and so ended all pretence of subordination to the empire.

The Visigoths, if not 'drunk with Romanism', were filled with respect for the imperial idea and bewildered by their own destruction of the great symbol of universalism. Paulus Orosius says that Ataulf had intended at first to replace the old Romania with a new 'Gothia', but finding the Goths 'incapable of obeying laws', chose the glory of restoring Rome with Gothic power. Thus although their rulers accepted the collaboration of Hispano-Roman advisers and officials, the Germanic peoples would not allow them to set up as Roman autocrats, but insisted on remaining a community of free warriors bound by their tribal customs and becoming a segregated military caste: there followed a long period of co-existence.

The Visigoths probably did not number more than 200,000 in a total population which may have reached nine millions. The first distributions of Spanish land among them took place between 419 and 431, when they were serving as allied soldiers and were probably settled according to Roman billetting usage, each family being placed in a house and receiving a third or two-thirds of the owner's land. Then or later they were probably awarded a large part of the old tribal territory of the Vaccei, the so-called Campi Gothici or Tierra de Campos, consisting of the plains north and south of the Douro, the wheatfields of the northern meseta. Their military duties against the troublesome peoples of Galicia led to the planting of settlements in the west and northwest, attested by the survival of place-names such as Godos and Villagodos. Elsewhere they formed garrisons in the chief towns or administrative centres, where each Gothic 'duke' or 'count' commanded a detachment of warriors. So long as they continued to govern from southern France Barcelona was an important point, and for a time they held court there; but two years after Euric's death Clovis, the king of the Salic Franks, advanced against Visigothic Aquitania and attracted the Gallo-Roman population by adopting catholicism. Although the Visigothic ruler, Alaric II, tried to counter this Frankish appeal by placing his Roman and German subjects on an equal footing before the law, Clovis defeated and killed him, and took Toulouse, and the Visigothic state was saved only by the intervention of the Ostrogoths of Italy. When in 526 their Ostrogothic protector died, their king Amalaric made terms with Clovis and married his daughter Clotilda. But the entry of a catholic into the Arian monarchy led to new troubles, and the Franks seized Narbonne and crossing the Pyrenees, occupied Pamplona and besieged Saragossa (? 541). During the crisis an Ostrogoth, Theudis, was made king of Spain and ruled long enough to save the Visigoths from collapse.

By now Byzantium was recovering its authority under Justinian. In 533 Belisarius had taken Carthage, destroyed the Vandal kingdom in Africa, and led its ruler captive to Constantinople. After his triumph, he invaded Sicily and even held Rome against the Ostrogoths, who offered to recognise him as emperor of the west. The revival of Roman rule in Africa inevitably threatened Spain; and Theudis, fearing a Byzantine attack from the south, crossed the straits and captured Septem (Ceuta) in 542, only to be driven out by the imperial troops. He had sought to conciliate the Hispano-Romans by marrying a Spanish catholic; but as eastern catholicism stretched out its arm along the African coast, the Arian Visigoths turned against him and murdered him in Seville. His successor, also an Ostrogoth, perished a year later.

The Visigoths now elected as their king one of themselves, Agila, who followed a policy of tribal nationalism. He oppressed the Hispano-Romans of the south, and they rebelled and defeated him as he marched on Córdoba. He was then rejected by his own people, who raised up Athanagild as king. The new ruler accepted the help of the Byzantines and defeated Agila near Seville (554). But the price of his success was the surrender of Baetica and part of Tarraconensis, and a Byzantine Spain continued to exist from 554 until the reign of Swinthila (621-31).

This contact with the east strengthened the southern catholics and did much to foster the revival of Spanish Romanism in the seventh century. Athanagild himself, having accepted a reduced Visigothic empire shorn of its former headquarters in Gaul, now established for the first time a capital of Spain at Toledo. This town, a minor Roman settlement, stood in mid-Spain at the centre of the criss-cross of military roads, and not far from the wheatlands of the Campi Gothici. The Arian capital was thus as safe as possible from its three catholic enemies, the Franks at the Pyrenees, the Byzantines in the south, and the Suevi in Galicia, now converted by St. Martin of Dume (c. 550-60). The setting up of this military headquarters probably led to a redeployment of the Visigoths settled in Spain, both to the centre and towards the new frontier in the south. Athanagild attacked the Byzantines on several occasions and recovered Seville, but on his death in 567 much of Baetica was still under the eastern empire.

The 'empire' of the Visigoths, though it was the first Spanish state, was in its origins as extra-national as the system it superseded. The new rulers of Spain were neither pagans like the free peoples of the north, nor catholics. Arianism was a 'natural' Christianity which had solved the conundrum of the three persons by subordinating the Son to the Father. The Bible had been translated into Gothic, and the church was national. Visigothic society was an association of free warriors, who cherished the right to elect their kings; their God was a moral force who revealed himself in judgements and ordeals. They had probably no written law of their own, and the military leader was also a judge, who called upon assessors or 'good men' to settle suits with him in public. The free men of a settlement were jointly responsible for any crime committed in it, and the clan or Sippe was collectively responsible for the honour of its members and so for their misdeeds. Their customs were literal and direct: brides were bought, wounds were compensable according to their place and depth, and punishments were often public and corporal. Honour was a man's most prized possession, and it was understood that he should take the law into his own hands to defend it.

All this was in complete contrast with Roman legal and social usage; and while the written codes promulgated by successive Visigothic kings reflect a growing tendency towards Romanism, the intense revival of Germanic customs which occurred after the Reconquest shows that in the north, where Roman civilisation rested lightly on the indigenous peoples, there was on the contrary a widespread reception of Germanism.

But in the Roman south a strong reaction followed. Its spearhead was the catholic church, reimpregnated with theocratic ideals by its contact with the Byzantines, and its leader was St. Leander, whose father had been a man of consequence in Byzantine Cartagena, and who, as Metropolitan of Seville, was able to introduce catholicism into the bosom of the royal family. The crown had fallen to Leovigild, who had married Athanagild's widow, and now recovered much of Baetica, including the city of Córdoba (572): after this only Granada and part of Cartaginensis remained in eastern hands. In the north he contained the Suevi and defeated the Basques, founding the town of Vitoria on their frontier (581). These successes were accompanied by a reform of Euric's code: in an attempt to lessen the gap between his two peoples Leovigild abolished the requirement of rebaptism for catholics who embraced Arianism and abrogated the old imperial law which forbade intermarriage between Romans and barbarians, though it may have been a dead letter long before. He then allowed his younger son Hermenegild to marry a catholic, Ingunda, and sent him to govern Baetica. But Ingunda, aided by St. Leander, converted her husband; and when Leovigild ordered him to return to Toledo, he came out in open rebellion with the support of the Byzantines, the catholic cities of the south and the Suevi. Leovigild marched the length of Spain from Vitoria to Seville and captured his son at Córdoba. The young man was held prisoner at Valencia, and when he refused to abjure, murdered by his jailor: outside Spain he was recognised as a catholic martyr and included in martyrologies, but in Spain itself the stigma of rebellion deprived him of this reward.

Because of his victories Leovigild enjoyed great prestige among his people. If he remained the champion of Arianism, he was none the less aware of the political attractions of catholicism and of the

Byzantine practice of hereditary monarchy. He and his successors repeatedly sought to circumvent the elective tradition by conferring power on their sons during their own lifetimes. Leovigild thus 'associated' his son Reccared, after whom he named his new city of Recopolis in Celtiberia. There was no immediate resistance to the hereditary succession; and within ten months, impelled by St. Leander, Reccared was converted to catholicism and summoned the Arian bishops and clergy to a council at which they were urged to follow his example. Many of the Visigoths refused to accept the change. Traditionalist insurrections in Lusitania and southern France were suppressed, but after Reccared's death in 601 the Arians rose up against his son Liuva II, whom they declared a bastard. The Visigothic traditionalists now deposed and killed the king, ending the attempt to create a royal dynasty and electing one of their own party, Witeric, to the throne. Seven years later, he too was killed, and in 612 the catholic party recovered power: their king Sisebut was to prove the most Romanising of the Visigothic rulers.

The 'Visigothic golden age' begun by St. Leander and carried to its summit by his brother and successor St Isidore was not a renascence of anything Visigothic, but a revival of Romanism. In the north and west Latin culture had petered out after the time of Hydatius and Paulus Orosius, both witnesses of the entry of the barbarians, and nothing more is heard of it until the arrival of St Martin of Dume (c. 550): in the north-east the silence extends until 567, when John of Bíclaro, Bishop of Gerona, composed a brief chronicle. But in the south academics of rhetoric may have continued to produce administrators as of old; and in the sixth century St. Leander established a school in which the classical trivium and quadrivium were taught side by side with theology and scriptural exegesis. Justinian's attempt to reconstitute the Roman world had now failed, and Spain was to remain independent of both Rome and Byzantium. But the ambition of the eastern emperors for a Christendom united by the twin bonds of citizenship and religion was firmly implanted in southern Spain, and Leander and Isidore set themselves the double task of capturing the Visigothic monarchy and restoring the Roman tradition. St. Isidore is chiefly remembered as the great preserver of classical learning, the compiler and encyclopaedist who seemed to proceed 'out of Antiquity itself'. But his influence was direct and political. His 'praise of Spain' and his commendation of Sisebut's successor Swinthila (621-31) as 'prince of peoples' and the 'first ruler to obtain the monarchy of all Spain' anticipate a new patriotism born of Visigothic authority and Hispano-Roman culture. Although Swinthila was elected in the Gothic fashion, St. Isidore declared that he had acceded by God's grace and anointed him with chrism according to the Old Testament ritual: the elected king was thus invested with a divine right, and the church associated itself with him by sealing the oaths of his nobles and laying anathema on his rivals.

The alliance of the Visigothic monarchy with the southern church found expression in the long series of Councils of Toledo. The first two Councils took place before the formal association of church and state; but the Third Council met in 587 to celebrate the conversion of Reccared and 'of the lineage of the Goths'. St. Isidore presided over the Fourth Council in 633, and it then became the custom for the Metropolitan of Toledo to act as head of the church. With the establishment of the dual authority, temporal and spiritual, and the removal of the headquarters of the church to the new political capital, the image of a Spanish state was already formed, and the Middle Ages were to look back to the Visigothic empire as a lost ideal. But although the surviving canons of the Councils show that the crown consulted the church on civil matters, the Visigothic nobility remained the arbitrators of secular power; and the Hispano-German duality of the seventh century was no more than an awkward compromise.

For reasons that remain obscure, Swinthila himself fell from grace, and his nobles, led by Sisnand, governor of Septimania, rose against him. The Fourth Council of Toledo denounced him as a tyrant, approved the sequestration of his possessions, and expelled him from the church. Both Sisnand and Isidore died in 636, and the nobles elected Khintila: his succession was confirmed by the Fifth and Sixth Councils, which pronounced an anathema against all who might try to depose him or seek the crown without being of pure Gothic descent or after having received the tonsure. Khintila attempted to dynasticise the succession, but his son Tulga was deposed and tonsured; and the throne was occupied by an elderly noble, Khindaswinth. The Visigoths were now divided into two irreconcilable factions, and the new king sought to assure himself and his party by killing five hundred nobles and two hundred free men. When he 'associated' his son Recceswinth with him, a new revolt occurred in the north, but it was repressed; and on the death of the old king in 653 Recceswinth continued to reign alone.

Of the two parties Khintila had represented the northern or 'purist' Visigoths, and Khindaswinth and his family the partisans of Romanisation. With the temporary victory of the latter, Recceswinth promulgated the *Liber Iudiciorum*, in which five hundred laws were arranged in twelve sections after the style of Justinian's code. The juridical distinction between Visigoths and natives was abolished, and the new code was made applicable, at least in theory, throughout the Peninsula.

Recceswinth died in 672 at the royal estate of Gerticos to the north-east of Salamanca on the edge of the Campi Gothici. A period of forty years, one of the most obscure in Spanish history, separates his death from the final collapse of the Visigothic state before the Muslim attack. Even allowing for the furious enthusiasm of the invaders, it is still remarkable that an area with a population of several millions, including tribes which had made so fierce a resistance to the Romans and were so often in the future to prove their military spirit, should have failed so abjectly to defend itself, especially when governed by a race which believed the military life to be the only noble one. The legal synthesis achieved by Recceswinth appears to cover a double decline. Among the Visigoths the elective monarchy was the very foundation of social order: the assembly of free warriors was the constitutional basis of society, and it was firmly opposed to dynasticism, with the possible succession of a woman or a minor. But when the tribal mass was dispersed over Spain, the primitive assembly could no longer function. For a time the assent of provincial authorities was sought when a new king was elected, but it was later decided that the election should be held wherever the old king had died, and only the nobles at court could participate. In the sixth century there was still a council of elder warriors or *seniores*, sometimes called a senate, but it seems to have been eclipsed by the *aula regia*, or royal council borrowed from the *palatium* of the lower empire. The kingship was thus confined to a political minority.

Meanwhile, in the course of the sixth century the last vestiges of the old Roman *municipium* also disappeared. The free middle class which had been responsible for the raising of taxes and the performance of civil duties, now collapsed. Although laws had been passed to prevent anyone from leaving the old curial caste and even to oblige those who entered it by marriage to assume municipal responsibilities, its numbers steadily declined, and it was now often impossible to find anyone qualified to attest municipal documents. The functions of the Roman municipal class passed to a Visigothic official, the *grefja* or judge, who acted as governor of the town. The only representative office was that of the *defensor*, or advocate for the populace: in the seventh century he was elected under the supervision of the bishop, but even this sole survivor of Hispano-Roman civic traditions may have become merely an appointee.

The Visigoths had come to Spain as a caste of warriors, and it was on the battlefield that their order was to perish. Their assumption of the Hispano-Roman roles of great landlords and provincial governors disrupted their primitive military organisation and the last Visigothic kings found it increasingly difficult to mobilise their followers: the rulers of the Romanising party even ordered their adherents to serve with slaves from the great estates.

On Recceswinth's death the royal council elected one of their number, Wamba, to succeed him. There followed a rebellion in Septimania; and when Wamba sent one Paul, a provincial governor of Byzantine stock, to repress it, he joined the rebels and won over the duke of Tarraconensis. Wamba carried a victorious campaign against his enemies as far as Nîmes, and paraded Paul and his fellow-traitors in disgrace through the streets of Toledo:

in 673 Wamba made enslavement the penalty for any noble who failed to present himself for military service. But seven years later he was overthrown, disqualified from ruling by being shorn and tonsured, and shut up in a monastery. His successor, Erwig, was the son of a 'Byzantine' by a niece of Khindaswinth, and thus represented the southern faction, now Gothic only in name. He modified Wamba's law of military service; and after the Thirteenth Council of Toledo had approved a canon which secured all the nobles of the palace against arrest, the two factions were reconciled, and Erwig's daughter married a nephew of the dethroned Wamba, Egica, who succeeded in 687.

Although the new king had taken an oath to defend his father-in-law's party, Wamba, still living in a monastery near Burgos, insisted that the feud should be resumed, and Egica asked the Fifteenth Council to absolve him from his oath. This was done, and there followed a series of plots and repressions. Probably in order to secure the succession of his son Witiza, Egica authorised the dignitaries of the palace to transmit their offices and privileges to their sons; and this final abandonment of the Visigothic tradition was followed by more disturbances in the provinces.

The social and political cleavage of the Visigoths was followed by a no less profound religious conflict in the south and east. St. Isidore, the first propounder of the Spanish state, was also the author of the first anti-Jewish treatise in the west. Eastern Romanism, with its insistence on secular and spiritual unity, had legislated against the Jews, while western Rome had remained tolerant. The earlier Visigothic kings had passed no discriminatory legislation, and under them the Spanish Jews received the same treatment as in the western empire. At this time the Jewish communities of the south and east probably formed a substantial proportion of the 'transmarini negotiatores' who controlled the Mediterranean trade of Spain. The first active anti-semitic legislation dates from the time of Isidore's pupil Sisebut, who in 613 decreed that Jews must accept conversion or leave Spain: few probably took the second alternative, and a form of composition may have been reached. But in 681 Erwig reminded the Twelfth Council of the need to enforce the existing legislation, and the law requiring baptism within a year was confirmed: in 693 unconverted Jews were denied access to the market-places and forbidden to trade with Christians, and the Seventeenth Council further decided that Jews should be deprived of their property and reduced to perpetual slavery. These penalties, analogous to those applied in cases of treason, were accompanied by accusations that the Spanish Jews were conspiring with those of Africa. If, or how, the Christian threat to Mediterranean trade was related to the sudden expansion of Islam remains obscure. Neither in Spain nor in Africa could the Jews have been ignorant that a place was reserved for them in the 'house of Islam', and after the Muslim conquest Spanish Jews quickly rallied to the new invaders. But so, too, did the traditionalist faction of the Visigoths, and it seems probable that in the legend-laden atmosphere that surrounds the 'ruin of Spain' opportunism has been often confused with treason.

Egica had associated his son Witiza with the crown since 693 and made him regent in 698. When Witiza succeeded in 702, he in turn seems to have attempted to 'associate' his son Akhila, whom he made governor of Tarraconensis. In this he was opposed by groups of nobles, who were defeated and punished. For a time also the laws against the Jews seem to have been moderated. But when in 710 Witiza died, Akhila was still in the north; and before he could reach Toledo, his family was driven out of the imperial city and took refuge in Galicia. The southern faction of the Visigoths then elected Roderic, who had probably been governor or duke of Baetica. Akhila sent troops against him, but they were defeated. But before Roderic had time to secure himself, a greater cataclysm was ready to burst.

III

THE MUSLIM ASCENDANCY

1. THE CONQUEST

THE thunderings of Islam had already been heard from across the straits. Since Muhammad's flight from Mecca in 622, his new faith had swept along the North African coast, encompassing the area that had belonged successively to Carthage, Rome, the Vandals and Byzantium. Within a generation of the Prophet's death, one of its generals, 'Uqba ibn Nafi', reached Tangier and raided the old Roman city of Volubilis and the plains of Atlantic Morocco (681–2: h.62). With the fall of Carthage in 698 Byzantine Africa ceased to exist, and only the port of Ceuta facing southern Spain remained independent. But the Berbers of the Atlas and central Morocco resisted, and it was only in 705 that the African north-west finally fell to Musa ibn Nuṣair. He appointed a freedman, Ṭariq ibn Ziyad, to govern Tangier, and himself returned to his headquarters in Tunisia. According to versions preserved by both Muslim and Christian writers, the governor of Ceuta, one Julian, possibly a Byzantine, proposed the conquest of Spain to Musa, and even made a small raid on the bay of Algeciras in November 709. But Musa had been forbidden by the Caliph to do more than reconnoitre; and he had already retired from the scene when in July 710 a scouting force of four hundred men, including a hundred horse and commanded by Ṭarif ibn Mulluk, were landed at the place now called Tarifa, using four ships supplied by Julian. On their return Ṭariq sent part of the booty to Musa and began to prepare a larger expedition, this time of seven thousand men, mostly Berbers, commanded by a few Arabs and freedmen. They were ferried over the straits in the same four ships in April and May 711 and seized the ancient town of Carteia, from which a camp was established on the 'green isle' of Algeciras. It was known that Roderic was fighting in the north, and as soon as news came that he was marching south Ṭariq sent urgently for more men, receiving another five thousand Berbers. Almost all his army was probably on foot, and he advanced about a day's march and awaited Roderic at the Guadalete, a stream near Arcos de la Frontera. The Visigothic horde appeared on July 19, and in the battle fought during the succeeding days, it was utterly routed. Roderic himself perished, possibly by drowning: his horse and regalia were found in a marsh.

Muslim writers say that both wings of Roderic's army were commanded by partisans of Akhila, who fled with their men. These may have been Witiza's brothers, Oppa and Sisbert. Whatever their conduct on the field, Witiza's family lived unmolested and protected by the conquerors. If Ṭariq did not give them the Visigothic throne, at least the royal estates passed back into their possession, and this reward was ratified by both Musa and the caliph.[1]

When Musa ibn Nuṣair was informed of the victory, he was jealous and angry. Collecting a force of eighteen thousand men, including many Arabs, 'successors' of the Prophet and their retainers, he crossed to the 'green isle' in June 712 and occupied Seville and the towns near it. The Visigoths retired upon Mérida, which surrendered in June 713. It was the last stand. After this victory Musa marched towards Toledo, where Ṭariq had forestalled him. At their meeting he struck the disobedient subordinate with his whip, possibly to cover himself against caliphal disapproval, and then entered the Visigothic capital. All the treasure of the kings was seized, and coins were struck bearing inscriptions in Arabic and Latin. In the spring Musa established a garrison in Saragossa and pressed on as far as Barcelona.

A messenger now arrived with orders for Musa and Ṭariq to

---

[1] The fact that these consisted of 3,000 farms illustrates the extreme concentration of the land in the hands of the Visigoths.

C

return to Damascus; but before obeying, Musa marched across the north and north-west of the Peninsula. In the spring of 714 the aged conqueror placed his son 'Abdu'l-'Aziz in charge of Spain and departed for Syria. The new Caliph disgraced him, and both he and Ṭariq died in obscurity.

The new religion was both spiritually and temporally an anti-Romanism. Christianity had been born in Judaea, on the very rim of the Roman world, and travelling by the tranquil seaways of the Mediterranean, had made a peaceful conquest of the ancient world. But in the east its reforming impulse had been lost in vain controversies, and it had degenerated into a despotic caesaropapism. The faith of Islam, formulated not far away, but a little outside the frontier of the old empire, reaffirmed the essential brotherhood of man, but sought to avoid metaphysical schisms by tolerating no speculation about the unity of God. It was a challenge to the Christian faith and to the legendary imperium of Rome: if the greatest power of the ancient world had accepted the mild pervasion of Christianity, how should it not succumb to a new and embattled theocracy? Whatever the caliph's own hesitations, his African subjects did not falter: within a few years of crossing the straits, the paladins of Islam were fighting in Gaul. The Arabs and their newly indoctrinated Berber armies were hardly more united than the Visigoths and the Hispano-Romans, and the secret of their triumph lay not in a greater social cohesion, but in the fact that they were joined in a large and profitable enterprise in which religious faith and military might were in harmony, not at variance: their dissensions were to come later.

The conquest was rapidly completed. Travelling by the system of Roman roads, the invaders marched from one administrative centre to the next, receiving the capitulations of the Visigothic counts as they went, or replacing them with small garrisons or trustworthy allies. Musa himself took Seville and Mérida and traversed the north as far as the land of the Basques, receiving the surrender of Asturica (Astorga), Legio and Amaya, the capital of the Cantabrians. Count Fortún, the governor of part of what is now Aragon, capitulated to Ṭariq and embraced Islam, while in the south-east another Visigothic count, Theodemir, who

THE MUSLIM ASCENDANCY

governed the modern Murcia from the town of Auriola (Orihuela), received a guarantee of full autonomy in return for the payment of tribute. When Musa left Spain, the capitulations probably covered all the Peninsula with the exception of the Basques and other hill-peoples of the Atlantic and Pyrenean zones, though there were still many places where the invaders had not yet been seen.

'Abdu'l-'Aziz set himself up as wali, or governor, with headquarters in Seville, where he married Roderic's widow Egilona. This may have been the proper course in legalistic Spain; but it gave Damascus the impression that the governor intended to act as king, and early in 716 he was murdered while praying in the cathedral-mosque in Seville. A wali was sent to take his place, and for the following forty years Spain was ruled by a succession of governors appointed either from Africa or directly from Damascus. Of a total of twenty, only three survived as long as five years: those who did not fall in battle were murdered by their rivals or died in feuds between the Yemenites and Qaisites, ancestral enemies.

The first governors attempted to carry the expansion of Islam into France. They ravaged Gascony and Poitou in 732, but after their defeat at the hands of Charles Martel this ambition had to be abandoned, and the Franks established themselves as far south as the Pyrenees.

Already in 716-19 the centre of Muslim authority had been advanced from Seville to the Roman administrative city of Córdoba, commanding the middle course of the Guadalquivir, the mines of the Sierra Morena and the pass leading to the meseta. Meanwhile, the Arab nobility settled in the towns of Andalusia and eastern Spain, assuming control of the estates of the Hispano-Romans. New contingents arrived with successive governors, but the 'first conquerors' resented the demands of these latecomers who had not fought for the land, much as the Spanish conquistadores strove to maintain their monopoly of Peru. So bitter were the quarrels that the Caliph is said to have thought of abandoning the whole enterprise.

But the majority of the invaders were Berbers from Mauretania, now called the Magrib or 'west'. They came from a variety of different tribes, speaking different languages and often still ignorant of Arabic. Many belonged to the great confederations of the Gumaras, Zanata, Hawwara, Matgara, Madyuna and Miknasa, but there were also smaller groups, such as the banu Razin who gave their name to Albarracín and the Walhaṣa of Ronda. Most were pastoral peoples who settled on the uplands of the central meseta or the Penibetic mountains rather than among the towns and fields of lower Andalusia. Within a generation of the conquest the whole Berber world rose in protest against the arrogance of the Arab nobility and embraced an Islamic heresy which laid emphasis on equality and brotherhood, and opposed the pretensions of the successors of the Prophet. In 740 the whole of the Magrib was in arms, and the Berbers of Galicia, Leon and central Spain marched against the Arabs of the cities, slaughtering those who stood in their way. As the Spanish Arabs retired upon Toledo and Córdoba, the caliph sent an army with some seven thousand Syrian cavalry to the Magrib; but being defeated there, it withdrew into Spain, where it succoured Córdoba and relieved Toledo. Having borne the brunt of the fighting, the new-comers demanded land, and there followed another struggle. At length a new governor made a fresh partition, dispersing the Arab tribal contingents or *junds* across the south from Portugal to Murcia. The main inflow of semitic settlers had now taken place. They were far fewer than the Visigoths who had revived Indo-European Spain three centuries earlier; but unlike them, the Arabs occupied the towns and spread their compact military communities throughout the Andalusian heartland, restoring the Tartessian and Roman urbanism of the south and establishing, not a segregated caste, but an open society which incorporated native Spaniards into its patrilineal system.

Meanwhile, the Berber population of northern and central Spain was much reduced. A new revolution occurred in 745, and it was followed by five years of famine, during which many more Berbers returned to Africa. Most of the Douro valley was probably evacuated, and a wide belt of no man's land now lay between the independent peoples of the north-west and the outposts of the Muslim state of al-Andalus.

2. ASTURIAS

In the first heat of the conquest the invaders thought mainly of attaching the existing divisions of the Visigothic state to their own system and not of a general occupation, for which their resources were quite inadequate. In their desire to challenge the Roman world they therefore neglected the isolated mountain regions of the Asturias and the Pyrenees. Both Romans and Visigoths had had to admit the independence of the Basques; and Musa too was content to leave them alone. He had received the capitulations of Astorga, Leon and Amaya, but he seems not to have ventured north of the Cantabrians, though a Berber leader called Munusa later appeared in Jejone (Gijón). In the midst of their own convulsions it was not difficult for the Arabs to dismiss the free peoples of the Asturias as a 'band of wild asses'.

According to tradition, the first to make a stand against the invaders was one Pelayo (Pelagius), who stirred up the Astures, the natives of the Picos de Europa, and was elected their leader at a tribal council in c. 718. He beat off a Muslim expedition into the mountains of Covadonga in 722; and the enemy did not return to these narrow and perilous valleys. Munusa may have abandoned Gijón long before the great Berber withdrawal. There can be little doubt that much of these northern fastnesses never submitted, except inasmuch as they were involuntarily included in wider capitulations.

Pelayo may have been a member of Witiza's or Roderic's guard, a fugitive from Córdoba, but this is uncertain.[1] His victory gave him local prestige, and he set up a village capital at Cangas de Onís, to which Visigothic refugees repaired. In neighbouring Cantabria there was also an independent governor or count, and his son Alfonso married Pelayo's daughter Ermesinda, uniting

---

[1] His name is not Germanic, but Latinised Celtic: cf. Pelagius (?Morgan), the stolid philosopher whom St. Jerome thought 'stuffed with British porridge'.

the two domains and giving rise to the royal line of Asturias. When the Berber rebellion of 740-1 drew away the invaders from the Douro valley, the small independent kingdom began to expand beyond the limits of the northern mountains; and in the middle of the century Alfonso I was able to advance over much of the north and north-west, entering Oporto, Braga and Viseu in modern Portugal, Astorga and Leon and part of what is now Castile, and even ranging as far south as Segovia and Avila. But he was unable to occupy more than a small proportion of this vast area, and therefore carried back part of the population which he resettled on his own frontiers.

The neo-Gothic kingdom thus came to consist of Asturias itself, flanked by Galicia to the west and Cantabria to the east: the Basques maintained relations with it, though they were still independent. In all this area the invaders had either not appeared or made only a short stay, and left no enduring mark of their presence. But further east, the valley of the Ebro, with its irrigated fields and its city of Saragossa, was a prize not to be let slip, and the Muslims maintained a garrison as far north as Pamplona. In the middle Pyrenees, the mountain communities perhaps paid tribute, but avoided occupation. Still further east, along the Mediterranean shore, lay the ancient road by which the Romans and Visigoths had entered Spain. This, for Islam, was the route of the Holy War; and although after the middle of the century the Franks drove the invaders from Septimania, both sides were to establish a fortified area between the sea and the Pyrenean foothills. From this 'Spanish march' the Franks were gradually to extend their control over the semi-autonomous mountain peoples. But little is heard of the Pyrenean communities until almost the end of the eighth century.

3. THE EMIRATE

Al-Andalus did not long remain a dependency of Damascus. In Syria the Umaiyad dynasty was overthrown and massacred by the descendants of Muhammad's cousin, the 'Abbasids. Only one escaped, a youth of twenty called 'Abdu'r-Raḥman: his mother had been a Berber, and he now made his way to the Magrib, where he conceived the idea of restoring the power of his house in the west. There were Syrian traditionalists in al-Andalus, and when he crossed the straits, most of the junds welcomed him. In 756 he defeated the governor at the gates of Córdoba and proclaimed himself Emir of al-Andalus.

The dynasty of 'Abdu'r-Raḥman, 'the immigrant', was to rule over Muslim Spain for two and a half centuries. Severed from Damascus and Baghdad by bitter clan-hatred, the Spanish Umaiyads were filled with nostalgia for their homeland and toiled restlessly to remake Spain in an eastern mould, resuming and intensifying the process begun by the Phoenicians. The founder of the emirate reigned from 756 until 788: he was an impressive figure, tall, loquacious, one-eyed, crowned with yellow curls and clad in white, the colour of his house. Many clients of his family rallied to him, but his 'Abbasid enemies did their best to stir up revolts against him. In 763 he was besieged in Carmona, but broke out, defeated his foes and sent their leader's head to be thrown down in the market-place at Qairwan. Four years later, the Berbers of the Tagus valley began to listen to the teaching of a village schoolmaster who preached simple faith and denounced Arab arrogance: from Sopetrán (Guadalajara) he occupied Coria, Medellín and Mérida, and nearly eight years passed before his followers were bribed to murder him and his movement collapsed.

Meanwhile, in 777 the 'Abbasids had sent more agents to provoke rebellion, and the governor of Saragossa was tempted to try his fortune, though not in the interests of the caliphs. He sought out Charlemagne at Paderborn, and persuaded him to send an army into Spain. So in 778 the Franks crossed the Pyrenees, subdued the Vascones or Navarrese of Pamplona, and reached Saragossa, only to find that the inhabitants had changed their minds and shut their gates. As the Frankish army retraced its steps, the Vascones fell on it in the long pass of Roncesvalles and won a famous victory. A few years later the people of Gerona opened their gates to the Franks: although the Muslims destroyed its walls in 793, its keep held out and the Frankish march remained secure.

When the first Umaiyad died, he left a kingdom now subdued, though far from unified, and had begun to raise a Syrian capital on the Visigothic shell of Córdoba. The old metropolitan church, which had long served Muslims on Fridays and Christians on Sundays, was now devoted entirely to Islam, and underwent the first of many extensions made necessary by the constant growth of the capital. Outside the city the Emir raised a garden-palace to remind him of the summer-houses of Palmyra.

For his successor, he chose his younger son Hisham I, possibly because he had been born in Spain. It fell to the second ruler to islamise the chequered provinces he had inherited, and he sent students to the east and invited theologians and jurists to Spain. In particular, a group of Spaniards studied at Medina with Malik ibn Anas (†795-6), who had developed a system of law based on the most literal reading of the Koran and Traditions: a compilation of Malik's teachings by a Cordobese Berber made Spain the citadel of this strict and dogmatic orthodoxy.

Hisham's successor, al-Hakam I (796-822) had inherited his grandfather's restless energies and hastened the process of Syrianisation. The frontier area from the Ebro to the Tagus, with its three capitals of Saragossa, Toledo and Mérida, all largely populated by converts (*muwalladun*) or subject Christians (mozarabs), rose in revolt; but al-Hakam defended himself with a professional army composed of Spaniards, Muslim and Christian, Berbers and slaves. These last, the 'Slavs', were prisoners or children sold by the tribes of north-eastern Europe to Jewish merchants who brought them by way of Verdun (where they were often castrated), Marseilles and Almería, to Córdoba. In the Emir's army they mingled with the mercenaries; but they were also admitted into his palace and came to occupy the great offices in the royal household.

The cost of maintaining this army and of the new palaces and the luxuries brought into Spain from the east was very great, and al-Hakam's taxation was resisted in the capital and in the provinces. In the north-east, disaffected governors surrendered Barcelona to the Franks, and Tarragona was temporarily lost (801-3). Toledo, if now as much Muslim as Christian, remained more Gothic than Arab: when it rebelled, al-Ḥakam bade the muwallad governor of Talavera to reduce it at all costs. Its leading citizens were lured to the citadel and murdered and their bodies flung into the ditch. This bloody 'day of the ditch' was stamped in the memories of the survivors, yet al-Ḥakam had to send troops to impose order in Toledo almost each year from 811 to 818. In Córdoba itself a plot to overthrow the Emir was betrayed, and the bodies of the conspirators exposed on crosses on the riverside promenade below the great mosque. In consequence al-Ḥakam bought more slaves and placed his guard under the command of the head of the Christian community.

In 818 the Christian general was entrusted with the task of collecting new tribute. Córdoba had now spread outwards round the mosque and beyond the river, where its proletariat occupied the old Roman settlement of Secunda, the 'suburb'. When their faqihs denounced the application of taxes not sanctioned by the Koran, they hooted al-Ḥakam as he came in from hunting cranes across the river, and seized the great Roman bridge. The royal army was called out to sack the southern suburb: it was rased and three hundred persons were crucified. The rest of its inhabitants were expelled from Spain, and some settled in Fez while others travelled to Alexandria and finally seized Crete, which they held until 961. Al-Ḥakam was remembered as 'the one of the suburb'. But later writers, looking back from the wreck of the Muslim state, commended his severity. According to a well-known poem he could tell his heir: "I have wielded my sword to unite my sundered provinces as a tailor uses his needle to sew pieces of cloth together. . . . I leave you my kingdom at peace, my son: it is a bed in which you may sleep quietly. . . ." His son, 'Abdu'r-Raḥman II, reigned for thirty years, a period of peace which poets likened to a honeymoon between the Emir and his people.

The Visigoths had brought to Spain a tribal military system, but had been forced to adopt the political and religious institutions of the Hispano-Romans: Islam provided a faith, a military organisation, and a new state. The ruler of Umaiyad Spain was an autocrat who possessed in his household all the organs of government, and was head of the state, leader of religion, the source of justice and commander of his own army. His administration, or diwan, of Persian origin, was a council of ministers, a treasury, and a civil service. The chief adviser was given the title of hajib (chamberlain)[1]: to him the royal secretaries, inspectors and collectors of taxes were responsible. The government of the capital depended directly on the emir, who appointed its qadi or judge of the city, and also the head of the police and officials of the markets. Outside the capital, each of the kuras, or provinces, consisted of a city and its surrounding area, with its governor appointed by the emir to stand in his stead. The governor himself settled questions of civil law, while a qadi applied Koranic law. He might also have a military leader (qa'id, Sp. *alcaide*) to command his garrison: the marches of the frontier were under purely military control. There was no representative municipal life in the Roman sense. The cities of al-Andalus were essentially centres of administration and markets, not municipalities.[2] Islam did however provide for the autonomous co-existence of the three 'peoples of the Book', and allowed both Christians and Jews to preserve their own communal organisation and apply their own law. Each community was required to acknowledge a responsible head and to provide a tax-gatherer: in the case of the subject Christians or mozarabs, the head of the community in Córdoba was regarded as the 'count of the Christians', who spoke in general for all his co-religionists.

The administrative unit, the town, and its economic centre, the market-place, were much more highly developed than their equivalents in the north. About the market-place, with its adjoining suks, its inspectors, police and porters, were placed the currency exchange, the toll-office, the mint, the warehouse for foreign merchandise, and the mosque with its school or university. At least from the time of 'Abdu'r-Rahman II al-Andalus had a money economy based on the gold dinar (imitated from the

---

[1] The word visir, so used in the east, was in Spain the title of each of the ministers.

[2] The sole institution of local representation was the trade-guild, probably derived from Byzantium, which broke across the rigid separation of the three religious confessions: but it does not seem to appear until the tenth century.

Byzantine aureus), the silver dirham (from the Persian drachma), and the bronze *fals*; of these, silver and bronze circulated in considerable quantities. While the Visigothic monarchy had conceived power in terms of the mere possession of land and hoarding of treasure, the fortunes of the Umaiyad rulers were linked to a freer economic system. The emir derived his revenues from personal estates, general taxation defined by the Koran, and income from buildings and land set aside for religious and charitable purposes. The sanctioned taxes included a tithe on produce paid by Muslims, a poll-tax and land-tax paid by non-Muslims, and tribute collected by the heads of communities of whatever confession. A special branch of the administration negotiated treaties by which communal leaders recognised the emir and undertook to pay him tribute: his prosperity and his military power were thus closely related, the more so since non-Koranic taxes, such as customs-duties and sales-taxes, derived from Roman or Byzantine models, were held to be illegal. 'Abdu'r-Raḥman II, profiting by his father's severity, saw his revenues rise to a million dinars a year, or almost double those of al-Ḥakam. This wealth permitted him to maintain a guard of some three thousand horse and two thousand foot in barracks attached to his palace.

It also hastened the Syrianisation of al-Andalus. To minister to the nostalgia of the Umaiyads, books, jewels, spices, fine textiles, furs, musicians and wives were brought in, largely by Jewish merchants. New industries were also set up in Spain. There already existed in the palace in Córdoba the *tiraz*, or royal factory of carpets and robes, which produced fine articles for the emir's own use and for him to bestow as presents on officials, visitors and foreign princes. Córdoba now also acquired fame for its leathers, metalwork and silk-weaving.

'Abdu'r-Raḥman's circle was remarkable for its variety of talents. Its inspirer was the Iraqi musician Ziryab, who had studied in Baghdad, excited the jealousy of the reigning arbiter of taste there, and fled to Spain soon after 'Abdu'r-Raḥman's accession: he founded a school of music, invented a new lute, replaced the old metal tableware with glass or glazed ware, introduced table-covers of fine leather, laid down rules for cooking, established the order of courses at table and designed dresses for the elegant. Among the Emir's philosophers and poets was Yahya ibn Ḥakam 'the gazelle', famous for the pungency of his satirical verse and chosen to be the Emir's ambassador to the Emperor of Byzantium. No less remarkable was 'Abbas ibn Firnas, of Berber descent, who excelled in all kinds of eccentric and original activities. His conjuring included both prestidigitation and the occult sciences, and he is said to have built a model of the firmament in glass. Perhaps his most surprising feat was an attempt to fly: dressed in a suit of silk feathers with movable wings, he leapt from a cliff and came to earth almost uninjured.

The fame of 'Abdu'r-Raḥman's court spread throughout western Europe and Africa. It also reached Byzantium, whence the Emperor sent to ask for the return of Crete, still held by the refugees of 'the suburb', and to propose an alliance against the 'Abbasids. The Emir disclaimed responsibility for the first and refused to engage himself against the second. But al-Andalus was soon assailed from another direction. In 844 the Norsemen, having seized Nantes, sailed southwards and attacked the ports of Galicia, whence they ranged the Atlantic sea-board and appeared with fifty-four longships in the estuary of the Tagus. The people of Lisbon held their own, and within a fortnight the raiders pursued their way southwards, entering the mouth of the Guadalquivir and pillaging the places of its great plain. Seville had no fleet, and its governor retreated to Carmona. But when the visitors had sacked the abandoned city and were scouring the villages, 'Abdu'r-Raḥman sent forward his army, which destroyed some of the longships and forced the rest to put to sea. The stragglers were spared on condition they abandoned paganism, and these Norse Muslims settled near Seville, where they applied themselves to the honest trade of cheese-making.

During the same age part of the Spanish mozarabic population also passed over to Islam. The origin of the crisis appears to have been economic, and it passed from the still restless towns of the frontier to Córdoba itself, and culminated in a long upheaval in the extreme south. It seems probable that the Emir had responded to the consolidation of the Frankish frontier and the campaigns of the Asturians by levying new taxes on the frontier towns. In 828 Louis the Pious wrote to the mozarabs of Mérida inciting them to rebel and reminding them that the Umaiyads had unjustly increased the tribute and exacted it by force, 'turning you from friends to enemies'. Some years later Toledo rebelled, and it and other towns were forced to pledge their loyalty by sending citizens to Córdoba to dwell in a 'house of the hostages'. This device appears to have been effective for some years, and in the middle of the century the centre of resistance moved to a group of religious leaders in Córdoba.

The Christian church had preserved its metropolitans in Toledo, Seville and Mérida, but many churches had been lost and some of the ancient dioceses had disappeared. In Córdoba at least the ranks of the faithful were thinned by the superior attractions of Muslim culture, which seduced the young from the now withered latinity of St. Isidore, and by discriminatory taxation. Frank theological discussions were not infrequent, though they almost invariably took place in private, and no conversion from Islam or public disrespect of it was permitted: Christianity was thus limited to the defensive. In 850 a Córdobese priest was beheaded for public disrespect to the prophet, and in the following year a number of mozarabs, inspired by the priest Eulogius, deliberately set themselves to gain the palm of martyrdom. At a Council held in Córdoba the tax-gatherer Gomes (who later embraced Islam) voiced the Emir's disapproval and, the church repudiated the martyrdoms as a form of suicide. However, Eulogius continued his campaign and was himself beheaded in 859, after which the movement rapidly declined.

'Abdu'r-Rahman died in 852, and was succeeded by his son Muhammad. Toledo rose again and seized its governor, demanding the return of its hostages in exchange for him. In the west one ibn Marwan, whose father had been governor of Mérida and who was himself a hostage, escaped, and set himself up at Badajoz, where he was for a time supported by the Asturian Christians. In the east the muwallad family of the banu Qasi, the descendants of that Count Fortún who had professed Islam and in return been promised autonomy, broke away from Córdoba, made an alliance with the Vascones of Pamplona, and built up a principality in the valley of the Ebro, with its capital at Saragossa. This new power, called the 'third kingdom of Spain', was essentially a Spanish reaction to the conflict between Franks and Syrians: the banu Qasi represented the ancient proprietors of the soil, who if Muslims, readily allied themselves with the free Navarrese, and as Spaniards, sacked Frankish Barcelona. But when the 'third kingdom' tried to expand westwards, it was defeated by the Asturians in the battle of Albelda; and a Córdobese army broke up its alliance with Pamplona, whose count was carried off to remain a guest in the house of hostages for twenty years.

The proprietors of the land waged a longer and intenser struggle against the emirate in the south where the muwallad 'Umar ibn Hafṣun maintained independence from 880 until his death in 917, after which his sons held out for a further decade. At the peak of his power he held most of upper Andalusia and part of the valley of the Guadalquivir: even the fields of Córdoba were not safe from his raids. His family had remained Christian until his father's time, and owned estates near Ronda. 'Umar's youthful exploits or *mocedades* included a murder, and he took to the hills and fled for a time to Africa; but he soon returned to live by brigandage in Andalusia, building himself a headquarters at Bobastro, an almost impregnable rock over the gorge of the Guadalhorce (Málaga). From it he took town after town as far as Priego, and formed an alliance with the governor of Cazlona (Jaén), also recently converted to Islam, provoking revolts of singular bitterness throughout Andalusia. But in 891 the new Emir 'Abdu'llah began to defeat him, and one by one his towns were whittled away. In 899 he proclaimed himself a Christian, but this did not improve his fortunes: the Andalusian Christians were no longer alone sufficient to defy the emirate, and the muwallads, or 'new Muslims', had no choice but to return to their allegiance. Ibn Hafṣun had come near to being a 'third king', but now and in the future all attempts to combine Islam with Spanish nationalism were to fail between the larger interests that confronted one another in the Peninsula. When the great rebel died, his domains were already much reduced, and Bobastro was finally rased in 928. Precarious as the Umaiyad state had seemed during parts of the ninth century, it was rapidly to recover in the tenth.

4. THE RESETTLEMENT

The annals of the northern kingdom in its early times are meagre in the extreme. Alfonso's successor Fruela resettled southern Galicia and the Bierzo, and was then assassinated by his cousin Aurelius. The Asturian peasants rebelled against Aurelius (774), and the Galicians against his successor, Silo, who moved the court from Cangas to the scarcely larger village of Pravia. On Silo's death the nobles elected Alfonso II to rule, but he was thrust aside by his uncle Mauregato (783) and took refuge with the Basques, his mother's people, resuming his interrupted reign in 791.

From these shadowy incidents we can detect the formation of a new monarchy, modestly imitative of the Visigothic state. The king was surrounded by a small court of nobles who 'elected' his successor, though in practice, their choice was restricted to the dynasty of Pelayo. The imposition of Visigothic traditions on the tribesmen of Asturias and Galicia was not carried out without resistance; but the natives were subdued and in part enserfed, and their own chiefs were probably replaced by Visigothic counts. The Galicians accepted the Visigothic *fuero juzgo*, but the Cantabrians perhaps proved recalcitrant, while the Basques remained in their pagan and primitive independence.

Alfonso II, who reigned until 842, consolidated the neo-Gothic monarchy, and enriched his new capital at Ovetao or Oviedo with palaces, a basilica, which he endowed with gold and silver plate and paintings, and other churches, and even baths. None of his palaces has survived, but the *cámara santa* at St. Julian reveals Carolingian influences with local variations. The building of these new churches followed a rift with the church of Toledo. Islamic monotheism clashed most violently with catholicism on the question of the Trinity. Already in the second century the rationalist theologians of Antioch had taught that Christ was a man filled with the Holy Spirit and so 'adopted' by God: this doctrine of adoptionism was now revived by Elipandus, Metropolitan of Toledo (c. 780), and his friend Felix, Bishop of Urgel, who tried unsuccessfully to introduce it to the Frankish court. The compromise was rejected in the Asturias, and the religious unity of Christian Spain was broken. But the need for a fresh religious tradition in the north was soon satisfied. A tomb found in Galicia between 810 and 830 was identified as that of St. James the Greater; and the conviction that this remote corner of the Roman world which had so long resisted orthodoxy belonged to the apostolic tradition was gradually to swell until Santiago vied with Rome itself. The primitive church of Compostela, built in about 850, was later enlarged and its endowment was extended by successive monarchs.

But while in the west the Asturian state was remote from the Muslim marches, and Alfonso II could take advantage of strife in al-Andalus to raid as far afield as Lisbon, to the east the frontier remained close to the Muslim stronghold of Saragossa which controlled the fertile middle valley of the Ebro. In this quarter Asturians, Cantabrians and Basques were already advancing through the gap between the Cantabrian mountains and the Basque hills and resettling the edge of the meseta, spreading out into the upper valley of the Ebro between its headwaters and the gorge of Haro, the oldest part of Old Castile. As the land was occupied by magnates or monasteries with their serfs or free colonists, it was defended by rough castles like the ancient *turres*, and it became known to the Muslims as *al-qila'*, 'the castles', or Castile, a word first recorded in a document of 800. The names of the settlers show that many of the leaders—counts, *infanzones* or bishops—were of Visigothic origin, while the mass of their followers were Asturo-Cantabrians or Basques. In some cases the ruler of Asturias licensed the expeditions and issued charters confirming the privileges of the settlers, but often the occupation of the land was carried out on the responsibility of a local leader and only received formal approval from the crown much later. During the reign of Alfonso's successor, Ramiro I (842–50) there were constant disorders in Asturias, and the new territories regulated their own affairs, choosing two 'judges' or leaders, one to command them in battle and the other to settle their disputes according to their own customs. These offices seem to revert to the Visigothic and Roman count (*comes*) and *judex*, but the decisions they handed down were based entirely on customary law, in contrast with the semi-Romanised code in use in Galicia and much of Asturias: the firm rejection of courtly or erudite practices and of Latin in favour of the broad vernacular clearly marked the Castilians off from their neighbours. Thus a 'new' and composite race largely Basque or Cantabrian in stock, but Visigothic in customs, and speaking its own romance (though in places it still used Basque) came to recolonise the old territory of the Autrigones and part of that of the Celtiberians.

Meanwhile, at the eastern end of the Pyrenees, the Franks had occupied Gerona and the valley of the Segre (793) and were soon to enter Barcelona. The lowlands of modern Catalonia still belonged to al-Andalus, and the military frontier ran from Barcelona to Urgel. Much of the hill-country that now came under Frankish protection was inhabited by 'hispani', some of whom were refugees from the south: allowance was made for their peculiar customs in the legislation of Charlemagne and Louis the Pious (*c.* 812–6). In 817 the province of Septimania was placed under a 'count of the March', who was thus interposed between the border counties and the counts or dukes of Toulouse. The chief counties thus loosely attached to the Frankish empire were Pallars, Ribagorza and Sobrarbe, while at Jaca a certain Aureolus or Oriol appears to have established the nucleus of the future state of Aragon.

The area between the Frankish march and the Asturian kingdom is of special interest, since it was to give birth to the three states of Castile, Aragon and Navarre. Straddling the Pyrenees, the Basque mountaineers were remarkable at once for their primitive conservatism and their power of association and absorption. In Roman times the western Basques had been at the end of the road. In their territory a few mines had been exploited, but no Roman settlement of any consequence had existed, and the native population slipped back easily into its rural isolation. To the east, however, the subjected Vascones of Pamplona and its plain had adopted Roman speech and ways. In the sixth century, if not earlier, their capital had a Christian community and a bishop, but with the decline in urban life which took place under the Visigoths, this Christian outpost was probably lost, and Pamplona seems to have alternated between native and Visigothic rule. It capitulated to the Muslim invaders in the year 718, and for a time was occupied by a governor and a garrison; but during the eighth century power again alternated, now between natives and Muslims. The shadowy figure of Eneco (Iñigo) Arista is credited with the founding of an independent county of Pamplona in about 800, within a few years of the Frankish defeat in the pass of Roncesvalles.

In its first moments Navarre was indeed a reaction against the Frankish protectorate; and the descendants of Eneco Arista regularly intermarried with the banu Qasi of nearby Tudela, through whom they were thus linked with Córdoba.

A third embryonic state, Aragon, had now begun to emerge to the east of Pamplona. These outer Vascones who came under Carolingian influence were distinguished as 'Gascones', and for a moment in the closing years of the eighth century their leader Velasco forced his way into Pamplona, killing its governor, Mutarrif, and establishing Frankish influence there. He was soon expelled, and in 820 the Navarrese and their Saragossan allies invaded Jaca and drove out its count, Aznar Galíndez, setting up a son-in-law of Eneco Arista in his place. In reply the Franks invaded Pamplona, and Aznar's son at length recovered Aragon. By the middle of the ninth century the pattern of three neo-Basque states, each a reaction to its neighbours, Asturians, Saragossan muwallads and Franks, had been worked out. To the west the Alavese Basques, now newly Christianised, were streaming southward to create Castile; in the centre Pamplona gave its hand to Saragossa; while to the east Aragon stood as a buffer state between Navarrese and Franks: it too began to receive Christianity through the monastery of Leire. Meanwhile, the Basque heartland in the crook of the Biscayan gulf remained untouched since the moment when Musa ibn Nuṣair had peered briefly into it and discovered 'a people like beasts'.

THE MUSLIM ASCENDANCY

In Oviedo Ramiro I was succeeded by Ordoño I (850–866) under whose rule the movement of expansion was resumed. The Count of the Castilians, one Roderic (85?–873), restored the old Cantabrian capital of Amaya, established a new line of castles, and won the pass of Pancorvo. By 880, the Castilian advance had reached the river Arlanzón, and the Emir of Córdoba sent his son to ravage the area. Although the Muslim campaigns of 882–3 wrought great havoc, the system of castles was now too strong to be destroyed; and Muhammad I duly made peace with the new King of Asturias, Alfonso III (866–911). Alfonso, who merited the title of the Great, took an active part in the repopulation of Castile, issuing charters to various monasteries, and curbing the independence of the Castilian counts. By the end of the century Asturian supremacy was restored, though Castile had no less firmly established its right to its own law. While Córdoba was occupied with the long rebellion of ibn Ḥafṣun, the Christians held the line of the Minho, where the Galicians restored Tuy, and resettled Leon, newly occupied and rewalled by Ordoño in 856. This expansion gave the Asturian monarchy a new capital, a small and poor town in comparison with caliphal Córdoba; but, unlike Oviedo and the earlier village-courts, a Roman city whose very name commemorated the long residence of the legionaries. South of Leon spread the vast expanses of the meseta, unfolding visions of future greatness, which, rather than the modest present, justified the neo-Gothic kings in assuming the title of emperors.

But while the western frontier offered this new dimension of conquest, the people of Castile were faced with more immediate problems. The Asturian kings were now persuaded of their imperial destiny as heirs to the Visigoths, and it was their ambition and obligation to restore the ancient capital of Toledo. Since this was so, the people of Castile looked towards Saragossa. In 859 the muwallads of the Ebro built a fortress at Albelda, south of Logroño; Ordoño came forth and met the challenge, destroying the stronghold and putting its garrison to the knife: His victory[1]

---

[1] A twelfth-century forger was to convert it into the 'battle of Clavijo' at which St James appeared mounted on a white charger and so justified the patronage of the Reconquest by the cathedral of Santiago.

asserted the claims of Castile to an eastward expansion beyond the ancient region of Celtiberia, and a century later its great paladin, the Cid, outdid the ancient Numantines by forcing a way to the sea at Valencia.

5. THE WESTERN CALIPHATE

During the ninth century the policy of Syrianisation pursued by the Umaiyads had provoked such resistance that al-Andalus seemed on the verge of disintegrating, as it was in fact to do when the Córdobese state finally collapsed.

But in the tenth century it reached new heights of power, its rulers assumed the caliphal title, challenging comparison with the Muslim states of Africa and the east, and its capital became the largest and wealthiest city in Europe.

The creator of the caliphate was 'Abdu'r-Raḥman III, the favourite grandson of the Emir 'Abdu'llah by his Navarrese wife Oneca, a daughter of the third Count of Pamplona, Fortún Garcés (c. 880). He acceded at the age of twenty in 912. Short of stature, he had blue eyes and reddish hair, which for political reasons he died black. A professing rather than a devout Muslim, he made his chief object the political integration of al-Andalus under the unquestioned authority of his house. His earliest campaigns were directed against the dissident Arab families of Carmona and Seville, which had been almost independent from 903 to 913. He settled the affair of ibn Ḥafṣun, and he removed the ambiguous banu Qasi from their control of the north-eastern frontier, which he placed under a rival family, the Tujibids, not of Gothic lineage.

When he had established his peace throughout Muslim Spain, 'Abdu'r-Raḥman ended the fictitious subordination to the eastern caliphate by assuming the title himself. The Fatimids of Egypt had already set up an anti-caliphate in 909, and thus pricked him to assert the honour of his house. But the title had the same transcendental significance as that of emperor in the Roman world, and it implied the rise of the Umaiyads above their co-religionists in Spain and a wider policy in Muslim Africa. Having reconstituted his administration on more autocratic lines, the new caliph justified his pretensions in war against the Christians. He had already attacked Navarre, and now imposed tribute on its ruler, Queen Tota. Thus Córdoba began to seek a superpolitical control over the northern states. But when in 939 he launched his 'campaign of omnipotence' against the Asturians, hoping to destroy their southern frontier of Zamora, he was defeated near Simancas, and left his coat of gilded mail on the field. Full of rage and indignation, he caused many of his followers to be crucified as traitors; but he could not prevent the Castilians from pressing forward to resettle Sepúlveda, within sight of the passes of the Guadarrama. His reply was to establish a forward military command at Medinaceli, which was heavily garrisoned and placed under a famous general, the freedman Galib. In 948 or 949 a Muslim raid reached as far north as Lugo in Galicia; and the Christians squabbled among themselves and renounced their allegiance to Sancho the Fat on the ground of his incapacity for war. He and his grandmother Tota and her son, the ruler of Navarre, turned to the Caliph for help, making the long journey to Córdoba, where they were received in the splendid new palace of Madina az-Zahra'. Here Sancho engaged himself to deliver ten castles in return for his restoration to the throne.

When the first Caliph died in 961, he had profited by the weakness of the northern states to open the frontiers, and had laid tribute on each of them by turn. Faced with the impossibility of uprooting the new Christian settlements or of absorbing their scattered territories, he had devised a military machine to harness them. With the Christian revival in the following century, the roles were to be reversed, and the quest for tribute replaced the settlement of land as the driving-force of the reconquest.

Under its new caliphate al-Andalus now began to play a new role in the Muslim world of the west. Hitherto, Africa had felt little affection for the Umaiyads. In Morocco the Idrisid kingdom, also founded by exiles from the east, owed nothing to Spain. To its east, Ifriqiya was ruled by the Aglabids, who, though now independent, had been officials of the 'Abbasids and were therefore hostile to the Umaiyads. Between these two large states, in the midst of what is now Algeria, lay the small Saharan kingdom of Tahart, which, because of its relative weakness, accepted the patronage of Córdoba and sent it supplies of wheat and contingents of Berber mercenaries. But the rise of the Fatimid empire overset the balance of power. The new conquerors seized Ifriqiya, annexed Tahart and overran the Magrib, driving the Idrisids to seek refuge in the mountains of the Riff (922). Al-Andalus itself was threatened, and although 'Abdu'r-Rahman built ships to stave off an invasion and sent troops to occupy the North African ports of Melilla (927) and Ceuta (931), he could do little more than hold his own, and the Fatimids even attacked the port of Almería and burnt its shipping. But during the reign of his successor, al-Hakam II, the Fatimids concentrated their forces in Egypt, leaving the African west in the hands of their Berber allies, the Sanhaja. Al-Hakam therefore made an alliance with the rival Berber confederation, the Zanata, who defeated the Sanhaja and sent the head of their general to Córdoba. After this success the Idrisids emerged from their fastnesses in the hope of recovering their former possessions; but they proved less formidable opponents, and when al-Hakam sent Galib to Africa they submitted and came to Córdoba to do homage. Thus when al-Hakam died in 976, the western caliphate had become the protecting power of the Magrib and could call upon its almost limitless supplies of fighting-men.

Al-Hakam II had acceded at the age of forty-six, after a long association with his father in the task of government. Like him, he was stocky and ruddy: his mother, Marjana, may not have been of Spanish stock, but his wife, Subh, the mother of his successor Hisham II, was a Basque and a woman of authority. Al-Hakam himself had poor health, and his chief fame was as a bibliophile: he is said to have accumulated and annotated four hundred thousand books. The assumption of the caliphal dignity turned the ruler into a semi-sacred figure imprisoned in an elaborate ritual and inaccessible except to a small clique of officials. The great families of the Arab nobility were generally excluded from the counsels of the palace, and power was shared between the holders of the few great offices and the Caliph's personal intimates, many of whom were Slavs.

When al-Ḥakam died, his son Hisham II was a boy of twelve. His father had obtained an oath of loyalty from the chief dignitaries: these were fully conscious of their power, and although two of them tried to press the claims of the late king's brother, a meeting of the rest, attended also by the Berber generals, decided to proclaim Hisham and had his uncle strangled. But Hisham II was, and would remain, unable to rule, and his mother had as her adviser the most ruthless and remarkable man of the day. He was Muhammad ibn Abi 'Amir al-Ma'afiri, later known as al-Manṣur or Almanzor, 'the victorious'. A member of a Yemenite family settled as landowners at Torrox, near Algeciras, he had become assistant to the qaḍi of Córdoba and administrator of the Basque queen's estates. By her influence he was placed in command of the police, and acquired great wealth and numerous clients, and built himself a palace. When Galib was sent to Morocco in 972, he accompanied the expedition as administrator, and on his return became supervisor of the mercenaries in Córdoba. In this way he acquired authority over the hordes of Berbers who formed the sinews of the caliphal army, and controlled the supplies sent forward to Galib at Medinaceli. As a favourite of Subḥ, he supported the succession of the boy Hisham, and emerged from the crisis as assistant to the ḥajib. He proved himself by conducting a military expedition against Salamanca, and was made governor of Córdoba. He was now able to overthrow the ḥajib al-Muṣḥafi, who had vainly tried to save himself by marrying his son to the daughter of the great soldier Galib. Almanzor prevented the match, married the bride himself, and soon after arrested and executed al-Muṣḥafi. He thus reached the pinnacle of power: he was not yet forty. His ruthlessness had caused a revulsion of feeling against him; but he now transferred the government offices to his own palace, built his own barracks, stables and granaries, and dominated the state through the Berber armies.

His rise was so outrageous that Galib, who was before all else a loyal servant of the Umaiyads, protested. But Almanzor brought in new contingents of Berbers and sent a Moroccan general to attack Medinaceli. Galib took refuge with the Christians, and when he returned with Leonese help, was defeated and died on the field. Having eliminated his father-in-law, Almanzor now led his own armies. In 981 he defeated the Christians near Simancas, and forced the Castilians to abandon Atienza and Sepúlveda. In 984 he levied tribute on Vermudo II of Leon. In 985 he invaded Barcelona and carried off its viscount. In 987 he destroyed Coimbra, and in 988 Leon and Zamora, forcing Vermudo to take refuge in Galicia. He had now married a daughter of Sancho Garcés, the ruler of Navarre, who bore him his son 'Abdu'r-Raḥman or 'Sanchul', and in 992 the Navarrese King visited his daughter and her redoubtable husband in Córdoba.

In 991 Almanzor had renounced the title of ḥajib, which he bestowed on his eldest son, as if he were himself king: everything he did was confirmed by Hisham, who lived secluded in his palace. In 996 Almanzor finally assumed the royal title and was mentioned in the Friday prayers in the mosques, and Hisham dutifully confirmed the usurpation: so long as Almanzor respected the source of his power, none dare touch him.

In 997 he embarked on his greatest campaign, the conquest of Santiago de Compostela, the shrine of the Asturo-Leonese monarchy. Part of his forces were transported by sea to central Portugal, where he himself joined them. Striking northward, he found Santiago undefended. The King of Leon could only ask for a new truce. Castile, which had discreetly held aloof, attempted to form a Christian league; but Almanzor marched to Medinaceli and offered battle at Calatanazor, where he apparently won his last major victory. Early in 1002 he began a campaign in the Rioja; but he was already ill, and returned to die at Medinaceli. His favourite son, 'Abdu'l-Malik, took his place.

For six years 'Abdu'l-Malik continued the war in the north and overran the foothills of the Pyrenees and Aragon and the neighbouring counties. But in 1008 he too died as he was about to leave Córdoba on a new expedition, and power passed to his younger brother Sanchul, the grandson of the King of Navarre, now aged twenty-four. He committed the capital error of persuading the Caliph to nominate him as his successor: despite the futility of Hisham, attachment to the house of the Umaiyads was still the main, perhaps even the only, unifying force in al-Andalus, and by his action Sanchul set all but the Berber generals, who had no respect for the Arab dynasty, against him. Before setting out to resume the war, he decreed that the court should wear Berber turbans instead of Arab caps (or so it was said: perhaps the phrase is a metaphor). While he was away in 1009 a revolution broke out in the capital. The mob attacked the palace, and although Hisham appeared between two retainers holding Korans, he was merely derided. The caliph's palace and barracks were sacked and destroyed, and a member of his family was set up in his place as Muhammad II.

Sanchul had now marched back from Toledo and might have entered Córdoba almost unopposed, but he hesitated and was abandoned by his Berbers, and captured and executed. But Muhammad II proved to be no more than the creature of the mob, which he could not govern. Some demanded the restoration of Hisham; and Muhammad gave out that he had died, producing a body which was solemnly buried. The Berbers held the key to power; but they needed a leader who would obey and pay them. When Muhammad outlawed them, they gave their support to another member of the Umaiyad house, Sulaiman, forming an alliance with the Count of Castile, Sancho García. The Christian and Berber forces assembled near Madrid, and marched south against Muhammad. He desperately produced Hisham II and pretended to have acted in his name. But the Berbers reminded him that Hisham was 'dead'; and they and their Christian allies entered the capital and Sulaiman was proclaimed caliph. Muhammad now raised an army in eastern Spain and hired a force of Frankish or Barcelonese mercenaries, who drove Sulaiman and the Berbers out of the capital. But as he pursued them towards Ronda, his Barcelonese were defeated, and he himself was soon after murdered in Córdoba.

The palace party of Slavs now restored Hisham II, but the magic of his line and title had gone. The Umaiyads, lately a symbol of invincible might, were now represented only by a powerless puppet, controlled by a clique of freedmen. The Berbers refused to respect the illusion; and the great Arab families hated the Slavs and feared the Africans. Hisham and his supporters soon found themselves besieged in Córdoba, while the Berbers, led by the Sanhaja Zawi ibn Ziri, occupied the ruins of the summer-palace at Madina az-Zahra' and subdued the towns of Jaén, Elvira (Granada) and Málaga. Faced with famine and bankruptcy, the capital surrendered a year later in 1013, when Sulaiman was restored and Hisham finally murdered. These were days of apocalyptic confusion, and the Berbers slaughtered and robbed the Arabs, the shops and the populace. In the following months Sulaiman appointed Berbers to all the principal offices and presented them with tracts of land, especially in Granada, which now became the home of the Sanhaja. Eastern Spain refused to accept this new domination and Córdoba found its authority severely reduced: in Africa only the seaports of Tangier, Ceuta and Arzila still acknowledged its sovereignty.

In 1016 the governor of Ceuta, 'Ali ibn Ḥammud, landed in Spain, entered Córdoba and put Sulaiman to death. Thus for the first time one who was not even an Umaiyad or a Spaniard, but a Berberised Arab, claimed to rule. Two years later he was murdered by the palace clique, and his brother and son fought for power. But by 1023 the Córdobese were weary of the Ḥammudites and expelled them; and in the following years various Umaiyads were raised up, torn down, and murdered or expelled. In 1027 the doubtful honour of the caliphate was bestowed on a third Hisham, who devoted himself to merry-making and left the conduct of affairs to a government of artisans led by a weaver. Soon after the weaver was murdered, and Hisham III took refuge in the mosque. The leading families of the city now decided that it was useless to elect another Umaiyad and constituted themselves into an oligarchical republic. Thus in November 1031 the caliphate of Córdoba came to an end, and the cloth so laboriously stitched together was rent into many pieces.

6. THE LEONESE EMPIRE

While the state of al-Andalus was soaring on its career from dissension to 'omnipotence' and relapsing into disintegration, the peoples of the north underwent the contrary experience. At the beginning of the tenth century the ruler of the Asturo-Leonese kingdom claimed, rather extravagantly, to be an emperor, though his territories were small and his state an agrarian monarchy of the simplest kind. Under the hammering of Almanzor, Leon became a mere tributary of Córdoba, incapable from its limited resources to match the professional armies recruited by the caliphate. But as the Umaiyad state collapsed, a new house, that of Navarre, picked up the imperial pretension and succeeded in unifying for a brief spell the whole of the north from Galicia to the Frankish frontiers.

Alfonso III, the restorer of Leon, seems first to have claimed the title of 'Imperator' in about 916, a decade before the erection of the western caliphate.

He had apparently even earlier been offered an imperial crown of gold and precious stones by the clergy of Tours, who happened to possess one and were short of money. The antecedents of the title are both Carolingian and Visigothic, but it seems probable that the context to which it should be referred is Alfonso's expedition to Toledo, whose inhabitants agreed to pay him tribute; this event took place towards the end of his reign, while the Emir 'Abdu'llah was still occupied with the rebellion of ibn Ḥafṣun. Moreover, in 905 the Count of Navarre, Sancho Garcés, had assumed the title of King, thus asserting Navarrese supremacy in the Pyrenean area. Alfonso III was on friendly terms with Navarre; but his new title reminded the world that the monarchy of Leon, with its Visigothic pretension, was still unique.

The rank of Emperor or 'king of kings' required that its possessor should have proved himself a conqueror or champion, but it also conferred on him the right to divide his realms among his sons as if they were his private patrimony. This custom was a Carolingian one; but it had also Spanish antecedents, harking back to the

Emperor Theodosius and his division of the Roman world. Although it is often regarded as a perverse and retrogressive practice, it was on the contrary intended to ensure that the whole of a great warrior's realms were not vested in a successor until he had proved his capacity. However, the division carried out by Alfonso seems to have been insisted on by his sons and it may have been introduced by his Basque Queen Ximena. His eldest son, who bore the Basque name of García, was called king in his father's lifetime, and succeeded to the throne of Leon. The second son, Ordoño, was called King of Galicia from 898; and a third, Fruela, was king in Asturias. When Alfonso, García and Ordoño all died, the three senior members of the dynasty Fruela, Ramiro (Alfonso's fourth son) and Sancho Ordoño (the son of Ordoño) succeeded respectively to Leon, Asturias and Galicia.[1]

This cumbersome succession, which was in a sense the opposite extreme from the Visigothic elective system, since it allowed the monarch not only to establish his dynasty but to delegate his functions, was especially unpopular in one part of the Leonese domains, Castile, which viewed the proliferation of kings with dislike. The free warriors of the frontier zone had habitually chosen their own judges and jealously preserved their own customs. Alfonso had attempted to check their independence by dividing the area between many counts, who, like all the magnates of his realms, were removable at the royal will. But on the death of the 'Emperor', an ambitious adventurer, Fernán González, took advantage of the divisions of the Leonese to unify the whole area, and by 931 he had forged the largest and most powerful single county in the Peninsula. Although Ramiro II, the last successful ruler of the Asturo-Leonese dynasty, several times deprived him of his authority, on the death of this king in 951, Fernán González made himself Count of Castile for life and transmitted the title to his heirs. His people seem to have been solidly behind him in the struggle to establish their rights against the old Visigothic nobility. This new society, with its passion for independence and social unity, could base its demands on a long record of military

[1] Cf. the attempts of the Emperor Charles V to establish an order of succession, p. 228-9.

success. As if in defiance of Leonese traditionalism, the founder's son, García Fernández, doubled the number of Castilian knights from 250 or 300 to 500 or 600, conferring the rank of *infanzonía*, or lesser nobility, on anyone who could serve with a horse. When Almanzor's Berbers ravaged Leon, Castile, with its towers and cavalry, was prepared for the shock and survived it.

Both in Leon and in Castile, the process of resettlement had proceeded rapidly until it was halted by the campaigns of the caliphate. In Leon Alfonso III reincorporated the old Campi Gothici and carried the frontier down to the Douro, restoring Zamora and Simancas in the last years of the ninth century. These places were colonised by northern magnates and prelates who brought down Galicians, Asturians and Basques, with whom they mingled Mozarabs from the south. Even Astorga had some 'Andalusians'; Leon possessed more, while in Zamora the great majority of the inhabitants were known by Arabic names. In contrast with the homogeneity of Castile, the southward extension of Leon shows a marked separation of regional groups. Whole villages bear regional names: Gallegos and Castellanos occur many times, and Arabic place-names are also frequent. Perhaps because of the attraction of the court and the greater conservatism of Leonese society, there is less evidence of individual enterprise than in Castile, and a greater proportion of the new settlements appear to have taken place under the patronage of monasteries.

During the first half of the tenth century the underlying divergencies between the societies of Leon and Castile took definite form as Castile attained unity under a hereditary count. In times of good fortune the loose 'imperial' framework of Leon served its purpose, but during the great adversities of the second half of the century the compact structure of Castile was to prove the more robust.

Meanwhile, the growth of Castile within the Leonese monarchy was matched by that of Navarre outside it. During the ninth century the presence of the Franks or their delegates in the Pyrenean counties had served to strengthen the connection between the counts of Pamplona and the banu Qasi of Saragossa. But with the conquests of Alfonso III and his marriage to the Basque

Ximena, the Navarrese came into the orbit of Leon. Sancho Garcés' assumption of the title of King of Navarre was a defiance of Córdoba, and when al-Andalus recovered from its prostration, 'Abdu'r-Raḥman set himself the task of abolishing the new 'kingdom'.

Alfonso III's grandson, Ordoño II of Leon, continued the alliance with Sancho Garcés, and in 917 joined with him in an attack on the Rioja. It seems likely that the Castilians regarded the venture with a jealous eye, for they too coveted this region, and in 920 after 'Abdu'r-Raḥman had invaded Navarre and defeated the Christians near its capital, Ordoño arrested some of the Castilian counts, who had possibly been lukewarm in their support of the Navarrese alliance. Three years later, Ordoño and Sancho Garcés reconquered the Rioja, and Navarre also acquired the county of Aragon by marriage.

But on Ordoño's death in 924, the Caliph again launched a furious assault against Pamplona, which was abandoned and sacked. The new King of Leon was himself dying of leprosy and could not intervene, and 'Abdu'r-Raḥman ended the Navarrese connection with Saragossa by removing the banu Qasi and placing the Tujibids in command of the frontier. The inter-confessional link was thus broken, and henceforth the only possible relationship between Christians and Muslims was that of lord and vassal.

When in 926 Sancho I died, and was succeeded by a child García Sánchez, whose grandmother, Queen Tota, acted as regent. Leon was involved in successorial problems and Navarre was prostrate. In 931, with the accession of Ramiro II, Leon began to recover, but the new king could not afford to ignore his Castilian subjects, and it was with the aid of Fernán González that he won the battle of Osma in 934 and laid tribute on Tujibid Saragossa in 937. No sooner did Ramiro renew the alliance with Navarre than the Caliph again struck at Pamplona, imposing tribute on Queen Tota and restoring his authority in Saragossa.

It was now that the Caliph made his first attempt to extend the system of tribute to all the Christian states by launching his 'campaign of omnipotence', frustrated by the Christian victory of Simancas. Ramiro was aided by contingents of Castilians and Navarrese, and after the victory he was able to extend the territories of Leon as far south as Salamanca, while the Castilians set up an outpost at Sepúlveda. But this was the last success of the old Leonese dynasty.

At this time the unified county of Castile was ruled by Fernán González whose power extended from the Basque border to the Muslim frontier at the Guadarramas. It was a formidable creation, and in 943 its count came out in open rebellion against the King of Leon. The immediate causes of this are unknown; but they were probably related to the tenure of the county and the disposal of its new conquests. Ramiro deposed Fernán González and for a time held him under arrest in Leon. A new count was appointed and the king sent his son Sancho to reside in Burgos.

News of the dissidences of the Christians soon reached Córdoba, and in 946 'Abdu'r-Raḥman began to build up his new base at Medinaceli for operations against Castile. But in the following year, Ramiro and the count came to terms, and Fernán González was restored to command the whole of Castile. Soon after, the king's eldest son Ordoño was married to Fernán González's daughter. This match assured the count of his power during the king's lifetime, but after a last campaign against Talavera Ramiro II died in Leon early in 951, and Fernán González was able to claim that his office was a hereditary possession and that Castile could no longer be divided.

Despite his relationship with the count, the new King of Leon, Ordoño III, was reluctant to concede these demands, and the Castilians, now aided by the Navarrese, gave their support to his younger brother Sancho, who had been sent to reside in Burgos some years before. The rebels marched on Leon, but they were defeated and Sancho was forced to take refuge with his grandmother, Queen Tota, in Navarre. Since Ordoño proved himself a successful warrior in an expedition against Lisbon, Fernán González came to terms with him and bided his time. In 956 both Ordoño and the count made truces with Córdoba, but in the same year Ordoño suddenly died, and since he was survived only by an infant son, the fugitive Sancho was able to claim the throne.

With the reign of Sancho I the Leonese monarchy lost control of its own subjects and sank into subservience to the caliphate. According to tradition, Sancho was repudiated by his barons because he was too fat to ride a horse and so to perform the primary function of a Leonese monarch, the winning of battles: however, two years earlier the same barons had not scrupled to set him up against his elder brother. In 957 Sancho rejected the truce imposed by the Caliph on his brother, and his troops were defeated by the Muslim governor of Toledo. In 958 a group of magnates led by Fernán González deposed him and set up his cousin(?) Ordoño IV, who, since he was no more than a puppet in the hands of one faction of the nobility, was remembered in Leon as 'the Bad'.

Sancho now repaired to the court of his grandmother at Pamplona, and she accompanied him to Córdoba, where he received both medical and military aid. Restored to a more kingly shape and supported by a Muslim army, he returned to Leon and took Zamora on its southern frontier, while the Navarrese invaded Castile. During the course of 959 the Leonese gradually abandoned Ordoño, who first retired into Asturias and later fled to his Castilian patron. But Fernán González himself was captured by the Navarrese and carried off to Pamplona, while his puppet made his way in turn to Córdoba to sue for help. He died there in obscurity.

The price of Sancho's throne was the delivery to the Caliph of ten castles. But when the time came, he refused to settle the debt and sought to form a league of the Christian states which included even the counts of Barcelona. Before it could concert its efforts, the caliphal armies entered Castile and took Gormaz and seized Calahorra from Navarre, also raiding the southern frontier of Leon and Barcelona. Sancho was forced to sue for peace, and faced by new disturbances in Galicia; and at the end of 966 he suddenly died. The succession of his son Ramiro III, a child of five, carried the hereditary idea to a point the old Visigoths would not have contemplated, and Leon was in effect ruled by a woman, the nun Doña Elvira, a daughter of Ramiro II, who like Tota of Navarre, came to terms with Córdoba in the hope of holding at bay the regional confederations of magnates.

During these years the counts who had formerly acknowledged the supremacy of Leon all came to terms with Córdoba, which now reached the zenith of its power. In 971 Borrell, Count of Barcelona, sent a present of thirty slaves to the Caliph, and there followed tributary missions from Ramiro III of Leon, from Sancho II of Navarre, from the Counts of Castile and Galicia. In 973 a Castilian mission to Córdoba was ignominiously arrested on the grounds that the frontier truce had been broken. Meanwhile, the Vikings commanded by Gundared again raided Galicia, and were finally driven off by St. Rosendo, Bishop of Santiago.

There followed the fulminating campaigns of Almanzor, who year after year devastated the territories of Leon. While Leon and Castile had for long accepted truces with Córdoba, the barons of Galicia had chafed at these conditions: they had supported Ordoño III's drive against Lisbon and they now led raids into southern Spain, as a result of which the Cordobese began to lay waste the Christian frontier. In 981, when the outer defences of both Leon and Castile, Zamora and Simancas, had been sacked, the Galicians rebelled and deposed Ramiro III in favour of a cousin, Vermudo II, who was annointed in the cathedral of Santiago in 982. There followed a war between the two kings, and Ramiro fled to the Asturias, where he died. But Vermudo could not impose himself on the Leonese barons, and was forced in turn to pay tribute to Córdoba in order to establish himself, and received a Muslim garrison to ensure his obedience. In 985 Barcelona was burnt and its inhabitants killed or enslaved; and when Vermudo turned out his protectors, Almanzor again invaded the west, sacking Coimbra, which stood empty for seven years, and forcing Vermudo to take refuge in Galicia. Many Leonese and Galicians made their own terms with the conqueror, and three years passed before Vermudo could re-enter his capital in 991. Four years later, the Count of Castile, García Fernández, the son

D

of the founder, was captured and carried off to Córdoba, where he died in captivity; and in 997 the great shrine of Santiago was sacked. All the inhabitants had fled when Almanzor entered the city, and the Muslims found only an old monk praying in the basilica. It was destroyed, and its bells and doors were taken to Córdoba to make lamps and roofing for the great mosque. Vermudo could only again ask for terms. He lived only two years longer, and was succeeded by a small child, Alfonso V.

But in the midst of the campaign of 1002, Almanzor died and was, as the *Chronicon Burgense* asserts, 'buried in hell'. In the course of the next generation all the might of Córdoba was to be obliterated, and the long-lost 'empire' of Leon was at last made real, not under the old Asturo-Leonese dynasty, but under a new house from Pamplona.

In Navarre, Queen Tota had appeased the Caliph while seeking to conserve Navarrese interests in Leon by restoring Sancho the Fat to the throne. But as the power of Leon collapsed, the rulers of Pamplona turned rather to Castile. In 981 Sancho II Garcés joined García Fernández of Castile in an attempt to support Galib against the rising power of Almanzor. They were defeated, and the Navarrese came to terms with the conqueror and sent one of his daughters to Córdoba to marry him: when his next attempt at revolt failed, he was at least able to go to Córdoba and offer his own explanations to his formidable son-in-law.

His successor García 'the Tremulous' (994–1000) made no open resistance to Córdoba, though he remained in close relations with the court of Castile. In 999, however, Almanzor sent an expedition against Pamplona; it was partially destroyed, and a few years later the dictator's son overran the Pyrenean counties of Sobrarbe and Ribagorza, which had hitherto gone free.

At this time the future maker of greater Navarre, Sancho III Garcés, was being educated at the court of Castile. He was born in about 990, the son of García the Tremulous and his queen Ximena, who was of Castilian stock. Owing to his father's early death, he was placed in the care of the third Count of Castile, Sancho García, and in due course married his elder daughter, Munia, called Mayor.[1] As the Muslim tide receded, the Navarrese took the opportunity to seize the disorganised counties of Sobrarbe and Ribagorza to the east, which had formerly been linked with the Frankish county of Barcelona. As a result of this acquisition, the young king claimed, quite extravagantly, to rule as far afield as Barcelona: his authority there went no further than a series of arbitrations between the young Count Berenguer Ramón and his possessive mother.

In 1017 the Count of Castile died, leaving a young son García; and Sancho III was able to set up as protector in his wife's county. For over a century Leon and Castile had disputed the possession of the border area between the rivers Pisuerga and Cea; and when Leon took advantage of the minority to seize this region, the Navarrese replied by occupying the Basque-speaking regions of eastern and northern Castile. In 1028 a further opportunity for aggrandisement occurred. Alfonso V of Leon died, leaving the child Vermudo III as his heir. The Leonese barons now sought to assure themselves of Castilian goodwill by marrying Vermudo's sister to the boy count and offering to settle the disputed frontier region on them. Had the match been concluded, Castile would again have been incorporated in the realms of Leon, and Sancho of Navarre's schemes would have been thwarted. However, he accepted the invitation to the wedding and repaired to Leon. One day as his young brother-in-law and protegé had just left the Leonese princess, there was a sudden affray in the street and García was assassinated by a band of Leonese malcontents. The male line of the counts of Castile thus came to an end: and Sancho promptly claimed it as his wife's inheritance and had no difficulty in having his second son Ferdinand recognised as the legitimate successor.

Having thus effectively detached Castile from Leon, Sancho turned his mind to the disputed Pisuerga-Cea area, and successfully pressed the hapless Vermudo to conclude a new marriage-treaty. In 1034 Sancho was again in Leon, and claimed to rule there as emperor, a title he had won, not by his exertions against

[1] Mayor used as a feminine Christian name implied the eldest daughter or heiress.

the Muslims, which were of the slightest, but by resolutely meddling in each of the Christian kingdoms. When he died in the following year, he divided his possessions between his sons. His eldest legitimate son García received Navarre; his second son Ferdinand, Castile, which he already held; a bastard, Ramiro, took Aragon, now again detached from Navarre; and Gonzalo, still a boy, received the counties of Sobrarbe and Ribagorza. The Navarrese dynasty was within a step of consolidating its power over the whole Visigothic heritage.

IV

THE GREAT RECONQUEST

1. THE FORMATION OF THE FIVE KINGDOMS

AT the time of Sancho's death Vermudo still reigned in Leon, but two years later Ferdinand of Castile assumed for the first time the title of king and challenged him to a pitched battle for the long-disputed Pisuerga area. Vermudo was defeated, and when he died by falling from his horse, the new King of Castile claimed also to be Emperor of Leon. From this time, the imperial pretension and the monarchy of Leon became a prize to be won by successive champions of the new dynasty.

Although their house was Navarrese by origin, both Sancho the Great and his son were Castilians on their mother's side, and the change of dynasty was a victory for Castile rather than for Navarre. Ferdinand had fought Vermudo for the Leonese-Castilian borderland and recovered it for Castile. In 1054 he fought his elder brother García for the Rioja and Bureba, parts of Castile which their father had attached to Navarre, and defeated and killed him in the battle of Atapuerca. Nine years later, the Castilians killed in battle a third brother, Ramiro of Aragon, as he disputed their control of the Muslim kingdom of Saragossa: by attaching the great city of the Ebro to Castile, Ferdinand blocked the expansion of Navarre and Aragon, and while the Castilians and Leonese were advancing towards Toledo and the central meseta, the Navarrese remained pinned back at the Ebro, and Aragon was confined to the Pyrenean foothills.

As the Caliphate dissolved into *taifas*, or principalities, those local divisions that had appeared and disappeared like submerging

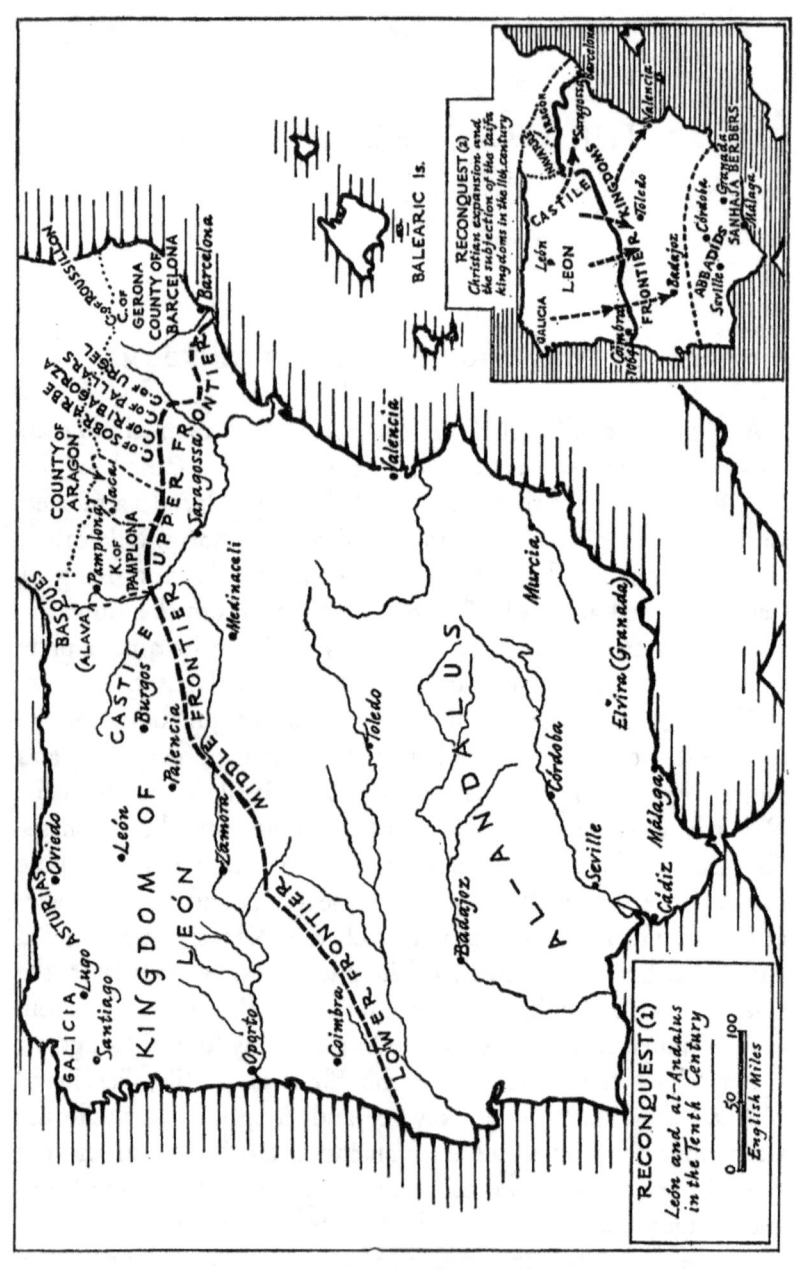

islands in the ninth century, the Muslim frontier came to consist of three separate states, Badajoz in the west, Toledo in the centre, and Saragossa in the north-east. Ferdinand was able to reduce all these to the status of tributaries, and his final achievements carried him to the two extremes of the Peninsula; in 1064 he reconquered Coimbra in the heart of Portugal, and in the following year he turned to the Mediterranean coast and besieged Valencia. There, however, he was forced to withdraw, and he died shortly after.

The founder of the Castilian monarchy divided his territories as his father had done, awarding the crown he had created to his eldest son, Sancho; Leon, to his second son, Alfonso; and Galicia to the third, García. His two daughters, Urraca and Elvira, were awarded the custody of monasteries and entitled queens. But unlike his father, Ferdinand was a conqueror of Muslims, and his division included the rights to the tribute he had laid on the Muslim states. With Castile went the vassalage and tribute of Saragossa; with Leon, Toledo of imperial memory; and with Galicia, Badajoz and Seville. This partition, with its north-east south-west axis, foreshadows a different Spain from the one we know, and it was to be modified half a century later with the rise of Aragon. Nevertheless, the assignment of vassal-kingdoms, and consequently of zones of reconquest, marks an important step in the development of both a Spanish and a European mind. The Spanish kingdoms, constantly preoccupied with the need to occupy and colonise new territories, had avoided that static society traditionally associated with the growth of European feudalism, and the settlement of the Peninsula was already a progressive undertaking which was to prepare communities for the future expansion overseas. Henceforth Castilians looked forward not merely to the acquisition of land but to the domination of alien states, and the granting of expectancies became a special feature of Spanish life. By the following century the Christian kingdoms were regulating by treaty not only their own future frontiers within the Peninsula, but also their claims to zones of influence in Africa, thus anticipating the system by which the New World was to be divided between Spain and Portugal.

Although Sancho the Great had given only a brief moment of

'omnipotence' to his native Navarre, his redistribution of the Christian territories determined the fortunes of the Peninsula during the middle ages. He had restored the monarchy of Navarre, created that of Aragon, and enabled his son to create that of Castile. He had also shown Ferdinand how to dominate Leon, and Ferdinand had applied the lesson by establishing another monarchy in the west, Galicia. Thus a pattern of Five Kingdoms was already set, though in the following century Portugal was to replace Galicia as the focus of independence in the west, and Aragon was to survive only by association with the county of Barcelona.[1]

[1] The peninsular 'nations' are in a sense new phenomena. None of the Five Kingdoms of Galicia-Portugal, Leon, Castile, Navarre and Aragon-Barcelona are mere geographical areas. Apart from the sea-coast they have no inexorable physical frontiers. Nor are they economic units like the taifas of the south: whereas al-Andalus consists of city-states each situated in the midst of its dependent irrigable area, the regions of the north are phases in an agrarian continuum. Nor are the new kingdoms simply cultural regions: in the west Galicia and Portugal form socially and linguistically a single area, but a political frontier was drawn rudely across it at the Minho. In the east, on the contrary, regions as distinct as the 'neo-Basque' kingdom of Aragon and the 'Frankish' county of Barcelona form a single, though never unified and always bilingual, monarchy.

The essence of each of the kingdoms lies in the defence of local traditions and customs recognised as forming separate 'jurisdictions.' Some of these 'customary' areas are of ancient origin and derive from tribal delimitations preserved in the Roman *conventus*: such is the case with the ancient frontier between Galicia and Leon. In Navarre the nucleus is ancient (the territory of the Romanised Vascones with its capital at Pamplona) but the delimitation is the result of modern struggles. Other areas, Castile and Aragon, are of relatively new formation. Whether ancient or new, the 'customary' area has a continuous existence independent of the vicissitudes of political power. Not all the jurisdictions attained independence, or having attained it, continued to keep it.

Castile may be regarded as the prototype of the modern national society in which the inhabitants participate consciously in the life of the community, while the Leonese empire preserved the supranational nature of the empires of antiquity. The imperialism (or anti-imperialism) of Sancho the Great brought the leadership of Spain from integralist Leon to autonomist Castile. But once Castile had attained its hegemony, it quickly adopted Leonese integralism. It was only with the supercession of the imperial idea in the twelfth century that the fluid monarchies of Navarre and Aragon and the new state of Portugal attained full sovereignty and recognition by Rome.

Sancho the Great's second achievement was to have reopened the western Peninsula to European influences, and especially to the reforms of Cluny. Since the 'ruin of Spain' the Visigothic church had altered little. The Hispanic liturgy, the rite of Toledo, now differed profoundly from that of Rome, while the old Visigothic uncial script was still the universal hand in Spanish monasteries. Separated from Rome, the Leonese church was now a purely national body dependent on the monarch, who appointed its bishops and endowed it with land and revenues.

The Cluniac reform, which sought to enforce the rule of St. Benedict and to make monastic houses dependent directly on the Holy See, first entered the Peninsula at the great Catalan monastery of Ripoll, whose abbot Oliva corresponded with Sancho, though the two men never met. It was implanted in Gascony in 997, and probably so first entered non-Frankish Spain. But in the Hispanic church there was strong resistance against the admission of foreigners, and it was only after Spaniards had gone to study at Cluny that the reform was admitted by Sancho at San Juan de la Peña in 1024. From this small beginning great changes were to follow. At first they proceeded slowly: in 1049 Leo IX denounced the claim of Santiago de Compostela to be an apostolic see and excommunicated its bishop, but this had little effect, and it was left to Ferdinand's son, Alfonso VI, to bring the Roman reforms into Leon.

On Ferdinand's death, Sancho II, the new King of Castile, first marched upon Saragossa to make good his claim to its tribute. He then challenged his brother Alfonso of Leon for the imperial title. The contest was fought at Llantada in 1068, and Sancho was the victor. But Alfonso sought to recompense himself by demanding the parias of Badajoz from their younger brother García, who as King of Galicia, had the difficult task of defending the headquarters of the national church at Santiago. Alfonso and Sancho now agreed to remove him, and in 1071 each occupied part of Galicia. A year later they again fought at Golpejera, and once more Alfonso was defeated. He now took refuge with his former tributary al-Ma'mun, King of Toledo.

But his exile was soon brought to an end by his sister Urraca, who was passionately devoted to him. She rebelled in Zamora, and when Sancho laid siege to the town, a certain Vellido Dolfós issued forth, pretending to have deserted the princess, and seized the opportunity to murder the king. Alfonso was at once summoned from Toledo, and resumed his reign in Leon and Castile, reannexing Galicia and holding García a captive until he died.

At this moment the Cluniac monk Hildebrand was elected to the papacy and began to press forward the policy of spiritual and temporal universalism, reasserting the supremacy of the Holy See and demanding vassalage and tribute from the rulers of Christendom. Already in 1068 the King of Aragon had visited Rome and declared himself a 'Knight of St. Peter', and in 1071 the Roman rite replaced the Spanish in the monastery of San Juan de la Peña. Four years later in Oviedo priests of both rites officiated at a ceremony performed before Alfonso. He himself was not disinclined to admit the Pope's demands. He had already concluded the first of his three French marriages, and he doubled the tribute which his father had already paid to Cluny. But when the Cluniac reform was introduced into Leon at Sahagún, there was open opposition to the surrender of the Spanish rite. Only after Alfonso's second marriage, to Constance of Burgundy, who brought various Cluniac monks to Spain, was the new liturgy adopted by a Council of the national church in 1080.

Five years later Alfonso VI achieved the ancient ambition of the Leonese kings, conquering Toledo and so becoming 'Emperor of all Spain'. At the time of his own exile, he had promised to respect the rights of his host, and had used the rivalry of the Muslim princes to impose tribute on Badajoz and Seville. But after the death of al-Ma'mun Toledo was torn between two parties, those who supported the Christian protectorate, even though it meant the payment of an oppressive tribute, and those who would have asked the Muslims of Morocco for aid, thus risking their political independence. The intransigent Muslims overthrew al-Ma'mun's grandson, and when Alfonso restored him by force in 1081, Toledo came virtually under Christian control: a northern army remained encamped outside its walls, and its kingdom was overrun. Finally in May 1085, it capitulated: its inhabitants were promised religious freedom and given the choice of remaining or taking their departure.

This was a turning-point in the reconquest. Toledo was the first great Muslim city to fall to the Christians. The Muslim princes now understood that the payment of tribute was no guarantee against a final spoliation, and their people were filled with revulsion against rulers who bought an illusory independence with gold. In the preceding years Alfonso had fought Navarre for the tribute of Saragossa, and had extracted parias from al-Mu'tamid of Seville and 'Abdu'llah of Granada: his adviser, the Mozarab Sisnand, had explained frankly to the latter that his policy was to exploit the Muslim princes until they were ready to submit completely. Alfonso had demanded that each of the Muslim vassals should receive a Christian lieutenant-governor to superintend the collection of tribute. His commander Alvar Fáñez controlled central Andalusia from his estates in the southern meseta, while García Jiménez held the fortress of Aledo, built in 1088 to dominate Almería and Murcia. The third and most famous of these Castilian warlords, Rodrigo Díaz de Bivar, known simply as Sidi, or 'My Lord', was shortly to establish a Christian-controlled taifa in Valencia.

The Cid had been born within a decade of the foundation of the Castilian monarchy, and in his youth served in the far-ranging campaigns of Ferdinand I. Under Sancho II, while still a young man, he was in high favour and commanded the royal host. Alfonso VI employed him on missions to enforce and collect parias but still mistrusted him; and after a quarrel with his master, the Cid and his followers left Castile and took service with the ruler of Saragossa. He twice defeated and captured the Count of Barcelona when he sought to infringe the Castilian monopoly of Saragossan tribute.

But already in 1086 Alfonso's demands had decided al-Mu'tamid of Seville that he would 'rather tend the camels of the Almoravids than graze swine in Castile'. He and the other Muslim princes, forced to levy unsanctioned taxation to pay parias, could no longer face the discontent of their faqihs and populace, and a mission was sent to Africa to invite the ruler of Morocco to intervene.

This was Yusuf ibn Tashfin, the leader of a confederation of Saharan peoples which had overrun part of West Africa, islamising the Negroes of upper Nigeria and pressing them to serve in the conquest of Morocco. These Almoravids, with their trains of baggage-camels, their alarming war-drums, and their black guards defended by shields of hippopotamus-hide, at length landed at Algeciras, and joined by contingents from Seville and Granada, fought the battle of Sacralias (Zallaka), near Badajoz, in which Alfonso was heavily defeated. His losses were so great that he appealed to France for help, and a force which included some of his wife's Burgundian relatives entered Spain. But Yusuf returned at once to Morocco, and most of the French crusaders also withdrew.

The immediate danger was past, but so also was the age of easily won tribute. In 1089 Yusuf returned to lead a campaign against the castle of Aledo, which remained like a thorn in the flank of al-Andalus. The Muslim siege failed to reduce it, but when Alfonso relieved it, he found it too badly damaged to be held.

Alfonso's object was now to wean the Muslim princes from Yusuf, who, having once entered Spain, was increasingly tempted by the men of religion to take it for himself. The Almoravids held strict views about the payment of taxes, and were shocked at the Spanish princes who subsidised the Christian armies. The rulers of Seville and Granada, feeling their thrones increasingly unsafe, began to negotiate secretly with Alfonso; but he was not strong enough to defend them. In the autumn of 1091 Seville and Granada passed under the Almoravids, and two years later the ruler of Badajoz, after vainly allying himself with Alfonso, was also overthrown. In Valencia the Cid held out until his death in 1099: but soon after his widow was forced to abandon his conquest.

Meanwhile, Alfonso, the self-styled 'Emperor of the Two Religions', could do little more than maintain his pretensions. He was now past middle life, and his three French wives had given him only one daughter, Urraca; he had also a bastard, Teresa. He now married the widow of al-Mu'tamid's son, who became

THE GREAT RECONQUEST

the mother of his heir, Sancho. This boy, whose birth symbolised Alfonso's claim to that 'third Spain' which was Muslim but not African, fell in battle against the Almoravids at Uclés in 1108, only a year before the old Emperor himself died.

The extraordinary monarch had entered Toledo as both exile and conqueror, had displaced his two brothers and outlived his five wives, had petulantly bullied and dismissed the great warriors of his day, had won half Spain and lost it again, had brought the Roman church into Castile and Leon and had filled them with Muslim gold. He had however never quite made his peace with Galicia, where in 1076 the national church still refused to receive the Roman rite, a resistance which was stiffened by the papal demand for tribute. In 1077 Gregory VII addressed the rulers of the Peninsula on the Roman claim to supremacy and their duty of vassalage. There was no immediate response, but in 1080 France admitted the claim and Gregory turned to England. The Bishop of Santiago, Diego Peláez, appears to have approached William the Conqueror for support in resisting the Holy See (1086?): such at least was the charge made against him when he was arrested as a traitor, and in 1088 he publicly acknowledged that he was unworthy of his office.

Holding under arrest both the temporal and spiritual authorities of Galicia, Alfonso now placed the whole of the north-west under the rule of two Burgundians, Raimundo and Henry, cousins of Queen Constance, who had come to the Peninsula to crusade and remained to marry his two daughters. Urraca's husband Raimundo held court in Santiago as Count of Galicia, while his cousin Henry, who arrived some years later, married the bastard Teresa and was awarded the frontier county of Portugal, which then extended from the Minho to Coimbra.

The division of the west was followed by a lengthy political and religious conflict. Santiago, long acknowledged as the heart of Spanish Christianity, was a modern creation. In Visigothic times, before St. James's preaching in Spain had ever been thought of, the primacy of Spain was held by Toledo, while Braga could claim to be the head of the church in the north-west. The restoration of the see of Toledo under a Cluniac was a blow to the pretensions of Santiago, which under Raimundo remained without a bishop. But its resourceful administrator, Diego Gelmírez, who was later to become its first archbishop, devoted himself whole-heartedly to the task of wringing privileges from Rome in return for his profession of orthodoxy, while Braga, at first the western outpost of the reform, protested vainly against his exorbitance.

These rivalries form the spiritual context for the separation of Portugal. Meanwhile, the two counts Raimundo and Henry had come into conflict. Raimundo and Urraca had expected to succeed Alfonso to the throne of Leon. But when the Emperor was at last blessed with a male heir, the half-Sevillian Sancho, they concluded a pact by which Raimundo promised Henry the kingdom of Toledo or an equivalent in return for his support. Raimundo soon died, leaving a child, the future Alfonso VII, as his heir; and on the death of Sancho, the old Emperor summoned Urraca and declared her his heiress.

Both she and her father had good reason to fear the ambitions of the restless Henry and her half-sister Teresa, who were given no advancement and therefore left to lead the Portuguese towards independence. Thus while the Galician barons made common cause with the boy Alfonso VII Raimundes, who had been reared among them, those of Portugal ranged themselves behind his cousin Afonso I Henriques. When Alfonso VII celebrated his coronation as Emperor in Leon, all the Christian rulers of the Peninsula except the Portuguese were present; and in 1139 Afonso Henriques claimed the title of King of Portugal and placed himself under the protection of the Holy See, which finally recognised the Portuguese monarchy forty years later.

Meanwhile, Urraca's succession in Leon had given rise to new conflicts. Ancient usage required that she should remarry and transmit her prerogatives of power to her husband. She was therefore wedded to the most redoubtable warrior of the day, Alfonso I of Aragon, known as the Battler, who was soon to match the late Emperor's conquest of Toledo by taking Saragossa: he was a great crusader, a loyal son of the church, and an unenthusiastic husband.

Aragon had first been constituted a kingdom for Ramiro, the bastard son of Sancho the Great, who had annexed the counties of Sobrarbe and Ribagorza from his young half-brother, Gonzalo. He had, however, made small progress against the Muslims, whose cavalry were too strong for him in the plains of Huesca: he had died at the siege of Graus in attempting to contest the Castilian protectorate over Saragossa in 1063. His successor, Sancho Ramírez (1063-94), a contemporary of the Cid, received the help of French crusaders in recovering Barbastro; but these allies soon succumbed to the ease of Muslim life and the place was again lost. It was only after Castile had been weakened by the onslaught of the Almoravids that Sancho Ramírez's son Pedro won Huesca and retook Barbastro (1096 and 1110), being then succeeded by his brother, the Battler, whose one thought was to serve the church militant.

Urraca, who had inherited her father's less ascetic temperament, soon quarrelled with her husband, and the Galicians raised up her young son Alfonso as their king in 1112(?). An anarchical struggle took place across the plains of Leon and Castile, and after temporary reconciliations the Battler retired defeated from his matrimonial campaign and returned to the east, where he took the opportunity to conquer Saragossa, so long held tributary to Castile, in 1118, and pushed his conquests beyond the Ebro, entering Tudela in 1119 and Calatayud and Daroca in 1120. A few years later he marched in triumph to Granada and Córdoba, reasserting Christian power in al-Andalus, where the Almoravids had held sway since the days of the old Emperor.

But in 1126 the young Alfonso VII crowned himself King in Leon and prepared to challenge the Battler for the tribute of Saragossa and the eastern fringe of Castile, which had remained in Aragonese hands. When the two finally met in battle in 1134, the Battler was defeated and died of his wounds. He characteristically bequeathed his kingdom to the Orders of St. John and the Temple, but his court ignored his testament and elected as his successor his brother Ramiro II, a Benedictine who was then bishop-elect of Roda. The Navarrese refused to acknowledge Ramiro the Monk, and raised up a king of their own, García

Ramírez. Nevertheless, the new ruler of Aragon came to terms with Castile and obtained recognition of his rights to Saragossa, for which he did homage to Leon. He also married a niece of the Count of Toulouse, Inés of Poitiers, and had by her a daughter Petronila, whose birth assured the continuity of the Aragonese line.

The papacy had neither granted Ramiro a dispensation from his vows, nor accepted the repudiation of the Battler's will. But since the Aragonese nobility refused to deliver their kingdom to the two Orders, a settlement was reached by betrothing the infant Petronila to the Count of Barcelona, Ramón Berenguer IV, who had himself become a Templar. The two Orders ceded their claim in return for a number of castles, and in 1137 the papacy recognised the Count of Barcelona as ruler of Aragon, while Ramiro resumed his monastic life. When Petronila's son Ramón Berenguer V of Barcelona came of age, he was recognised as king in Aragon and took the Aragonese name of Alfonso II. Henceforth, the kingdom and county continued to be ruled together by the house of Barcelona, though they retained their separate institutions.

Meanwhile, in Leon the young Alfonso VII, having vanquished the Battler, was crowned Emperor in 1136. By the following decade the Spanish Muslims were already tiring of their Almoravid masters, and were ready to resume the payment of tribute to the new emperor. From Toledo Alfonso conducted expeditions towards Extremadura, taking Coria in 1142. Two years later a revolt against the Almoravid generals began in southern Portugal, and spread to Valencia and Murcia. In Córdoba, the African governor was besieged by a Spanish Muslim, Zafadola, a member of the northern family of the banu Hud, who summoned the Christians to his aid. Alfonso now traversed the whole of Andalusia, thus eclipsing the Battler's feat. While he was before Córdoba in 1146, Genoese representatives proposed a joint expedition for the conquest of Almería, then the richest port of Muslim Andalusia, and in 1147 the cradle of ancient civilisations was captured and held until the Emperor's death ten years later.

Like his predecessors, Alfonso VII divided his empire between his sons, awarding Castile to the elder, Sancho III, and Leon to the younger, Ferdinand II. The former died after a reign of barely a year, and left the throne to an infant son, Alfonso VIII (1158-1214). There was not now, or again in the future, a formal contest for the imperial title. By now the papacy had established its universalist principles. If the whole of Christendom was to be united in one spiritual and one temporal order, there was no more place for two emperors than for two popes, and the peculiar pretensions of the rulers of Leon must disappear. A century later a Spanish king would pursue the imperial title in Germany and Rome, but it was not to be assumed again in Spain until the coming of the Hapsburgs.

But if the title was superseded, the aspiration survived. The kingdom of Toledo had remained in the possession of Castile, which was thus compensated for the Aragonese seizure of Saragossa. But Toledo had from time immemorial been a Leonese claim, and it was a prize not lightly to be renounced. The papal delegates who now frequently appeared in the courts of the Peninsula strove to adjust the claims of the Five Kings, and to replace the abhorred competitive system of the empire by negotiated settlements. In 1151 Castile had admitted the Aragonese conquest of Saragossa in return for homage. Seven years later the brothers Ferdinand II of Leon and Sancho III planned to partition Portugal, thus partially compensating Leon for the loss of Toledo. But when Sancho died immediately afterwards and his infant son Alfonso VIII succeeded in Castile, the Leonese were again tempted to intervene in Toledo. Profiting by the quarrels of the Castilian magnates, Ferdinand made himself guardian of his infant nephew, and for a time held the imperial city, referring to himself by the anticipatory title of *nondum imperator*. But in 1166 his nephew was proclaimed of age and he was obliged to withdraw.

During the minority, two great families, the Laras and Castros, had disputed the tutorship of Alfonso VIII, and their quarrels had enabled the Navarrese to occupy the part of the Bureba and Rioja that Sancho the Great had won for them. When Alfonso came to the throne his first task was to recover this territory. He had already been betrothed to Eleanor, daughter of Henry II of

England, who brought as her dowry the duchy of Gascony, and his dispute with Navarre was now submitted to Henry for judgement, and Logroño reverted to Castile. He also made a new treaty with Aragon: at Cazorla in 1179 the Aragonese were relieved of the obligation to do homage for Saragossa, and Castile recognised their rights to the conquest of Valencia and Alicante, while Aragon accepted Castile's claims to Murcia and Andalusia. Leon was still left unsatisfied; and when in 1179 the papacy finally acknowledged the Portuguese monarchy, the former imperial power was tightly encased between two states that had once been her frontier counties. When Ferdinand II died, his successor, Alfonso IX (1188–1230) conducted a long and bitter struggle against Castilian hegemony.

In this period of apparent decline Leon was to produce two important innovations, one military and the other political. If in the middle of the century Almoravid power had collapsed and al-Andalus was disintegrating in a second age of taifas, a new Moroccan dynasty was at hand to take up the challenge. These were the Almohads, who drew their strength not from wild and fanatical converts, but from the sedentary tribes of the Moroccan plains. They began to appear in the Peninsula as early as 1146, and in the succeeding years they drove the Christians out of Andalusia, which they attached to their new empire of Marrakesh. They attempted a slower and intenser occupation than that of their exotic predecessors, expelling the last mozarabs from the south and restoring the fortifications of the Andalusian cities.

There was now no single Christian champion to oppose the new African invasion; and the greater responsibilities of the Christian world had been assumed by the church. Papal delegates appeared in Spain to conduct negotiations between the princes for the definition of frontiers, and their alliances were controlled by the strict application of the canonical impediments to their marriages. The church also provided new means of defence. The military Orders of St John and the Temple, an international force organised in national 'Provinces', had entered Spain from Catalonia and Aragon and shared in some of the notable feats of arms of the first half of the century. Already in the time of Alfonso VI bands of

THE GREAT RECONQUEST

French knights, responding to the exhortations of the Cluniac reformers, had visited Spain, and the King of Portugal had had the temporary aid of a large force of northern crusaders sailing to Palestine when he reconquered Lisbon in 1147. But in 1158, when the Templars were unable to hold Calatrava against Almohad attacks, the Cistercian abbot of Fitero declared a crusade and a small army of knights was organised under his patronage. As a result, Ferdinand II gave his approval to the constitution of the Order of Calatrava, a monastic society of knights like that of St John of Jerusalem. In 1164 a group of knights from Salamanca established themselves at San Julián de Pereiro on the Portuguese frontier and founded the Order later called Alcántara, while in 1176 another band at Cáceres was taken under the protection of the Archbishop of Compostela and assumed the title of Santiago.

These societies of knights, dwelling in strongly fortified priory-towns, were in origin the Christian reply to the Almoravids and Almohads. They were all of Leonese origin, and perhaps reflect the weakness of its secular military forces: although they soon formed Provinces in the other kingdoms, attempts to create 'national' orders in Castile were unsuccessful. The Orders proved peculiarly suited to occupy the vast expanses of the lower meseta. This since prehistoric times had been grazing-land, as the crude figures of the *berracos* show. More recently it had supplied meat and leather for the armies of Córdoba and the Muslim frontier; and the military orders and secular magnates who resettled it became proprietors of herds of half-wild cattle, flocks of migrant sheep and droves of hogs.[1] The transhumant sheep grazed in Extremadura in the winter, and were driven to summer pastures in the northern mountains, their migratory cycle coinciding with the alternation of peace and campaigning in the military life. Sheep-ranging was to grow into a great collective enterprise with its own Council at court.

While new forms of society were thus beginning to appear in Leonese Extremadura and the southern meseta, a step was taken

[1] This, and similar regions of Andalusia, became the original home of the cattle-ranch, which was later to be carried to the islands of the Caribbean, Mexico and South America.

towards a reordering of the old society of the north, when in the first year of the reign of Alfonso IX representatives of the municipalities were summoned for the first time to an assembly at court, the forerunner of the future *cortes*.

Since its origins the Asturian monarchy had been accompanied by a *curia* or court, consisting of the holders of the great offices and such other nobles or prelates as were summoned or happened to be present. In addition, greater assemblies were called from time to time, either to exchange oaths with a new king or to give their opinion or consent in dynastic or political matters, such as the conclusion of marriages and treaties and the opening of war. During the agrarian period matters of state concerned only the court, the more powerful counts and prelates and a small number of royal officials, and no 'representation' existed. But the municipalities which had been granted charters from the ninth and tenth centuries onwards now became a new force in the life of the state, and were of particular importance in sustaining the crown with tribute. With the Almoravid and Almohad invasions the quantities of gold and silver that had formerly flowed from al-Andalus into the royal treasuries of the north were cut off, and the crown was forced regularly to debase the currency. These arbitrary changes were resisted by the municipalities, whose fueros presumed a system of permanently fixed values; and as a result, the crown received a compensation from the towns in return for an undertaking not to 'break' the coin, usually for seven years, and even disposed of the right to mint coin, a privilege which, in the days of Alfonso VI, it had jealously preserved. It is believed that the summoning of representatives of the towns to cortes arose from their claims to be consulted about the conditions under which tribute was paid, especially monetary values and rates of exchange; but this is not certain.[1]

[1] The later cortes had three principal functions: (1) the exchange of oaths, the recognition of the heir to the throne and other dynastic matters; (2) the presentation of grievances or proposals of legislation; and (3) the voting of supply or 'service'. From what is known of the cortes of 1188, they appear to have been in part a 'curia' of the old type in which the new king received the oath of his nobles and prelates, and in part a prefiguration of the cortes of three estates. Alfonso swore to respect the existing customs and privileges of the

Leon still found the ascendancy of Castile hard to bear. Both Ferdinand II and Alfonso IX cultivated Portuguese friendship and married Portuguese princesses, but in each case Rome invoked the canonical impediment and forced a separation. In 1194 the visiting legate also negotiated a truce for ten years between Castile and Leon at Tordehumos. The Holy See undertook to study the great issue between Leon and Castile, but in its anxiety for the resumption of the crusade, it hesitated to pronounce. Both kings now made important grants to the Order of Santiago[1], but when in the following year the Almohads delivered a great attack against Alarcos, the Castilians took the field before the Leonese could arrive and were heavily defeated. There followed a stormy interview between the two Alfonsos at Toledo; and in the next year Alfonso IX made terms with the Almohads and invaded his cousin's territory. He was promptly excommunicated, and the Castilians invaded Leon: in 1197 both kings visited the Almohad Caliph in Seville, and soon after Alfonso IX married Berenguela of Castile, the daughter of his cousin and enemy.

This marriage was evidently as uncanonical as the last, but its legality was solemnly discussed by a council at Salamanca in 1201, and when the King and Queen were finally separated three years later, four children had been born to them, including the prince, who, as Ferdinand III, was permanently to unite the two crowns. The divorce was followed by a new quarrel about the territories which constituted the dowry, but by 1209 peace was restored, and Pope Innocent III commissioned Rodrigo Jiménez de Rada,

kingdom, and he also promised to revoke alienations of the royal patrimony made by Ferdinand II. There is no direct reference to tributary negotiations. The presence of the municipalities may be related with the political crisis in Leon, since the king swore not to make peace or war without first seeking the opinion of the nobility, clergy and 'good men.' The appearance of representatives of the towns is first recorded in Catalonia in 1214-8(?) in Portugal in 1254, in Aragon in 1274, in Valencia in 1283 and in Navarre in 1300. The Leonese cortes were resumed in Castile after the union of the two crowns under Ferdinand III. For a brief period at the end of the 13th century, those of Leon again met separately, but after 1300 the Leonese and Castilians sat as one body.

[1] Alfonso IX awarded it a tenth of all money coined in Leon.

Archbishop of Toledo and Primate of Spain, to organise a crusade. This was the campaign of Las Navas de Tolosa, which opened the gates of Andalusia to the Christians in 1212.

The final unification of the two kingdoms was to come about with the extinction of the Castilian, not the Leonese, line. In Leon, Alfonso IX's son by Teresa of Portugal died, and his heir was therefore Ferdinand, the son of Berenguela of Castile. In Castile, Alfonso VIII and his Queen died within a few months of one another, and their young son, Henry I, named after his English grandfather, was killed in an accident in 1217. He had fallen under the control of his *alférez*, Don Alvaro Núñez, and a rival party now bestowed the throne on Berenguela, who transferred her rights to her son Ferdinand. This prince was already heir to the throne of Leon, but his father, the wayward Alfonso IX, now saw the opportunity to claim both thrones and attempted unsuccessfully to invade Castile. Disappointed in these ambitions, he tried to deprive his son of the succession to Leon, which he bequeathed to his two daughters; but when he at last died in 1230, Berenguela persuaded the princesses to relinquish their rights in favour of Ferdinand III, who thus finally ended the long dispute and ruled over both Leon and Castile.

2. AL-ANDALUS AND AFRICA

At the fall of the caliphate al-Andalus still comprised more than two-thirds of Spain. The frontier stretched from the mouth of the Douro to its headwaters, where it curved north to Tudela on the Ebro and ran along the foothills of the Pyrenees: here Huesca and Barbastro defended Saragossa, and the strongholds of Lérida and Tarragona, still in Muslim hands, defied Barcelona.

Within this area Umaiyad civilisation flourished in a network of cities and towns supported by the intensive cultivation of irrigated vegas and huertas. It was thus a revival of Roman and pre-Roman Spain, but the ancient practice of irrigation had been extended and perfected, and the economy of al-Andalus had been enriched by the introduction of new crops, the orange, lemon, saffron, sugar-cane, cotton and silk. The growth of industry at Córdoba had been imitated in other cities, and the Spanish ports conducted a prosperous trade with Africa and the east. There were in addition many specialised activities: Toledo, the old military capital of the Visigoths and now the centre of the frontier, became famous for its arms, Málaga for its preserved fruits, Córdoba for leatherware, Granada and Almería for silks, and Málaga and later Valencia for glazed pottery.

Al-Andalus they composed a series of separate and different economic regions, linked to Córdoba by bonds of administration and religious duty. In its desire for 'omnipotence', the caliphate had ceased to rely on the military service of its subjects, using its resources of tribute to build up a professional army. In 991 Almanzor finally suppressed the old military circumscriptions, the Arab junds, and placed the destiny of Muslim Spain entirely in the hands of his Africans. Unlike the early Berber settlers, these newcomers were not given land, but lived in barracks near the capital. Once the Christians ceased to supply them with tribute or booty, they rapidly exhausted the resources of Córdoba and the provincial governors could afford to stand aloof. The collapse of the caliphate was thus followed by the disintegration of al-Andalus which fell apart into its administrative divisions.

The *taifa*-states numbered at one time as many as twenty-six, though some of these enjoyed only a brief spell of independence before being annexed by their more powerful neighbours. At first almost all the rulers of taifas pretended to be ḥajibs, or vizirs of a now non-existent overlord, but as new dynasties were established their successors assumed the title of kings.

At the moment of dissolution the various taifas were dominated by members of the several parties which had lately struggled for power: Berbers, Arabs, Slavs and members of Almanzor's family. Of the Berbers the strongest group was the Sanhaja horde, brought to Spain by Almanzor. They had supported his son Sanchul and had ravaged Córdoba in the terrible year of 1013. They had been promised land and followed their leader Zawi ibn Ziri to the district of Granada or Elvira, where they founded a new state of Berbers, Christians and Jews: other Berber groups held a few towns on its western rim. In Málaga, the family of 'Ali ibn Ḥammud, who had briefly usurped the caliphate, carved out a small principality with its Berber followers, the Zanata. Another group of taifas was formed by the palace Slavs: one Khayran and his successor Zuhayr held Almería and Murcia; al-Mujahid took Denia and the Balearics, and Nabil Tortosa. In the midst of these Arabised Russians, a grandson of Almanzor set himself up in Valencia.

All the rest of al-Andalus was governed by long-established Hispano-Muslim families, Arabs, Berbers or muwallads. In Córdoba and Seville these families formed a council of elders or senate; and since no one was at first able or willing to rule, they practised an oligarchical republicanism. These two taifas remained on hostile terms with the Berbers who had destroyed Arab supremacy. In the west a group of Arab families set up small city-states, which were later absorbed by Seville. The three frontier areas established kingdoms with their capitals at the centres of the upper, middle and lower marches, Saragossa, Toledo and Badajoz. Saragossa was seized in 1039 by the banu Hud, an Arab family of the first conquerors; Toledo by the banu Di'n-Nun, who claimed similar descent; and Badajoz by the Berber family of ibn al-Aftas, 'sons of the ape'.

The intricate pattern of the taifas was soon much simplified. While Seville annexed the minor Arab principalities, Granada took Málaga and Almería, forming a neo-African whole. The growth of this block separated Córdoba from its ports, and assured the rise of Seville, which still enjoyed free access to the Muslim world. The Sevillians had been spared a Berber occupation by the diplomacy of their qaḍi, who after some hesitation agreed to rule the city, thus founding the 'Abbadid dynasty. Both he and the president of Córdoba realised that only an Umaiyad could reunite Arab Spain. They therefore countenanced the imposture of a mat-maker named Khalaf who had pretended to be Hisham in the small town of Calatrava. He was brought to Seville and 'recognised' by the Caliph's widows. But in Córdoba the governing body refused to admit him; and although the fiction was kept up for a time in Seville, the qaḍi's successor, al-Mu'tadid, finally announced that the 'Caliph' had died and had appointed himself to be Emir of all Spain.

The reign of al-Mu'tadid saw the gradual annexation of all the neighbouring taifas from the Atlantic coast to Córdoba itself. But the Kings of Seville, though they built up a mercenary army, were still unable to face the power of Castile, and Ferdinand I ravaged their fields and forced them to pay tribute: he also asked for the relics of Santa Justa, thought to be preserved there, but they could not be found, though the body of St. Isidore was conveniently revealed and the great proponent of the old universalism was solemnly conveyed to Leon to inaugurate the new.

Meanwhile, the Berber taifa of Granada had also expanded. Its founder Zawi returned in 1019 to his native Ifriqiya in quest of a throne, and going 'like one led to his ruin without knowing it,' was poisoned by rivals. To succeed him, the shaikhs of the Sanhaja chose his nephew Habus, and whilst the subtle Arab al-Mu'tadid was enhancing Seville, this rude autocrat divided the old *kura* of Elvira into tribal districts and made the qadi of each responsible for raising a contingent of troops. The capital (Iliberris, Elvira, Granada) was largely Jewish and Christian, and for affairs of state Habus depended on the head of the Jewish community, Samuel ben Negralla, who had studied at Córdoba, set up as a spice-merchant in Málaga, and been called upon by the Berber commander there to write his letters. Because of his mastery of the florid ceremonial style he was summoned to Granada, where he succeeded to the vizirate, an office that could scarcely have been held by a Jew anywhere else in Spain: when Habus died in 1038, Samuel secured the election of his elder son Badis.

Hitherto Granada had remained on amicable terms with Zuhayr, the ruler of Almería and Murcia, who had also refused to credit the 'resurrection' of Hisham II. But when Zuhayr and his Arab vizir visited Granada they gave offence by their assumption of superiority and Badis sent a force which fell on them as they withdrew: Zuhayr was killed and his estates were shared between Granada and Valencia.

There followed open war with Seville. Al-Mu'tadid attacked the Berber taifas of Ronda, Arcos and Morón and killed their rulers; and Badis in reply planned to murder all the Arabs in Granada, but was prevented by his vizir. The celebrated Jew, mathematician, astrologer and philosopher as well as statesman, died in 1056, and his son Joseph inherited his office. But the new minister lacked his father's discretion, and the scandal of a Muslim state governed by a Jew provoked the faqihs to protest. 'When I came to Granada,' sang Abu Ishaq in a well-known poem, 'I saw that the Jews reigned there. They had divided the capital and the provinces among themselves, and one of these accursed ones reigned everywhere. They laid on the taxes and ate well: they dressed magnificently while you, O Muslims, were clad in rags. All the secrets of the state were known to them. . . .' Soon after, the mob attacked Badis' palace, the old *alcazaba*, in search of the hated vizir. Joseph had fled, but he was found hiding in a charcoal store: four thousand Jews are said to have been murdered with him (December 30, 1066).

On the death of Badis in 1073, his possessions were divided between his two grandsons, the elder, 'Abdu'llah, reigning in Granada, while the younger, Tamim, received Málaga. The Sevillians at once attempted to invade Granada, but they were defeated not far from the city and driven off. Their last king, al-Mu'tamid, made Seville famous as the centre of Hispano-Muslim culture. His literary court attracted the poets of the day, and his Queen, Rumaikiya, was renowned for her extravagant caprices. Having added Córdoba to his domains, he hoped to annex Murcia, thus encircling Granada. In 1078 he sought Catalan mercenaries from Ramón Berenguer II, and Murcia was at length captured. But al-Mu'tamid was doubtful about his own power to defeat the Sanhaja, and he proposed to his overlord Alfonso VI that they should together despoil Granada. A Castilian embassy accepted an agreement by which Granada would pass to the 'Abbadids and its treasury to Alfonso. But the Emperor had no desire to strengthen Seville, and imposed his own tribute on Granada. After this al-Mu'tamid grew defiant and arrested a Castilian embassy: in reply Alfonso laid waste the fields of Seville and advanced to the extreme limit of Spain at Tarifa, riding his horse into the sea in token of his pretensions.

THE GREAT RECONQUEST

This exploit was followed by the occupation of Toledo in May 1085. The fall of the first great Muslim city sent a shiver of horror thoughout the taifa-princes; and in the following year all but al-Mu'tamid paid Alfonso tribute and received governors appointed by the self-styled 'Emperor of the Two Religions'. The King of Seville had already decided to appeal to Africa for help. A generation earlier, in 1039, a Moroccan enthusiast had gone out to reislamise the tribes of the Sahara, preaching strict attention to the Koran, the ablutions, the giving of alms and the fear of hell. His followers were called Almoravids (*al-murabitin*, 'those who gather in the fortress to carry out the holy war'). They went as far afield as Nigeria and converted and mobilised the Negro peoples. In 1042 the Sahara accepted the revival, which drew its generals and faqihs from the Lamtuna Berbers. They then began to conquer Morocco, abolishing unsanctioned taxation and destroying wineshops and musical instruments. In 1061 the first ruler of the Almoravids returned to the desert to die, but his governor in Morocco, Yusuf ibn Tashfin, went on to found the new capital of Marrakesh. Already in 1075 al-Mu'tamid had approached Yusuf, who refused to involve himself in Spain until he should have won Tangier and Ceuta. Tangier fell to him in 1077 and Ceuta in 1084. Now that the new power was so near, al-Mu'tamid was hesitant, but the faqihs, perturbed by the fall of Toledo, the transigence of the Andalusian princes and the payment of tribute to the Christians, forced his hand. A deputation went to Africa, and in June 1086 the new conqueror arrived in Spain. Shrivelled, bushy-browed and squeaky-voiced, he wore a veil and ate barley-bread and camel-meat. His forces were vast: immense trains of camels carried arms, ovens and flour; the black guards carried impenetrable shields, and a system of signalling with drums enabled large masses of men to be concentrated suddenly at a given point. These forces crushed Alfonso's army at Zallaka in October, 1086.

Yusuf's victory was received with rejoicing throughout al-Andalus, where within living memory Islam had achieved nothing more than defensive successes. The taifa-princes were relieved when Yusuf himself returned to Morocco on the morrow of the battle, retaining only the town of Algeciras as a bridgehead in the Peninsula. But the Spanish Muslims could still not fend for themselves: Toledo remained in Christian hands, and the Cid held Valencia. The faqihs pressed for the recall of the Almoravids, and in 1090 Yusuf returned to Spain for the campaign of Aledo: when it was over, he once more withdrew to Africa.

There now began the same process of dispossession by which the Almoravids had won Morocco. In Granada 'Abdu'llah was denounced by his own qaḍi, and although he threw himself on the clemency of the African generals, they dethroned him and shared the riches of the Alhambra. The rulers of Seville and Badajoz hastened to congratulate Yusuf, but he scarcely deigned to acknowledge their flatteries. Seville was soon invested, and al-Muʻtamid and Rumaikiya were carried off to Morocco, where the once splendid kinglet died in misery at Agmat. With the conquest of Badajoz in 1094, all the independent taifas except two small states in Aragon disappeared. On the death of the Cid, his widow found herself unable to hold Valencia, and it too was relinquished to the Almoravids.

The Almoravid empire in Spain lasted for only fifty years. The great victory of Zallaka was never repeated: the later successes of the Almoravids were either inconclusive or won against their own co-religionists. Nor did they succeed in revitalising the Hispano-Muslim state. They appointed military governors to each province, and these men, whether they preserved their desert puritanism or succumbed to the ease of Andalusian life, were no more than petty tyrants. In Spanish eyes their only merit lay in their military power. But after they had killed the Emperor's heir at Ucles, their might soon declined. In the following decade the Aragonese Battler took Saragossa, and in the next he marched through Andalusia, bringing back many of the surviving mozarabs. After his death, his stepson Alfonso VII plundered the south. The power of the Almoravids was already declining in Morocco, and they could no longer defend the Spanish Muslims. The people of al-Andalus began to sigh for the relative peace they had enjoyed under their own princes. There were revolts in southern Portugal, and in 1144 Alfonso placed a member of the banu Hud as governor of Granada, and soon after captured Almería. A second age of taifas, whose princes were now no more than Christian appointees, seemed about to dawn.

But these successes were at once swept away by a new invasion from Africa. In 1126 the peoples of the Atlas were stirred by a new religious leader, who claimed to be the Mahdi, the uniter of Islam. His followers, the Almohads (*al-muwahhidun* or unitarians), were drawn mainly from agricultural tribes, stirred not so much by the desire for conquest and plunder, as for order and the obligatory religious war. Within a quarter of a century they demolished the declining Almoravid empire, capturing Marrakesh in 1147. Before ibn Hud and the heirs of the 'third Spain' could consolidate themselves, the Almohads crossed the straits and laid claim to al-Andalus. For them the Holy War was a social duty, and Spain a land dyed with the blood of the martyrs. They built the town of Gibraltar to defend the road into the Peninsula, and secured access from it to Seville by planting colonies of trustworthy tribesmen in the vicinity of Jerez. Each of their tribes was required to participate in the religious war, originally by contributing a contingent of a thousand men; and the idea of holding Spain by permanent but renewable garrisons was to take firm root. Having summoned the representatives of Muslim Spain to do him homage at Gibraltar, the Almohad caliph appointed his heir as his regent in Seville: during the next half-century the governors of the Spanish cities were usually members of his lineage.

Thus when his heir Abu Ya'qub succeeded to the throne, he took with him to Morocco a Spanish upbringing and a profound attachment to Arabic literature and culture gained in the city of the 'Abbadids. Averroes, the great reviver of Islamic thought, tells how, on first being presented to Abu Ya'qub, he found him alone with ibn Tufayl, and 'after a few kindly enquiries about my family, the Emir suddenly asked my opinion about the nature of Heaven and the Creation'. Aware of the narrow views of the faqihs, Averroes cautiously replied that he had not given much thought to these matters, whereupon Abu Ya'qub opened the discussion by stating the opinions of Plato and Aristotle.

But while this Hispano-Moroccan renascence forms the background of the return of Greek learning to Europe a century later, eastern Spain, which was less directly linked with Morocco, inclined towards the creation of a non-African and 'national' Islamic state. One Muhammad ibn Mardanish (Martínez), born at Peñíscola in 1124 of mixed descent, set up a new kingdom in Murcia and Valencia. At the height of his powers he defeated the Almohad governors of the upper Guadalquivir valley and laid siege to Córdoba and Seville. His greatest exploit was his capture of Granada in 1162: the city capitulated after negotiations with the Jews, but the Almohad garrison continued to hold the keep of the Alhambra. A first Almohad relief expedition was defeated, but a second destroyed the besieging force, and thereafter ibn Mardanish's fortunes declined. He became a vassal of Aragon, and Valencia broke away from him. Left only with Murcia, he recommended his heir to submit, and soon after his death in 1172 this last 'third Spain' disappeared.

Like the Almoravids, the Almohads won one great victory against the Christians. This was the battle of Alarcos, fought in 1195, when the flower of the Christian army was left on the field and Alfonso VIII of Castile narrowly escaped capture. But this defeat was less extenuating than Zallaka, and the military Orders, if they were pushed back, continued to form a barrier across the middle of the meseta. A few years later in 1212 the Christians replied with the victory of Las Navas de Tolosa, which opened the road from the tablelands into the valley of the Guadalquivir and exposed the heart of al-Andalus.

3. THE COMPLETION OF THE RECONQUEST

The final subjection of Muslim Spain quickly followed. As Almohad power declined, Ferdinand III of Castile (1217-54) and Leon (1230-54) reunited the two central kingdoms and joined their forces to reconquer Andalusia; in the east, James I of Aragon (1213-76) conquered Valencia and the Balearic Islands; and in the west, Sancho II and Afonso III completed the Portuguese reconquest.

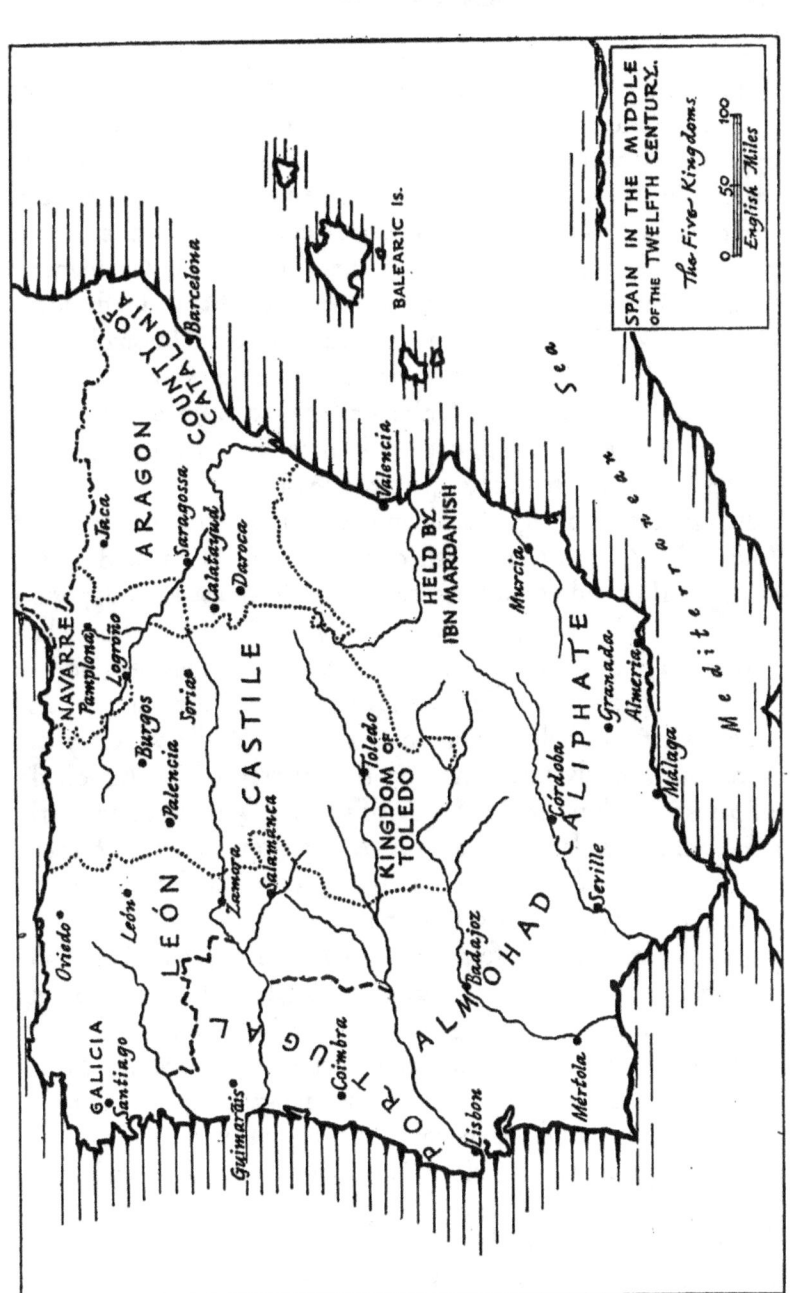

After the battle of Las Navas the Almohad caliph had concluded a truce in 1214, and it was renewed in 1221. His death three years later and the accession of a young boy gave Ferdinand the opportunity to intervene in the affairs of Morocco and to resume the war in Andalusia. During the first years of his reign Ferdinand had been faced with a rebellion of the Laras and other nobles, and his jealous father, Alfonso IX, had invaded Castile and had almost reached Burgos. But peace was at last restored and the dissident Count Alvaro Núñez de Lara went to serve the Almohad caliph in Morocco, where he died. In 1219 Ferdinand married Beatrice of Swabia, whose father, Duke Philip, had been elected Holy Roman Emperor in 1197: a legitimate imperialism was thus placed within reach of the Spanish dynasty.

In his first campaign Ferdinand descended into the valley of Andalusia through the breach opened at Las Navas and raided Jaén. Its Almohad governor accepted Ferdinand's aid in opposing a brother, who was proclaimed caliph in Morocco. But when Ferdinand had occupied several towns near Jaén, his protégé was murdered, and a new caliph was proclaimed at Córdoba, who also sought Christian help in winning Morocco. While the Castilians were thus actively intervening in the quarrels of the Almohads, a Spanish Muslim, ibn Hud, one of the family that had formerly ruled Saragossa, launched an anti-African revolution in Murcia, sweeping all al-Andalus within the space of a few years and virtually ending Almohad power in Spain.

At this moment Alfonso IX died in Leon and Ferdinand departed to visit and pacify his new kingdom. In the following year he resumed his war against the Muslims, taking Trujillo in Extremadura and forcing ibn Hud to pay a heavy tribute. Meanwhile, the salient in mid-Andalusia was strengthened and extended. In 1236 a Christian force approached the suburbs of Córdoba, and finding no resistance, set siege to the old Umaiyad capital, summoning Ferdinand to help. Although ibn Hud advanced towards the scene of the struggle, he was unable to face the Christian armies and retired, and Córdoba surrendered. Having failed in the field, ibn Hud was murdered in Murcia or Almería. Al-Andalus again dissolved into localisms, while in 1240–1 Ferdinand spent

THE GREAT RECONQUEST

over a year in Córdoba, granting it a municipal organisation and receiving tribute from a number of neighbouring towns.

Meanwhile, Aragon had returned to the war. The first ruler of the joint house of Barcelona, Ramón Berenguer V or Alfonso II of Aragon (1162–96), had won Teruel from the Muslims and reserved the conquest of Valencia for his house by the treaty of Cazorla of 1179. But he also became Count of Provence by inheritance in 1167, and Aragon was thereafter to hesitate between a Peninsular and a French destiny. On his death he left his kingdom to his elder son, Pedro II, and Provence to the younger. But at this time the states of southern France were already threatened with absorption by the Capetian north, and Pedro was drawn into a new alliance with Toulouse. In order to secure support for his French ambitions he paid a tribute to the Holy See and was crowned in Rome in 1204. But he hesitated to become the instrument for the suppression of the Catharist heresy now spreading through southern France. When at length the Pope called on the rulers of northern France to crusade against the southern dissenters, Philippe-Auguste and his nobles needed no second bidding, and invited Pedro to collaborate in purifying his own vassals. Simon de Montfort took Carcassonne in 1209, and offered Pedro homage for it. But the Aragonese delayed his recognition of the conquest; and after he had taken part in the victory of Las Navas and so proved his zeal as a crusader, he found that de Montfort had attacked Toulouse. In August 1213 he marched towards the city, and was completely defeated in the battle of Muret. He himself was killed, and his heir, the future James the Conqueror, a boy of six, remained in the hands of de Montfort, to be returned in the following year.

During his minority a papal legate arranged that a great-uncle should act as his procurator and that there should be governors in each of his realms. But this was no substitute for royal power, and the barons of Aragon and Catalonia constantly had recourse to private wars. It was only in 1227 that peace was at last restored at Alcalá. James then organised a Catalan expedition with the aid of ships and men from Genoa and Marseilles and took Majorca from the Almohads in 1229: Minorca was conquered a year or two later, and Ibiza in 1235. This maritime expansion fulfilled the aspirations of his Catalan subjects, and the city of Barcelona now began its great mercantile career. With the King's encouragement it developed a new municipal and trading organisation and soon extended its network of merchant colonies governed by elected consuls round the ports of the Mediterranean. Its sea-law was now probably first committed to writing.

James' other realm, Old Aragon, bred warriors rather than seafarers, and its nobility cast their eyes towards the Muslim kingdom of Valencia. One of them had already seized Morella on the frontier; and in 1233 James obtained a bull to crusade and occupied northern Valencia as far as the Sierra de Espadán. In 1235 he restored the old fortress of Puig de Cebolla, a few miles from the capital, but it was only in September 1238 that the people of Valencia finally capitulated. Like Córdoba, it was unsuccoured, and many of the inhabitants went into exile. The Aragonese barons received shares in the city and in the surrounding huerta, and the see founded by the Cid was restored.

As James partitioned Valencia and Ferdinand disposed his forces in Córdoba, the surviving Muslim territories each followed its own fortune. The governor of Murcia, seeing no possibility of obtaining help from Africa, decided to capitulate to Ferdinand; and in 1243 the heir to Leon and Castile, the future Alfonso X, advanced to receive the keys of the city and its surrounding towns. A few of these resisted, but they were soon reduced: by the treaty of Almizra (1245), the Aragonese recognised the Castilian acquisition of Murcia.

Ferdinand now laid siege to Jaén, which had constituted itself a separate taifa. Meanwhile, at the time of the fall of Córdoba, a Muslim frontiersman, Muhammad ibn al-Aḥmar, who had hitherto defended the small town of Arjona, was received by the people of Granada. His entry almost certainly had the consent of Ferdinand, who gladly saw this mountain kingdom reappear to divide lower Andalusia from Murcia and the east. As Ferdinand camped before Jaén, the new ruler came to him and undertook to pay tribute and to collaborate in the siege of Seville. In this way Granada obtained a limited autonomy, and remained the last of the taifas, governed by the Naṣrids, the descendants of ibn al-Aḥmar, until its final suppression in 1492.

With the fall of Jaén and the vassalage of Granada, only Seville and the area to its south and west remained independent. In 1247 its neighbour Carmona capitulated, and the Christian armies began to lay siege to it. Its leaders had long wavered between war and peace, and in case of war between various allegiances. Thus at the last they were alone in the field. The city was cut off from all help and Christian ships brought from the Biscayan coast blockaded the river and broke the bridge of boats which linked the city with its suburb of Triana. Finally in December 1248, it surrendered, and its leading citizens took their departure, while throngs of gaping northerners trooped through its narrow streets. and surveyed its wonderful extent from the lofty tower of the Giralda. Soon after, the towns to its south also capitulated, and only a foothold on the north shore of the straits remained in Moroccan hands. Ferdinand had proposed to follow his conquest with a great expedition to Morocco, where Christian troops had already replaced Negroes as the guard of the Almohads, and Franciscan missions for the ransoming of captives had been active since at least 1220. But before anything could be achieved Ferdinand died in his new capital of Seville in 1254: a century was still to pass before the northern Pillar of Hercules was firmly held by Castile.

V

MEDIAEVAL SPAIN—PART ONE

1. CASTILE AND LEON

THE final conquest of the Muslim south and east had been accomplished in the space of scarcely two decades. During the period that followed, the destinies of the Five Kingdoms diverged. Navarre, long excluded from the great advance, had already turned towards France. In Aragon, Catalonia had begun to establish its merchant colonies in the wake of those of Genoa at all the trading-centres from Seville to Alexandria, and the Aragonese crown, after being rebuffed in France and Tunisia, turned its energies to the annexation of the Mediterranean islands and thence to the conquest of southern Italy. Leon, having vested her imperialism in Castile, was slowly to surrender her political individuality, and later writers, in seeking to identify the Five Kingdoms, would introduce Muslim Granada to complete the tally. Meanwhile, Portugal remained in association with the central kingdom until the Pillars of Hercules were secure: once there was safe transit between the inland sea and the outer ocean, the confluence of Mediterranean and Atlantic shipping in her ports would give her a new mission of oceanic discovery.

On the death of Ferdinand III, Castile and Leon were preparing to enter Africa. But within a few years a new dynasty, the banu Marin or Marinids, rose up in Morocco, and inheriting the Almohad preoccupation with the Holy War, firmly planted its foot at the southern tip of Spain and on the road into Europe. For eighty years the Castilians attempted to parry its invasions and to dislodge it. This crusade kept alive the military habit of life in Andalusia; but it offered few material rewards, and the ancient impetus derived from ambition, religious fervour and land-hunger lost its force.

Castile, like Aragon, had become aware of the importance of sea-power. Already in 1146 the Genoese had sent ships to collaborate in the conquest of Almería, and a century later Ferdinand III brought Basque, Cantabrian and Galician vessels to blockade Seville: his son Alfonso X planted colonies of northern fishermen on the Atlantic coast of Andalusia in readiness for a new expansion. The first full use of the straits was made in 1284 when a Genoese, Benedetto Zaccaria, made the earliest recorded voyage since Phoenician or Roman times from the Mediterranean to the ports of northern Europe. After he had won a victory over the Muslims in 1291, the king of Castile granted him the title of 'chief emir of the sea', the first admiral.[1] The shipyards of Seville were restored and in the second half of the fourteenth century Castile became a great naval power.

But Castilian shipping was essentially a military instrument rendered necessary by the struggle for the straits. The trade of Andalusia remained in the hands of Muslims or of Genoese and Pisans, who since the middle of the twelfth century had created an active tri-continental traffic, bringing the spices of the near east to Italy and North Africa, taking Italian fustians and Spanish dyes and paper to the Magrib and Ifriqiya, and bringing back African sheep and goatskins. After the first dislocation of the conquest, the economy of Andalusia was at least in part restored, and the Castilian court was attracted to settle in Seville no less by its wealth than by its proximity to the new frontier and the peculiar problems of the resettlement.

In the wake of the conquering soldiers came colonists from Castile, Leon, Galicia, Portugal, Aragon and the Basque country. From some regions of the north there were large migrations: in particular Galicia supplied Seville with plentiful settlers, as had been foreseen by Ferdinand I. These groups brought their own customs and speech, but in the melting-pot of Andalusia they slowly surrendered their regionalisms and became the first

[1] Admiral, from Sp. *almirante*, and so from Arabic *amir*, ruler, commander.

Spaniards by nationality 'because they could not be anything else,' adopting the language of Castile which was thus to become 'Spanish'. The capital of this first 'new world' remained Seville, still entirely Muslim in aspect and considered 'the noblest city on earth'. It was the favourite seat of the Spanish monarchy for a century.

In the course of the reconquest, the Five Kingdoms evolved far from their original state as phases in an 'agrarian continuum'. As their frontiers were extended, their national centres tended also to shift southward towards the richer and larger cities of the mudéjar zone. In the west, the earliest capital of Portugal had been Guimarãis, north of the Douro; it was followed by mozarabic Coimbra, and later by the Roman, mozarabic and Muslim sea-port of Lisbon. This southward movement of the Portuguese capital appears to result from the long survival in the west of the practices of the earliest phase of the reconquest, when the rural north proposed to absorb new settlers and integrate them into its society. Galician monasteries preserve long genealogies of former Muslims brought north as captives and settled as labourers and artisans. They intermarried with the existing population and when they embraced Christianity ascended from slavery to serfdom. This practice of integration was characteristic of western society: although the social unity of the west could not prevent the truncation of Galicia, it remained an essential condition of Portuguese nationhood, and its fruit is to be seen in modern Brazil.

In eastern Spain, the reabsorption of Muslims was slower and less complete. In Catalonia few Muslims were reincorporated, and the capital remained always at Barcelona. The centre of Navarre remained at the ancient capital of Pamplona, though it annexed a small mudéjar zone in the Ebro valley. In Aragon the former Muslim capital of Saragossa replaced Jaca as the capital, but the mediaeval history of Aragon shows that the old nobility of the north strove tenaciously to maintain their ancient privileges. Because of the late expansion of Aragon, there was no extensive area of rural settlement, and it survived as an independent state only by associating with the enlarged county of Barcelona.

Greater Aragon was thus a political, not a social creation; and when the dual state acquired Valencia, it had no hesitation in constituting it a third, though subordinate kingdom.[1] Thus while Portugal remained an integrated state formed of a single (though still incompletely unified) society, greater Aragon remained a composite monarchy formed by the federation of three distinct societies.

Between these two extremes lay the reconstituted kingdom of Castile and Leon, which contained elements of both its neighbours. Since the early days of the reconquest the Leonese monarchy had claimed to be the heirs of the northern Visigoths, thus maintaining a vague tradition of racial superiority, which was in the future to be consecrated in the same way as the myth of 'Norman blood'. But Leonese society, like that of Galicia, had no hesitation in reincorporating Arabised Christians or even muwallads, who often formed separate villages in the midst of the northern settlers. In the frontier area of Castile, however, the constant threat of attack made loyalty or conformity the first consideration. There is little doubt that Castilian society was not originally exclusive, and that the special quality on which it prides itself, purity of caste, 'castizo', meant not racial consistency, but undivided loyalty. This attitude was doubtless hardened by the pitiless campaigns of Almanzor; and it was as a compact military society that Castile came to the fore in the eleventh century.

But in the second half of the eleventh century the character of the reconquest changed. Great Muslim cities began to fall into northern hands, and there could no longer be any question of merely redistributing their population as captives or colonists. After Ferdinand I's conquest of Coimbra in 1064, several thousands of its inhabitants were still sold into slavery; but twenty years later when Toledo capitulated to his son a large Muslim population was incorporated into Castile. There was in fact no choice but to adopt the Muslim solution by which the three 'Peoples of the Book' dwelt side by side in segregated communities. But in the immediately following years al-Andalus passed out of the hands

---

[1] In strict fact, a second kingdom, since Catalonia was a county, or later, a principality.

of its Spanish princes and into those of African intruders, who could not by any stretch of the imagination be regarded as Spaniards or proprietors of the land. Thus while Alfonso VI began his reign by promoting a Christian reform, he ended it as the would-be patron of the Spanish Muslims. His successors, Alfonso the Battler and Alfonso VII, did their best to relieve the new pressure on the mozarabs or Andalusian Christians by bringing them back and resettling them in the north. As a result, when Andalusia, Murcia and Valencia were at last reconquered, they had long been denuded of their Christian populations and it was necessary to apply a much vaster and more rapid policy of colonisation than ever before. If, therefore, the central belt of Spain was in the first half of the twelfth century southernised by the resettlement of groups of redeemed Christians, Andalusia was even more intensively northernised in the thirteenth. The Andalusian metempsychosis is difficult to describe for lack of documentation. Both Muslims and Christians recognised the distinction between capitulation, by which the conquered retained certain rights, and surrender, which was often followed by summary expulsion. But these general principles were in practice modified by more immediate considerations: it was often possible to expel the inhabitants of towns but impossible to do without the labour of the country people. Christian garrisons might buy supplies across the frontier or they might occupy walled towns and allow the former inhabitants to resettle outside the fortifications. Even in cases where the document describing the redistribution of property (repartimiento) has survived and suggests that a complete evacuation took place, it cannot be assumed that numbers of Muslims did not remain or return.

In the second half of the thirteenth century Castile therefore consisted of three principal zones: the first, Old Castile, was the area of intense rural resettlement which recognised Burgos as its capital; the second, the earliest of the great conquests, the kingdom of Toledo, known as 'New Castile'; and the third, Andalusia. Old Castile contained many towns and villages whose usages were laid down in municipal charters granted in perpetuity by successive magnates and monarchs. In New Castile this pattern was adapted to include the tri-communal system inherited from Islam. In Andalusia the northern municipality was introduced by the crown, but the tri-communal system had already largely disappeared; and if the Jews continued to occupy their special quarters, the Christians took over most of the Muslim towns and reduced the former inhabitants to an inferior and extra-municipal status, or used their services as rural labourers, artisans and carriers. Emerging from the simple social unity of Old Castile, the peoples of the central kingdom had attained a form of domestic imperialism. These phases of expansion were not confined to Castile; but whereas Aragon adopted a tripartite political form and Portugal proceeded on its course of gradual social assimilation, Castile resolutely set its face against any form of territorial division and as resolutely insisted on the preservation of 'Castilian' hegemony. The bond which united the three phases of Castile was the crown, but its power was already limited in the sense that it could not divest itself of its realms, and it constituted at once a symbol of national unity and a guarantee of local rights.

Ferdinand III was himself conscious of having transcended the limits of Old Castile and Leon, and his unfulfilled ambitions included not only the subjugation of Morocco, but also the creation of a royal law for all his realms and the acquisition of the imperial title. But the execution of these designs fell to his son Alfonso X, 'the Learned' (1252-84), who surrounded himself with the trappings of universal monarchy, absolute power, patrimonial magnificence and encyclopaedic 'learning' and the patronage of culture, only to end his long quest in a miserable deposition.

Alfonso's first undertaking was an attempt to annex Navarre on the death of its ruler Theobald I in 1253. It failed, and in the following year he again disappointed the Castilians by abandoning Gascony, which had come to Alfonso VIII as the dowry of Eleanor of England and was now returned with a Spanish bride to Edward, Prince of Wales. He did indeed conquer the south-western tip of the Peninsula, the Algarve, in 1257, but gave it as a dowry to his daughter on her marriage to the King of Portugal, and later waived the small tribute that was paid for it.

He had already begun his quest for the crown of the Holy Roman Empire, which was constantly to elude him for twenty years. His ambition for the title held by his maternal grandfather must have been known before 1256, when a mission from Pisa seeking a commercial agreement addressed him, without any authority to do so, by the imperial title. Thereafter his representative in Germany, the Archdeacon of Morocco, bought over several electors at twenty thousand marks apiece, and they adhered to him even after his rival Richard of Cornwall was proclaimed at Frankfurt. All efforts to induce Rome to pronounce between the contestants failed. When Richard died in 1272, Alfonso was once more thwarted, and on the election of Rudolph of Hapsburg in the following year he sought to intervene in the struggle in Italy. At length in 1275, discouraged and faced with the threat of rebellion and invasion, he withdrew his pretensions.

He had meanwhile attempted to establish absolute power in Castile by forming a new and general system of laws. In Andalusia his father had revived the Visigothic *fuero juzgo*, a royal law which had long kept Galicia faithful and subservient to the crown: the new municipalities of Seville and Córdoba had been erected on the basis of the statute-law of Toledo. But while in Andalusia a motley population acknowledged one law, Castile, with its 'castizo' people, had a multiplicity of different usages, which to the Romanist jurisconsults seemed 'godless' in their neo-Gothic variety and pragmatism. In 1255 Alfonso produced the *Fuero Real*, a collection of the common law of Castile, supplemented by 'new laws' applicable to all his dominions. Ten years later, his jurisconsults, trained in Italy and versed in Justinian and Roman and canon law, produced an alternative code in the *Siete Partidas*, which formed a universal system of royal justice intended ultimately to replace the jealously guarded privileges of the Castilian municipalities and the private jurisdictions of the nobility. But the novelty of royal absolutism incensed both classes of Castilian traditionalists, and the *Partidas* were accordingly never promulgated, but remained a mere compendium or guide, intended to supplement the existing laws or serve as a reference in case of conflict.

Alfonso was to be denied the absolute authority he desired. His assault on the laws of the land, carried out under the autocratic camouflage of 'learning', cost him the sympathy of Castilians; and his attempts to dispose of his patrimony without having won fame as a conqueror caused his nobles to rebel. The precarious nature of his power was shown in 1264 when the Muslims of Andalusia and Murcia, in collusion with his vassal of Granada, rose against him in a general rebellion, and hundreds of villages and towns passed temporarily out of Christian control. They were gradually reduced, but Murcia was recovered only with the help of James I of Aragon.

This rebellion was followed by the Marinid revival in Africa. In 1275 the King of Granada solicited the aid of the new dynasty, whose leaders desired only to renew the holy war. They crossed the straits to Tarifa and laid waste the fields about Jerez, carrying their prisoners in chains to Africa.

The campaign had unexpected consequences. As Alfonso's eldest son, Fernando de la Cerda, advanced to meet them, he was taken ill and died. According to the Roman code, the next heir was Fernando's infant son. Alfonso himself was absent from the kingdom, having gone, still in pursuit of his imperial ambition, to interview Pope Gregory X at Beaucaire. The nobility seized the opportunity to vindicate their own traditions, and elected Ferdinand's younger brother, Sancho, to lead them. When Alfonso returned, now disillusioned, he prepared to accommodate himself, but Ferdinand's widow, Blanche of France, a daughter of St Louis, stirred up influences in favour of her son, and Alfonso at length proposed to set up a kingdom at Jaén so that his grandson might have the royal title. But Castile had set its face firmly against patrimonial divisions, and there followed open war between the Romanist ruler and his traditionalist son. The unlucky autocrat remained in Seville while cortes met at Valladolid in 1282 and deposed him. In his last months he negotiated for the help of the Marinids, and was accused of having pledged his crown with them. He died in 1284: even his testament, in which he again sought to divide his realms, was ignored.

His successor, Sancho IV (1284-95), known as *el bravo*, 'the fierce', on account of his displays of royal ire, set aside his Roman pretensions and became the defender of neo-Gothicism supported by the old nobility and the leagues of *hermandades*, now formed by the towns to protect their rights. The French princess fled with her small son to Aragon and although she left behind a champion, he too was soon expelled. Meanwhile, Sancho's favourite Lope Díaz de Haro, Lord of Biscay, aroused the discontent of nobility and clergy by farming the royal taxes to his Jew, Abraham de Barchilón. A faction of the nobility rebelled, and in 1288 Sancho quarrelled with his favourite and murdered him. Meanwhile, Philip IV of France had taken up the cause of the Infantes de la Cerda, who, after spending seven years in captivity in Aragon, were at last released, and the elder, Alfonso, attempted to invade Castile. He was repulsed: peace was made at Bayonne, and he retired to France.

Meanwhile, the battle for the straits was resumed. Alfonso X's attempt to find allies in Morocco led to a second Marinid invasion in 1285, when the area between Tarifa and Seville was again devastated. Sancho IV was still unsure of the allegiance of the south, and he therefore concluded a seven-years truce, which gave security to Moroccans trading in Spain. When this truce expired in 1292, his throne was assured, and he prepared to attack Tarifa, obtaining the help of Aragonese galleys and the favourable neutrality of his vassal, the Sultan of Granada, to whom he promised Tarifa in exchange for other places. In October 1292, the town was taken after a long siege, but Sancho now refused to deliver it, and the defrauded Sultan turned to the Moroccans. The two Muslim parties were joined by Sancho's brother John, and they together attacked Tarifa. It was held for Sancho by an Andalusian captain, Pérez de Guzmán, who refused to surrender it even when John had his captive son slain before his eyes: his singular loyalty to the crown earned him fame as 'Guzmán the Good'. Tarifa held firm, and the Marinids returned to Africa.

Sancho IV died of tuberculosis at Toledo in April 1295, leaving his son Ferdinand IV, a boy of nine, in the charge of his widow, María de Molina. Since Sancho himself had seized power on the pretext of his nephew's youth, his son and widow had to face a counter-attack. Alfonso de la Cerda returned from France and obtained the help of James II of Aragon and Muhammad II of Granada. He also undertook to share his claim with John, the traitor of Tarifa: he would keep the Castiles and eastern Andalusia, and John should have Leon, Galicia and Seville, while Aragon would take Murcia. The prospects of the young king were not hopeful: a brother of Alfonso the Learned, Henry, who had long sojourned in Rome and had acquired the title of 'the Senator', obtained the tutorship at the cortes of Valladolid (1295) and proposed to surrender Tarifa to Granada. But the staunch queen-mother held out, and finally made peace with Aragon. The pretender returned to France, and John 'of Tarifa' took the oath of allegiance to his nephew in 1300.

When Ferdinand came of age the ruler of Granada, Muhammad III, renewed his submission and recognised the Castilian claim to Tarifa, dispersing part of his Berber garrisons (1304). But at this time Morocco again fell into disorder, and Muhammad III seized the southern shore of the straits at Ceuta (1306): against this Granadine bridgehead the Moroccans founded the town of Tetuán. Ferdinand now hoped to extinguish Granada and seize control of the straits at a single blow, and he obtained Aragonese help by offering to cede Almería. But in Granada Muhammad was overthrown by a palace revolution, and his successor, Naṣr, faced with a siege of Algeciras by Ferdinand and of Almería by James II, hastily came to terms with the Marinid sultan, granting him the towns of Algeciras and Ronda. Thus the three forces were interlocked as before: Naṣr resumed the payment of tribute to Ferdinand, who accordingly guaranteed his throne. In the struggle Gibraltar passed to Ferdinand, while the Aragonese retired from Almería and abandoned the contest for the straits.

Ferdinand IV died at Jaén in 1312: according to legend, he was 'emplazado' or cited to die by two brothers he had wrongfully executed. His son Alfonso was less than two years old, and there followed another troubled minority. The throne itself was not now seriously disputed, for Alfonso de la Cerda had withdrawn his claims, and his reappearance met with little response. But the regency conferred royal powers for a period of years, together with the possibility of controlling the young king's inclinations and perhaps of winning a permanent alliance through marriage. The three contestants were: John 'of Tarifa'; Juan Manuel, a nephew of Alfonso X, and like him a patron of letters and student of statecraft; and Pedro, a son of Sancho IV. On the death of the Queen, each claimed to be regent, and John and Pedro were finally recognised.

In 1316 Pedro attacked Granada, which had again slipped from Castilian control, and two years later, when he and John launched separate raids, both perished in the 'disaster of the vega'. A convocation of frontier towns meeting at Baena hastily made peace and undertook to recognise no regent who would not ratify it. The depletion of regents was quickly made good, and the new claimants were: John '*el tuerto*', the son of John of Tarifa; Juan Manuel: and Philip, another son of Sancho IV. The learned king had laid down in the *Partidas* that there should be 'one, or three, or five regents'; and cortes were summoned to decide the issue. As they were about to meet, the Dowager Queen, María de Molina, herself died, and the three claimants divided the country between them: John 'el tuerto' governed in Leon; Juan Manuel in Toledo and Extremadura, and Philip in Andalusia, divisions which corresponded to the three phases of Castilian growth.

Alfonso XI was declared of age at fourteen, and the cortes of 1325 sanctioned a reorganisation of his household, as a result of which power was held by the 'Andalusian' party of Philip, though he himself retired. The other regents left the court and conspired: John was killed in an ambush, while Juan Manuel was conciliated by the offer of a marriage between the King and his daughter. On finding himself deluded, he raised a rebellion and sought alliances in Portugal and Aragon, but finally surrendered at his castle of Peñafiel in 1337.

The struggles of the regents cover a complex period during which power was exercised temporarily by regional governors: the absolutist ambitions of the crown were suspended, and the nobility extended its powers wherever it could, challenged only by the traditionalist influence of cortes, now representing the northern municipalities, strongly banded in defence of their rights.

Alfonso XI was the last of the kings of the reconquest who established a personal ascendancy by virtue of his deeds against the Muslims: he was also the reviver of Alfonso X's absolutism, and now at last began to establish a royal law. He had been brought up in Valladolid, but in 1325 he passed under the influence of Prince Philip's 'Andalusian' party, and from 1327 he was firmly attached to Seville by his association with Leonor de Guzmán. Since the defeat of 1319 the struggle against Granada had been abandoned, and the Naṣrids had taken Baza and Martos (1324–5). But in 1327 Alfonso also began his military career, and he soon forced the Granadines to pay him a tribute of 15,000 *doblas*. Within a few years they tired of paying, and again turned to Morocco. In 1333 Castile lost Gibraltar, and Alfonso made peace. At this time the Genoese served the Moroccans with ships, and defeated the Castilian fleet in Algeciras. Thus encouraged, the Marinids prepared for a supreme effort, and assembling an army that recalled the great hosts of the Almoravids and Almohads, they laid siege to Tarifa. But Alfonso, aided by the Portuguese, defeated them in the battle of the Salado, fought not far from the scene of the 'ruin of Spain' six centuries before. After it, the Moroccans never again attempted a large invasion of the Peninsula, but contented themselves with reinforcing Granada. They still held their foothold north of the straits, but Alfonso captured Algeciras after a siege lasting nearly two years (June 1342–March 1344), and in 1350 he invested Gibraltar: he died of the Black Death before its walls, and it remained in Muslim hands for a further century.

During the long reign of Alfonso XI the monarchy recovered its lost authority, and steadily reduced its barons to order. The military Orders, which claimed to belong to the church and so to enjoy autonomy, were compelled to do homage, and an attempt was made to found a national Order. Meanwhile, the Castilian municipalities, which had joined with the nobility in defying Alfonso X's absolutist pretensions, had now experienced the abuses of an unchecked nobility long enough to seek the protection of the crown. The chief fear of the towns that formed the royal patrimony was that a weak monarch would bestow them on his favourites, and at their request Alfonso promised not to alienate the *tierras de realengo*. He also returned to the vexed question of a royal law. His father had attempted to clarify the Fuero Real by producing another partial compendium, the 'Leyes de Estilo'. Now, at the cortes of Villa Real (Ciudad Real) of 1346, Segovia (1347) and Alcalá (1348) new ordinances were adopted and the various systems of law were placed in order of precedence: first, the new laws of Alfonso XI, agreed by his jurisconsults and cortes; second, the 'fuero juzgo', the royal law which ran in Galicia and Andalusia; third, municipal statute-law; and fourth, the *Partidas*. Although the unpopular Partidas were thus subordinated to the rest, the Castilian towns remained dissatisfied, and gave only lukewarm support to the crown in the great struggle of the following reign.

On his death Alfonso XI left an heir by his Portuguese Queen, Pedro, then a youth of sixteen. Of his family by Leonor de Guzmán, the eldest was Henry, Count of Trastámara, who had a younger twin, Fadrique; they were about a year older than their half-brother, and Henry was to devote most of his life to a single-minded, unscrupulous and finally successful struggle to supplant him. The old school of royal regents had now died out; and Pedro fell under the influence of Juan Alfonso de Albuquerque, the son of a bastard of King Denis of Portugal, who had been given charge of his education in 1338. He was perhaps the first of the 'validos', favourites whose power derived from an ascendancy established during the king's youth. Albuquerque promptly placed his Jew, Samuel Levi, as Pedro's treasurer. Scarcely had the reign begun when the young king fell seriously ill, and parties at once formed round possible successors. Albuquerque favoured Pedro's cousin, but a rival group put forward a descendant of the La Cerdas, still regarded by strict legitimists as the true line. But Pedro recovered, and in 1351, perhaps at the instigation of his favourite, connived at the murder of Leonor de Guzmán.

This crime set her son off on his long quest for vengeance and power. His first rebellion was in the Asturias in 1352, and it was easily quelled. But while the King was in the north, Albuquerque introduced him to María de Padilla, whose family, led by her uncle, Juan Fernández de Hinestrosa, quickly established their own power and threatened to undo the favourite. Albuquerque now turned to France and betrothed the young king to Blanche of Bourbon; but two days after the wedding, celebrated in Valladolid in 1353, Pedro abandoned his new queen, and she was shut up in the alcázar at Toledo, while Albuquerque fled to Portugal.

The architect of the French alliance now joined Henry of Trastámara, and gathering a league of malcontents, launched a new rising, in which Henry and Fadrique, now Master of Santiago, were joined by the citizens of Toledo. For a time Pedro was little more than a prisoner at Toro, but the rebellion slowly subsided and he recovered Toledo. At this time his rival began to identify himself with the old nobility of the north who resented the rise of the new class of legists: Pedro on the contrary seems to have appointed members of this new caste of functionaries even to the great offices of his court, and against them the bastard Henry was to pose as the champion of Castilian traditionalism.

The great struggle was now to involve the whole of the Peninsula. The French, engaged in mortal conflict with England, coveted the naval forces of the Peninsular powers. As early as 1342-3 Duke Henry of Lancaster had arrived at the siege of Algeciras and proposed an Anglo-Spanish marriage, which was not concluded. Alfonso XI had thereafter avoided entanglements with either side, but Albuquerque had proved venal, and by arranging the marriage of Pedro and Blanche, enabled the French to enjoy a brief triumph. Frustrated in Castile, they came to terms with Aragon, and in 1356 a fleet of Catalan galleys was sent to attack England. As they sailed through the straits and passed Sanlúcar, where Pedro was watching the tunny-fishing, they had a brush with Castilian ships. Pedro at once protested in Aragon, where his rival Henry had been received. The complaint was rejected, and he launched an invasion of the neighbouring kingdom, driving Henry to take refuge in France, where for the following six years he bided his time.

In the meantime, both Blanche of Bourbon and María de Padilla died, and Pedro took an oath that he had been married to the latter and that his children by her were legitimate. Henry was thus deprived of any hope of legal succession, and negotiated in

France for the use of the Free Companies to invade Spain. In return, Pedro concluded an alliance with Edward III in June 1362, and forestalled his enemy by invading Aragon and reaching Valencia: in order to keep Aragonese support, Henry now offered to cede part of Castile.

But there were too many aggrieved nobles in Castile for Pedro to risk a long campaign, and in 1365 Henry struck back. The Free Companies under du Guesclin entered Catalonia and marched across Aragon: as they reached Castilian soil, Henry declared himself king and showered rewards on them. For the first time French titles of nobility were introduced into Spain, and Henry made du Guesclin Duke of Trastámara. Faced with foreign knights in plate-armour and unsure of his supporters, Pedro abandoned Burgos and fell back on Toledo, which he soon also quitted. Even in Seville he was not safe, for his Italian admiral seized his treasure and declared for his rival. He therefore withdrew to Portugal, where he was coolly received by his namesake and passed on to Galicia. Here he was among loyalists, and applying for the fulfilment of his English alliance, soon joined the Black Prince in Bordeaux.

Henry had attempted to reduce the whole of Castile, but Galicia was unyielding. As the Black Prince began to march through Navarre, Henry faced him at Nájera on April 3, 1367, and suffered a shattering defeat, after which he fled to Aragon, leaving du Guesclin and other notables prisoners in English hands. This success was followed by a bitter quarrel between the victors. Pedro had engaged to pay for the expedition, and the bill was quickly presented. It proved immensely more expensive than had been anticipated, and he had no money and could not afford to maintain an English garrison. While he wrote to the Castilian towns for aid, the Black Prince was proposing to the unreliable Pedro of Aragon, lately the ally of Henry, that they should partition Castile if Pedro could not pay his debts.

In the meanwhile Henry had obtained new help in France, and re-entered Castile in September 1367. He occupied Burgos, and compensated for the general lack of enthusiasm for his cause by taking savage reprisals. Most of the towns now favoured

Pedro, and in Asturias an hermandad was formed against the usurper.

From Burgos Henry marched on Toledo, but this time the old capital did not surrender, and he spent almost a year encamped before its walls. Much of Spain, especially Galicia and Andalusia, remained with Pedro, but much more was passive. The bastard now set himself up as the restorer of traditionalism. His propagandists maintained that he had been 'elected' to the throne in the old Visigothic manner, that he was the true heir of the La Cerdas, since whose time all the kings of Spain had been illegitimate, and that his rival was the tool and protector of Muslims and Jews, and had corrupted the faith: this time the French had not made the mistake of backing the innovating party.

Now Leon and Córdoba went over to Henry, and although Pedro sent his Granadine allies against the latter city, they could not take it. The decisive factor was the help of France, and France needed the Castilian galleys in Seville. Henry had already pledged himself to make war on England, and to send ships from northern Spain if he could not take Seville. Meanwhile, England, the former ally and present creditor, refused to renew her help for Pedro. By the end of 1368 Pedro was forced to succour Toledo or face defeat. He therefore marched into New Castile, and Henry abandoned the siege and went forth to meet him. At Montiel Pedro was taken by surprise; his scattered army was defeated, and he himself was taken prisoner. The half-brothers met in a tent on the field, and Henry settled the long conflict by stabbing Pedro with his own hand.

2. ARAGON, 1272–1412

The kingdom of Aragon was at this time by far the most complex of the Peninsular states. In Portugal the monarchy presided over a single, if not yet homogeneous, society. In Castile, the crown expressed an over-riding national unity, though it was also the guarantor of differing societies. But in Aragon the state itself was a political, not a social creation, formed by the association of two peoples of different language and traditions, and now enlarged by a third area, Valencia. While in the central kingdom Castile and Leon were represented in unified cortes[1], Aragon not only had General Cortes for the three realms, but also separate meetings for each of them. Far from attaining homogeneity, the county of Barcelona and the kingdoms of Aragon and Valencia each developed on different lines.

Although the kings of the house of Barcelona usually resided in Saragossa, the foreign and economic policy of the union was dominated by Catalonia. This was at once the most feudal and the most enterprising of the three areas. The group of Frankish counties which were associated to form the territory of Catalonia under the leadership of Barcelona acknowledged the feudal overlordship of the Barcelonese counts, but not their sovereignty. Thus a great variety of local jurisdictions was preserved, and their proprietors long continued to enjoy the right to use and abuse a downtrodden and servile peasantry. But in the city of Barcelona itself a rapid expansion of commerce and industry gave rise to a vigorous urban society, itself divided into three classes (the great merchants and liberal professions, traders and artisans[2]), and endowed with special institutions largely derived from those of the mercantile communities of Italy. As in other parts of Catalonia, the royal authority was represented by a 'veguer' or vicar, but from 1274 this official was assisted not only by a small council but by a consultative committee, the Concell de Cent, consisting of a hundred citizens chosen annually to represent the various classes and interests. The municipality minted its own currency and controlled the conduct of overseas trade through the appointment of the consuls who governed the Catalan merchant colonies abroad and by the application of the sea-law of Barcelona. By the process of *carreratge*, under which smaller places were incorporated as 'streets' of the city, the capital threw its mantle over almost all the ports of the east coast as far south as Alicante.

---

[1] Those of Leon met separately four times in the last quarter of the thirteenth century, but not at all after 1300.

[2] These were known as 'hands', greater, middle and lesser. The three estates of the cortes were 'arms'.

Old Aragon was a land-locked kingdom. It consisted of two principal zones. The rural north, like that of Catalonia, had been formed by the fusion of several counties, each subdivided into Pyrenean compartments in which local jurisdictions were firmly entrenched. Because of the long Castilian protectorate over Saragossa, the expansion of Aragon had been delayed until the last years of the eleventh century: consequently it knew little of the long period of rural resettlement out of which the municipalities of Portugal and Castile, with their elaborate local fueros, had developed. Rural Aragon was dominated by its nobility, which acquired formal hereditary rights to its lands in 1196, and it was this class that fought most bitterly for the 'privileges of Aragon', now menaced by the desire of the crown for absolute powers. Old Aragon had had its capital at Jaca, which had received a charter in 1064, but the towns of Saragossa and southern Aragon had been reconquered only in the first half of the following century, when they were resettled and granted fueros in the same way as Toledo. Their laws were thus of royal and relatively recent origin, and they received justice from a variety of officials some of whom, such as the *zalmedina* of Saragossa, owed their existence to the convergence of the northern governors with Muslim qaḍis. In contrast to the north the towns of southern Aragon were *mudéjar*, bourgeois and royalist. The kingdom as a whole was much poorer than the county of Catalonia.

Valencia, the new conquest, was a taifa kingdom colonised by both Aragonese and Catalans. Northern nobles took possession of its estates and of the fertile huertas of its river-valleys, where they continued to exploit the industry and skill of the Muslim farmers, forming a colonial oligarchy less independent of the crown than the old north. The commerce and industry of the cities passed gradually into Catalan hands.

Before and during this conquest James I had attempted to create a new and less powerful class of nobility of *caballeros* attached to his house; but this was opposed by the old nobility, and at the cortes of Egea in 1265, he promised not to elevate those who were not already of noble birth. He also undertook to entrust a member of his council with the task of applying the ancient privileges of Aragon. This official, the *justicia*, stood at the centre of the struggle between traditional and royal law, and for a long period represented the baronial prick within the king's conscience.

James I long survived his fellow-conqueror, Ferdinand III. After the occupation of Valencia, he turned to French affairs, vainly looking for an opportunity to avenge the defeat of Muret. Many southern French had taken refuge at his court, and he hoped to contain the northern French by forming a system of alliances from Toulouse to Provence. But the Pope refused to abet his dynastic plans, and James could do no more than attempt to preserve his town of Montpellier. St. Louis retorted by demanding the 'return' of the ancient Frankish march of Barcelona; and by the treaty of Corbeil in 1249 both sides renounced their pretensions: under it the border counties of Roussillon and Cerdagne remained with Catalonia.

But James' rivalry with France was to lead him to embark on a foreign policy even more far-reaching than Alfonso's quest for the imperial crown. He married his heir Pedro to the daughter of King Manfred, who in 1250 had received Naples and Sicily from his father the Emperor Frederick II Stauffen. The papacy, which claimed the patronage of the kingdom of Naples, awarded it to Charles of Anjou, a brother of St Louis, who 'crusaded' against the imperialists, and having killed Manfred at Benevento in 1266, imposed French rule in southern Italy, and planned with the aid of Rome to attack the Emperor of Byzantium.

When James I died in 1276, leaving Aragon to his eldest son Pedro III (1276-85) and his new conquests of Majorca and the Pyrenean counties to his second son James, the former repudiated the Aragonese vassalage to the Holy See at his coronation and welcomed the Ghibelline refugees from Sicily at his court. For a moment the line of French popes who had supported Charles of Anjou was broken, and Gregory X attempted to reconcile the jealous princes of the west and pave the way for a new crusade. But on his death Charles arranged for the election of another complaisant Frenchman, with whom he again planned the conquest of the eastern empire.

Meanwhile, the Sicilian refugees had warned the Byzantine

Emperor of Charles' intentions and had arranged a tentative alliance between him and the Aragonese. In 1280 Pedro III prepared with their aid to establish a protectorate over the Muslim kingdom of Tunisia, which had been reserved for Aragon in treaties with Castile; but when in March 1282, the Sicilians rebelled against French rule in the famous 'Vespers', and offered their crown to him, Pedro at once diverted his attention from Africa, landed at Trapani and forced the French to abandon the island. The French Pope excommunicated him, and Charles challenged him to single combat. But this solution was forbidden by the Pope, and when Pedro repaired to the trysting-place at Bordeaux, his rival did not appear. Instead the Pope declared a crusade against Aragon and 'deposed' its king, offering his crown to a son of Philip III of France.

To a nation accustomed to receiving the indulgence of Rome for its exertions against Islam, the ban was disturbing. The Aragonese nobles disowned the Sicilian adventure, and at the cortes of Saragossa in 1283 Pedro granted the General Privilege by which he renounced absolutism and confirmed the independence of the justicia. When at last the French did invade Aragon, Pedro was able to resist; and despite the defection of his brother James of Majorca and Roussillon, his admiral Roger de Lauria defeated the French fleet, and his son recovered Majorca.

Pedro died in 1285, leaving Aragon to his eldest son, Alfonso III, and Sicily to a younger son, James II. Although his father had sought a deathbed reconciliation with Rome and promised to relinquish Sicily, Alfonso had no intention of complying. When he returned from Majorca to meet cortes at Saragossa in 1286, his nobles demanded that he should receive their nominees as irremovable members of his council and even claimed the right to depose him, recently exercised against Alfonso X in Castile. They formed a Union, and when it broke into rebellion and threatened to secede to France or Castile he was obliged to grant the 'Privileges of the Union', by which he undertook to summon cortes annually and to receive their nominees as his advisers.

Meanwhile, James of Sicily, supported by the sea-power of Catalonia, continued to defy the Pope. Long negotiations between

Edward I of England, the French, the King of Aragon and the Holy See bore little fruit, and in 1286 the war was renewed. James besieged Brindisi, while Lauria destroyed the French fleet; and the French claimant, Charles the Lame, was captured and delivered to Alfonso. A new Pope, Nicholas IV, still insisted that James should abandon Sicily, and when Alfonso was induced to release Charles, at once crowned him King of Naples. Once more the struggle was renewed, and at last Alfonso was persuaded to come to terms. By the treaty of Tarascon of 1291 he abandoned his brother and was reconciled with Rome, promising to recall all his subjects from Sicily.

This peace compromised the supremacy of Catalan sea-power, and when five months later Alfonso suddenly died in Barcelona the Catalans immediately sent a mission to offer the crown to James of Sicily. He accepted not as his brother's heir, but as the eldest surviving son of Pedro III, and thus avoided acknowledging the privileges recently wrung from his brother. Once more the French and the anti-imperialists demanded that the Pope should declare a crusade against Aragon and prohibit the Aragonese clergy from recognising the new king. But the election of a new Pope, Boniface VIII, and the need of the French for shipping finally brought a settlement. By the treaty of Agnani, James II gave up his claim to Sicily, and received in exchange the right to conquer Sardinia and Corsica. He soon after married a French princess and undertook to send forty Catalan galleys to fight the English.

This arrangement left James' younger brother Fadrique, who was governing Sicily, and the Sicilians themselves, unappeased. Boniface offered Fadrique a marriage through which he would acquire the French claim to Byzantium, but he preferred a small reality to a large illusion, and in 1296 the Sicilians elected him their King. James II now went to Rome and received the title to Sardinia and Corsica in exchange for Sicily. He thus assumed the obligation to remove his brother, but his attempt to invade the island in 1298 was a failure, and it was only in 1302 by the peace of Caltabellotta that the French admitted Fadrique's claim and agreed that he should marry a Neapolitan Angevin, thus reuniting the two areas.

The peace led directly to the most remarkable expansion of the Aragonese. The Catalan *almogáveres* now disengaged were contracted by a German freebooter, Rutger von Blum, or Roger de Flor, for service with the Byzantine emperor, who was disturbed by the attacks of the Turks on the Greek cities of Asia Minor. Some 6,500 members of the Catalan Grand Company arrived in Constantinople in 1303. Rutger had driven a hard bargain, including marriage with the emperor's niece, and after several small victories he was named Caesar. But he and his men soon outstayed their welcome, and in 1305 he and many of his followers were massacred. The survivors remained encamped at Gallipoli until June 1307, attracting many new recruits, among them several thousand Turks. In 1309 they moved from Macedonia into Thessaly, and from Thessaly into central Greece, where they were engaged by the Burgundian ruler of Athens, but when he dismissed them, they turned upon Franks and Greeks and cut them to pieces in the battle of the Cephissos, near Thebes. They then seized the towns and castles of the Duchy of Athens, sharing out the wives and property of their victims. For two generations, supported by the Catalans in Sicily, they continued to dominate this part of Greece, playing their part in the Latinisation of Athens, where by 1370 about a third of the population was of Catalan origin.

Meanwhile, James II of Aragon had made good his claims to Sardinia and Corsica. These islands had been won from the Almohads by Pisa and Genoa in 1150, and had long been a bone of contention between the two republics. In 1309 the Pisans ransomed Sardinia, but thirteen years later James rejected a similar offer and annexed the island. The Sardinians, who included large colonies of Genoese, soon grew dissatisfied with Aragonese rule. Under James' successor Alfonso IV (1327–36) there was open war between Catalans and Genoese, and after a short peace Alfonso's son Pedro IV (1336–1387) made an alliance with the strongest rival of Genoa, the republic of Venice. In 1352 a combined Catalan and Venetian fleet pursued the Genoese as far as Constantinople. After this, much of Sardinia renounced Aragonese rule, and although Pedro took Alghero in 1354, a strong local party refused to acknowledge him and came to terms only thirty years later. Pedro also reannexed Majorca and Roussillon, which had been constituted into a separate kingdom since the days of James I and were now finally incorporated into the kingdom of Aragon.

Pedro IV, known as *el Ceremoniós,* or 'the punctilious', set himself the task of recovering for the crown the royal prerogatives usurped by the Union. The issue was joined over the question of the succession; in 1347 Pedro's only child was a daughter, whose succession he was determined to ensure despite the law of James I in favour of the male line. The baronial party gave its support to his brother James, who in return encouraged them to restore the Union, while the nobles of Valencia put forth a demand that they should have a *justicia* of their own. Pedro could count on the support of Catalonia, but Aragon and Valencia were banded together against him and sought at the cortes of Saragossa of 1347 to force him to renew the Privilege of the Union. This he refused to do, and cortes threatened to elect another king. Since they had his brother at hand, he gave way, granting the Union's demands and retiring to Catalonia. His brother was soon after poisoned, and in Valencia, which was divided between royalists and Unionists, there was civil war. As the Aragonese threatened to intervene, Pedro again gave way, confirming the Union of Valencia, acknowledging its right to associate with that of Aragon, and conceding the demand for a justicia. He himself was held in Valencia, and was unable to escape until in May 1348 the Black Death spread confusion there. He now collected a strong army in Catalonia and marched against the Aragonese Unionists, who were defeated at Epila. In his reprisals many of the defenders of traditionalism were put to death, and the Union and its Privilege were abolished. New cortes were summoned at Saragossa to ratify the change; and Pedro assured himself of the subservience of the justicia by demanding his written resignation which he always held. In course of time the office lost its contentious nature and became a hereditary conservatorship of the laws of Aragon.

Having thus assured the Aragonese monarchy of powers it had

scarcely enjoyed since the accession of the Catalan house, Pedro devoted himself to questions of foreign policy. His constant intrigues brought him close to defeat at the hands of Pedro of Castile, involved him in a long dispute with Henry II, and almost lost him the Roussillon. In 1374 he made a weak peace with Castile at Almazán.

Three years later, on the death of Fadrique III of Sicily, Pedro at once revived the Aragonese claim to the island and having occupied it, placed his younger son Martin as governor of it in his name.

His successor was his elder son, John I (1387-95), whose inclinations were towards literature, astrology, luxury and courtly pursuits. If he introduced the Provençal *jocs florals* into Barcelona, he also allowed the affairs of Sicily and Sardinia to lapse into disorder. In 1391 Sardinian patriots almost drove the Aragonese out of their island, while in Sicily Martin was faced by a general uprising of the islanders: this was suppressed in 1394. John I died while hunting and as his son had predeceased him, cortes offered the crown of Aragon to Martin of Sicily, who accepted it, leaving his son, Martin the younger, as governor of the island. The choice was challenged by John's son-in-law, the Count of Foix, who was forced to take refuge beyond the Pyrenees.

Meanwhile, the Great Schism touched Aragon closely, for in 1394 Pedro de Luna, Cardinal of Aragon, was elected Pope and set himself up in Avignon, where with true Aragonese obstinacy he resisted all suggestions that he should follow the example of his rivals and abdicate. When most of the French cardinals withdrew their allegiance and he was threatened with eviction from Avignon, he appealed to Martin, who prevailed upon the French to desist. Benedict still stood firm and his clergy, tiring of dependence on the French kings, returned to his side. Avignon was garrisoned with Aragonese men-at-arms, and for a time the French again recognised Benedict. Even after the Council of Pisa had deposed him in 1409, he persisted in his refusal to resign and withdrew to the stronghold of Peñíscola on the luminous Valencian coast, and was still composing arguments in his own favour when the Council of Constance declared him a schismatic in 1417.

Meanwhile, the Angevins of Naples had stirred up new troubles in Sicily, and King Martin had been obliged to send reinforcements to his son. In the midst of the struggle the latter died in 1409, and his father survived him by less than a year. With his death the line of the counts of Barcelona, which had ruled Aragon for two and a half centuries, came to an end.

3. NAVARRE AND THE BASQUE PROVINCES

The kingdom of Navarre which had briefly dominated northern Spain disappeared as an independent state only forty years after the death of Sancho III, when in 1076 his grandson Sancho IV was hurled from a rock at Peñalén, and the Navarrese, fearing the ambitions of Castile, accepted the rule of Sancho Ramírez, the second king of Aragon. It was restored sixty years later when they rejected the testament of Alfonso the Battler and set up a descendant of Sancho 'of Peñalén', García Ramírez.

In the early reconquest both Leon and Navarre had drawn upon the resources of the three Basque provinces: Alava in particular had contributed to make the frontier area of Castile. But by the time of Sancho the Great all three provinces were associated with Navarre, and during the following two centuries, they fluctuated between the rulers of Pamplona and Burgos. This fluctuation corresponds to the practice of *behetría*, current in Castile, by which the holders of certain fueros were entitled to choose their own overlord. Thus Alava returned to Castile in 1200. Its counts and ecclesiastics formed a governing oligarchy, the 'Cofradía of Arriaga'. In 1332 this body merged itself permanently with Castile, granting high justice and certain tributes to the crown, which in turn accepted the right of local juntas to decide whether or not its orders were in accordance with the ancient fueros (*pase foral*). Guipúzcoa likewise claimed the right to choose its overlord and was finally also vested in the crown of Castile, which appointed an 'adelantado', again with powers limited by the '*pase foral*'. In the westernmost of the Basque Provinces, Biscay, overlordship passed from Navarre to the counts of Haro, whose rights were finally inherited by Henry III of Castile.

The three provinces remained distinct and always refused to coalesce. Each protected its internal autonomy by general juntas composed of representatives of towns and rural districts, who scrutinised all new legislation in the light of their existing rights. In general the towns had royal fueros, while the rural areas continued to conduct their affairs by juntas of elders according to ancient tradition: the customs of rural Biscay were committed to writing only in 1452.

Meanwhile, Navarre passed on the death of Sancho the Strong in 1234 to his nephew Theobald of Champagne, and in 1285, when its heiress was an infant, her mother, alarmed by the rivalries of parties favouring Castile and Aragon, betrothed her to the dauphin, the future Philip III: Navarre remained as a seneschalship of the French crown until 1328. On the death of Charles IV the Bold, the Navarrese refused to accept the Salic succession and broke away from the French crown, acknowledging as their queen Charles' niece, Joan II, whose consort, Philip of Evreux, died in the great siege of Algeciras in 1343.

Charles II, the Bad, possessed territories in Normandy and aspired to succeed to the French throne, but his intrigues with the English and with Pedro and Henry of Castile finally cost him his northern possessions: his successor Charles III the Noble (1387–1425) restored peace and built the new palaces of Olite and Tafalla.

Medieval Navarre consisted of five 'merindades', (the equivalent of the Castilian 'partidos'), one, St. Jean Pied-de-Port or Ultrapuertos, north of the Pyrenees, and the rest in Spain. Its three cities and twenty-four *villas* were inhabited mainly by free Basques, who also assimilated colonies of Gascons, northern French, Jews and mudéjares. The latter were numerous at Tudela on the Ebro, and enjoyed full civil liberties, including the attainment of nobility and the right to hold office, in return for the payment of heavy taxes.

Although the total population of Navarre probably did not

exceed a hundred thousand, it acquired a full range of Castilian institutions (cortes, alcaldes, merinos) as well as some French introductions. These foreign absorptions are not uncharacteristic of Basque society: the survival of an older order seems to be represented by the general pretension to nobility and a parallel refusal to take it seriously, the survival of family authority, a dislike of the Roman form of marriage, and an intense sense of obligation between neighbours. Against this ancient background, the court and its circle presents a picture of agreeable unreality.

Charles III's heiress Blanche was married to the ambitious Aragonese Trastámara, John, whose dispute with his heir, the ill-fated Prince of Viana, forms part of the history of Aragon.

4. NAṢRID GRANADA

The new state established in upper Andalusia by Muhammad ibn al-Aḥmar (1238–72) was the last of the taifas, created by a Spanish Muslim under Christian protection, and settled by colonies of Muslim refugees from other parts of Spain. Its founder collaborated closely with his Castilian master, and his troops adopted Christian dress and arms, but with the death of Ferdinand and the rise of Marinid power in Morocco, the opportunity occurred to pursue a more equivocal policy; and while Alfonso X intrigued with dissident members of the Naṣrid clan, Muhammad II (1272–1302) sought the aid of the Marinids and of Aragon. Thereafter the sultans of Granada constantly adjusted themselves to the ebb and flow of power in Castile and the Magrib. The very precariousness of Granadine life brought a concentration of Muslim orthodoxy and an intensification of political life: sultans appointed vizirs of opposing policies, and when they compromised themselves too deeply with either Moroccans or Castilians they were often removed by sudden revolutions. Changes of sultans were not infrequent, though Granada remained always faithful to the Naṣrid dynasty.

Muhammad II had received Marinid garrisons, and from his time Berber volunteers (*guzat*) regularly occupied its western frontier. When his successor Muhammad III seized a bridgehead in Africa, his Castilian overlord deprived him of Tarifa and he was overthrown: his successor Naṣr came to terms with the Marinids and then submitted to Ferdinand IV, whom he assisted in an attack on Algeciras. After this Naṣr himself was supplanted by a relative more in sympathy with the Marinids, Abu'l-Walid Isma'il I (1314-25).

Not content with holding a bridgehead in Europe, the Moroccans now pervaded the Granadine state, in which members of the Marinid family who commanded the Berber garrisons began to play a political role. When in 1319 they killed both regents of Castile in the battle of the vega and forced the Christian towns of the frontier to sue for peace, there was an intensification of patriotic spirit and of Moroccan influence. Under Muhammad IV (1325-33), the commander of the *guzat* usurped the functions of the vizirate and treated Granada as occupied territory. The Granadines ejected him, and resumed the payment of tribute to Castile. But Muhammad soon repaired to Morocco and negotiated for a fresh Muslim force which seized Gibraltar: Alfonso XI arrived too late to save the town, but negotiated with his evasive vassal before the walls: hardly had the two kings parted when Muhammad was murdered by the Berbers.

His brother Yusuf I (1333-54) made new terms with Castile and the Berber contingents were restricted in number: no new troops were now to cross from Africa except as replacements. But Marinid fervour for the Holy War was unabated, and in 1340 the sultan of Morocco prepared the great invasion which was to end in the defeat of the Salado. Yusuf emerged from the rout with honour, and devoted himself to the restoration of his state: a university was founded in the capital; the country districts were re-islamised; the crown was enriched by the growth of industries and the expansion of foreign trade; and the Alhambra, to which Isma'il I had added the Generalife, was further embellished and extended. Yusuf's vizirs included Abu'l-Nu'ayr Ridwan, of Christian descent, and ibn al-Khatib, the last great writer of Muslim Spain.

When Yusuf was murdered by a madman, his son Muhammad

V (1354-59: 1362-91) continued his father's policy, preserving the balance between his overlord and his allies. But in 1359 he was expelled by a revolt instigated by an ambitious cousin, Muhammad VI, known as the 'Red King', and fled first to the Magrib where his plans were frustrated by the death of the Sultan, and then to Pedro I of Castile. With Pedro's aid Muhammad V set himself up at Ronda. But it was dangerous to be imposed in Granada by Christian arms; and only when the Castilian forces withdrew did the towns declare for him. The Red King fled to Pedro, taking with him the royal jewels,[1] only to be executed as a traitor. During the Castilian civil war, Muhammad V raided lower Andalusia and sacked Jaén, ostensibly on behalf of Pedro: he also added Algeciras to his possessions before making terms with Henry II.

At the end of the century the tranquillity of Granada was disturbed by a revival of Moroccan influence. Muhammad VII (1392-1408) sought the friendship of both Castile and Fez, but the war between the two faiths continued in the form of frontier engagements. When finally the regent of Castile, Ferdinand, captured the town of Antequera, a wedge was driven into the territory of Granada, and its survival became doubly precarious. Little is known of the internal history of Granada in its final phase, but the reign of Yusuf III (1408-17) appears to have been its last period of tranquillity. In Morocco the later Marinids became mere pawns in the hands of rival viziers, and the troubled reign of Muhammad VIII (1417-45), who thrice occupied the throne and was thrice dethroned, probably reflects parallel dissensions in Granada.

For all the apparent instability of its political life, Granadine society showed remarkable vitality. Many of its inhabitants were descendants of aristocratic houses of Muslim Spain, who, though reduced to artisanship, preserved their old pride. The concentration of population left little room for large estates, and round the capital the fertile gardens of the villas (cármenes, al-qarm, 'a vineyard') were intensively cultivated. In the crowded city itself

---

[1] His great ruby was presented by Pedro to the Black Prince and still forms part of the English crown jewels.

the sultan and his vizirs dispensing justice from the Sublime Door of the great fortress-palace of the Alhambra, presided over a mercantile, administrative and intellectual bourgeoisie which bravely sustained a doomed culture, a microcosm of occidental Islam.

VI

MEDIAEVAL SPAIN—PART TWO

1. CASTILE: THE TRASTÁMARAS, 1368–1474

A CENTURY had now passed since the reunited forces of Leon and Castile had surged forward to the Pillars of Hercules. The Marinids still held their bridgehead in Europe, and the crusading spirit of the Christians had begun to fail: although in 1340 the Portuguese had joined in the defensive campaign of the Salado, the Aragonese, immersed in other schemes, did not appear, and with the death of Alfonso XI even Castile abandoned the traditional struggle for half a century.

The new bastard house reverted on the contrary to that older imperialism that sought to restore the Gothic imperium over all Spain. It was now recognised that war between Christian princes could not be followed by conquest, and the only legitimate means of annexing a kingdom was by dynastic acquisition on the failure of a royal line: it was however possible to use war in order to bring about a favourable marriage, and Henry II and his son were now to attempt to annex Portugal in this way. The attachment might seem a natural one: both kingdoms were unitarian states whose main interests were still in the Peninsula. But when the crisis occurred, the social unity of the Portuguese proved an unsurmountable obstacle and the Castilian campaign was an ignominious failure. A generation later, when the house of Barcelona also failed, a Castilian Trastámara was appointed to occupy the vacant throne: it was this junior branch of the house that finally achieved the union of Aragon with Castile when its heir, Ferdinand II (V of Castile) married the Castilian heiress Isabella in 1469.

The regicide at Montiel did not at once assure the victory of the Trastámaras. Galicia was still staunchly legitimist, and when a group of Petrists offered their allegiance to the young King of Portugal, both it and the frontier towns of Zamora and Ciudad Rodrigo readily acknowledged him. Other towns on the eastern frontier accepted Aragonese rule. Meanwhile, Henry II had marched to Seville, but on learning that the Portuguese were in Galicia he hastened to invade northern Portugal, only to be in turn diverted by the raids of Muhammad V in Andalusia. Many of the Castilian towns sent no representatives to his first cortes at Toro in 1369, where as a result of his rewards a group of Frenchmen sat on the nobles' benches, rejoicing in their new titles. Such towns as did appear complained of the depredations of the barons, the collapse of royal justice and the debasement of the coin.

But in 1371 Henry's affairs began to improve. Zamora and Carmona (where Pedro's closest adherents had taken refuge) gave in, and even Galicia was the scene of disorders, when the dignitaries of the cathedral of Santiago displayed Trastámaran inclinations and the loyalist populace locked them in the cathedral for nine days. In March peace was imposed on Ferdinand of Portugal, who renounced his pretensions in Castile and consented to marry Henry's daughter. The Petrist claim now passed to the dead king's legitimised daughters by María de Padilla, whom he had left in Gascony. The elder of these married John of Lancaster, and for sixteen years the old cause was upheld in the palace of the Savoy and in successive campaigns in Portugal and Galicia.

In 1372-3 John of Gaunt concluded an alliance with Portugal and sent a small English force to the Peninsula. It was insufficient to face Henry II's armies, and in March 1373 Ferdinand was forced to accept the treaty of Santarem, by which he undertook to join the French side and treat the English as enemies. This treaty remained in force, at least in theory, until 1379, but the Portuguese used the respite to strengthen the defences of Lisbon, and when Henry II died both Ferdinand and John of Gaunt prepared to try their fortunes with his successor.

The founder of the new house, compelled by his alliance with the old nobility and his inability to restore internal prosperity to embark on an aggressive foreign policy, had forced favourable treaties on Portugal, Aragon and Navarre, while in 1377–79 the Sevillian galleys commanded by Sancho de Tovar ravaged the English coast from Cornwall to the Thames, burning Winchelsea and Gravesend. But Henry's adventures and his munificence towards his supporters resulted in constant inflation and the impoverishment of the towns, which, in spite of his attempts to appease them, were now united as never before.

Henry's son, John I (1379–90), found himself unable to depart from his father's policies. He did not dare to dispossess the beneficiaries of the civil war: although he called in their privileges for inspection, he ended by confirming them all. At the same time he resumed and sought to consummate his father's Portuguese policy.

King Ferdinand of Portugal was now dominated by an ambitious wife, whose first object was to ensure the succession of her small daughter Beatriz and her own regency. This child had been betrothed to a bastard of Henry II; but in the first year of his reign, John put forward a new bridegroom, his own heir, thus bringing the union of the two crowns much nearer. But having submitted to this change, Ferdinand again turned to the English alliance, and preparations were made in London to send a new force to the Peninsula. In 1381 the Castilian navy defeated the Portuguese at the mouth of the Guadiana, but a few months later the Earl of Cambridge arrived in Lisbon at the head of an English expeditionary force. Its conduct was far from exemplary, and when the allies advanced towards the frontier to meet a Castilian invasion early in 1383, Ferdinand, who was now seriously ill, was induced by his queen to come to terms. The wife of John I had recently died, and by the Treaty of Salvaterra it was arranged that the Portuguese heiress should be betrothed to the ruler of Castile. On her accession John would become consort in Portugal, but an heir of the match would inherit both kingdoms: if there were none, Portugal would go to John's successor. Meanwhile, the Castilians supplied ships to speed the departure of the English troops. Six months later, the King of Portugal died (October 1383).

Although John was recommended to proceed cautiously, since the Portuguese people were opposed to Castilian domination, he at once had himself and Beatriz proclaimed and sent orders to the governors of the Portuguese towns. The Portuguese nobility were well disposed towards a house which had so generously rewarded the Castilian aristocracy for its support, but the Portuguese legalists and towns had profited from the lessons of the Spanish civil war. A bastard half-brother of Ferdinand, the Master of Avis, was raised up as Defender of the Realm and finally elected King by the cortes of Coimbra in March 1385. His cause was plausibly argued by the jurist João das Regras, who had returned to Portugal from Bologna three years before and was able to produce documents of questionable authenticity in support of his candidate. The Portuguese people at once rallied to their new ruler, and when John of Castile invaded their country, he was defeated in the battle of Aljubarrota (August 1385) in which the flower of Castilian chivalry perished. The new order in Portugal was saved, and John of Gaunt promptly entered into a new Portuguese alliance in the hope of at last gaining his long-sought Castilian crown. In July 1386 he landed at Corunna and marched through Galicia: his daughter, Philippa of Lancaster, was married to the King of Portugal at Oporto in the following February, and the two allies prepared to invade Castile. But their campaign was a failure: although John of Castile lacked fame, men and money after his great defeat, his subjects felt no enthusiasm for the Lancastrian intruder. In September the rivals came to terms: Catherine of Lancaster, the grand-daughter of Pedro, would marry the heir to Castile, the grandson of Henry II, and in addition, John of Gaunt received a large indemnity in silver and gold, paid to him in Bayonne: thus the great feud was closed.

For Castile, Aljubarrota meant the end of her imperialist ambitions and the disgrace of the old aristocracy. John himself was profoundly shaken by his defeat, and at the cortes of Valladolid

(1385) he confessed his deficiencies as the representative of God and the guardian of peace, order and justice in Castile. He regretted having conducted affairs 'out of our own head and without taking advice', and said that he had wished to redress wrongs, but had found it a 'very hard thing to win men from the things they are accustomed to, even if such things be evil'. These speeches, and his elaborate penances, were probably the result of Franciscan preaching. With the eclipse of the old nobility, the king and his state were ruled by the church, which readily explained how he had offended God, the jurists, who now found the traditionalist resistance to Romanism greatly reduced, and the municipalities, on whose subsidies John depended in order to pay the Lancastrian indemnity.

The four cortes of Segovia (1386), Briviesca (1387), Palencia (1388) and Guadalajara (1390) illustrate the great development of 'national' government and especially the rise of the municipalities as a result of the loss of prestige of the crown and the eclipse of the old nobility. A royal council of twelve members, four from each estate, was set up, and the monarch's prerogatives were limited to the appointment of governors and judges, presentations to sees and abbeys, the donation of lands, and the royal pardon. At Briviesca four 'doctores legistas' were added to the council; and when John died in 1390, leaving a boy of eleven as his heir, the council of regency was formed not by members of the royal family or the great officers of the state, but by a small 'cortes' consisting of three nobles, four ecclesiastics and eight procurators of the towns.

Nevertheless, as the crisis receded, it became clear that the gains made by the towns were in the field of economic policy, not in that of legislative power, which was now increasingly exercised by the Romanist lawyers. The royal treasury had gained a deplorable reputation for debasement and dishonesty. In 1386 it had issued a new base currency, the 'blancos', which it used for disbursements, though it would only accept old coin at its face value for payments: in practice no one received the new coin at its official value, and a complicated system or rates of exchange was practised. When two years later the procurators voted a new subsidy to meet the 'Duke of Lancaster's payments', they insisted that the bullion should not enter the treasury but should be sent direct to Bayonne.

It was against this background that a balance was struck between the crown and its tax-payers. Cortes did assign revenues for a royal army to consist of four thousand Castilian 'lances' and fifteen hundred Andalusian light cavalry, but they refused to grant any extraordinary revenues to the crown. Thus the pattern was established for a periodical debate between the ruler and his towns on the question of redress and supply.

Meanwhile, the legists of the Roman tradition were now firmly entrenched as the interpreters of Spanish law. The reception of Roman law was facilitated by the founding of a college for Spanish students at Bologna in 1364, and by the reform of the statutes of the university of Salamanca undertaken by don Pedro de Luna, the future Pope Benedict 'XIII'. As a result of Alfonso XI's arrangement of the four codes in order of precedence, many cases were referred to the crown, and Henry II had set up a special court, the *chancellería*, consisting of four jurists and three bishops, to hear appeals. This was to form the basis for the growth of a royal administration and the future bureaucratic state.

While the church lent its learning to the state, the crown attempted to collaborate in a revival of religious observance. At the cortes of Briviesca it was agreed that when a member of the royal family arrived in a town the cross should not be brought out to him, but he should repair to the church: other recommendations were that travellers should not be allowed to lodge in churches and that no one should work or trade on Sundays. At the same time Pedro de Luna attempted at the Council of Palencia to tighten ecclesiastical discipline.

A less agreeable consequence of the reception of Romanism was the revival of the ancient theme of a single state and an exclusive spiritual authority. The Lateran Councils, reverting to the laws of Justinian, had aimed especially at the suppression of Judaism, Pedro de Luna had convoked Jewish theologians to a dispute at Tortosa, as a result of which they were declared to have been vanquished, and a long campaign of preaching and persecution brought about the gradual decline of the great jewries of eastern Spain. In Castile cortes called for the segregation of both Muslims and Jews in 1387; and four years later the impassioned preaching of the archdeacon of Ecija caused a fearful massacre in Seville, which was soon imitated in other cities of the south and east. This was the beginning of the final breakdown of the old tri-communal system inherited from Islam, and in the course of the following century there followed many conversions, especially in Castile and other parts of northern Spain. As *conversos* or 'New Christians', Jewish administrators continued to exercise influence at court and in the church, and even to intensify the pressure against the communities from which they had sprung.

The reign of Henry III, known as the Ailing, seemed about to bring Castile into conformity with the Roman pattern of the Christian state, in which the crown, the divinely inspired source of Roman justice, aided by jurists trained in a uniform school, regulated a nation divided into three orders, whose hierarchies assembled to deliberate for the general good in cortes. The young king, despite his ill-health, had a lively spirit: when one day he found his brother Ferdinand, the future king of Aragon, occupying the royal stool he flung it through the window with the traditional display of ire. By his marriage to Catherine of Lancaster the dynastic feud was closed. At the beginning of his reign he was defied by a new baronial leader, the Count of Noreña, a bastard of Henry II, who was attacked and defeated in his Asturian fastness; and although other magnates continued to abuse the rights of towns and impede the execution of royal justice, their trespasses were reduced by the appointment of 'corregidores', officials whose first mission was to defend the municipalities against force and corruption, but who also served to secure the supremacy of the crown.

Meanwhile, a truce with Portugal had been concluded in 1393, and was extended by successive treaties, though a permanent settlement was not reached until 1431. In Granada this was also a moment of revival, and when in 1394 the Master of Alcántara had led forth a crusade in a mood of exaltation he was ignominiously defeated. There followed a pause in the frontier war till

1406, when the Granadines attacked Murcia: four years later, Henry's younger brother, Ferdinand, won renown by reducing Antequera after a famous siege. Already in 1400 Castile had attempted a descent on Africa, when her fleet attacked Tetuán, while the adventurous Don Pero Niño harassed Muslim shipping in the Mediterranean. Meanwhile, the prospect of concluding an alliance with enemies of Islam in Asia or Africa, which had been canvassed since the time of the crusades, was revived by news of the feats of Tamerlane. Two Castilian envoys witnessed his victory at Angora and were also present at his death soon afterwards. To the west, the Genoese had a generation earlier made expeditions into the Atlantic which had resulted in the rediscovery of the Canaries; and in 1404 two French adventurers, Jean de Bethencourt and Gadifer de la Salle, were licensed to occupy them in the name of Castile.

But on the death of Henry III Castile once more fell into civil strife, and the last two rulers of the house of Trastámara brought the dynasty to a miserable end. John II (1406–54) acceded as a child, and for a time his uncle Ferdinand saw to it that the regency was not disturbed, but in 1410, after his victory at Antequera, he was awarded the crown of Aragon, and so removed from the Castilian scene.

Thereafter Castile was governed by the stout Lancastrian Queen-mother until her death in 1418. She in 1412 promulgated the Ordenamientos of Valladolid by which Jewish communities were deprived of their financial and juridical autonomy, and those who had fled from the jewries after the great persecution were forced to return and to wear a badge. These laws were very irregularly applied, and twenty years later many Jewish communities still administered their own affairs. Nevertheless, the old security was gone: in central Spain Jews either accepted conversion or abandoned the dangerous cities and sought refuge in smaller towns and villages: only Andalusia kept its large urban communities.

With the majority of John II the reforming impulse weakened, and the crown passed under the influence of a powerful favourite. On the death of the Queen-mother, the revival of the old council of regency had led at once to rivalries, and in 1419 the King was declared of age. The example for royal favourites had been given by Albuquerque, and it was now applied by Alvaro de Luna, a bastard of the great Aragonese house who had entered the service of John II in 1409, when he was eighteen and his master ten years younger. The child conceived such an attachment for him that it could not bear to be separated from him, and Don Alvaro was well launched on his career.

There were however other contenders for power. Before departing for Aragon, Ferdinand had carefully provided his younger sons with ample territories in his native Castile. One of these, Henry, seized the young king, married his sister, and called tame cortes at Avila, which bestowed on him the rich marquisate of Villena on the Aragonese frontier. Alvaro de Luna, who had remained with the King, enabled him to escape, and after calling cortes at Madrid in 1422, succeeded in arresting Henry. But Henry's eldest brother, who had now succeeded to the Aragonese throne, lost no time in succouring the 'Aragonese' faction in Castile, and in 1425 the captive was released and formed a new league against the favourite, who for a moment was overthrown. But his rivals could not control the King, and he soon returned to power. Although a third 'Aragonese' brother, John, had now acquired the throne of Navarre by marrying the heiress of Charles the Noble, and joined in an invasion of Castile, a settlement was reached in 1430: Don Alvaro remained in power and the Aragonese Trastámaras were allowed to keep their estates in Castile.

The peace gave Don Alvaro the opportunity to launch a campaign against Granada in justification of the ancient rights of the crown. On July 1, 1431 the Castilians set up their camp in the Sierra Elvira not far from the Naṣrid capital. When Muhammad VII came out to do battle, he was heavily defeated at the Higueruela, and much of his cavalry, built up during the years of Castilian weakness, was destroyed.

There followed five years of relative tranquillity. The favourite, holding the great office of Constable of Castile, held the willing King in thrall and exercised a dictatorship over his rivals. John II lacked utterly the ruthless will of the founder of the line and the tender conscience of his grandfather. He devoted himself to pleasure-seeking and fashionable literature, and his peripatetic court began to acquire the refinements with which Catalan civilisation had reached its height half a century before. The eccentric figure of Enrique de Villena (†1434) who arranged the festivities for the coronation of Ferdinand of Antequera in Saragossa and wrote the first Spanish cookery-book, translated the Aeneid and dabbled in astrology, serves to link the social luxuriance of the Aragonese golden age with the Castile of John II. It was an age in which secular traditionalism was again dominant, and the desire for a vigorous religious and social reform had died down. The king, divided from his subjects by his favourite, thought little of meddling in their affairs. The Castilian nobility varied their feuds with jousts and tourneys: the most famous of these was the 'Paso Honroso' of 1434 in which Suero de Quiñones and his nine companions ran seven hundred and twenty-seven courses against sixty-eight challengers and broke a hundred and sixty-six lances. This athletic extravagance was perhaps more characteristic of Castile than the sybaritism of John's court. The northern towns, associated in leagues for their own protection, were wedded to their ancient austerity, and rural life remained exceedingly simple and conservative, and in the eyes of foreign travellers, strikingly archaic.

Not content with his control of John II, the Constable also made himself guardian of the infant prince, the future Henry IV, born in 1425, and appointed his brother, whose professional qualifications were negligible, Archbishop of Toledo. These extensions of his authority caused scandal, and when in 1437 he persuaded John to arrest the Adelantado Pero Manrique, the head of a powerful clan, an opposition party again forced him to leave court. But John remained loyal to him, and he was brought back, only to be expelled again by the Aragonese faction, who set up a court to pass formal sentence of banishment on him. When John again attempted to recall his favourite, the Admiral placed him under restraint, and this violence to the royal person quickly revived support for Don Alvaro. The heir to the throne escaped from the king's captors and the Constable raised a royal army in his name and faced his enemies at Olmedo in 1445. When battle was finally joined, the Constable and the prince were victorious: Henry died of his wounds and the Admiral and other magnates were captured.

After Olmedo the opposition forces were disbanded, and for several years the Constable was again dictator. But his very success caused his rivals to look to the next ruler. As page to Prince Henry, he had appointed one Juan Pacheco, of Portuguese descent, who had done good service by arranging Henry's escape before Olmedo. In the division of the spoils, Pacheco had been given the marquisate of Villena. while the Constable reserved for himself the Mastership of Santiago, the richest prize Spain had to offer. At this time John was a widower, and the Constable arranged for him to marry a Portuguese princess, hoping perhaps to obtain new support against Aragon, but the young queen, far from proving an ally to the Constable, became the instrument of his fall. Although Don Alvaro formed a temporary alliance with Pacheco against their rivals, it was only a question of time until the great magnates led by the Admiral should separate the two favourites. In 1453 the queen persuaded John to consent to the Constable's arrest, and Don Alvaro was at once executed by royal order, on a charge of having bewitched the king. He died bravely; and John, consumed with remorse at his own weakness, survived him by only a year.

John left three children: Henry IV, the child of his first wife, María of Aragon; and Isabella and Alfonso, by his second wife, Isabella of Portugal. The heir, a large shambling creature, physically repellent and morally perverted, was even less capable of effective government than his father. Pacheco, perhaps partly responsible for his corruption, lacked the intense will of the Constable, but exceeded even him in cupidity. He owed his position to a natural talent for intrigue, and had involved his master in all the rivalries and dissensions of his father's reign. Nevertheless, he succeeded in making peace with Aragon and Navarre, and the Aragonese royal family at last surrendered its estates in Castile.

The new king now made the customary campaign against

Granada in 1455. After their victory in 1431 the Constable and John II had installed a puppet ruler in the Alhambra, but he had been quickly overthrown, and while the Castilian monarchy was engaged in its own strife the frontier war had been carried on by the *adelantados* or marchers and the Military Orders. In 1453 the adelantado of Murcia had defeated Muhammad IX, who was promptly forced to abdicate; his successor, Sa'd, came to terms with John II and probably submitted to Henry, whose expedition to the south seems to have been no more than a demonstration. The Castilian council probably sought to stir up dissension in Granada by protecting the deposed Muhammad IX, while the Christian frontiersmen, irked by Henry's lack of warlike spirit, began to organise their own offensive in 1457. As a result an agreement was made by which Sa'd paid tribute at half the former rate, and part of the frontier, at Jaén, was left open for the campaigns which brought honour and profit to the élite of both sides: soon after, Sa'd's son, Abu'l-Ḥasan (Mulay Hasen) captured the governor and Bishop of Jaén and forced Henry to contribute to a heavy ransom.

These events added little to the prestige of Henry IV, but the final decline of royal power and public order in Castile occurred only after the reconstitution of the 'Aragonese' party in 1458, when John, lately King of Navarre, had followed his brother Alfonso to the throne of Aragon. Alfonso, immersed in the affairs of Italy, had lost interest in Castile, and even almost in Aragon itself; but John had both inherited the ambitions of the third brother Henry, and had taken as his second wife the daughter of the Admiral of Castile, Juana Enríquez, a woman of overriding ambition. From the small balcony of Pamplona he had long surveyed the panorama of the Peninsula with the same acquisitive interest as his remote ancestor, Sancho the Great.

Meanwhile, in Castile, Henry's unnatural tendencies had presented a new problem of succession. In his youth, he had been married to Blanche of Navarre, from whom he had been divorced on grounds of incapacity. After his accession, he had married Joana, a sister of Afonso V of Portugal, and had established a luxurious and allegedly disorderly court in the mudéjar town of

Madrid, dividing his attentions between his queen and two of her ladies. In this semi-polygamous situation Pacheco continued to influence Henry through the queen, while the Archbishop of Seville exercised a countervailing influence through one of her rivals. In addition, a new favourite presented himself in the person of a young Andalusian, Beltrán de la Cueva. Six years passed before the queen gave birth to a daughter, also Juana, and as it had been commonly rumoured that Henry was impotent, the report that the father of the new princess was in fact Cueva fell upon willing ears. A powerful faction, which included the Archbishop of Toledo, Marquis of Santillana and Master of Calatrava, now joined in the league of Tudela (1460), demanding that Henry should declare his half-brother Alfonso his heir.

In reply Henry made an alliance with the Prince of Viana, the heir to Navarre, whose rights had been usurped by his stepfather, now John II of Aragon. Castilian troops entered Navarre, and would probably have had little difficulty in forestalling the Aragonese had not Louis XI of France become alarmed at the possibility of Castilian control of the Pyrenean kingdom and arranged an arbitration, by which only the district of Estella remained in Castilian hands.

During the following years the power of the Castilian crown sank to its nadir. The cortes of Madrid had recognised the infant Juana as heiress to the throne, opening the prospect of a troubled minority and a new struggle for power. But the rise of Cueva caused Pacheco to go over to the malcontents, who revived the league of Tudela and came out in open rebellion when Henry bestowed the mastership of Santiago on his new favourite. In negotiations with the rebels the king agreed that his brother Alfonso should marry his daughter and so inherit the crown. This solution was a traditional one; but as a guarantee, Henry was required to deliver Alfonso over to the nobles and to deprive Cueva of his mastership.

This agreement was soon followed by further strife. At this time the outlying parts of the kingdom enjoyed complete independence. Murcia went five years without receiving a royal communication. The towns of Castile upheld their own version of royal justice with their hermandades, whose bands of crossbowmen pursued malefactors across the land and shot their victims to death where they found them. In Galicia visitors to Santiago found a local count besieging the Archbishop in his city and as they passed from one camp to the other were informed by the prelate's mother that they had been excommunicated. In Andalusia rival noblemen settled their differences at Granada under the patronage of the Naṣrid sultan, and lived with a certain lavish grandeur: a famous frontiersman celebrated carnival with a battle for a wooden tower in which ten thousand eggs were thrown.

Ignored by his subjects, Henry seems to have turned to his Granadine vassals for aid. He had already shown his preference for the mudéjar region of New Castile, and when a Granadine faction offered him their services he settled them in the region of Toledo: this delivery of land to strangers was much resented and the baronial struggle gradually acquired a wider significance. In April 1465 a faction solemnly deposed Henry in effigy at the 'farce of Avila', branding him as a 'heathen', and proclaimed his half-brother king as 'Alfonso XII'.

Castilian royalism was deeply offended at this outrage, and the towns formed a league on behalf of the rightful king. Once more Henry attempted to negotiate, and the egregious Pacheco offered to recognise him and hand over Alfonso, provided that the king's sister Isabella should marry Pacheco's brother, the Master of Calatrava. This scheme was prevented by the Master's sudden death. Nothing daunted, Pacheco seized the Mastership of Santiago for himself and defied the royal forces in a new battle of Olmedo (August 1467). Although Henry's troops were victorious, his own authority was little strengthened; but in 1468 the sudden death of Alfonso, the 'Christian King', deprived the malcontents of their figurehead and expectations.

There was now no male heir. Of the two females Juana was an infant in the hands of her 'heathen' father, while Henry's half-sister Isabella was of marriageable age and had her own household in a Castilian town. The rebel leaders offered her the crown, but she prudently refused to usurp her half-brother's prerogatives.

However, Pacheco succeeded in persuading Henry to accept the treaty of Toros de Guisando (September 1468), by which he again repudiated his daughter and recognised Isabella as his heiress. The Portuguese queen was dismissed from the court, and Isabella patiently waited her turn at Valladolid. Pacheco proposed that she should be married to Afonso V of Portugal, and induced Henry to agree. But Isabella had no intention of becoming a pawn in the hands of the intolerable schemer and was easily persuaded by the Archbishop of Toledo to accept the candidate of the Aragonese party: in October 1469 she made a clandestine marriage with Ferdinand, the son and heir of John II of Aragon.

Henry had not been consulted, and in a last attempt to save his crown from passing into Aragonese hands, he again recognised his daughter Juana and betrothed her to the Duke of Guyenne, the brother and heir-apparent to the King of France. This card might have outplayed the Aragonese hand, but Guyenne died in 1471 without having set foot in Spain. Pacheco was now at last resourceless, and left the court frustrated as Henry accepted a reconciliation with Isabella and even addressed a letter to her husband. When Henry died in 1474, Isabella was at once acclaimed, and five years later, with the accession of Ferdinand in Aragon, the two crowns were finally joined.

2. THE TRASTÁMARAS IN ARAGON, 1412–79

On the extinction of the Catalan house the Aragonese crown was disposed of, not by cortes in the traditionalist fashion, but by a commission of nine theologians and jurists representing the three divisions of the state. Assembled at Caspe on the Ebro, they acted as judges between the rival candidates, not as electors, and they finally decided in favour of the younger brother of Henry III of Castile, Ferdinand, who had recently won Antequera from the Muslims. His chief rival, the Count of Urgel, had already claimed the office of primogènit or Lieutenant of Catalonia, customarily held by the heir to the throne, and had the support of the Lunas, the family of the Aragonese anti-Pope. But when his supporters murdered the head of the Aragonese church, the Archbishop of Saragossa, his cause lost ground; and although on the entry of Ferdinand he gathered troops in Gascony and invaded Aragon, he was defeated and ended his days in captivity.

Meanwhile, the Trastámaran succession was accepted in the three Peninsular realms, and in the Balearics, Sardinia and Sicily. Owing his elevation to the church, Ferdinand set his face firmly against Benedict 'XIII' and prohibited all reference to his pretensions, though there was still in Aragon much feeling in favour of one who had been a famous native churchman. He also in his short reign gave deep offence to the Catalans. Since Pedro IV's defeat of the rebellious Aragonese and Valencians, Catalonia had been closely identified with the fortunes of the old house, and in the later years of the fourteenth century Barcelona had reached the peak of its prosperity and Catalan culture had had its golden age. But the new ruler brought in Castilian advisers and still continued to interest himself in the affairs of his native country, where he had endowed his younger sons with estates. His subjects (and especially the Catalans) attempted to press new advisers on him, but they had met with small success when he died in 1416.

He was succeeded by his two sons, Alfonso V (1416–58) and John II (1458–1479). The first of these continued to treat Pope Luna as a schismatic, but it was only in 1429, after Benedict's death, that his successor, Clement 'VIII', desisted from his claims. The Aragonese cortes had still not made their peace with the new dynasty, and in 1420 Alfonso turned his attention to Mediterranean affairs, first invading Corsica, which had been in Genoese hands for many years, and then embarking on the conquest of Naples.

Since the death of King Robert in 1343 Naples had been bequeathed to Louis of Anjou, but conquered by the Duke of Durazzo, whose sister and heiress, Queen Joan, now appealed to Aragon for help against the Angevins. In consequence Alfonso landed in Sicily, challenged the Duke of Anjou and drove the French out of Naples (1421). But the wayward queen soon quarrelled with her deliverer and entered a new league for the expulsion of the Aragonese. On her death in 1435 the Pope awarded her crown to the nearest Angevin claimant, King René of Provence, then a captive in the hands of the Duke of Burgundy. But by dint of promises and presents Alfonso built up a party in Naples and landed at Gaeta, only to be captured by the Genoese in the sea-battle of Ponza.

This was a fortunate reverse, for his captors delivered him to the Duke of Milan, who decided that more was to be gained from Aragon than was to be feared from the French. Alfonso and the Duke became allies, and Naples was finally conquered in 1442. René, who had ransomed himself in order to make good his claim, fled to Florence; and the Pope, apprehensive of the possible rise of a new Aragonese anti-Pope, invested Alfonso with the kingdom of Naples in the following year.

From this time Alfonso identified himself completely with the affairs of his new conquest. Although he was now famous as a conqueror in the Mediterranean world, his Peninsular subjects were by no means reconciled to his absence, and when in 1445 it was reported that he intended to move the seat of his government to Naples, the justicia of Aragon, the custodian of the national privileges, was sent to remonstrate with him. Nevertheless, he continued to rule in splendour in his new conquest, leaving his wife and later his brother, John II, to govern his possessions in Spain. On the fall of Constantinople to the Turks, the Holy See again attempted to draw the warring princes of Christendom into a crusade, but Alfonso refused to take part, turning his forces against the Genoese, who since the battle of Ponza had remained independent of Milan and flung in their lot with the Angevins. In the siege of Genoa Alfonso 'the Magnanimous' met his end in 1458, leaving behind a prodigious reputation as a patron of culture, and a bastard son, Ferdinand (Ferrante), to inherit the crown of Naples. As a result of his adventures, Aragon was entrenched in southern Italy, whilst the French threatened to force their way into the north, and the stage was thus set for the long series of conflicts between the heirs of Franks and Visigoths for the hegemony of Europe.

Meanwhile, Alfonso's brother John had remained immersed in the politics of the Peninsula. In 1409 he had married the gentle

Blanche, heiress of Navarre; and on the death of her father, Charles the Noble, in 1425, he at once claimed the title of king. When she died in 1441, he continued to reign, while their son was known as Prince of Viana, the title assumed by the heirs to the Navarrese throne.[1]

John had been the ally of his brother Henry in his long struggle with the Constable of Castile, and he now married the daughter of the Admiral, Juana Enríquez, who bore him another son, the future Ferdinand the Catholic, in 1453. At its birth this child was sure of nothing: Navarre belonged to his half-brother; his uncle Alfonso of Aragon might still have legitimate children; and Castile had a king, a prince and a princess. Yet he was to rule all three.

John's earlier attempts to recreate the Aragonese party in Castile had been frustrated by the reverse at Olmedo, after which he was deprived of his Castilian estates. For some years he vainly endeavoured to induce the cortes of Navarre and Aragon to go to war on his behalf, but neither would support him, and when in 1451 his schemes involved Navarre in a Castilian invasion, his son, the Prince of Viana, was compelled to give assurances that Navarre did not support his pretensions, after which the Castilians withdrew. This peace was followed by a bitter persecution of the Prince by his father and stepmother. Juana Enríquez went to Navarre, provoked the Prince to take up arms, and defeated and captured him. He was soon released, but under her influence, John II was filled with hatred for the Prince, and in 1455 he authorised the Count of Foix to invade Navarre and depose him. As a result Charles took refuge with his uncle Alfonso in Italy.

Three years later, Alfonso died and John was duly recognised as King of Aragon, while Naples was inherited by Alfonso's bastard, Ferdinand. Charles of Navarre, who had inherited his mother's patient character, remained in Sicily, where he was offered, and refused the crown. But his father and stepmother could not rest while he was free; and he was at length induced to return to Aragon by a feigned reconciliation. John then

---

[1] Cf. the attitude of his son to the accession of Isabella in Castille: in Aragon the male succession had been prescribed by James I, but Pedro IV had asserted the right to set this aside in 1347. Navarre admitted the female succession.

summoned cortes, at which Sardinia and Sicily were permanently incorporated in the Aragonese crown. His Catalan subjects insisted that he should also proclaim Charles primogènit and thus acknowledge him as heir to Aragon; but this John refused to admit, and shortly after Charles was arrested.

As a result, the Catalan government, the Generalitat, claimed that its privileges had been infringed and began to take up arms on Charles' behalf. Although John was obliged to release his son, both the Prince's rights and the autonomy of Catalonia were now doomed. Juana Enríquez was appointed governor of the Principality, thus reserving the heirship for her young son. There followed long negotiations between the King and the Prince, amidst increasing excitement on the part of the Catalans. When at length John apparently gave way before the rising storm, Charles suddenly died, and it was generally supposed that he had been poisoned by his stepmother's orders (September 1461): he was popularly regarded as a saint and it was said that his bones worked miracles.

The crisis was reached when the young Ferdinand was declared primogènit. Barcelona now turned sharply against John and began to move towards revolution. The possibility of a disintegration of the Aragonese state could not fail to interest the French crown, which remembered that by the treaty of Corbeil St Louis had left the Roussillon in Aragonese hands. Louis XI now offered his protection to the Catalans; and when they refused it, turned to John II, proposing that he should suppress the revolution and occupy the Roussillon as a guarantee that he would be paid for his trouble.

Meanwhile, the Catalans were in open rebellion. The territorial army or *somatent* was called out under the command of the Count of Pallars, and John was formally deposed in June 1462. For a time he and his queen were blockaded in Gerona. The French prepared to seize the Roussillon, and the Catalans offered their allegiance to the King of Castile. But while the Principality was raising his banner and minting coin in his name, Henry IV was on the verge of capitulating to his own rebels and disowning his infant daughter. Louis XI pressed home his advantage, and having appeased Henry with a small section of Navarre, sent his own armies into Catalonia.

Having occupied the Roussillon, Louis held his hand. The Generalitat had boldly declared that it would rather pass under the Grand Turk than return to John II. In fact it chose as its king Pedro, Constable of Portugal, a descendant of the Count of Urgel, who reached Barcelona in 1464 and endeavoured to carry on a war despite lack of money and supplies. Early in 1465 he was defeated at Calaf, and he died in the following year. Barcelona, separated from Aragon and from Sicily, was now short of wheat, and therefore decided to offer its crown to René of Provence. He accepted and sent his son as primogènit, receiving a promise of French support in return for accepting the cession of the Roussillon.

But with the sudden capture of the King of France by Charles of Burgundy the situation took a new turn. John II was old and infirm, but he was still ready to fight for his possessions, and he now forestalled a renewal of the Franco-Castilian alliance by marrying his heir to Isabella of Castile. Dispensations were rapidly forged, and the match was concluded in October 1469. Louis, having recovered his liberty, made a last effort to detach Aragon from Castile, but the marriage remained.

Moreover, the resistance of the Catalans was now weakening. King René's primogènit died in 1470, and Catalonia, now led by Pallars, was a republic in all but name. John had continued to hold the town of Lérida, and in April 1472 he was able to blockade Barcelona. In October the capital gave in and returned to its allegiance. The old king could not afford to be ungenerous, and he made a settlement which attached the Catalan capital firmly to the interests of his successor. Meanwhile, Ferdinand and Isabella had already an heiress born in 1470, and four years later their prestige was greatly increased when Isabella acceded to the Castilian throne.

In Catalonia such enthusiasm as had been felt for Louis XI was soon dissipated. He had not legitimised his annexation of the Roussillon, and the inhabitants found French absolutism little to their taste. In 1471 a general rising restored the rule of Aragon everywhere except in Perpignan, and finally in September 1473 John agreed to pay an indemnity for its return, the whole area being neutralised until this had been satisfied. He was however unable to meet the obligation; and while he was engaged in the more important task of placing his son on the throne of Castile, the French again occupied the area. It was only after John himself had died in 1479, that his son finally recovered the old frontier as part of an advantageous bargain with Charles VIII in 1493.

VII

FERDINAND AND ISABELLA

BOTH of the states now brought together by the reunion of the two branches of the Trastámaras had been shaken by great crises. In Aragon the conflict was a political one: Pedro IV had consolidated the authority of the house of Barcelona at Epila, but only at the cost of acknowledging the hegemony of Catalonia. By securing the heir to the throne as its governor, the Principality had legitimately exercised an influence long sought by ambitious favourites in Castile. The new dynasty of the Trastámaras had refused to admit the special influence of the Catalans, and the capitulation of Barcelona had been the revenge for Epila: John II had won the right to set his Peninsular policy above the Mediterranean interests of Catalonia. But the essential structure of the eastern kingdom was not altered. It remained constituted in three distinct areas: Old Aragon, where the tenacity of the old nobility in defence of their privileges had produced cortes of four estates, two of them noble; Catalonia, where the third estate had eclipsed the rest and formed a new urban 'nation'; and Valencia, still largely a colonial society in which Aragonese nobles and Catalan merchants exploited, each after their own fashion, the labours of a Muslim majority.

In Castile, the struggle was less clearly defined. The central kingdom had stood firm on the principle of political union, and the monarch represented the essential integrity of a series of differing societies under the domination of Old Castile. He was in theory less trammelled by regional interests than the ruler of Aragon, but over much of Castile royal power was a matter of faith rather than of fact. The land was rich in warlords; and in

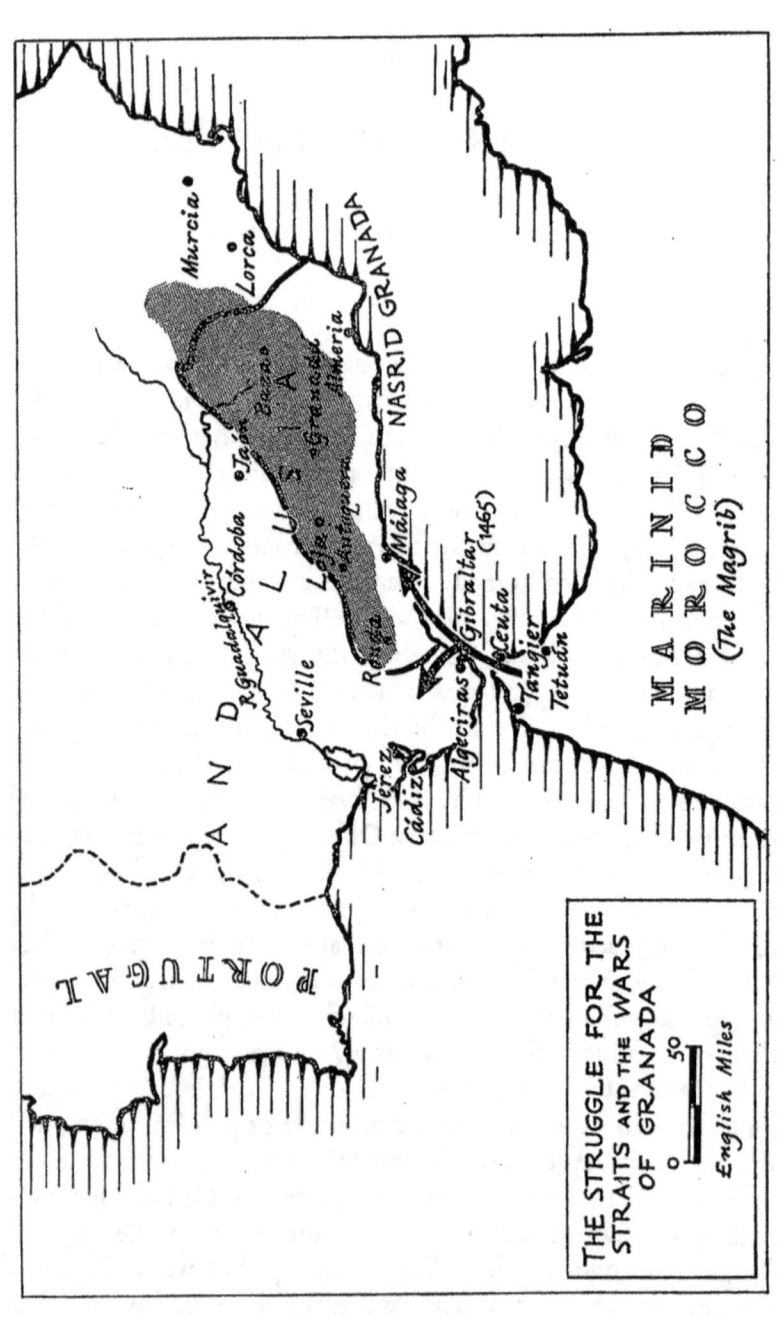

the long struggle between Germanism and Romanism, the momentary success of the latter during the reigns of John I and Henry III had been followed by a violent reaction. Under Alvaro de Luna absolute power was wielded not by the monarch but by a nobleman whose aims and methods were those of generations of Castilian magnates: his dictatorship had no constitutional basis and it was followed by anarchy. Meanwhile, in the absence of a royal 'will', the ambitions of the Trastámaras to dominate in the Peninsula had also degenerated into factional interests: Don Alvaro, by origin an Aragonese, inclined towards the Portuguese alliance; his successor, of Portuguese descent, wavered between Portugal and Aragon.

Unlike the localised nobility of Aragon, who pitted themselves against the authority of the crown, the Castilian nobles were broadcast over the whole realm. In the north they claimed greater antiquity, but enjoyed less wealth: in the conquests they were fewer, but dominated great estates and were masters of numerous mudéjar artisans and serfs. Over much of Spain they were immersed in local rivalries and feuds. The essential contest for power turned on the possession of the great offices of court and state. But far from being contained within the limits of their own order, they had overflowed into the church by seizing the great prelacies and the military Orders, which, though nominally ecclesiastical, were turned into private appanages in time of trouble. Against these forces the crown's physical resources were small. The royal army provided by cortes for John I was inadequate: Alvaro de Luna had contracted a Spanish adventurer who had led an international company in France, while Henry IV relied on his Muslim guard.

There was in Castile no dominant capital such as Barcelona or even Saragossa, each of which held five votes in their respective cortes. The strength of Castile lay not in the growth of highly developed or specialised cities, but in the alliance of a group of homogeneous 'county-towns', whose leagues or hermandades were sufficiently strong to execute justice in the king's name, even when he was incapacitated. For administrative purposes the kingdom had been divided into: Old Castile, Leon, Galicia,

Asturias, the Basque Provinces, Toledo, the Extremaduras and Andalusia, and these areas were represented at court on a 'federal' basis: in 1406 Henry III established a council with two good men from each of the main non-Castilian areas (Leon, Asturias, Galicia, Toledo, Extremadura and Andalusia). In cortes, almost all the towns of Castile had claimed representation at the beginning of the fifteenth century, but by its end these had been reduced to eighteen 'cortes-towns', each of which appointed two procurators. There was no question of municipal representation, but rather of a conference of jurisdictions. While the main capitals of the Castiles, basing their claims on ancient privileges, expected to receive the royal summons, each 'kingdom' of the reconquest was represented by its capital. Thus Seville, Córdoba and Jaén could stand for the whole of Andalusia, and the city of Murcia for its 'kingdom'. In the north, therefore, cortes was 'parliamentary' but in the rest of the country 'federalist' in tendency.[1]

Many of the Castilian towns were administrative centres of purely agrarian districts, though some possessed rising industries: in Segovia, a favourite residence of the court of Henry IV, there was a thriving woollen industry. However, in much of Castile the artisanate remained largely Muslim; and the Christian guild-organisation was still relatively undeveloped. In contrast with Aragon, where the lesser nobility or *caballeros* had their own 'arm' in cortes, the third estate of Castile was composed of both *caballeros* and men of peasant stock or *labradores*. At the end of the fourteenth century the procurators for a time consisted of equal numbers from each class, but this proportion seems not to have been firmly established, and many of the procurators were probably officials or legists, who might be either *caballeros* or *labradores* by origin.

Whilst in Aragon the crown was obliged to call cortes every two years, in Castile the summons was a royal prerogative. Provided that the crown was prepared to forgo service, it might dispense with cortes for several years, though it then ran the

[1] In the Basque area, each province had its own assembly composed of members elected by urban or rural communities. These miniature parliaments voted their own laws and administered their own fiscal system.

danger of losing its reputation as an 'undoer of wrongs'. The influence of the procurators thus varied considerably; there was no debate in the parliamentary sense, and no precise obligation on the crown to adopt the suggestions of cortes, though it was thought that the imposition of new taxation without the sanction of the 'nation' was illegal. On questions of subsidy, the procurators might specify the period over which collection should be made, or insist on safeguards against the corruption of the collectors, or demand that Galicia, which had no representative in cortes, should pay its share.

The system thus evolved was eminently suited to a conservative people, most of whom dwelt in rural towns maintained by a stable agricultural and stock-raising economy, and felt no enthusiasm for the vicissitudes of mercantile life. Its whole interest lay in the preservation of ancient privileges, rather than in the acquisition of new rights or opportunities.

Such was the Castile to which Isabella acceded five years after her marriage. This had been no love-match. Isabella, plump, countrified and devout, was filled with an absorbing sense of religious duty. Her conscience did not permit her to question the rights of her brother, King Henry, but she was easily persuaded of the bastardy of her niece, the infant Juana. It was with her a matter of doctrine that her enemies were traitors.[1] Through her the resourceful Ferdinand acquired as much power as a foreign consort could hope to hold in Castile. On her accession he promptly demanded the exercise of royal authority for himself (as his father had done in Navarre), notwithstanding the provisions of the marriage contract. The question was referred to Cardinal Mendoza and the Archbishop of Toledo, who decided in favour of a joint title: both names would appear in ecclesiastical and administrative appointments and on seals and coins, but Isabella alone should receive homage in Castile and authorise disbursements. When Ferdinand succeeded to the throne of Aragon, it was arranged that both rulers should do justice if they were together, and each in his own realm if they were apart. No

[1] Not all her subjects shared this conviction: at a critical moment, the Duke of Alba reminded her: 'If we are defeated, we shall be the traitors.'

constitutional union of the two kingdoms took place, though they now received common laws under a joint seal. An heir would inherit each crown on the death of its proprietor.

Isabella's succession did not go uncontested. Even after the failure of the French match, the child Juana remained the symbol for inveterate enemies of the Aragonese connection. She had been betrothed to her uncle, Afonso V of Portugal, who entered the field on her behalf, temporarily encouraged by Louis XI, in 1475. Zamora and other towns in the west went over to the Portuguese. The new rulers had still only a small army, and among the suggestions put forward for settling the challenge were that of a single combat between Ferdinand and Afonso, or the cession of Galicia by Castile. But the victory of Toro on 1 March, 1476 checked the Portuguese advance, and it was soon followed by the surrender of Zamora. By the summer the invaders had withdrawn, and Afonso himself departed for France to ask Louis XI for military aid. He failed to obtain more than evasive civilities and retired, Amadis-like, to do penance in a village in Normandy. When in 1479 he attempted to repeat the invasion of Castile, Isabella, now securely established, was able to settle his claim on very favourable terms. By the treaty of the Alcáçovas, Afonso renounced his betrothal to Juana, who remained immured in a convent at Coimbra until her death in 1530, and undertook to marry his grandson to a daughter of Ferdinand and Isabella, thus providing for an eventual fusion of the two kingdoms. At the same time the Portuguese acknowledged the Castilian claim to the Canaries, and Castile recognised Portuguese rights in the other Atlantic Islands and the African mainland, a division which anticipated the treaty of 1494 for the partition of the New World.

Isabella was now firmly supported by the towns of Castile, the lower nobility and the church. At her first cortes at Madrigal in 1476 she took under her protection the union of the towns, the 'new hermandad' formed in the stormy days of 1465-7. It had attained unprecedented strength in Castile, the Asturias and Galicia, and was governed by a central committee or junta. Isabella now made the presidency of this junta a royal appointment and required that all classes should contribute to sustain it.

Despite the statutory privileges of the municipalities, the hermandad was required to apply everywhere equal penalties for equal crimes, and its posses of crossbowmen remained the principal instrument for enforcing royal authority until 1498, when, having served its purpose, it was dissolved.

In the meantime, the crown had begun to obtain control of the military Orders. In 1476, on the death of the Master of Santiago, Isabella demanded that the knights should elect her husband as his successor, and forced the issue with the aid of a papal bull. The remaining orders were similarly attached on the death of the existing masters, Calatrava in 1487 and Alcántara in 1494. In 1480 the cortes of Toledo took steps to enhance the prestige of the monarchy by depriving the nobility of the right to include crowns in their arms. They were forbidden to build castles without royal licence, and alienations of royal property made by Henry IV were revised. Local rivalries did not disappear, but after Ferdinand and Isabella had made a progress through Extremadura, where they confiscated the estates of their enemies and visited Seville to end the feud between the Marquis of Cádiz and the Duke of Medina Sidonia, no nobles openly defied the crown.

The reality of power now lay with the legalistic class and its allies, the church and the lesser nobility of Castile. The cortes of Madrigal and Toledo (1480) consecrated the power of the legists by awarding them eight or nine places in their Council, as compared with three for the nobility and one for the church. All the administration of Castile was concentrated as far as possible in the hands of this body, which in effect controlled the municipalities through the appointment of corregidores. This office, used by Alfonso XI and Henry III to defend the municipalities from the intrusions of the nobility and from corrupt influences, now became the chief instrument for assuring royal authority. From 1480 onwards corregidores, never members of the great nobility, were steadily appointed to the principal towns. Meanwhile, a collection of royal ordinances was compiled by Alfonso Díaz de Montalvo and a copy was sent to the Alcalde of every place with more than two hundred inhabitants to serve as a reference in all criminal and civil judgements. However, the ordinances still failed to become the sole and undisputed law of the land, and the people remained passionately attached to their traditional statutes.

For fourteen years, from 1483 to 1497, cortes did not meet at all. This was the phase during which the crown made great steps in its control of municipal government: enriched by the revenues of Santiago and the recovery of alienated land, it waged the war of Granada without new subsidies from cortes and legislated entirely through the royal council. When cortes were finally resumed, the nobility and clergy no longer attended, and the procurators were assembled principally to acknowledge successive heirs to the throne.

Under the new absolutism, the idea of an organic monarchy replaced that of an organic society, and the crown resolutely strengthened the instruments of control, the Royal Council, the courts of appeal (*audiencias* or *chancillerías*), the corregidores, the masterships and the hermandades. All these were existing institutions; all that was new was the spirit that controlled and remoulded them. The most remarkable of these contrivances was the Sacred Office of the Holy Inquisition, authorised by Sixtus IV in 1478 to ensure the sincerity of Jews and Muslims converted to Christianity: these were originally the only consciences that it was empowered to test, though its functions were later extended. At the time of the Albigensian war Aragon had received a mediaeval inquisition under papal control, but Castile, then untouched by reformist ideas, had never known the institution. The new tribunal was not an extension of the Aragonese, but a separate body controlled directly by the Castilian crown. This fact was both a reflection of the contemporary passion for extending royal authority, and of the confidence of the Holy See in the rulers of Castile.

Isabella's anti-semitism, like others of her policies, was a resumption of measures first taken in the time of Henry III and his widow, and inspired by the Lateran Councils. During the reigns of John II and Henry IV this legislation had been very irregularly applied: many conversions had taken place, and while some 'New Christians' had risen to occupy high rank in the church itself, others had returned to the old faith. In 1476 Castilian Jews were again deprived of their independent courts for criminal cases, and in 1480 they were once more required to live in special quarters. Three years later all Jews were ordered to leave Andalusia, though few if any did so, and Ferdinand's order for their expulsion from Saragossa in 1486 was not applied. During their war against Granada, Ferdinand and Isabella still contracted Jewish loans to finance the crusade, but as the struggle drew to a close they prepared for more drastic measures. In 1490 the ancient fable of the ritual sacrifice of a Christian child was revived, and seven persons were burnt alive at Avila.[1] Soon after, in March 1492, Ferdinand and Isabella ordered the expulsion of all Jews from Spain. As of old, the victims offered to redeem the sentence by means of a subsidy of 30,000 ducats; but this time no general settlement (as distinct from bargains with individuals) was accepted, and there followed a great diaspora of the Spanish Jews to Portugal (from which they were expelled under Spanish pressure four years later), to Africa, Turkey and northern Europe. The number of refugees may have reached 160,000; some of these returned in the course of the sixteenth and seventeenth centuries. Of the great mass of 'New Christians' who remained, some fervently embraced their new opportunities, while others continued to practise the old faith in secret, and were from time to time denounced and suffered the penalties of the Inquisition.

In Isabella's eyes the crowning achievement of her reign was the conquest of Granada. The extinction of the Naṣrid kingdom linked her and her husband with the great rulers of the Reconquest and revived the vision of a Spanish empire in Africa. Following the example of Ferdinand III, who had been buried in his reconquered capital of Seville, Ferdinand and Isabella endowed a pantheon for their house in Granada, and the first title inscribed on their tomb was that of 'extirpators of the Muhammadan heresy'. Around it Isabella intended that a new capital for all Spain should arise.

Since the beginning of the fifteenth century there had been two

[1] The case of the 'Santo Niño de la Guardia' was preceded by that of San Dominguito del Val in Saragossa, and evidently derives from the same source as the tale of Little St Hugh of Lincoln and many other innocents.

royal successes against the Naṣrid kingdom, the capture of Antequera in 1410 and the battle of Sierra Elvira in 1431: in 1462 Gibraltar had been taken by the Duke of Medina Sidonia, but when Henry IV died no tribute had been paid for some years. On the accession of Isabella, the King of Portugal's challenge made it necessary to conclude a truce with Granada, and this was renewed in 1478.

But in September 1479 peace was made with Portugal, and two months later Isabella asked the Pope for a renewal of the crusading privileges for the struggle against Granada. Soon after, instructions were given for the seizure of a frontier fortress without declaration of war. To this the Muslims replied with a sudden attack against the Christian outpost of Zahara in the last days of 1481 or first of 1482, and at the end of February Rodrigo Ponce de León, later Marquis of Cádiz, replied by advancing on Alhama and taking it by surprise. This feat cut the direct road from Granada to Málaga and threatened to divide the Naṣrid kingdom in two. But its precarious internal unity was also threatened. Mulay Ḥasan (1466–85), had two sons by his first wife Aisha and another family by a second wife of Christian origin, Isabel de Solís, to whom he had rashly given precedence. He himself was now old and infirm; and when he went forth to contest the recent Christian success, Aisha and the supporters of her son Abu 'Abdu'llah (Boabdil) took advantage of the unrest in the capital to seize the Alhambra. Mulay Ḥasan therefore took refuge with his brother az-Zagal, the governor of Málaga. This town was well garrisoned with African troops, and in April 1483 az-Zagal restored his brother's fortunes by defeating Cádiz as he advanced into the vega of Granada. But a month later, when Boabdil tried to emulate his uncle by striking into Christian territory, he was defeated and captured at Lucena. His removal permitted az-Zagal to seize most of the kingdom, though part of the capital was still held by Aisha.

Among the Christians the capture of Boabdil caused great elation, but after long discussion the royal council decided to keep alive the divisions of the Granadines by releasing him, having first extracted from him an oath of allegiance. When he re-entered

Granada there was a bitter conflict between his supporters and those of his father, and he was forced to withdraw to Almería. By now the Christians had overrun the area between Ronda and Málaga, and all attempts to reduce the salient of Alhama had failed. Mulay Ḥasan was blind and ill; and since his death would bring Boabdil to the throne, az-Zagal made a desperate effort to capture his nephew: he succeeded in taking Aisha, but the last of the Naṣrids escaped and fled once more to his Christian patrons.

In 1485 most of western Granada passed into Christian hands; and when Mulay Ḥasan died, Ferdinand again released Boabdil to rejoin his mother and claim his throne. Faced with the double danger of invasion and civil war, the religious leaders in Granada attempted to set up a dual monarchy. Boabdil, the vassal of Castile, would hold the northern part of the kingdom as a buffer-state to be governed from the Albaicín, while his uncle would rule the rest from the Alhambra. But Ferdinand refused to accept this expedient, and accusing Boabdil of breaking his bond, pressed on with the war.

In 1486 Ferdinand besieged Boabdil in Loja, within full view of the Alhambra, and the vassal King again surrendered. In the following spring Málaga, the second city of the kingdom, with a strong Berber garrison, gave in after a siege of nearly four months: a small group of merchants and officials who had sued for peace was allowed to remain under the protection of the conquerors, but the majority of the population received the harsh treatment which was the conventional reward for a long resistance.

All western Granada had now fallen, and in the capital there was again fighting in the streets. Boabdil returned to the Alhambra, while az-Zagal attempted to place eastern Granada on a war-footing. But some of the governors favoured Boabdil, and when Ferdinand launched an attack from Murcia in June 1488 the frontier began to crumble. The surrender of Almería was frustrated by az-Zagal, and this temporary success filled the Granadines with desperate exaltation. But in the following year Ferdinand led forth a force of thirteen thousand cavalry and forty thousand foot, and finally reduced the stronghold of Baza after a siege of five months. The resistance of eastern Granada now

G

ended, and az-Zagal himself capitulated and departed to end his days in Africa.

In the capital, emotions now ran so high that even Boabdil prepared to fight. Ferdinand published the news that he had promised to surrender after the fall of Baza, and relations between lord and vassal were broken off. In 1490 a Christian army devastated the vega before Granada and Boabdil won a small success against a party of English archers holding the village of Alhendín. His only hope of survival was to break through to the sea and restore contact with Africa, but as he advanced to the coast, Ferdinand's armies again closed in on the capital. In 1491 the formal siege began: in April the Castilians camped on the site that was to become Santa Fe, and devastated the fields and gardens round the city. By the autumn hunger and anarchy were rife among the Muslims, and secret negotiations were begun. The capitulation was finally signed on November 25, and Boabdil undertook to deliver up the Alhambra on the following Epiphany, receiving for himself an estate in the Alpujarras and for his subjects full guarantees for the preservation of the Muslim religion, laws and institutions. Owing to the difficulty of maintaining order, the entry was advanced, and on January 2, 1492, Boabdil delivered the keys to Ferdinand. He soon tired of his small estate in the stark Alpujarras, and selling it to his vanquishers (who cheated him of part of the price) he retired, like many of his subjects, to Africa.

A Christian governor, the Count of Tendilla, was placed in the Alhambra to safeguard the collection of tribute and the valuable silk-industry, and Isabella's confessor, the saintly converso, Fr Hernando de Talavera, was appointed Archbishop of Granada. But despite his ministrations and example, the conquered Muslims showed no disposition to accept Christianity, and when eight years later the Catholic Monarchs revisited their conquest, they left a less unworldly representative to aid him, Cardinal Ximénez de Cisneros, who speedily goaded the Granadines into revolt, thus providing a pretext for the annulment of the capitulations and the mass-baptism of the whole population: after April 1502 all Granadines were thus supposedly Christians.

As they embarked on the conquest of Granada, Ferdinand and

Isabella had reassured the rulers of Egypt, who might otherwise have intervened, that their object was to repossess territory that was properly theirs. However, as soon as the war was done, preparations were made for a possible descent on the African coast. That this expansion was deferred until after Isabella's death was due partly to the demands of Aragonese foreign policy and partly to the opening of a new and greater perspective. For seven years an importunate Italian visionary had been attempting to persuade Isabella to finance an expedition to open direct trade with Asia, which he was persuaded could be easily reached by sailing west from the Canaries. But he pitched his demands high, and Isabella insisted on deferring the discovery of America until Granada should have fallen.

During the long period of Castilian introversion, the Portuguese had established themselves in Africa by conquering Ceuta in 1415, to which they later added a handful of other towns on the Moroccan coast. They had also ventured out into the Atlantic to colonise the hitherto uninhabited Madeiras and Azores, and had probed their way southwards down the coast of west Africa, building a fortress at Mina, whence they traded in gold-dust and other commodities with the peoples of Guiné (Ghana). After the French attempt to colonise the Canaries, one of the pioneers had bequeathed his rights to the Andalusian Count of Niebla, while a nephew had transferred his claim to Prince Henry of Portugal. In 1454 a Castilian attempt to occupy Grand Canary and Tenerife had failed, but in 1477 Isabella bought out the existing proprietors and the conquest of Grand Canary was completed during the following five years. During this time the seamen of Atlantic Andalusia competed with the Portuguese for the trade in Guinea-gold; but in 1479 the war between Castile and Portugal ended with the Portuguese acceptance of the Castilian claim to the Canaries and the Castilian admission of Portuguese rights on the African mainland, to the exclusion of the Andalusian navigators.

In the following year Christopher Columbus married the daughter of the Portuguese proprietor of the island of Porto Santo in the Madeiras, and began to elaborate his plan to discover India by crossing the Atlantic. Both because he himself did not carry conviction, and because the Portuguese were intent on reaching India by way of the Cape of Good Hope, his attempts to interest the Portuguese court failed and in 1485 he came to the court of Castile and obtained his first audience with Ferdinand and Isabella. After many rebuffs, his almost fanatical insistence was finally rewarded; and in April 1492 he received a contract by which he was entitled to call himself Admiral of the seas and islands he might discover off the coast of Asia and to receive a tenth of such cargo as he should bring back. The seamen of the small port of Palos were compelled to furnish three ships, which sailed in the autumn. Columbus sighted land, at Watling Island in the Bahamas, on October 12, and established a settlement in 'Hispaniola', the present Santo Domingo. In May 1493 he arrived in Lisbon with the tidings that he had been to Asia, and brought six 'Indians' back to Spain. He was received by Ferdinand and Isabella in Barcelona, and the new discoveries were at once attached to the crown of Castile. Columbus himself was confirmed in his rank and office of admiral, viceroy and governor. No sooner had Ferdinand and Isabella reported the discovery to Rome than the Aragonese Pope Alexander VI conferred the supposed 'Indies' on Castile.

Meanwhile, in 1489 Bartolomeu Dias had rounded the Cape of Good Hope and so demonstrated that Africa could be circumnavigated, while other Portuguese travellers had set out to verify the position of India and Ethiopia by land. The Portuguese seaway to the East was thus vindicated; and John II at once protested against the papal award, which infringed the rights granted by earlier popes to his predecessors. After lengthy negotiations the Castilians and Portuguese concluded the Treaty of Tordesillas of 1494, which established a line of demarcation first fixed at one hundred, and later adjusted to three hundred and seventy, leagues west of the Cape Verde Islands: all discoveries to the west of this line were awarded to Castile, and those to the east to Portugal. The amplification secured the navigation of the south Atlantic and the possession of Brazil for Portugal.

During the following decade Columbus made three further expeditions to the Indies. In 1493 he found that the garrison he left in Hispaniola had been murdered, and made the discovery of the lesser Antilles, Jamaica and Puerto Rico. In 1498-1500 he visited Trinidad and Tobago and touched the mainland of South America at the mouth of the Orinoco: he recognised from the great volume of fresh water that he lay off a continental land-mass, and identified it as one of the rivers of paradise flowing out of the Asiatic Eden. On his final voyage in 1502-4 he reached the Honduras and Nombre de Dios on the mainland.

Meanwhile, other explorers were probing the trans-Atlantic coast north and south, and it fell to another Italian, Amerigo Vespucci, who sailed in both Portuguese and Spanish expeditions, to establish the continuity of the southern coastline. It first received his name in a treatise by the German geographer Waldseemuller in 1507. Columbus himself had died in the belief that the land-mass he had discovered was Asia, and that some of its many natives must be able to direct him to the Cipango, or Japan, of Marco Polo. Although his own faith was unshaken, it was now well known that what he had found was not Asia, which was reached by Vasco da Gama in 1498-1500, but a 'new', and it seemed, vacant world. However, Castile adhered to the name that Columbus had bestowed on it: for her America remained 'the Indies' and its peoples 'Indians'. The full effect of his prodigious serendipity became clear only a quarter of a century later.

The war of Granada and the discovery of the New World were Castilian enterprises. In 1493 Ferdinand turned his attention to the affairs of Aragon, and by the Treaty of Barcelona induced Charles VIII of France to accept the loss of the provinces of the Roussillon and Cerdagne and the restoration of the old Pyrenean frontier in return for an undertaking to make no alliance contrary to French interests, the Pope only excepted. Charles VIII, intent on schemes of conquest in Italy, supposed that he had purchased the acquiescence of the traditional rival, and on the death of King Ferdinand of Naples in January 1494, he prepared to cross the Alps into Italy. His army was the largest seen there since the barbarian invasions.

Since the death of Alfonso the Magnanimous the Aragonese

house of Naples had, like its relatives in the Peninsula, attempted to increase its power at the expense of its nobles. Ferdinand I and his son Alfonso engaged a Turkish guard, and in 1485 arrested and executed some of their leading nobles: the kingdom was therefore divided and ripe for a renewal of the Angevin claim. A French intervention had been brought nearer by a quarrel between Naples and the Duke of Milan, Ludovico Sforza; and on the death of Lorenzo de Medici of Florence, who had hitherto maintained an unpopular alliance with Naples, Charles VIII was able to enter Florence almost without opposition, and on the last day of 1494 he reached Rome itself. The 'Spanish' Pope refused to grant him the investiture of Naples, but he marched forward, and in February 1495 entered the city and was crowned King of Sicily and Jerusalem, while its Aragonese ruler, Ferdinand II, fled to Ischia.

But Ferdinand of Aragon had now no intention of admitting the Angevin intrusion, and at once entered into a league with the Pope, the Duke of Milan, the Emperor Maximilian and Venice. At this time the Pope conferred on him and his Queen the title of the 'Catholic Monarchs', which seemed to establish Spain's claim to defend papal interests and so to resist the pretensions of France to be the eldest daughter of the church.

While Charles hastily withdrew, leaving only a garrison in his new conquest, a Spanish army was sent to Italy to restore the Aragonese house. It was led by an Andalusian soldier who had won fame on the frontier and in the conquest of Granada, Gonzalo Fernández de Córdoba, who was to be remembered as the Grand Captain. After a first check, he overran Sicily, and by the end of 1496 the French régime was overthrown.

But on the death of Charles VIII, his successor Louis XII claimed to be both King of Naples and Duke of Milan; and when the French had isolated Ludovico Sforza and occupied his territories, Ferdinand concluded with them the secret treaty of Granada of 1500 which provided for the spoliation of the Aragonese house of Naples. The young Ferdinand II had died and been succeeded by his uncle Frederick, who had vainly offered to pay tribute to Louis and sought the aid of the Turks. In 1501 the French occupied the northern half of the kingdom, while the Spaniards took Apulia and Calabria. A year later, a dispute about the province of the Capitanata led to a quarrel between the two accomplices, and although the Spaniards were at first besieged by Namours in Barletta, the Grand Captain was victorious at Cerignola in April 1503 and entered Naples itself a fortnight later. The French garrisons were shut up in Gaeta, and although Louis desperately sought to relieve them, the Spaniards held the line of the Garigliano river, and finally destroyed the whole of the opposing army. Gaeta at once surrendered on January 1, 1504. Although Louis had attempted a diversionary attack in the Roussillon, it did not save him from conceding defeat in the Treaty of Lyons a month later. Thus when Isabella died in the following November the Spanish dyarchy was at the peak of its power.

Its future, however, was veiled. In 1496, as the struggle with France was renewed, the Catholic Monarchs had concluded an alliance with the Emperor Maximilian, marrying their son and daughter, Juan and Juana, to his daughter and son, Margaret and Philip. The two bridegrooms were the heirs to their respective kingdoms, so that a lasting alliance was envisaged. However, within six months of his marriage Juan of Castile died, and the heir of the Catholic Monarchs became their eldest daughter Isabella, Queen of Portugal, who died after giving birth to a son. This child, Miguel da Paz, was recognised as heir by the cortes of each of the Peninsular kingdoms (except Navarre), and would have crowned the work of unification had he not died in 1500. The new heir was Juana, whose husband, the Archduke Philip, governed the Emperor's patrimonial estates from his capital at Brussels; and instead of absorbing Portugal, Castile and Aragon were now launched on a career of European expansion and imperialism.

The Emperor Maximilian was a descendant of that Rudolph of Hapsburg who had defrauded Alfonso the Learned of his imperial aspirations in 1273. Although his family sprang from a modest castle in what is now northern Switzerland, it had prospered by a series of fortunate marriages. Maximilian's father, the Emperor Frederick III, had restored relations with the Peninsula by marrying a Portuguese princess, and Maximilian himself had married the heiress of Charles the Bold, Duke of Burgundy, whose attempt to reunite the scattered Burgundian possessions in the face of French opposition had ended in his death in battle in 1477. The Archduke Philip's Burgundy therefore consisted of the complex territories of the Low Countries, Artois and Franche-Comté: the old county of Burgundy or Bourgogne had remained in French hands, but its recovery was ardently desired by the traditionalists of the family. For this reason and because his southern frontier was within two days' march of Paris, the ruler of Burgundy was regarded as a useful ally against the French.

Six months before the death of the Portuguese prince a son, the future Charles I of Spain and Emperor Charles V, had been born to Philip and Juana at Ghent. However, the new heirs had definite shortcomings. Juana showed signs of mental instability which were aggravated by her husband's infidelities; and Philip, far from proving a stable ally against France, inclined towards friendship with the Valois. In 1502 they visited Spain; and after observing them, Isabella decided to appoint her husband regent of Castile on her death. This solution was opposed by a faction of the Castilian magnates, who distrusted Ferdinand and had already begun to cultivate Philip. On Isabella's death, the Archduke at once claimed to be King of Castile, and arrived there with his wife in April 1505.

Ferdinand at first attempted to negotiate with his son-in-law, but the Castilian nobles deserted him and he had no choice but to withdraw to Aragon. Under Philip I, and his favourite, Juan Manuel, Lord of Belmonte, the nobility again made inroads on the royal patrimony. Fearing a resumption of the Franco-Castilian alliance, Ferdinand parried it in advance by marrying Germaine of Foix and settling the possessions of Aragon on the heirs of this match (October 1505). A prince was indeed born, but death removed the child of disunion as it had removed the child of union six years earlier. It also removed Philip I within a year of his arrival in Spain, and Isabella's close adviser, Cardinal Ximénez de Cisneros, was now made regent of Castile, and prepared to hand power back to Ferdinand. The Castilians themselves were divided, and Ferdinand was forced to conquer Burgos, to send troops against the rebellious dukes of Nájera and Niebla, and to go in person to reduce two Andalusian nobles.

During the period of separation Ferdinand had busied himself with the interests of Aragon in Italy. He had dispensed with the services of the Castilian Grand Captain, who was ungraciously sent back to his native Andalusia. Thus when in 1509 the forces of Castile were mobilised to attack Oran, the expedition was commanded by Cardinal Cisneros, while the greatest soldier of the day counted his beads in Granada. This exploit, Castile's first conquest on the African mainland, fired the imagination of Spaniards like a second Granada; but when García de Toledo attacked Los Gelves in 1510, he was worsted and the crusading fervour again subsided.

Ferdinand was first and foremost the master of Aragonese foreign policy, and his great achievement was to have involved Castile inextricably in it. His French marriage was followed by an alliance with both France and Maximilian in the League of Cambrai of 1508, by which, under pretext of pursuing the crusade, the three parties proposed to partition the republic of Venice, which five years earlier had incurred papal displeasure by seizing the towns of Rimini and Faenza. But although Julius II excommunicated the Venetians in 1509, he soon became alarmed at the preponderance of France, and first made terms with Venice and then detached Spain from the League. A new alliance, the Holy League, received the support of the Spanish armies of Naples, who drove their way into northern Italy. Near Ravenna the French were again completely defeated and their commander killed. All the French acquisitions in northern Italy, except the fortresses of Milan and Genoa, were lost, and the Congress of Mantua proceeded to restore Italy with Spanish arms. A new Pope, Leo X, continued the anti-French policy of his predecessor, and in 1513 a Swiss army defeated the French at Novara and placed the young son of Ludovico Sforza on the ducal throne of Milan. Southern Italy was firmly in Spanish hands and the north was again free.

G*

Ferdinand's final success was the recovery of Navarre. His father had long ruled it, but had surrendered it to his younger daughter and her husband Gaston of Foix, in the hope of securing a powerful military ally north of the Pyrenees. But Gaston had died almost at once, and his heir, Francis-Phœbus, was a boy of twelve. At that time, the Navarrese were divided into a French party led by the Agramonts, and the Spanish party of the Beaumonts, and on the death of the boy king, his sister and heiress was married to Jean d'Albret, who attempted to steer a hazardous course between his powerful neighbours. In 1512 Ferdinand demanded guarantees from him, drove him into the arms of the French, declared him deposed by a forged papal bull, and annexed the whole of Navarre south of the Pyrenees, attaching it not to Aragon, but to Castile. In 1515 the acquisition was approved by the cortes of Burgos, and the incorporation of the small state which had given a royal house to both Castile and Aragon, and was in some sense the parent of both, strengthened the union of the two crowns and gave Castile a bone of contention against France.

Ferdinand's last year was not unclouded. In France Louis XII was succeeded in January 1515 by Francis I, who at once asserted his claim to Milan and began to collect new and greater armies which in August crossed the Alps under their veteran leaders, the Constable of Bourbon, Bayard and Trivulzio, and finding the army of the Holy League unprepared, defeated the Milanese Swiss at Marignano in September. When Ferdinand died in November, the French challenger had already entered Milan in triumph and was planning new wars in Navarre and Naples.

Since the death of Philip I, his widow Queen Juana had remained in melancholy semi-seclusion at Tordesillas, while her son Charles was reared in the Netherlands and acknowledged as Duke of Burgundy in 1507. The boy's paternal grandfather, the mercurial Emperor Maximilian, had intense dynastic ambitions, and was resolved that Charles should succeed him as emperor, thus assuring the supremacy of the house of Hapsburg from Hispaniola to the confines of Hungary. This possibility was not popular in Castile, where the brief career of Philip and the reappearance of the old feuds had strengthened popular prejudice against foreign-born rulers. Ferdinand, although he had brought up Charles' younger brother, also Ferdinand, in Spain, can scarcely have thought seriously of altering the succession, and on his deathbed he arranged for Charles' assumption of power. He did indeed think that his namesake might act as governor until Charles' arrival, but his advisers feared that factions would form round the two brothers, and he therefore left Castile in the care of the aged Cardinal Cisneros and Aragon in that of the Archbishop of Saragossa.

PART TWO

VIII

THE HAPSBURGS—PART ONE

1. CHARLES I

MORE than a year and a half passed between the death of Ferdinand V and the arrival in Spain of his grandson. Fortunately for Charles, the regent of Castile was a firm legalist and resisted strong pressure against the Burgundian succession. The brief reign of Philip I had filled the Castilian towns with distrust of the Hapsburgs, and this was increased during the interregnum. In Brussels, the baronial leader Juan Manuel, Ferdinand's enemy, who had been arrested during Charles' minority, was released and recompensed. The Castilian towns impatiently demanded to hold cortes and objected to the assumption of the royal title by the young Archduke since his mother, the mad Queen Juana, was still alive, and he had not yet taken the traditional oaths. Cisneros vainly urged that he should come at once to Spain: when he called cortes for December 1516, he was instructed from Brussels to withdraw the summons, and four months later he was forced to prevent the procurators from assembling unconvoked. The towns had already attempted to revive their hermandad, and they now sent a delegation to Charles to ask that he should appear in Spain and undertake not to introduce foreign officials into Castile or send Spanish treasure out of it: these requests were evaded.

When at last, in September 1517, Charles landed at a small port near Santander, he and his company made an uncomfortable march from village to village to visit his mother at Tordesillas and ascertain the extent of her madness. On his arrival he sent a curt letter of dismissal to the regent, but Cisneros died before it reached his hands.

Charles was now a smallish, ungainly lad of seventeen. He had been brought up with his sisters at Malines and still knew nothing of the language he was later to think fit for addressing God, but defended himself in public with a sullen silence. His education had been quite unSpanish. The ruler of the Netherlands was a nobleman, not a crusader or a justicer, and the most famous institution of his court was the Order of the Golden Fleece, a select club of aristocrats united by the oath of the mystic Pheasant, who discussed one another's achievements at their chapters and gorged themselves at interminable banquets. It was another world from the anarchical jealousies of the Castilian nobles and the sobriety of daily life on the meseta. But Charles was by blood more a Spaniard than anything else and in course of time he accommodated himself to the world of his ancestors.

Charles came to Spain surrounded by Flemish courtiers: Guillaume de Croy, Lord of Chièvres, his closest adviser, who outraged Castilian sentiment by bestowing the Archbishopric of Toledo, the wealthiest see in Europe, on his nephew, a youth in the Netherlands; Jean Sauvage, Grand Chancellor of all his realms, whose very office was a slight to Spaniards, but who died in June 1518; and his tutor, the virtuous Adrian of Utrecht. Spaniards were quick to resent the existence of this Flemish barrier, but it at least served to protect the young king from irremediable entanglements with Spanish factions. Chièvres quickly became famous for his rapacity, a vice much resented in a foreigner. His gravest fault was his attempt to levy taxation on the nobility and church and to raise the rate of the *alcabala*, or sales-tax. The very name of the Castilian tribute, the service, shows that it was freely granted; but the alcabala, of southern origin, was undisguisably an imposition. Isabella had levied it, but had not been fully convinced that the crown was entitled to impose new taxation in Castile without consent: Chièvres had no such scruples. He also called in the good gold coin of Ferdinand and Isabella, which it was generally believed was destined to leave Spain for the north.

There was therefore a widespread sense of grievance when

Charles held his first Castilian cortes in 1518 at Valladolid. The hidalgos of the municipalities were stung by the extension to them of the alcabala: in Toledo, in particular, part of the municipal council was alleged to have been bribed to accept the change. Now that Cisneros was dead, Charles had no adequate Castilian intermediary, and he nominated Sauvage to preside and Adrian to act as assessor to cortes. The procurators objected strongly to the appointment of the Flemings and reminded Charles that his mother was still 'Queen-proprietress' of Castile. But having aired their grievances, they finally granted service and the court moved on to Aragon. Here there were similar difficulties: at one stage the courtiers talked of using force and provoked a small riot, but by dint of corruption service was at last obtained in July 1518. In Catalonia progress was no more rapid: Charles was still at Lérida when word came of the death of the Emperor Maximilian, which occurred in January 1519. This news caused him to return to Castile to raise support for his campaign for the imperial succession: consequently, he failed altogether to visit Valencia and his attempts to satisfy the complaints of both the Valencian aristocracy and the towns without first-hand knowledge had disastrous results.

His long sojourns in Aragon and Catalonia restored the confidence of those kingdoms and impressed him with their intense pride and independence. Had his grandfather not died, he might have returned to make his peace with Castile at leisure. But his one object was now to obtain the imperial title: he required first to be elected, then to receive the approval of the Pope, and finally to be crowned in Italy. His rivals were a challenger, Francis I of France, and an outsider, Henry VIII of England; and the bribes were driven to unprecedented heights. But the struggle was a short one: Charles' dynastically-minded grandfather had cleared the way for him, and in July 1519 he was elected. It was the last of the mediaeval 'elections', for he was to make the empire hereditary in his family; but when it was over he owed nearly a million florins, largely to the German banking-house of Fugger.

The election aroused bitter resentment in Castile, where it was held that a Spanish king had no right to accept an alien crown without reference to cortes, and a foreigner had no right to pledge Spanish revenues for cash. The old Emperor had been a famous spendthrift who maintained his dignity on loans from his bankers, but Castile had come to expect a certain parsimony from her rulers. Isabella had seized the wealth of the dissident nobles and of the military Orders, and had devoted it to the war against Islam and the exploitation of the Antilles, going long years without asking cortes for service. During the reign of Philip I and the regency of Ferdinand the nobility had again made inroads on the royal patrimony; and the towns were justifiably alarmed when Charles rudely mortgaged the crown's resources and summoned the Castilian cortes to ask for a new vote before he had even completed the round of the Peninsula, and less than two years since he had first sought their aid.

The new cortes were summoned to meet at Santiago de Compostela. This was the national shrine to which the ancient emperors of Leon had repaired to pray or give thanks for great undertakings: it also lay conveniently remote from politically-minded Castile in a region that had not even representation in cortes. As soon as he had received his service, Charles intended to sail from Corunna for the north. Scarcely were cortes announced when the city of Toledo petitioned for the redress of grievances. It received no satisfaction, and a general unrest spread from it to the allied towns. Charles had almost to fight his way in places along the road to Galicia. In the absence of the monarch, the order imposed by Ferdinand and Isabella seemed likely again to dissolve into anarchy.

Thus when cortes assembled on March 31, 1519, under the presidency of Charles' new Grand Chancellor, the Piedmontese, Mercurino Gattinara, who was to shape his thoughts for the next decade, only three cities gave their support to the subsidy and twelve opposed it. Cajolery and bribery could secure no more than eight out of the sixteen cities entitled to vote; but Gattinara declared that consent had been given, and the procurators dispersed. Charles left his Dutch preceptor, Adrian, to govern Castile, and on May 20 sailed for England and the north.

When Charles had departed the smouldering discontent of the

Castilian towns burst into open rebellion. In April 1520 the royal administration was overthrown in Toledo. Each parish elected a representative to sit on a communal committee, and power was given to Pedro Lasso and Juan de Padilla, members of noble Toledan families: other towns—Segovia, Madrid, Alcalá, Soria, Guadalajara, Avila, Salamanca, Toro, Zamora, Cuenca and Murcia—at once joined the movement. The 'comuneros', as the rebels were called, were Castilians. Aragon did not stir: even Galicia and Andalusia, the regions which had the royal 'fuero juzgo' and were traditionally subservient to the crown, stood aside. In Castile itself the movement was complicated by local rivalries and feuds. Toledo, the first of the cortes towns, was the head of the movement: its rival Burgos, the ancient capital of Old Castile, remained lukewarm. Some of the nobles and prelates joined the rebellion, so that it appeared at first to have a national rather than a social significance; but most of these nursed personal grievances, and in its essence the movement was a protest by the populace of the cortes-towns, and especially by the tax-paying class. As the struggle proceeded, and it assumed the form of a social war, the hidalgos wavered and the greater nobility, which had at first watched the strife between the crown and its former allies, the municipalities, with some satisfaction, grew alarmed, and threw in its weight on the royalist side. Thus the struggle was at large waged by defenders of a conservative and popular form of social organisation. When it was over, peasants and artisans were quickly excluded from representation in cortes, which in the following generation came to be composed wholly of 'hidalgos', the loyalist squirearchy which combined a strong sense of Castilian nationalism with a no less intense devotion to the crown.

As the movement spread, the Royal Council in Valladolid decided to take action against Segovia, where the wool-workers had murdered one of their procurators for taking bribes at Santiago. Rodrigo Ronquillo, a well-known martinet, was sent with a thousand horse to impose discipline, but the Segovians were reinforced by contingents from other towns, and it became necessary to bring up cannon from the deposit at Medina del

Campo. But the townspeople of Medina refused to allow the cannon to leave, and as the royal troops scuffled with them, part of the place was fired, and the flames spread among the storehouses containing goods for the famous fair, many of which were gutted. This disaster, threatening the prosperity of all Castile, brought in such towns as Palencia, Cáceres and Badajoz. Whereas earlier attempts to form an hermandad had met with only limited success, there was now general support for the 'Holy Junta', which met at Avila, declared Adrian deposed, and appointed Padilla to command the municipal levies. The so-called 'constitution of Avila' protested loyalty to Charles, but laid down four demands: that the two procurators of each town should be one hidalgo and one labrador; that the King should not appoint corregidors freely, but choose two, one from either class; that there should be no export of Castilian treasure; and that both classes should have the right to bear arms. The nature of these demands indicates the social implications of the struggle: the Castilian 'labradores' were seeking equal treatment and representation with the hidalgos and opposing the enforcement of a formal system of four classes.

The rebels attempted to legitimise the movement by obtaining the approval of mad Queen Juana in Tordesillas. Adrian sent to forestall them; but the people of the town joined the revolt, and Padilla brought the comunero army to her and explained their aims. She gave her consent to the summoning of cortes, and when they assembled on September 24, she read a speech from the throne. But she would not sign documents; and as the populace pressed on towards a social war the middle classes began to hesitate. When news came that Charles had rejected the demands of Avila and appointed the two great officers of Castile, the Constable and Admiral, to sit with Adrian, the nobility rallied to the throne. The cleavage was sharpened as the populace of seigneurial towns repudiated their overlords, and the rebels petitioned Charles to revoke grants of land made since the death of Isabella. The Junta, aware of its peril, now found a disgruntled nobleman, Don Pedro Girón, a nephew of the Constable, to take command of its troops, but he resigned without having accomplished anything. The royalists had taken Tordesillas: and Padilla, who had retired in dudgeon to Toledo, returned and won a minor success. The Bishop of Zamora, a swashbuckling cleric at the head of a priestly army which recalled the old military Orders, came out for the rebels. But when Padilla was brought to battle by the royalists at Villalar, his municipal levies made only a half-hearted resistance (April 23, 1521). The comuneros were routed: he and the other leaders were executed on the following day and the Castilian towns soon submitted. Only Padilla's widow and the Bishop of Zamora (who had declared himself Archbishop of Toledo) held out for a while in the imperial capital.

The crisis in Castile gave the French King the opportunity to invade Navarre, and in May his troops crossed the Pyrenees and advanced to the Ebro. But his offer of support came too late to save the comuneros. The Governors of Castile countered it by allowing Girón and other compromised nobles to redeem themselves by fighting the invader. In June 1521 the Spanish victory of Noain completed the recovery of Navarre and drew a veil of national sentiment over the events of the last year. In most of the rebel cities a general pardon was granted; but in each a dozen exceptions were made, usually of 'labradores' who could find no patrons.

The struggle in Castile was followed by another and bitterer conflict in Valencia and the Balearics. Charles' failure to visit Valencia confused an already complex situation. The towns, and especially the capital, were populated largely by Catalans, who had introduced the fueros of Barcelona, while the countryside was owned by an Aragonese nobility and tilled by mudéjares. With the temporary decline of Barcelona, Valencia had acquired a prosperous cloth industry and a highly developed Christian guild-organisation; and when Muslim corsairs attacked the Valencian coast, the artisans were armed. But as a result of their aggressiveness against the native mudéjares, orders were given that they must surrender their weapons. The guildsmen resisted and forming a 'germania' (or hermandad), appealed to the king. Charles was then in Catalonia, but had already decided not to visit Valencia: he therefore sought to satisfy the Valencians by concessions. The triumphant guildsmen at once appointed a

Junta of Thirteen to govern their own affairs. Charles was informed of this and revised his order, but on their appeal he again gave way and sent Adrian to receive the homage of Valencia on his behalf. But the appeasement of the artisans annoyed the Valencian nobility, and from Corunna Charles sent Don Diego Hurtado de Mendoza, Count of Mélito, to govern the troubled kingdom. On his arrival the Viceroy was refused admittance into the capital and retired to Játiva and Denia: all southern Valencia was now controlled by the rebellious artisans, who vainly appealed to the comuneros and to Aragon for help. Attempts to negotiate failed; and the municipal troops, led by a cloth-worker, Vicente Peris, attacked the royalists with success. But once the extremists had left the capital, the moderates appealed to the Viceroy's brother, who entered it while Peris and his army ravaged the great estates, terrorising the mudéjares and forcing them to accept baptism. Peris then returned to the city and was acclaimed by his fellow guildsmen, only to be defeated by the royalists.

The rebellion was now limited to the towns of Játiva and Alcira; but as the royalists laid siege to them, Peris again entered Valencia and was this time defeated and killed (March 1522). In Játiva and Alcira the struggle was carried on by 'el Encobert', an impostor who pretended to be Prince Juan, the dead heir of Ferdinand and Isabella. A price was put upon his head, and he was finally murdered (May 1523), and the recapture of his two towns was followed by a harsh repression.

The only other region which obeyed the Valencians' call to arms was Majorca, where somewhat similar conditions existed. There was unrest on the island in 1520, and in February 1521 artisans and peasants rebelled against the taxes imposed on them and their exploitation by the nobility and bourgeoisie. They chose a cloth-trader to be their leader, and deposing the governor, raised a nobleman of Palma, Pedro Pachs, in his stead. But Pachs lost control of the populace and was murdered, whereupon the rebels demanded that the rich should be put to death and their wealth divided. They took the castle of Bellver by assault, and most of the surviving nobles fled. When finally a royal force of four galleys and eight hundred men was landed, the people of

Palma still resisted, surrendering only after a long siege in March 1523.

These disturbances brought Charles back to Spain and forced him to give close attention to its affairs. He was now to spend seven full years in the Peninsula. In obedience to the desires of his subjects he married the daughter of the King of Portugal in 1526; and his heir, Prince Philip, born in 1527, was educated entirely in Spain. He had already loosened his hold on Austria by appointing his brother Ferdinand to represent him there in 1522: after this he drew no revenues from it and his influence was virtually limited to questions of defence from Turks or Lutherans. Meanwhile, in Spain he took steps to raise his own standing by establishing degrees of nobility, by reorganising the system of Councils and by closer collaboration with the church and cortes. In return, Spain, not the Netherlands or Germany, became the point of departure for his wider policies.

Although Spain now accepted her imperial destiny, her first fears were fully justified. Charles' whole reign was consistently deficitary, and his great designs and small journeys were alike contingent on supply. On his accession, the flow of bullion from the Indies was actually declining, and it was only with the opening of the great silver-mines of Peru in the last decade of his reign that he began to receive large revenues from this source. For a quarter of a century his main wealth was drawn from the service of cortes, grants by the clergy and increases in internal taxation. His expenditure, coupled with the rising level of contribution, produced a general inflation and helped to stimulate the rise of Castilian industry. This in turn rendered cortes able and willing to contribute. But cortes no longer stood for the artisans and guildsmen: the procurators themselves were now hidalgos, and as this class was of Charles' own making they were usually ready to meet his demands.

Charles was also dependent on Castile for men, and he constantly used his Spanish subjects as soldiers, administrators and ambassadors. His own interests were, however, distinct from the traditional policies of Spain. Aragon had brought him the crown of Naples: but Gattinara, the Italian proponent of his imperialism, was convinced that the key to universal power lay in the control of all Italy, and that this could be achieved only by holding the French out of the north, as well as the south. Possession of Milan and Genoa would not only guarantee the Emperor's ascendancy over the Pope, but also assure communications between Spain and Austria, and virtually enclose France.

Thus for some years Charles' great object was to establish himself against his rival, Francis I, and to claim his imperial coronation in Italy. But to do this he must hold Germany loyal to his family and to Rome. When he had gone to the north in 1520 Martin Luther had looked to him as the possible protector of the German national and spiritual revival, and so long as Luther's views seemed 'reasonable' Charles' advisers had hoped for a conciliatory reform. But when Luther took his stand at Worms, Charles, not without hesitation, denounced him as a 'notorious heretic' (May 1521). Once this step had been taken, Charles did all he could to restore Christian unity by means of a reformation of the church. He had received from his tutor Adrian the idea of summoning a General Council of the church, which he came to regard as a supreme parliament of Christendom capable of overruling the Pope himself. Such Councils had been summoned in the previous century, but they had been more effective in removing undesirable popes than in reforming the scandals of the church; and although Charles persisted in his object for a quarter of a century, no pope would submit to a council not under his exclusive authority, while the Lutherans refused to accept any but a free assembly. In this extreme, southern autocracy and northern nationalism proved irreconcilable: and it says much for Charles' good sense and loyalty that he patiently strove to heal the breach while successive popes baited him with the Turcophile kings of France.

Already during the electoral campaign the papacy had favoured France: but Charles' denunciation of Luther enabled him to form an alliance with Rome. Now Leo X desired to resist French encroachments from Milan into Ferrara, and by a secret treaty (June 28, 1521) he invested Charles with the sovereignty of Naples. Consequently Charles and Francis resumed the ancient feud between Aragonese and Angevins; and after Gattinara had formulated exaggerated demands, the imperial troops entered Milan and drove Charles' rival out of Italy.

The death of Leo X in December 1521 opened the way for an even closer relationship with Rome, for his successor was the regent of Spain, Adrian of Utrecht. Charles had not intervened in the election, but he expected much of it. He did receive the Spanish military Orders, which Adrian now vested permanently in the crown. Moreover, the severe Adrian found much to criticise in Rome, and in 1522 he both demanded the execution of the edict against Luther and admitted the need for reforms in the church itself. Once this admission was made, Charles became not so much the secular arm of the church as the arbiter of Christendom, a temporal potentate with a direct spiritual responsibility, and the idea of calling a General Council as a sort of parliament of western Christianity took firm root in his mind.

But the affairs of Italy did not run smoothly. Adrian could neither remedy the abuses of the church, nor bring about peace between the Emperor and the King of France. His papacy was no more than a well-meaning failure, and after his death no non-Italian was ever elected to the Holy See. To his successor, Clement VII, a Medici, both Charles and Francis were barbarians to be expelled from Italy; but Francis, being the weaker, was preferable.

In 1524 the Spaniards recovered Fuenterrabía and they and their allies again overran the Milanese and invaded Provence, but failed to capture Marseilles. By the autumn Francis had prepared a new army and re-entered Milan, and Clement VII agreed to submit to him. Charles was now forced to decide whether to take action against the Pope. He had still not been crowned emperor. 'Peace', he decided, 'is beautiful to talk of, but hard to have', and as he pondered, his armies came up with the enemy and won the great victory of Pavia in February 1525, in which much of the French nobility fell or was captured and Francis himself was brought a prisoner to Madrid.

In the spring of 1526 Charles, travelling to Seville to marry the daughter of King Manoel of Portugal, seemed to be the arbiter of Europe. By the Treaty of Madrid, Francis, after a year's imprisonment, had ceded the French county of Burgundy to him, renounced his own claims in Italy and the Low Countries, and delivered up his two sons as hostages. The terms, had they been honoured, would have assured Charles of the Hapsburg territorial aspiration and of his own coronation and hegemony in Italy. But on setting foot in his own country Francis refused to deliver Burgundy and was promptly absolved by the Pope from his oath: in the same year he renewed the struggle.

Charles' conquest of Milan and his victory over his challenger had drawn together the Italian rulers, who now joined the Clementine League at Cognac (May 1526) for the recovery of Francis' sons and the ejection of the imperialists from Naples: and Francis and the Pope were secretly joined by Henry VIII, who now desired to divorce his Spanish Queen. At this moment Charles was, for all his apparent might, paralysed by lack of money to pay his northern mercenaries. His Castilian subjects were still wayward: the nobility would fight for him, but not, as he desired, replenish his treasury; the military Orders would only do their traditional duty against the infidel; the towns he had already tapped. Instead of repairing to Rome to be crowned, Charles found himself faced with a new French war.

Francis had reasserted his claim to Naples, and all Charles' efforts could not wean Clement from the League. As the months went by, disorder prevailed in the cockpit of northern Italy and the imperial mercenaries, long unpaid, began to advance on Rome. Clement offered them money: they demanded more. On May 6th 1527, they scaled the walls and began to sack the city: the plundering lasted many weeks, and the Pope himself, who had taken refuge in Sant'Angelo, was made prisoner.

In this strange crisis Charles had vacillated until his troops were out of hand. Gattinara, who was absent in Provence, had already braced the Spanish cortes for a clash with the papacy, and he now hesitated whether to justify the deed, but decided to repudiate it. It was, however, easier to stir Spanish patriotism than to satisfy Spanish scruples. In his own mind Gattinara was one of those moderates who 'cherished God's word', neither a blind adherent of the papacy, nor an obstinate Lutheran. Such views were held by a small group in the Emperor's council, and by individualists such as the *converso* Luis Vives, who rejoiced that the Pope's opposition to Charles' design for unifying Europe had been broken. But they were not destined to prevail in the Spanish church: Spaniards, secure in their own nationalistic Romanism, were shocked when rude hands, their own among them, were laid on the Pope.

Meanwhile, under pretext of releasing Clement, French armies again marched southwards to conquer Naples. The city was blockaded and its Aragonese viceroy perished at sea in an attempt to relieve it. Fortunately for Charles, the powerful Genoese Admiral, Andrea Doria, now quarrelled with the French and came over to his side. Control of the Mediterranean then passed to the imperialists, and a year later the war was ended with the Peace of the Ladies at Cambrai (August 1529). Both sides were exhausted, but there was now no impediment to Charles' coronation in Italy. In 1529 the Castilian cortes granted him 400,000 ducats for the Italian war, and those of Aragon followed suit, asking however for a reduction in the number of religious holidays and an increase in the working days.[1] Meanwhile, Cortés had newly returned to Europe with the treasure of the Aztecs; and, much against the wishes of his people, Charles accepted a large sum from the Portuguese in settlement of the Castilian claim to the Moluccas. Thus relieved, Charles was able to embark at Palamós for Genoa and advance in a triumphal progress to Bologna, where Clement VII invested him first with the iron crown of Lombardy and second with the imperial crown (February 1530). Charles now held more of Europe than any other ruler since Charlemagne. He had twice defeated his rival, and his possessions virtually encircled France. The grand design of Gattinara seemed to have been achieved.

On Gattinara's death in June 1530 Charles did not appoint another Grand Chancellor for all his realms, following the advice

[1] While in Saragossa, Charles undertook to pay for the Imperial canal, for the irrigation of part of the Ebro valley: like his palace in Granada, it was never completed.

of his former confessor, the Spaniard Loaysa. Instead of being guided by the universalist aims of the friend of Erasmus, he relied on the more orthodox and restricted counsels of another Burgundian, Granvelle, who, however subtle and comprehensive in single questions or negotiations, never attempted to transcend his master's outlook.

From his coronation at Bologna Charles made his way to Germany. Here the diet of Speyer in 1526 had adopted the principle of *cuius regio, eius religio* as a temporary expedient until the summoning of a General Council of the church. This granted each of the German princes a local absolutism in matters of religion and consequently of social order.

Charles' advisers had hoped that it would halt the spread of the reformation, but its effect was rather the reverse. The declaration of the Protestants gave the movement a political form, and when Charles again tried reconciliation at the diet of Augsburg in 1530 he failed. Each side drew up a declaration, and at its close the protestant princes formed the League of Schmalkalde. Charles himself had foreseen three possibilities: submission to an imperial judgement, the calling of a General Council of the church, and the use of force. In view of his own commitment to Rome the first was unacceptable, while the papacy remained shy of a Council. The third choice was advocated by Loaysa, who reminded Charles that 'force alone had settled the revolt against the King in Spain, and force alone will put an end to Germany's revolt against God'. But Charles could not afford to accept this simplification: he reported to the Empress that the Pope's refusal of a Council had done great harm, and still hoped for a reconciliation.

For Spaniards the direct threat to Christianity came from the Turks. During the reign of Selim I (1512–20), they had been occupied in the annexation of Egypt and Arabia, but with the accession of Sulaiman II, they again turned against eastern Europe. In 1521 they captured Belgrade, thus opening up the Danubian plain, and in the following years, they defeated and killed the King of Hungary at Mohács, entering Buda and threatening Vienna itself. Charles' brother Ferdinand, now elected King of Bohemia, also received the Sacred Crown of Hungary, but the Hungarian plain remained in Turkish hands. Meanwhile, Francis I, while still a prisoner at Madrid, had begun to cultivate Sulaiman as an ally against Charles, and eventually concluded agreements with the Turks through their Hungarian vassals, while Charles sent a mission to propose a military understanding with Persia (1529).

When news came of fresh Turkish preparations Francis continued to negotiate with Constantinople through his Spanish renegade, Rincón, assuring the Pope of his readiness to occupy Naples as his part of a crusade. However, as Charles advanced to join his brother for the defence of Vienna, the Turkish armies withdrew without offering battle (1532). In 1533 Sulaiman concluded a peace with Ferdinand in order to disengage his forces for the assault on Persia; but he remained at war with Charles, and the scene of hostilities between the Ottoman empire and the Christians was transferred to the Mediterranean.

Here the renegade Kairuddin (Barbarossa 'II') continued to threaten the shipping of Spain and Italy, and in the following years raids on the Spanish coast were resumed and numbers of Spanish Christians and Moriscos fled or were abducted. But with the adhesion of Andrea Doria and the Genoese to Charles' side, the balance of sea-power in the Mediterranean turned in favour of the Christians, who raided Cherchel (1530), and Honeine, near Oran (1531): in 1533 a Genoese fleet and Spanish troops occupied Coron and other places in the Peloponnese, which were held for a short time.

But Barbarossa, now strongly supported by the Turks, replied in 1534 by conquering Tunis, whose ruler had been in alliance with the Emperor. Its loss exposed the shipping of southern Sicily to constant attack, and Charles began to assemble an armament in Sardinia for its recovery. This time the Castilian cortes voted a large service, and a fleet of 400 galleys and transports was gathered. Charles himself accompanied the expedition, which landed near Carthage, took La Goletta by storm after a short siege, and entered Tunis itself a week later (July 1535). Much of Barbarossa's fleet was destroyed, though he and his army escaped to Algiers. The conquest was a resounding one, but it neither crippled the Turkish assault, nor ended Barbarossa's raids on Spain itself.

It was soon followed by a renewal of the war with France. For a decade Francis had been the friend of the Turks, and the cannon captured at La Goletta bore the stamp of the lily-flower on their barrels. But the pretext for the third contest was the death of Francesco Sforza, the aged Duke of Milan. Francis again advanced his claim to the duchy, and Charles, who had learned from Gattinara to regard it as the key to imperial power in Italy, ordered Leyva to occupy it. From his Tunisian campaign, Charles had passed to Naples and Rome, where he attempted to persuade Paul III to enter a Hapsburg league for defence against the Turks and French. But the Pope reproached Charles for his dilatoriness in preventing the secession of the north: he, not Charles, was the arbiter of Christendom, and he would not take sides. In April 1536, Charles delivered a great harangue before the Sacred College and the ambassadors in Rome: he spoke in Spanish, denouncing Francis I for disturbing the peace, and offering to save bloodshed by challenging him to single combat, the gages being the county of Burgundy against Milan. This offer, springing from Charles' mediaeval and Germanic notions of chivalry, was not countenanced by Paul III, or accepted by his rival. The French had already entered Savoy, and Charles now despatched Leyva to invade Provence. The attack was at first successful, but it was checked at Aix, and the defenders laid the land waste.

Leyva himself died, and the imperial troops were forced to retire. In the following year Charles' armies attacked through Roussillon, while in the north the French had invaded the Netherlands and forced the Regent, Charles' sister Mary, to ask for an armistice. Finally in June 1538, a truce for ten years was concluded at Nice, and France remained in possession of the greater part of Savoy. The question of Milan, which had prompted the war, remained unsolved.

This inconclusive war and its inconclusive peace was followed by a meeting between the two rulers, who now temporarily became cordial friends, and Charles traversed the whole of

Francis' kingdom on his way to impose order in the Netherlands. The war and Charles' sojourn in Italy had proved extremely costly, and in 1539 his birthplace, the city of Ghent, refused to meet the contribution required of it and rose in rebellion, offering homage to Francis I; but the French King sent its compromising letters on to his new-found ally, and Charles severely punished the rebels.

In Castile too, Charles' expenditure was resisted: in 1537 he had tussles with the cortes of Castile and Aragon. When new cortes were summoned in the following year, Charles proposed the introduction of a new tax, the *sisa*, which should apply to all three estates: the Castilian nobility resisted, and although the clergy had been disposed to support the crown, Charles was obliged to give way, still believing, as he advised his son, that the *sisa* would solve all his troubles.[1]

Meanwhile, Sulaiman had prepared an attack on the Venetian possessions, and when the Muslims landed in Italy itself and took Otranto, the countries of the west were shocked and alarmed (July 1537). The assault was not followed up, and the Holy League, in which the Emperor, the Pope and Venice joined for the war against the infidel, had a brief and unhappy career: the allies were constantly at odds until Venice made a separate peace in 1540.

Charles had long nursed the imperial idea of a grand expedition against Constantinople, but this was quite beyond his means. Since he could not do what he felt his honour required of him, he decided to return to Spain to raise more money, and on his way to conquer Algiers at the expense of his subjects in Naples and Sicily. Although the Pope sought to dissuade him, and his best commanders opposed him because of the lateness of the season, in October 1541 he led an army of 24,000 men supported by 65 galleys against the city. He had perhaps expected an immediate surrender by the governor, a Sardinian renegade; but if so,

---

[1] The *sisa*, of Aragonese origin, was collected by traders, who were required to give their customers short weight and pay what they saved to the treasury. It had the advantage of not appearing to be a tax, and the subtle effect of legalising the instinct towards dishonesty.

he was disappointed, and a sudden storm wrecked many of his ships as they rode at anchor in the bay. Deprived of their cannon and almost without supplies, the imperial forces could only withdraw and re-embark in what was left of the fleet. Half of the men and a third of the ships were lost.

Although Cortés, the conqueror of Mexico, urged that the day could still be won, Charles insisted on the withdrawal. The reverse was a serious one: not only was the Christian champion worsted, but he never found the opportunity to reassert himself in North Africa. Muslim raids on Spain continued irregularly for another generation, and were ended only by the victory of Lepanto. And as the defeat went unavenged, so the Christian hold on Africa was weakened: Tripoli was abandoned by the knights of St John in 1551.

This reverse was followed by a fourth and final war with Francis I. Milan had been the subject of negotiations for a dynastic alliance; but Charles had perhaps never intended to relinquish his grip on the precious duchy, and in October 1540 he bestowed it on his heir, Prince Philip. By this decision he entrusted Spain, not Austria, with the defence of Hapsburg interests in Italy, and foreshadowed the future division of the imperial domains. A new challenge from France was now inevitable, and a pretext was given when two of Francis' envoys to Constantinople were murdered as they passed through Pavia in 1541. In July 1542 French troops entered the Netherlands and took Luxemburg, while a force led by the Duke of Orleans invaded Roussillon. In the following year, Charles rallied the Germans, formed a secret alliance with England, and launched a drive against Paris. Although his first impulse was halted at Landrécy (November 1543), a second campaign from Metz brought the imperial troops to Soissons, within two days of the capital, and their light cavalry reached Meaux (September 1544). Meanwhile, in Italy, the Duke of Enghien had defeated the Marqués del Vasto at Cerisolas (May 1544) and half-destroyed the Spanish forces in northern Italy. The peace of Crépy which ended the war was thus less favourable to Charles than might have been expected. It restored the treaties of Madrid and Cambrai, and the Emperor renounced his claim to the county of Burgundy and Francis the Angevin pretensions in Italy. Charles' relinquishment of his ancestral ambition was made in the hope of achieving a settlement of the religious question and of the Milanese dispute; and Francis at last undertook to oppose the Turks and to collaborate in the reform of the church and in furthering the Council on which Charles had set such high hopes. To seal their association, it was arranged that Francis' heir should marry a Hapsburg and receive either the Netherlands or Milan.

For Charles the results of this treaty were disappointing. The death of the Duke of Orleans annulled the dynastic plan, and by his support for the conciliar idea Francis gained the opportunity to meddle in the affairs of the north. But it was from this settlement that Charles proceeded to seek the pacification of Germany to which he was to devote the last ten years of his life. Owing to his preoccupations with France and the Turks, he had hitherto been content to prolong the truce in Germany. In the days of Clement VII he had vainly pressed for a Council of the church: now that Paul III was ready to accede, the breach between the German parties had attained political as well as theological dimensions, and Charles found himself attempting to apply remedies that had long been superseded. It was not for nothing that his fellow-members of the Golden Fleece reproached him for that dilatoriness which he conceived to be a virtue. Since the Pope had already condemned Lutheranism, the Germans saw little ground for a compromise, and hoped to gain much more from a German national assembly which Charles had also offered: by 1537 the cherished Council seemed already hopeless, and in the following year the formation of the Catholic League at Nürnberg drew the political lines even more clearly. Stricken with indecision, Charles now urged Ferdinand not to provoke an issue, and in the following years, as his mind was filled with unrealisable crusading dreams, he accepted the contributions of the Protestants to the struggle against the Turks (1541–4): in return he undertook to cope with the religious problem in the following diet at Worms. When Francis I fulfilled his part of the peace of Crépy by asking the Pope to call a Council, Paul III at once complied, and it was convened for March 15, 1545, at Trent. Meanwhile, the Pope's grandson negotiated with Charles for a solution by force, and Charles was offered not only troops but a million ducats from the revenues of the Spanish church for the campaign.

Charles again hesitated. He was unready for war and had pretended to the Protestants that he desired peace: German Catholics chafed at his lukewarmness and protestants mistrusted him. His Spanish ambassador in Rome reminded him that it lay with the Vatican to make the empire hereditary in his family, and that the Pope, Emperor and King of France could together impose order on Germany and England. At Trent no Protestants appeared, and the first deliberations turned on a treaty between the Emperor and Pope to provide for a war of enforcement.

The protestant princes, still united in the League of Schmalkalde, held their own discussions at Frankfurt, and their differences encouraged the catholic war-party. Luther himself, who had never approved of forcible resistance to the Emperor, died in February 1546; and the defection of Maurice of Saxony from the Lutherans, together with the threat of an Anglo-French alliance, now combined to precipitate open conflict. In August 1546 the Protestant League formally challenged the Emperor, and after a series of marchings and counter-marchings during the winter, Charles and Alba defeated the League at Muhlberg in April 1547.

But the victory was a hollow one. Charles still regarded himself as a moderator. If his dreams of universalism were now dissolving, he was still responsible for the integrity of his possessions. Having striven so long for a Council, he had found himself seeking to postpone a dogmatic definition of justification, in the hope that the Lutherans might still be prevailed upon to attend. But the Council accepted the uncompromising Roman definition in January 1547, and three months later adhered to its general doctrine of the sacraments. In consequence Charles fought the battle of Muhlberg in a spirit of disillusionment, and three weeks after the battle the Council was moved from Trent to Bologna, no longer on the frontier between north and south, but within the papal domains. Finding only intransigence in Rome, Charles was forced to reach his own understanding with the Lutherans and in 1548 he gave his support to the Interim of Augsburg, which admitted communion under both species, accepted the confiscation of church property, and approved the marriage of the clergy. These concessions went far beyond anything that had been propounded at Trent, yet they achieved no permanent security for protestantism: when it was too late, Paul III did shortly before his death recognise the Interim, but the decisions of Trent still stood; and neither the suspension of the Council in 1549, nor its resumption, with a few protestant participants, under Julius III, in 1551, brought a settlement any nearer. Charles' ambassador at Trent, the humanist Diego Hurtado de Mendoza, left with the feeling that the Council had done more harm to the Church than Luther himself: for all Charles' efforts Christian unity had ceased to exist.

Francis I had died in 1546, and his successor Henry II proceeded to challenge the Emperor, no longer in Italy, but by negotiation with the German princes. By the treaty of Lochau, Henry promised to subsidise them in the expectation that they would overrun the Netherlands and thus remove the threat to Paris. Accordingly, the princes issued a challenge in the Germanic style: 'our two armies shall fight, calling on God to decide between us', and the league was confirmed in the Treaty of Chambord (July 1552). Charles, though he had often feared an alliance between the French and Germans, was taken by surprise: he believed that Maurice of Saxony and his colleagues would negotiate or that the towns would stand by him. But he had no money to pay troops and when Maurice struck, he was almost captured at Innsbruck and could only flee over the Brenner to Villach. He left his brother Ferdinand to negotiate the peace of Passau, by which the principle of '*cuius regio, eius religio*' was reiterated, and catholic Europe accepted co-existence with the protestant north: Charles himself would never regard the religious duality as more than a temporary measure until a settlement should bring reunion. One more bitter humiliation awaited him. Henry II had seized Metz, at the extreme of the imperial Netherlands, and Charles decided, on the advice of Alba, to attack it. But all his efforts to bombard or mine the city in the midst of winter proved unsuccessful, and in January

1553 he was forced to raise the siege and return to the Netherlands. His German policy had now completely failed, and in the following year he did not even attend the diet, but left his brother to negotiate the settlement of Augsburg, which in 1555 finally established both religions side by side in Germany. For more than thirty years Charles had personified an anachronism, and the strain on his indecisive and meticulous mind had been very great: old before his time, he was now in a state of mental and physical collapse, and the thought of retirement to the relative stability of Spain and of the abdication of his wider responsibilities dominated his mind and actions.

As early as 1540, when he had made the twelve-year-old Philip his regent in Spain, he had given thought to the future of his domains. His vision was of a Europe dominated by the head of the house of Hapsburg and consisting essentially of two ancestral areas, the Hapsburg empire and France, flanked by England and Portugal. The imperial crown, it seemed, would go to the senior member of his house, his brother Ferdinand, who had governed Austria since 1522, was elected King of Bohemia and Hungary after the battle of Mohács, and received the title of King of the Romans after Charles had been crowned in Bologna in 1531. In 1540 Charles decided that Italy should go with Spain. There remained the Burgundian Netherlands. These he had first intended for Philip, but in 1548 he brought Ferdinand's son Maximilian to Spain to marry his daughter María, and planned to make the pair Archduke and Archduchess of the Netherlands in order that Philip might succeed to the empire. But Ferdinand was determined that his branch of the family, which now enjoyed the confidence of the Germans, should retain the empire, and there followed a long dispute between the two brothers. In 1549 Maximilian was elected King of Bohemia, and very belatedly Charles summoned Philip from Spain to visit Flanders and Germany. The experiment was not successful: the Netherlands now wanted a Spaniard even less than Castile had wanted a Fleming a generation earlier. Philip was a courtly but retiring youth, with small skill in jousting, and he did not impress the northern barons. However, in 1551 a secret agreement was reached whereby the successive heads of the family, Ferdinand, Philip, Maximilian, should succeed in order to the empire. But Charles still distrusted his brother, and feared the Lutheran inclinations of his nephew, Maximilian; and as late as 1553 he again attempted to make Philip Archduke of Austria.

He now no longer thought of rearing some imperishable edifice, but only of perpetuating what already existed. Since he had been forced almost to abandon Germany, the Netherlands could no longer be safely approached from Milan by way of Switzerland, and if they still hung suspended like a threat above Paris, they were too vulnerable to survive as an independent state. Since 1548 they had been detached from the Empire, and it now became vital to secure their connection with Spain. Only an alliance with England could assure the sea-passage from the Netherlands to Spain from French attack and in 1553 the opportunity offered to establish this. Charles had been in his youth the friend of Henry VIII, and the rift between them caused by the divorce of Catherine of Aragon had been closed by her death. Under Edward VI the great barrier had been English religious nationalism, but on the accession of Catherine's daughter, Mary Tudor, these difficulties were removed. By marrying his son Philip, a widower at eighteen from his first marriage, to Mary, Charles hoped that their heir might come to inherit England and the Burgundian territories, and thus govern a secure and predominantly catholic state on both sides of the Narrow Seas. In the event of the death of the pathetic Don Carlos, this heir would also inherit Spain.

To Philip the match was an unpleasant duty which he undertook with reluctant obedience. During the negotiations he delayed answering his father's letters as long as possible, and the Emperor feared that his conduct might spoil the cherished scheme, or that it might be frustrated by excessive zeal for the catholic restoration on the part of Rome. Great pains were taken not to offend the English Protestants: there was to be no question of the return of church property, and Philip was to be satisfied with the mere title of King of England during Mary's life, and to bring her a dowry. He undertook by the marriage-treaty not to intervene in English affairs, but before leaving Spain he took the precaution of making a secret declaration that he did not regard himself as bound by this provision.

The disparate marriage was celebrated at Winchester on July 25, 1554. Philip's appearance and conduct made a not unfavourable impression: perhaps his politely suppressed repugnance passed for reserve. He knew no French and did not learn English, but gestured courteously and found pensions for his adherents. But the hoped-for child was never born, and after a year Philip left England: the alliance had failed.

The Emperor was now a broken and superseded man, and in 1555 at a great assembly in Brussels, he began his series of abdications, placing his first possessions of the Burgundian Netherlands in the hands of Philip and departing for Spain. The failure of his policies in Germany and England and the election of a new and vehemently anti-Spanish Pope, Paul IV Caraffa, in May 1555 opened the prospect of a new competition with France and added to the gloom of his final year. His mother, the mad Juana, had survived until April 1555, and it was only on her death that he was free to dispose of the Spanish crown, which in 1556 he transferred to Philip. Retiring to the modest but comfortable semi-seclusion of the monastery of Yuste, he now divested himself of the imperial crown and his brother Ferdinand at last became Emperor in February 1558. Charles himself died seven months later.

2. PHILIP II

The concept of an emperor of chivalry died with Charles V, but already by the middle of his reign the mediaeval ideal of a 'universal' order belonged to the past. The climax of Charles' career had been that solemn assembly in Rome when he had defied Francis I to meet him in single combat. The very gesture recalled an outmoded order: the horse, from which chivalry took its name, had won Mexico, but the fate of Peru was settled by that equalising and authoritarian weapon, the arquebus, with which Spanish infantry were to dominate Europe for a century. In Spain the realism of the reconquest had curbed many, but not all, of the exaggerations of chivalry, which lingered on as a literary convention or was revived to fight the battle of the spirit by St Ignatius of Loyola.

Prince Philip was bred in quite a different school from his father. His tutor was a scholar of Salamanca, Juan Martínez Silíceo: his counsellors ecclesiastics; a noble soldier, Don Juan de Zúñiga, taught him to ride and fence. His disposition, his father was informed, was 'good, but not great'. He was amiable, pleasure-loving and obedient: his closest friend was an agreeable Portuguese boy, Rui Gomes da Silva, and he enjoyed chess, aesthetic pursuits and contemplation: he failed to impress the athletic barons of the north, though not for want of trying.[1] He acquired his father's apparent impassivity and cultivated the professional reserve on which the legend of greatness rested. But in Philip his father's chronic scruples, hesitations and dilatoriness were reduced to a general lack of decision, and an all-engulfing preoccupation with details, in which he sought to relieve himself from his burden of responsibilities. He was inevitably compared with his father, and as time passed and the Emperor became a legend, men thought of him as a great conqueror and warrior. This was certainly a distortion of the truth, but it fostered Philip's sense of inadequacy and caused him increasingly to shut himself off from stronger and more positive minds than his own. His own respect for his father concealed depths of resentment, and he himself had to endure the obsessionate knight-errantry and twisted hatred of his son Don Carlos: though Philip was naturally kind within his own family circle, he was led by his own 'reason of state' to imprison, and perhaps destroy, the unfortunate monster he had begotten.

Although Philip's religious orthodoxy had contributed to lose him the sympathy of the German princes, it did not at once assure him of the blessing of the Holy See. The new Pope, the passionate old Neapolitan 'Angevin', Paul IV, had nursed a bitter grievance

---

[1] 'Our prince is doing his best with the electors and the German princes.... If this goes on it looks as if all may yet be saved.... He often goes out to join their sports, and is to take part in a tourney next Thursday.' Granvelle, *State Papers*, X. 83.

towards the Emperor since the sack of Rome. To him, Charles had sought to impose his will on the papacy and was the 'heretic and schismatic' supporter of the Interim of Augsburg. Paul at once entered into relations with the King of France, persecuted the imperial party in Rome, flouted the regalist monopoly so jealously prized in Spain, and finally prepared to excommunicate both the Emperor and his son, though the documents were never drawn.

In February 1556 Charles had concluded the truce of Vaucelles with France, but the Pope now offered to recognise Henry II as King of Naples, thus inviting a new French invasion of Italy. In the autumn, the truce was broken and Guise prepared for the attack, while Alba, now Viceroy of Naples, entered the Papal States. The French armies, harassed by plague, soon withdrew; and Paul gave in, ending his alliance with France and promising to remain neutral.

Meanwhile, in the north, Philip had raised a great army of Spaniards, Flemings, Germans and English, which he placed under the command of Prince Philibert-Emmanuel of Savoy. It laid siege to the stronghold of Saint-Quentin, and on August 2, 1557 completely destroyed the French army sent to its relief. This victory, which inspired Philip to build the vast monument of the Escorial and so to fix the capital of Spain in Madrid, was an auspicious opening to his reign. He himself visited the battlefield, but he let slip the opportunity to march on Paris, which was undefended and in panic. Thus at the beginning of 1558 the French were able to recover Calais, the last English possession beyond the Channel. In July the Anglo-Spanish forces won the victory of Gravelines; but the death of Charles V in September made it necessary for Philip to return to Spain, while that of Mary Tudor two months later released him from his obligation to recover Calais before making peace. Freed from the ties of father and wife, Philip concluded the peace of Cateau-Cambrésis (April 1559) by which he and Henry II undertook to collaborate in the suppression of heresy, now spreading throughout France, and sealed their alliance with the marriage of Philip to Henry's daughter Elizabeth of Valois, while the Prince of Savoy married Henry's sister and so established a buffer-state between France and Italy, allied to both France and Spain. Thus at last the long series of competitive wars for the mastery of Italy was brought to an end, and Spanish paramountcy in Milan and Naples was accepted. In the following years France, divided by the growth of Calvinism, was no longer dangerous, and only in the time of Richelieu was the ancient rivalry renewed.

Philip had spent nearly four years (1555-9) as governor of the ancestral Burgundian domains, but he had still failed to overcome the distrust of his northern subjects. They now desired to resume the perpetual confederation with the empire from which Charles had divided them in 1548, and demanded this privilege of representation and the withdrawal of foreign troops as a condition of paying their subsidy. Philip feared to grant either demand. Far from allowing the Netherlands to associate with the empire, he sought when he left to place a Spaniard as governor over them. They resisted, maintaining that they should be governed either by a member of his own family or by a Fleming. He sent for his son, Don Carlos, then fourteen, but the boy was incapable of governing, and he finally appointed his aunt, Margaret, the widowed Duchess of Parma. This done, he took his departure for the Peninsula. He was never to leave it again.

The Spain to which Philip returned had enjoyed internal peace for a generation. Many Spaniards rejoiced in a sense of exaltation and accomplishment. The strange adventures of their compatriots in Mexico and Peru had culminated in the discovery of the great silver mountain of Potosí, which now began to pour its riches into Spain: its revenues, when farmed out, yielded the crown half a million ducats, as much as the whole of the Indies in the past. Nevertheless, Charles had left his son a formidable legacy of debt amounting to twenty million ducats, a large annual deficit and innumerable encumbrances[1]. Philip had accepted these liabilities, but in 1557 he attempted to clear away all charges on his revenues, replacing them with *juros* or bonds carrying five per cent interest. This forced conversion caused a depreciation of the bonds, which

---

[1] Especially the *juros*, which provided Spaniards with annuities: these were estimated at 50 m. ducats.

became saleable only at a discount, and a sharp decline in the credit of the state.

But on his return Philip found the cortes acquiescent in his own plans: the replacement of universalism by a policy of national concentration and the resumption of the traditional crusade against the Muslims. After his clash with Paul IV, in which he merely shouldered his father's burden, he had shown his readiness to collaborate with Rome: and Paul, fearing that the new Emperor Ferdinand would make a further compromise with the German protestants, also inclined towards Philip. The Council of Trent was recalled to a third session, and far from attempting to impede its deliberations as his father had done, Philip sought an undertaking that all previous decisions should be regarded as inviolable. This was granted in 1560; and while Ferdinand tried to delay the condemnation of the confession of Augsburg, the Spanish theologians took their stand firmly on doctrinal orthodoxy. For a time Philip thought of raising the delicate question of church and state, in the hope of having Spain's peculiar regalism acknowledged, but he refrained from doing so, and at length promulgated the decrees of Trent 'without prejudice to the rights' of his crown.

Dissociated from the problems of the north, except in so far as he continued to aid his uncle Ferdinand and to defend his Burgundian heritage in the Netherlands, Philip now actively applied the principle of *cuius regio, eius religio* in Spain. There religious dissidence meant Hebraism and Islam, and Lutheranism was long regarded as a purely German theological quarrel. But the entry of Calvinism, with its severe and uncompromising dogma, into France, could scarcely be ignored, and it was especially after its appearance that the Inquisition turned its forces against protestantism. To Spanish Jews it seemed that the reformed Christianity was more monotheistic, and so closer to Judaism, than the old faith, and they welcomed Charles' attempt at conciliation. A few openly embraced the new beliefs, among them the Navarrese Jew, Miguel Servet (1511-53), who was burnt in Geneva by Calvin, but in Spain itself the doctrinal disquiet of the conversos was diffused in the new movement of mysticism.

The first trial of an alleged protestant in Spain was that of a canon of the cathedral of Seville, Dr Egidio, who abjured in 1550 and was sentenced to a year's imprisonment. In 1557 the investigation of a protestant community in Seville was followed by several hundred examinations, and in September 1559 sixteen persons were executed and burnt. Meanwhile, shortly before the Emperor's death, it was reported that his former chaplain, Dr Agustín Cazalla, who had accompanied him on his travels in Germany and was now a canon of Salamanca, had formed a Lutheran circle in Valladolid. The investigation was followed by the execution of Cazalla and several members of his group. By now Philip himself had returned to Spain, and he was present at one of the ceremonial punishments in October 1559. In the following year a pragmatic was issued by which Spaniards were prohibited from going abroad to study.

Apart from these cases, which constitute almost the whole history of protestantism in sixteenth-century Spain, the Inquisition engaged in a variety of disciplinary activities, ranging from the repression of witchcraft to the persecution of the Archbishop of Toledo, Fray Bartolomé de Carranza, a converso who had inspected the libraries of Oxford, been chaplain to Queen Mary and given the Emperor absolution on his deathbed. Allegedly because his *Commentaries on the Catechism* (1558), which criticised abuses in the church, was heretical, he was arrested in August 1559, and disappeared into the dungeons of the Inquisition. He resisted the evidence of his fellow-Dominican, the Inquisitor-General Valdés, as a personal enemy, and his case was transferred to Rome: even so, sentence was not passed until 1576. The use of the Inquisition to settle a private feud or to remove a converso from the titular headship of the Castilian church, did much to make the Inquisition loathed outside Spain. Nevertheless, within Spain, its revival was generally popular: Spaniards believed that 'most of the heresiarchs and heretics of this present century' had been Jews, and they applauded the punishment of those found guilty of relapse, and the reassertion of a severe Castilianism.

Philip's desire for orthodoxy and nationalism was clearly expressed at the cortes of Toledo in 1560, when he declared his preference for his native Spain, announced that he had freed Europe from cares and given it peace, and promised that his own victories would be against the Turks and Moors. He thereupon asked for money to build a fleet for the defence of the Mediterranean, and received, though not with alacrity, a grant of 1·2 m. ducats over three years. He had already asked the Pope for a subsidy for Spain's war against the Turks and for the renewal of the *cruzada*.

These efforts had been stimulated by the loss of Tripoli in 1551, which Philip promised to restore to the Knights of St John, and the renewed raids of the corsairs; the most dangerous of these, Dragut Reis, scourged the coasts of Italy with a hundred galleys in 1558, and in the following years sent many expeditions against Spain itself. But Philip's first fleet of seventy vessels was lost by storm in 1561 before it had even been paid for, and in the following year many more galleys were lost by storm or burnt at Seville: almost his whole force was whittled away, and in 1563 he found himself again asking cortes to pay for a new fleet.

In the same year he convoked the General Cortes of Aragon, which had been consistently ignored for the past decade. The experience was not a happy one. He had hoped to receive a large service and to have Don Carlos acknowledged as his heir, but the Aragonese vehemently criticised the Inquisition, and accused him of enlarging its jurisdiction to deal with all criminal cases: so strong was the feeling against this infringement of the Aragonese fueros that the nobility threatened to end the union with Castile. Finally, after an extended session, Philip obtained a limited service in exchange for a promise to enquire into the functioning of the Inquisition and to respect the fueros. His attempt to have Carlos recognised by proxy as his heir ended in complete failure.

The Aragonese refusal to accept Don Carlos had ensued from the Prince's disordered conduct on receiving the oath in Castile in the previous year. Dwarfish and deformed, Don Carlos already displayed an unhealthy propensity to acts of cruelty. In 1562 he injured his head in a fall: and although his life was saved by the removal of a piece of skull, he became subject to fits of uncontrollable fury. Philip seems to have hoped that he would recover and reign, but the boy had turned violently against his father, and demanded to go to the Netherlands to impose peace there. When this was forbidden, he began to make secret plans for the journey, confiding in his uncle, Don John of Austria. It seemed that he must inevitably perpetrate some mischief, and after Christmas 1567 his father, attended by various nobles, arrested him: for a time he was kept in a closed room, but in July 1568 he suddenly died, whether by suicide, illness or 'reason of state' is not certainly known. It is only necessary to think of the disastrous career of his cousin, Sebastian of Portugal, also descended from the mad Queen and also obsessed with imperial delusions of knight-errantry, to realise what might have been the consequences if he had acceded.

At the time of this gloomy episode Philip had left behind him the retiring indolence of his youth and was, like his father, saddled with a vast complexity of affairs, many of which he could only solve by procrastination. He had carefully observed Charles' advice to avoid favourites, and was therefore in the hands of his secretaries. His court was divided into two sets, the traditionalists, led by the Duke of Alba, and the 'modernists' who followed Philip's boyhood friend, Rui Gomes, now Prince of Eboli. The two cliques conform to a familiar pattern. Rui Gomes' following was international, Italian, and legalistic, while Alba's tended towards Castilian nationalism, northern, military and conservative: but no fixed principle other than interest and ambition divided them, and the lines were never sharply drawn. Rui Gomes was a courtier rather than a politician, and Alba a soldier: although the former never lost Philip's confidence, the latter was once exiled for an apparently trivial cause, and finally dismissed with the special ingratitude reserved for grandees. If Philip had a favourite, it was the Inquisition, that busy and secretive instrument which could be used to extend the limits of royal power.

This new manifestation of southern authoritarianism had long alarmed the Netherlands, where catholicism was of a moderate character and, still influenced by the Erasmist tradition, felt little affection for the rigid purism of the south. In Germany the religious struggle had worked itself out: Lutheranism had been tamed, and German catholics had reconciled themselves to its existence. It had entered the Low Countries early and its first two martyrs were burned in Brussels in 1523, but it had remained a popular movement, and by 1530 the Roman Inquisition had stamped it out. Calvinism had first appeared a little later, but it was only in 1550 that the Emperor issued stringent regulations, the 'Placards', which made the spreading of dissent punishable by death.

As the rivalry of Calvinists and Catholics threatened to engulf France, Philip confirmed the Placards, and from 1556, when the Jesuits entered the Netherlands, Calvinism became identified with the anti-Spanish party. The nobility of the Low Countries now desired the same independence as the German princes. They had spent their wealth during the Emperor's wars and had followed his example by incurring great debts. With the return of peace they had no means of meeting their obligations and were disposed to seek the secularisation of church property, which had so enriched the German princes. Their leader, William of Orange, dissembled and still remained a member of Margaret's Council of State, but his object was the expulsion of the Spaniards.

Philip in return attempted to strengthen and centralise his power. The seventeen provinces of the Netherlands had all recognised the Emperor under different titles, and this extreme localism was reflected in a loosely organised and vulnerable church. When Philip raised the number of sees from four to thirteen in 1559, the dissident nobility strenuously opposed his reforms. Under their pressure Margaret persuaded him to allow her to dismiss Granvelle, his chief adviser on Netherlands affairs, in 1564, and this concession was followed by a campaign against the Placards and the decrees of Trent. Philip sustained all the measures already in force against heresy; and the leaders of the opposition, William of Orange and the Counts of Egmont and Horn, now withdrew from Margaret's Council.

The regent herself, alarmed by the rapid spread of opposition, granted a suspension of the Placards. This retreat led at once to a series of riots in which native and foreign Calvinists sought to disrupt catholicism by raiding and destroying churches and monasteries: in August 1566 some four hundred buildings were attacked within four days, and a great destruction of images and symbols occurred. Although the disturbances gradually subsided, Philip resolved to send a Spanish military commander to take his aunt's place: this was the Duke of Alba, who arrived in Brussels in August 1567, accompanied by ten thousand Spanish troops. He duly set up a special court, the Tribunal of Tumults, or of Blood, to castigate the rioters and instigators, and during the years 1568 and 1569 a devastating purge was carried out. Among those executed were Egmont and Horn, notwithstanding their privileges as Knights of the Golden Fleece. William of Orange withdrew to Germany; and when he returned at the head of an army, he was easily defeated and put to flight by Alba. At this moment, it appeared as if the Netherlands would once again be united as the northern outpost of catholicism: the dissident nobles were dead or dispersed, the south generally loyal, and Alba's army apparently unchallengeable. But the government of the Netherlands was now without money, and Alba attempted to introduce a levy on capital and a sales tax similar to the Castilian *alcabala*, to consist of ten per cent on each sale of movable goods and twenty per cent on that of property, and to be applied to all classes, nobility and people alike. The States-General were bitterly opposed to Alba's scheme, and for three years only the traditional subsidies were paid: when finally in 1572 the new tax was imposed, rebellion followed.[1]

The Dutch dissidents, who accepted for themselves the scornful epithet of 'gueux', beggars, outcasts, had taken refuge in a fleet of ships, and fortified by letters of marque issued by William, and favoured by the English government, privateered against loyalist shipping. But in 1572 the English ports were closed, and the 'Sea-Beggars' seized Brill and held the surrounding district in defiance of Alba. An open struggle for the independence of the northern Netherlands now began, and it was to continue for almost forty years.

[1] As it almost did in Castile when Charles attempted to impose the *sisa* on all classes at once: Charles had advised his son that the *sisa* was the true solution to his financial problems.

Alba's forces had been sufficient for their task. But the fame of his repression made it necessary to replace him, and in 1573 the more conciliatory Requesens, who had governed the Milanese, went to the Netherlands to restore civil government and abolish the 'Tribunal of Blood'. But by now William held the Calvinist provinces of Holland and Zealand and called himself 'Stathouder'; and although Requesens recovered part of Zealand, he died in March 1576 without having exploited his success. In the previous year the cost of the war had been sufficient to drive Philip into insolvency: he owed his bankers about thirty-seven million ducats, and therefore suspended all obligations on the treasury and loans for the war, making it impossible to pay the troops. On November 4, 1576, the Spanish garrison in Antwerp ran loose and sacked the city, and their comrades in other places soon followed their example. Although Philip now sent his half-brother, Don John of Austria, to govern the Netherlands, the States-General refused to admit him unless the garrisons were withdrawn, and this was accepted by the Perpetual Edict of February 1577. His governorship thus carried only a semblance of power. William of Orange was in effective control of all the north, and in September he entered Brussels in triumph and placed himself under the protection of a brother of the Emperor. Thereafter the struggles between Calvinists and catholics led to the secession of the Belgian provinces, and Don John was able to defeat the States-General in January 1578. But little had been made of this victory when he died at Namur on October 1st; and it was left to Margaret's son, Alexander Farnese, to rebuild catholic Flanders by patient diplomacy.

Meanwhile, Philip sought to purge Spain of her own dissidents. Two great morisco areas still existed, Granada in Castile and Valencia in Aragon. The second had been reconquered for four centuries, yet it possessed villages where only the notary and innkeeper were Old Christians: even after the germanía, when many Muslims had accepted Christianity, the great landowners had prevented church and state from harassing their industrious serfs. In Granada, where the memory of independence and prosperity was still preserved, conversion had been offered as an alternative to exile after the revolt of 1500: and all Granadines were now in theory Christians. However, most of those in the city Islamised in secret, while in the remote valleys of the Alpujarras, from which much of the raw silk for its chief industry was drawn, the villages remained for many years virtually unindoctrinated. The hereditary captains-general of the Alhambra, the Marquises of Mondéjar, who were responsible for the safety of the silk-trade and the collection of the royal tributes, became the natural guardians of Morisco interests; and whenever civil or ecclesiastical authority bore down on them, it was not difficult to obtain a suspension, usually in return for a subsidy. In 1526 an ecclesiastical council had decided that all Moriscos must practise the Christian religion unless, exceptionally, they could prove that they had been baptised by force. This announcement caused many Valencians to take to the hills, while in Granada a second council recommended that all practices which impeded true conversion should be forbidden: the use of the Arabic language, books and names, the possession of Berber slaves, the wearing of Morisco dress, customs such as public baths, the use of henna, and the celebration of traditional festivities and dances. These prohibitions were embodied in a new pragmatic, but before it was published the Granadines offered a subsidy for its suspension, and their offer was promptly accepted: the Valencians had lately made a similar bargain for forty years. During the period of grace, it was conventionally accepted that the peculiar features of Morisco life were 'regional', not religious: and appeals to the Emperor secured fairly complete protection for them. However, in the middle of his reign a long dispute took place about the sum to be contributed to the Inquisition as compensation[1], and when he abdicated the Moriscos promptly sent a mission to Flanders to offer Philip 100,000 ducats and 3,000 a year to support the Inquisition.

But a less transient regime had now begun. The Inquisition resumed its work, and those who fell foul of it fled to the sierra, where they were either protected by landowners or became bandits: others joined the Berber raiders who descended on the

[1] For the confiscations it failed to make in cases covered by an automatic pardon.

Granadine coast to trade, smuggle, rob or visit their relatives. The authorities replied by sequestrating the property of the fugitives and organising man-hunts against the bandits; and a gradual deline of public order followed. In 1563 the Archbishop of Granada, returning from Trent by way of Rome and Madrid, conveyed to Philip a message expressing papal concern for the souls of the Moriscos. A new council recommended the enforcement of the pragmatic of 1526: Philip II, guided by his Inquisitor-General, Diego de Espinosa, allowed the matter to be laid as a charge on his conscience, and a member of the Council of the Inquisition, Pedro de Deza, was appointed president of the audiencia in Granada in order to see the affair through.

Deza reached Granada in May 1566, and prepared to publish the pragmatic on January 1st, 1567. Its regulations affecting customs and dress were to be enforced a year later, when the Morisco women would be forced to lay aside their conspicuous veiled bonnet, *haik* and padded trousers and put their children to Christian schools. At Easter there were rumours of rebellion; but when Mondéjar attempted to appeal, Espinosa refused to allow him to see the King. At Christmas 1567 the villages of the Alpujarras suddenly rose, murdering many of the priests and other Christians who dwelt among them: a force of outlaws descended on the city and entered it by night, but the urban Moriscos shut their doors and the attack failed. Mondéjar had only 350 men in the Alhambra, and though he gave pursuit in the morning, he found the Alpujarras in arms and had to retire.

The rebels chose as their king Don Fernando de Válor, a regidor of Granada who claimed descent from the Umaiyad caliphs. He led an irregular campaign for several weeks, while Mondéjar, calling out the municipal levies of Andalusia, reinforced Granada and pacified most of the rebels with the promise of a pardon. But this promise, with its implication of a return to the old system, provoked Deza to new steps. Under pretext of a crisis he summoned Mondéjar's personal rival, the Marquis of Los Vélez, to enter the Alpujarras from the east. The rebellion flared up again; and as the municipal troops, whose only hope of reward was plunder, fell on the villagers or deserted, Deza stirred up the central government, which now decided to treat the rebellion as a formal war. After long pondering, Philip sent his young half-brother, Don John of Austria, to take over the command, appointing Mondéjar, Los Vélez and Deza to his council. But a formal war required seasoned troops, which had to be brought from Italy; money, which was scarcely to be found; and a plan of campaign, which, in view of the rivalry of the two Andalusians, had to be dictated from Madrid. Mondéjar soon retired; and the rebels, now deprived of any hope of favourable terms, desperately resisted Los Vélez in their inaccessible hills. In 1569 the movement spread to the valley of the Almanzora and threatened to reach Murcia and Valencia. Don John, who had not yet been allowed to take the field, was now permitted to do so. Most of the Morisco population of the city of Granada was transported to other parts of Spain. Finally, by the middle of 1570, the rebel cause became hopeless and the last resisters surrendered or were hunted like animals from rock to rock. A force of several hundred Turkish volunteers who had joined them was repatriated, and the Morisco population of the Alpujarras distributed throughout central Spain. Colonies of Galicians and other Old Christians were brought in to replace them, but many of the villages remained abandoned. A large part of the Granadine Muslims had been scattered over poorer areas of central Spain where they were slowly absorbed: Granada itself was much impoverished, and in the war Spanish arms, directed by Espinosa and Deza, had hardly shone: as Philip's historian noted, an affair for helmets had been botched by two priests' caps.

At the moment of the Granadine war, the Turks had again turned the brunt of their attack from the Mediterranean to Hungary. For some years Christian and Turk had had alternating successes in the central Mediterranean: in 1560 the Viceroy of Sicily had recovered Gelves (Jerba), which the corsair Dragut Reis had won from the Knights of Malta: it remained only briefly in Christian hands, and in 1568 Sulaiman made his last great attack in the Mediterranean against Malta. The Knights held out from May until September, when Philip at last justified his claim to the *cruzada* by bringing a force to their relief. Thereafter the Turks resumed their campaigns along the Danube, levying tribute on Maximilian and forcing him to seek a subsidy from his cousin in Spain. But Sulaiman's successor, Selim, now gave up the Hungarian war. His vizir Sokolli urged him to support the Granadines; but his own ambition was to take the Venetian outpost of Cyprus, and when by a lucky chance the arsenals of Venice were destroyed by an explosion, Selim issued an ultimatum for its surrender (February 1570). Although Venice had traditionally been the rival of Spain and ally of France, the Pope now put forth a plan for a new league, and after lengthy negotiations agreement was reached in May 1571. Even so, all Cyprus had been lost when the combined fleet was ready to sail four months later. The Christian command was given to Don John of Austria, and he was attended by García de Toledo, the reliever of Malta, and the Marquis of Santa Cruz. They had over two hundred galleys and a hundred small ships, carrying an army of 28,000. On October 7, 1571, this force sighted the enemy in the bay of Lepanto, in the gulf of Corinth, not far from the classical site of Actium. At ten in the morning the Turks were sighted, their galleys high in the water. The allied fleet rode low so as to avoid the enemy's fire, and when battle was joined at mid-day most of the Turkish ships were engaged and sunk or captured: half their men were said to have been lost and only one squadron escaped. One of the Christian wounded was a young soldier named Cervantes who thought his participation in 'the greatest occasion the centuries have ever seen' well worth the loss of an arm.

The victory opened brilliant possibilities. The Pope and García de Toledo dreamed of the Holy Land, and Don John of winning a kingdom for himself in the Balkans. But on the death of Pius V in May 1572 the League fell asunder. Don John remained with the fleet, but without money, at Messina, while the Venetians chafed at his unwillingness or inability to defend Crete; and Turks and French negotiated for a resumption of their old alliance, which would have placed Algiers in French hands.

By March 1573 the Venetians had lost patience with their

Spanish allies, and were treating for a separate peace through the good offices of the French ambassador in Constantinople. By paying a large indemnity and consenting to leave Cyprus in Turkish hands, they now recovered the right to trade with the Levant. When finally Don John left Messina, he was able to occupy Tunis and Bizerta almost without resistance, and was urged by his friends to set himself up as king there: his brother, however, instructed him to return to Naples. Although a garrison of 8,000 Spaniards and Italians was left to hold the new conquest, it proved insufficient for the task. Tunis soon returned to Turkish control; and Spain, now immersed in her struggle with the Dutch, was content to negotiate for a permanent peace with the Sultan, who, if he had 'had his beard shaven', had not lost an inch of land. His beard recovered so well that by 1572 he had again a hundred galleys at sea.

The Granadine war, Lepanto and the repression of the Netherlands strained Philip's resources to the utmost. Since his first insolvency in 1557 his bankers had stiffened their terms. In 1575, when the steady increase in the inflow of American treasure was momentarily halted, and his revenues were committed to his creditors for a decade ahead, a new suspension of payments was necessary; and when a composition was at last reached in December 1577 many bankers in Spain, Genoa and Antwerp had been ruined. But in the following years the expansion of the bullion trade was resumed, and by the end of the reign these revenues had increased almost fourfold.

Meanwhile, Philip was at last able to fulfil the ambitions of the Catholic Monarchs for the annexation of Portugal. Its young ruler Sebastian, fired with the combined examples of the Emperor, St Ignatius and Don John, determined to invade Africa as Christ's captain and overturn the Moroccan empire. In the summer of 1578 he mobilised all the resources Portugal could provide and landed his forces at Larache. They met a great Moroccan array at Alcazarquivir, where on August 4, 1578, the Christian army was destroyed and Sebastian himself disappeared in the fray.

He was succeeded by his only surviving legitimate male heir, the aged Cardinal Henry, who lived little more than a year. During this interval Philip was actively preparing his own succession. The support of part of the Portuguese nobility was bought through the agency of his ambassador, Cristóvão de Moura. The Portuguese clergy were on the whole well disposed. The third estate alone held that their crown could only be worn by a Portuguese. But the towns and artisans no longer enjoyed the power they had had in 1385, and after the shattering defeat of Alcazar war was impossible. Nor did a suitable rival present himself. The Prior of Crato, a bastard grandson of King Manoel, claimed the throne, but his supporters were disorganised and the troops he mustered proved no match for Alba's veterans. When the Cardinal-King died, he left the government to a regency of five. While they temporised, harassed by Moura's persistent pressure for the recognition of Philip, the Prior brought his army of ill-equipped irregulars to defend the capital; and Alba, advancing from Badajoz to the port of Setúbal, where he was joined by the Spanish fleet, broke their resistance in a short skirmish at Alcántara (August 1580). Lisbon at once surrendered and the Prior fled north to France.

In the following year Philip himself attended the Portuguese cortes at Tomar and was crowned in Lisbon. The fact that he was half Portuguese, his willingness to make a long sojourn among his new subjects, and the general guarantees he gave for the preservation of national autonomy largely reconciled them to the change of dynasty. Although the Portuguese people yearned for Sebastian, whom they now idealised and mystically believed would 'come again', there was little response to the efforts of the Prior of Crato and his foreign allies to exploit their aspirations. His negotiations with England and France caused Catherine de Medici to send a fleet against the Azores in 1582, but it was decisively defeated by the Marquis of Santa Cruz; and when, after the Armada, Elizabeth sent Drake and Norris with the Prior against Lisbon, the Portuguese showed no disposition to join the invading heretics, and the expedition withdrew with heavy losses (1589).

The third episode in Philip's series of actions to concentrate and unify the Peninsula, the curtailment of the privileges of Aragon, developed from the scandalous affair of his secretary, Antonio

Pérez. The bastard son of the Aragonese Archdeacon of Sepúlveda, from whom he inherited his office, Pérez was a man of unusual vigour and ambition. By receiving presents, selling information and misappropriating funds, he maintained a flamboyant style of living; but his positive qualities proved invaluable to the hesitant and slow-moving King, and when in 1578 he was arrested for complicity in the murder of Don John of Austria's secretary, Juan de Escobedo, he had become so indispensable that he was allowed to continue his work under house-arrest. Escobedo had been sent to Spain to urge Philip to find more money and men for the Flemish war, and whether his removal was the result of a personal intrigue or an act of 'reason of state' remains obscure. Four years passed before an inspection revealed the extent of Pérez's misdeeds, and he was then banished from court for ten years and ordered to reimburse the vast sum of twelve million maravedis. Once he was condemned, the family of Escobedo renewed its demand for vengeance, and he was formally accused of murder. He confessed under torture, but two months later escaped from prison and fled to Saragossa, where in 1590 he claimed the ancient privilege of *manifestación*, whereby an Aragonese accused by the crown was held in the special prison of the justicia, to be judged under Aragonese law.

In Castile itself the affair of Antonio Pérez throws a curious light on the network of devious interests which had grown up at court. Philip's own hesitations and fears were reflected in the apparently contradictory attachments of the governing group. Of the Castilian conservative party, the Duke of Alba had alarmed Philip by his violence in the Netherlands, and even his success in conducting the Portuguese campaign did not regain him the King's confidence: however, a group of the secretaries, Mateo Vázquez and Zayas, belonged to his clique. Rui Gomes, the King's most intimate personal friend, died in 1573, leaving an extravagant widow and many ambitious hangers-on: they now attached themselves to Pérez, who had owed his promotion to Gomes. This faction included many persons with Aragonese and Italian interests, and such Andalusian nobles as Los Vélez and the Duke of Sessa. Pérez's own rise had come at a time when Philip wa depressed by the death of his third wife, the affair of Don Carlos, the Morisco war and the threat of war in the Netherlands. Having established his ascendancy, he had to struggle to keep it and therefore plunged deeply into corruption, taking bribes from place-hunters (even the Duke of Medina Sidonia on being made viceroy in Milan) and involving himself with Genoese bankers. He was also cultivated by the Pope and the nuncio, whose main interest lay contrary to the prevailing regalism of the Spanish church and Inquisition. He was warmly protected by the Archbishop of Toledo, who was also Inquisitor-General, and he himself cultivated the Jesuits, who had their own problems.[1] Many other individuals, representative or private, denied access to the retiring King, gladly plied his amenable secretary.

But if in Castile the affair was confused by the conflicting interests of individuals and institutions, in Aragon there was a simple issue. The Aragonese, with their traditional order of society unaffected by the rebellion of the comuneros, and their powerful barrier of fueros still intact, were strongly entrenched against any form of Castilianisation. At the cortes of 1563 there had been an uproar against the use of the Inquisition as an instrument for extending the royal prerogatives in Aragon and Philip had had to promise an investigation: more than twenty years passed before the Aragonese cortes were summoned again in 1585, when Philip made all offices open to Castilians available also to natives of Aragon, vainly hoping that this would induce the Aragonese to desist from their traditional right to have a viceroy of their own race. On this fundamental issue of authority, the Aragonese were well agreed, though the immediate problem was primarily one which affected the nobility. The great lords, who retained feudal powers long since surrendered in Castile, enjoyed virtual exemption from royal justice, and the entry of a Castilian viceroy would inevitably lead to the diminution of their privileges: their leader, the Duke of Villahermosa, had recently been deprived

[1] As an order which was neither secular, regular nor lay the traditional church desired to exclude them from the pulpit and confessional. Their own universalistic ideals made them challenge the theory of racial purism supported by the Dominicans and the Inquisition.

of his estates in Ribagorza and was therefore aggrieved.[1] The lower nobility feared that Castilianisation would reduce them in rank or abolish their representation in cortes; and they were the most passionate opponents of royal interference. The duty of reaching a decision lay with the justicia of Aragon, who, with his court, was arbitrator of the Aragonese fueros, and Philip sent the Marquis of Almenara to Saragossa to put the case for appointing a 'foreign' viceroy before the justicia's court. While the king thus exposed his claim to a possible rebuff, his representative sought to influence opinion by lavish entertainment, but this policy only made him suspected and mocked and his table-companions were dubbed 'Knights of the Soup'.

It needed little to convince the Aragonese that Philip was a tyrant. Pérez was condemned to death for murder and treason in Madrid, and Philip demanded his extradition: but the Aragonese readily believed his own version that Philip had been privy to the death of Escobedo, and they refused to give him up. Consequently in 1591 Pérez was moved from the justicia's prison to the Inquisition. At once the Aragonese traditionalists spread word that their fueros had been violated and turned an angry mob against the house of Almenara (who died of the wounds he received) and the palace of the Inquisition: when they threatened to burn the latter down, Pérez was released and escorted back to the prison of the justicia.

These riots gave Philip a justification for breaking through the network of privileges. He had now moved Castilian forces to the frontier and was with his usual deliberation consulting his councils before he 'invaded' Aragon and its fueros. With the death of Almenara there was sufficient evidence of lack of public order in Saragossa. Philip carefully sounded the Council of Aragon and the more subservient cities of the kingdom about the punishment of the rioters, and they issued declarations in his favour; but in Saragossa itself there was still strong feeling in favour of Pérez and

---

[1] His brother the Count of Ribagorza had been hanged on a false charge of unnatural vice. He had murdered his adulterous wife: this was not a crime, but she was a sister-in-law to Philip's friend and adviser, the Count of Chinchón, so an accusation had to be fabricated.

resistance. Already the moderates had been alarmed by the rebellious cries of 'Liberty!', and after several months they arranged that Pérez should be restored to the Inquisition: however, a group of his friends had little difficulty in staging a riot to cover his escape to France, where he devoted the rest of his life to waging a war of propaganda against Philip, whom he presented to the world as a monster of iniquity. The King's attempts to have him murdered were foiled, and he died in Paris in 1611.

His escape had been facilitated by the death of the old justicia, whose young son fell entirely into the hands of extreme autonomists and decided to match Philip's show of force with force, proclaiming that the impending invasion was an infringement of the fueros and hurriedly forming an army of resistance. The young justicia accepted the command, but took fright and fled, and the Castilians had no difficulty in entering the city.[1] The pacification was easily completed. A group of the nobility was imprisoned, including Villahermosa, who was accused of seeking to set up a republic. The Inquisition instituted numerous trials and condemned eighty persons to die; but Philip exercised his clemency and spared all but a handful. One of those who perished was the justicia, the unfortunate symbol of autonomy, who was executed, but buried with all the pomp due to his office.

In the following year the cortes of Tarazona (June 1592) approved the abolition of the hereditary office of the justicia and radical changes in the government of Aragon. It was now accepted that the viceroy might be non-Aragonese and the justicia became a royal appointment terminable at the royal pleasure; the judges of his court were all also appointees and the right of appeal to them was restricted. In cortes, the representation of the great nobles was limited to eight, or more if the king chose to summon them, and the separate estate of the lower nobility disappeared. The number of towns entitled to appear was reduced and the Aragonese principle that redress must precede supply was weakened by setting a limit to the time to be spent in the discussion of

[1] As Spain was then at war with France it was declared that they would enter Aragon on their way to the front: this, Philip's legalists pronounced, would be no breach of the fueros.

grievances, so that although the main object of the crown was still to get a closure, it could not henceforth be subjected to unseemly indignities in doing so.

These reforms established the King of Castile in place of the justicia as the fountain of justice in Aragon and greatly extended his political powers at the expense of the Aragonese nobility. A kingdom without a king, Aragon had scarcely modified its constitution since the beginning of the century, and its defiance of Castile was rather a defence of an archaic baronialism than the expression of a deep-seated sense of national interest. Now the attenuation of its political and juridicial autonomy led to a steady process of Castilianisation: in 1701 it inclined to Castile rather than to Catalonia in the War of the Spanish Succession, and by 1812 it surpassed even Castile in the dourness of its resistance to Napoleon. In Catalonia, however, the desire for independence remained obdurate; and Philip was content merely to drive a wedge between the two ancient divisions of the eastern kingdom.

Philip's respect for Catalan susceptibilities was rooted in his fear of a renewal of French power, which had so often exploited the discontent of the Principality. Until 1572 he had watched the dissensions of the French with some detachment, but the prospect of a protestant succession in Paris caused him to open negotiations with the Duke of Guise and the French catholic party, who readily agreed to recognise Spanish preponderance in the Netherlands in return for his moral and material support. This in turn stiffened his policy towards England. True to the Emperor's principle of friendship with England against France, Philip had suffered Elizabeth's protection of the Sea-Beggars, the attacks of her privateers on his shipping and ports in the New World, and her seizure of bullion consigned to the Netherlands: he had even dissuaded the Pope from excommunicating her. This long-suffering policy was dictated by his fear that the French catholics might succeed in placing Mary Queen of Scots on the English throne and so in barring his access to the Netherlands. But as Elizabeth, while returning his expressions of friendship, allowed her corsairs to harass, smuggle and rob the length and breadth of his possessions in America, and France continued to be rent with religious and political dissensions, the danger of the Franco-Scottish catholic league gave way to the more disturbing possibility of an Anglo-French protestant alliance. When the Queen of France sheltered the Portuguese pretender and sent her expedition to the Azores on his behalf, Philip was forced to seal his alliance with the Catholic League in France, while supporting the Irish rebels against the English queen. Elizabeth had now to accept the consequences of her double policy: in 1584 she dismissed Philip's ambassador and made an alliance with the Dutch, sending Leicester with a small army to their aid. This was a clear alignment, for in 1579, Alexander Farnese had drawn together the catholics of the southern Netherlands, and William of Orange had ranged the protestant provinces against them in the League of Utrecht. Alexander won Antwerp and was threatening the very existence of the northern provinces when he was killed in 1584: Elizabeth's intervention was timed to prevent the total collapse of the Dutch provinces.

Now that he had friends in France, Philip decided on a direct invasion of England. Since the naval victories of Santa Cruz at Lepanto and the Azores, confidence in Castilian sea-power had mounted, and a great fleet was now prepared in the yards of Lisbon and northern Spain to carry an army from the Peninsula and transport Farnese's veterans from Flanders. The conception was a military one, and provided that the armies could land, it promised success. Early in 1587 Drake attacked the ships building in Lisbon and Cádiz, and did such damage as to force a postponement, but in May 1588 the Invincible Armada was finally ready to sail, carrying a force of about 30,000. It was obliged by storm to put in at Corunna, and was intercepted as it sailed up the Channel to embark Farnese's contingents. In a series of running actions fought from the Isle of Wight to Calais, the Spaniards suffered serious, though not fatal, losses. A Dutch diversion held up Farnese, and his troops were not ready to leave; and as the Spanish waited, an English attack, coupled with an unexpected gale, spread confusion among them. Abandoning the Netherlands contingents, the Armada sailed north to round Scotland and so regain Spain without risking the narrows. The route was unfamiliar, and many of the ships unsupplied for such an enterprise: some sixty-three of them, and about a third of the troops, were lost.

The Armada had been a supreme effort: its cost added enormously to Philip's debts, and after it he could make only half-hearted attempts against Elizabeth. Her own attempt to establish the Prior of Crato in Lisbon in the following year was a wretched failure; but in 1596 Essex' raid on Cádiz dealt a fatal blow to Spanish sea-power.

In France, the year of the Armada had also seen the murder of the Duke of Guise, who for the past four years had received a pension from Philip II as the head of the catholic movement against a protestant succession. Throwing off their tutelage, the last of the Valois, Henry III, now made an alliance with the Huguenots and accepted the succession of his distant relative Henry of Navarre. In reply, the catholics stirred up the people of Paris, and in August 1589 Henry was murdered by a Dominican monk.

At this moment Philip II entertained strong hopes that he would himself be elected to the vacant throne, thus gaining by patient diplomacy what his father's many victories had never achieved. But the new head of the house of Guise had his own ambitions and the Catholic League dare not risk placing a Spaniard on the throne. Meanwhile, Henry of Navarre won over the 'politiques' who stood between the two religious factions, defeated the Catholic League at Ivry and laid siege to Paris.

Philip now bade Farnese advance from the Netherlands and drive off the Huguenots; and on August 30, 1590, the French capital was occupied by a Spanish garrison. Although Philip's agents did their best to win popularity by distributing gifts, this very demonstration of his power sufficed to ruin his cause. The Catholic League now rejected even the accession of a French prince married to Philip's daughter, the niece of Henry III, and Philip's proposal that Brittany should be detached for her, proved no more acceptable. In 1592 Farnese, his outstanding soldier and diplomat, saved Rouen from Henry of Navarre, but soon after was wounded and died. He had temporarily persuaded the French catholics to accept the claim of the Spanish princess, but their real intentions were to retain Philip's support without being committed to his candidate. When the States-General assembled in Paris in January 1593, the Spanish case was presented by the Duke of Feria, whose proposals for the marriage of the princess to the Austrian heir and for her immediate recognition were received with diminishing sympathy. Meanwhile, Henry of Navarre had agreed to adopt catholicism and was duly crowned at Chartres in 1594: in the following year the Pope accepted this expedient conversion despite the interested protests of Philip against its insincerity.

Philip had perhaps prevented a Huguenot from reigning in France, but the accession of Henry IV was followed by a renewal of war between the two countries early in 1595. Although Philip won Amiens two years later, his French supporters dwindled and Henry steadily consolidated his throne. In May 1598 Philip, now within a few months of his own end, concluded the peace of Vervins: by it he virtually restored that of Cateau-Cambrésis with which his reign had begun.

During the last years the shrunken figure who governed a vast empire from a modest apartment in the massive mausoleum he had built to his father's memory had become almost a legend among his people. They approved his resumption of Castilian sobriety after the Emperor's Burgundian extravagance; they identified themselves with his ambitions; and they respected his love of justice, even if they grew tired of waiting for it. But it may be doubted if this affection existed among his courtiers: the great nobility had too long been held at arm's length; the seekers of sinecures had too long witnessed successive retrenchments in the royal household; and, above all, Philip had consistently shown himself jealous of competence. His few trusted servants were all survivors of an older generation: newcomers felt themselves underrated by 'a brain that thought it knew all that could be known and treated everyone else as a blockhead'.

So in August 1598, the King entered upon his last illness, a distressing and disgusting one, which he bore with fortitude.

On September 13th, this small man cast in a great mould breathed his last.

3. THE NEW WORLD

Soon after the accession of the Emperor the empty world which Columbus had presented to the Catholic Monarchs became suddenly scarcely less valuable than the splendid East for which he had mistaken it.

In the first stages of the discovery, the only Spanish settlements had been on the islands of Hispaniola and Cuba. Coastal navigation had revealed the general outline of the eastern coast of the Americas as far south as the River Plate—an apparently endless shore with great forests, torpid rivers and primitive Indian tribes. Since 1508, when the fact of the new land-mass was already understood, preparations were made to cross it. In that year Nicuesa led an expedition to Panama, where a permanent settlement was made by Vasco Núñez de Balboa, and in 1512 Ponce de León explored Florida, still hoping that the continent of North America might yield the key to Marco Polo's Cipango.

Hitherto the whole adventure of America had brought many hardships and no large rewards. There was ample land in the Antilles, and an agricultural exploitation like that of the Azores and Madeiras was simplified by the presence of an Indian population. But in 1513 Núñez de Balboa made his way from Darien across the isthmus of Panama and became the first European to behold the Pacific. The problems of reaching the true India and of possessing the New World now bifurcated. In 1518 Charles accepted the plan of a Portuguese, Fernando de Magalhãis, who had sailed to India by way of Africa and taken part in the conquest of Malacca, but afterwards quarrelled with his own king and came to Castile. He proposed to reach the Spice Islands from the west and by forestalling his fellow-countrymen to close the gap left by the Treaty of Tordesillas, which had divided the Atlantic, but not Asia itself. Magellan sailed from Sanlúcar in September 1519, rounded Cape Horn by the straits that bear his name and entered the waters of the ocean which he christened Pacific.[1] Three months later he touched the archipelago of the Marianas and landed in the Philippines, where he was to die in a fight with the natives. The command passed to his Basque pilot, Juan Sebastián de Elcano, who, after visiting Borneo and obtaining a cargo of spices in the Moluccas, crossed the Indian ocean to Moçambique and returned by the Portuguese route round the Cape of Good Hope. Magellan himself did not quite complete the circumnavigation of the world: his service with the Portuguese had taken him as far east as Malacca and he died in the Philippines; consequently the Emperor awarded Elcano the arms of the globe with the motto *Primus me circumdedisti*.

This achievement crowned the great campaign of maritime discovery that had followed the forcing of the straits. Meanwhile, the Spaniards had begun the task of conquering America, the imperial enterprise which was to transfer the energies and experiences of the reconquest to the New World. In 1517 Hernández de Córdoba had fought his way to the Peninsula of Yucatan and come upon the high native civilisation of the Mayas, then in decline. The exploits of Hernández and his successor Grijalba determined Hernán Cortés to attempt his own conquest, and he obtained permission from the governor of Cuba to organise an expedition. Cortés, born at Medellín in Extremadura of a family of poor hidalgos of Aragonese origin, had come to the Antilles in 1504, and had proved his character and enterprise in the royal service. He raised eleven ships with six hundred men, sixteen horses and a few small cannon, and so sailed for the mainland, ignoring the governor's demand that he should return. Landing near Tabasco, he made contact with and defeated the Tlaxcaltecs, a people formerly independent, but now subject to the Aztecs. From them he took a native mistress and learned of the great Indian empire with its capital at the lake-city of Mexico. At Veracruz he received an embassy from Montezuma, and accordingly renounced the authority of the governor of Cuba and established his own colony, sending a report to Spain in order to

---

[1] This name displaced that given by the Spaniards of Panama, the Southern Sea.

obtain royal countenance for his insubordination. Leaving a small garrison behind, he began his famous march against Mexico, which he entered on November 8, 1519. This great capital reminded the Spaniards of an imaginary city in some novel of chivalry. Its ruler had heard of Cortés' victories and of his mysterious cannon and horses, and welcomed him for what he pretended to be, the messenger of the greatest ruler in the world and of God's vicar on earth. The Spaniards were lodged in a palace, which they proceeded to fortify, and when one of them was killed in a scuffle with the Indians, Cortés demanded that Montezuma should become a hostage, acknowledge the Emperor, adopt Christianity and pay tribute.

Montezuma was disposed to give way, short of renouncing his own gods. But after four months Cortés received news that the governor of Cuba had sent an expedition of 1,400 men under Pánfilo de Narváez to put an end to his unofficial conquest. He therefore left a garrison in Mexico, and taking about half his total force, marched on Narváez and surprised him. Most of the newcomers at once acclaimed Cortés as their leader. But in his absence the garrison left in the Aztec capital was attacked by the Mexicans. Cortés returned and entered the city: he attempted to use Montezuma to pacify his subjects, but the captive emperor was wounded and died. Without this weapon the Spaniards had no control over the Indians, and on July 1st, 1520, Cortés fought his way across the causeways with heavy losses and retired to Otumba. But the prospect of losing the capital and its treasures stirred the Spaniards to a new effort. Collecting an auxiliary army from tribes subdued by the Aztecs, Cortés dispersed the Mexican forces and returned to the city: this time it was conquered and plundered.

Once the ruling race had been dominated, Cortés devoted himself to the erection of a Spanish town and a Spanish administration. In spite of the opposition of his rivals, he was given great honours and full powers by the Emperor, becoming Marquis of the Valley of Oaxaca and adelantado of the Pacific. But in 1535 Charles sent out an aristocrat, Don Antonio de Mendoza, with the title of Viceroy, and the quarrels between the conqueror and his superior grew so bitter that Cortés came to Europe to appeal to the Emperor. He took part in the unsuccessful attack on Algiers, and died in Spain in 1547.

Securely established on the foundations of the Aztec civilisation, Spanish power was rapidly extended throughout Mexico. Cortés himself campaigned in what is now Guatemala, annexing new peoples to the Viceroyalty of New Spain and appointing commanders to the frontier areas of Central America. Within a generation of its discovery, Mexico was already a Spanish city, with its soldiers, officials, merchants, priests, printing-press and university.

The conquest of Mexico filled Spaniards with a sense of wonder and pride. Mexicans in robes of feathers were seen at court; a hoard of strange carvings in jade was presented by Cortés to the Emperor, and tales of Spanish heroism against the Aztecs were repeated far and wide. A certain unreality, as of a story or dream come true, overhung the conquest, and invested it, for all its brutality, with an air of romantic predestination.

The second great conquest of the New World, that of the Inca empire of Peru, if it lacked these qualities of surprise and delight, satisfied even more amply the desire for wealth and power. The kingdom of Tahuantinsuyu (the Four Quarters) had been built up by an active military caste, whose capital was at Cuzco in the high Andes. They had developed an extraordinary capacity for social organisation and had imposed their rule on all their neighbours, the heirs of a long series of indigenous civilisations, from the border of what is now Ecuador to central Chile, and from the fringes of the Amazonian forest to the sea. The head of the dominant caste was worshipped as a Child of the Sun, and a strict hierarchy of officials apportioned work and rewards among their subject peoples. At the time of the Spanish conquest the throne of the Incas had been the subject of a contest between Huáscar, the heir to the old kingdom of Cuzco, and his half-brother, Atahuallpa, the ruler of the north, who had recently been victorious and captured the ancestral capital.

Rumours of the existence of this empire were received by Spaniards navigating in the 'Southern Sea' from the Isthmus in 1520 or shortly before. The right to explore what is now northern

Colombia had first been held by Pascual de Andagoya, but was acquired by a partnership consisting of Francisco Pizarro, a native of Trujillo in Extremadura and a distant kinsman of Cortés, Diego de Almagro, a soldier of fortune of humble origins, and Hernando de Luque, a priest in Panama. In 1524 they signed a contract by which Luque supplied capital, and the others undertook to share the proceeds of the conquest with him. The first attempts of this 'Southern Enterprise' were unsuccessful,[1] but in 1526 Pizarro reached an island, the Gallo, where all but thirteen of his companions turned back. The discovery of Túmbez confirmed the existence of the Inca empire and proved the inadequacy of the adventurers' resources; and Pizarro was sent to Spain to obtain the Emperor's support. At Toledo in 1529 he received extensive concessions; his thirteen loyal companions were made 'hidalgos'; he himself became governor and captain-general of whatever he should conquer, while Almagro was accorded the modest distinction of governor of Túmbez; the crown contributed half a million maravedis towards the cost of the expedition. In January 1530 Pizarro, now accompanied by his brothers, rejoined Almagro, and a year later they sailed from Panama and landed at Túmbez, whence 168 Spaniards set out to conquer an empire of many millions. Nothing was yet known of Cuzco, and Pizarro therefore marched towards the former northern capital at Tomebamba, which had probably been destroyed during the civil wars. Meanwhile, Atahuallpa advanced to Cajamarca, and the Spaniards set out to meet him there. Pizarro knew from Cortés' experience that the secret of success lay in capturing the source of authority; and on meeting Atahuallpa he ordered his men to seize him. The handful of horses and small troop of men with firearms put the Indian army to flight. Atahuallpa was dragged to the Spanish camp, and readily undertook to fill the room in which he was placed with gold and silver in order to obtain his release. The arrest took place on November 16, 1532, and within a few months the room was almost filled. But Spaniards sent out

[1] Its participants were known as 'the men of Peru' from some chieftain or river on the way: the word was thus popularly applied to the Inca empire. Attempts to impose the official titles of 'New Castile' and 'New Toledo' failed.

to assess the inflow of treasure brought reports of an Inca plan to release the King, and in August 1533 Pizarro accused him of the murder of his half-brother and had him baptised and garrotted.

The removal of Atahuallpa enabled Pizarro to appoint a captive Inca and to send Almagro forward to capture Cuzco. But the capital was extremely remote from his base, and in 1535 he decided to found a new city at the mouth of the river Rímac, or Lima. His claim to govern Cuzco was now disputed by Almagro, and the boundary between their two jurisdictions as laid down by royal grant proved impossible to determine. Almagro at first agreed to march southwards into what is now Chile, but this expedition demonstrated that there were no new sources of bullion there and he hastily returned to renew his claim to Cuzco. At the same time, the Indians rebelled against the Spaniards, and for a moment both cities were almost lost. But at Lima the Incas were driven off, and in Cuzco Almagro remained master of the old capital, with Pizarro's brothers his captives. He still refused to cede his claims, and was finally defeated, tried and executed by Hernando Pizarro. After his death his son, Diego the younger, rallied the Almagrists and murdered Francisco Pizarro in Lima (1541).

In order to end the strife between the two factions, the Emperor now sent out a governor, Vaca de Castro, who formed a royalist army and defeated the younger Almagro. But many of the first conquerors remained extremely dissatisfied with the rewards they had received; and the sending of the first Viceroy, the choleric Blasco Núñez de Vela, caused them to rebel, choosing as their leader Pizarro's youngest brother, Gonzalo. In the course of the struggle, the Viceroy was first deported, and when he imprudently attempted to return, defeated and killed. A pacification was finally achieved by a new governor, Pedro de la Gasca, a modest priest, whose energy and subtlety were too much for the warring conquerors. Even he scarcely dared judge the importunate demands put forward by the jealous settlers, and departed for Spain, leaving others to enforce his redistribution of the land. For some years yet disgruntled captains formed 'Armies of Liberation' and made *pronunciamientos* against an ungrateful crown; but finally, the long viceroyalty of Don Francisco de Toledo suppressed the troubles, satisfied the Spaniards at the expense of the mestizos, ended the independence of the fugitive Incas and established a colonial order that was to last for more than two centuries.

The great centres of Spanish power in the Americas were built upon the seats of Indian civilisations, where the principal stores of treasure were accumulated; but before the end of the sixteenth century much of the South American continent, most of Central America, and a large part of North America had been explored and occupied. From Mexico, Alvarado and Cortés had entered Guatemala, whence Nicaragua and Honduras were partly explored (1523). In 1527 Charles, in an attempt to satisfy his German creditors, granted the Welsers rights to settle Venezuela, where their governors conducted a bloody war with the Indians.

After the conquest of Peru many adventurers from Central America were attracted there, and some passed into the service of Pizarro, who gave his followers the opportunity to make new conquests to the north, east and south of the Inca empire. In 1534 Belalcázar entered Quito, formerly Atahuallpa's northern capital, and explored the southern valleys of Colombia, and in 1540 Pedro de Valdivia occupied Chile and founded Santiago, whence the Spaniards fought a long and difficult war against the Araucanians. In Colombia, the rumoured existence of the Golden Man, el Dorado, attracted many adventurers. Jiménez de Quesada, following the Magdalena river from Santa Marta on the Caribbean coast, entered the land of the Chibchas, the highest South American civilisation outside the Inca empire, in 1536, and other expeditions from Ecuador and Venezuela reached the same region within the next few years. So persistent was the legend of el Dorado that Pizarro's youngest brother, Gonzalo, who had already explored much of Los Charcos (Bolivia), on assuming the governorship of Quito, began to drive eastward into the forests of the Upper Amazon (1539). Having marched and floated some way down the river, he was abandoned by his follower Orellana, who took their improvised launch and became the first man to sail down the greatest river system in the world, eventually reaching the Spanish settlement at Trinidad. Returning to Spain, Orellana was granted a commission to colonise Amazonia, only to die in the attempt.

In the south-eastern quarter of the continent, Juan Díaz de Solís had sailed up the River Plate in 1515, and survivors of his expedition later reached the uplands of Bolivia, there to perish. A first fort was established on the shores of the River Plate by Sebastian Cabot, who sailed in the wake of Magellan in 1527, but stayed to explore the system of the Paraná and Paraguay, on which he bestowed the misleading title of the River of Silver (Río de la Plata). A group of Díaz de Solís' men reached the fringe of the Inca empire and returned to Spain, where they found that the Emperor had already given his support to Pizarro. Once news of Pizarro's conquest was learned in Europe, the prospect of tapping its resources from the River Plate became an alluring one, and in 1536 Pedro de Mendoza was awarded the right to colonise Buenos Aires: his expedition succumbed to disease and starvation, but one of his followers established the first colony in Paraguay at Asunción. Ten years later explorers from Peru discovered Mendoza's ruined fort: for a moment 'Peruvians' came into conflict with 'Paraguayans'; but the claims of the latter were at last upheld, and it was they who succeeded in establishing a permanent colony at Buenos Aires in 1580, thus completing the cycle of foundations of the cities which now form the capitals of Latin America.

Except for the German settlers in Venezuela and a scattering of Portuguese and Italians, the conquest and civilisation of America was achieved entirely by Spaniards. In theory, Moriscos and Jews were excluded; but these regulations were perhaps never fully effective. Emigration no longer followed the Madeiran pattern, in which a landowner would take with him his household and labourers, but certain areas were colonised by regional groups, Extremadurans, Galicians or Leonese: many emigrants of the generation of Cortés and Pizarro were from Extremadura, and for years the mere fact of being a native of that province opened all doors in Peru. In parts of Central America, especially Costa Rica, Galician peasant practices still survive, while the seafaring

Basques were soon found in most of the ports of America. At the time of the conquest of Peru there was great mobility among the settlers, but this gradually diminished, especially after the regular entry of European women in the second half of the century.

The pattern of discovery and conquest inevitably dictated that of administration. Columbus vainly strove to keep the exclusive rights he had acquired from Isabella: the Antilles required not an Admiral of the Ocean, but a series of governors able to keep order among the colonists and speed the work of establishment. Once the mainland was reached, the acquisition of the Mexican and Peruvian states presented new problems. The 'first conquerors' claimed exclusive rights to what they had won, sending their subordinates out to make new discoveries, and resisting the attempts of the crown to dispose of their lands. Absolute monarchs quickly ended this new baronialism by restricting the original grants to one or two lives, and by the middle of the century royal power was well established in Mexico and the feudalism of Peru was on the wane. Conquerors gave way to administrators; and while the heirs of the first settlers became a land-owning society dominating only the municipal government of the scattered towns, all important offices in the civil administration were held by Peninsular Spaniards, whose duty was to uphold the royal authority and whose ambition was to enrich themselves before returning home. Each new viceroy or governor[1] brought with him a new train of clients and functionaries, of whom only a relatively small proportion intended to settle in the New World.

In Europe, control of navigation to the New World was soon established at Seville. In view of the monopoly claimed by the crown it was inevitable that American affairs should be concentrated at a single port under royal jurisdiction in Castile. Columbus himself had sailed from the fishing-town of Palos, near Huelva, and for a moment the American trade was awarded to the open-sea

[1] The 'kingdoms' of the new world were *reinos* in the same sense as those of Toledo, Jaén or Murcia; i.e. areas regarded as independent states at the time of their conquest. Their governors were only entitled viceroys when they happened to be of the highest social rank: only later was the word viceroyalty applied to the territory.

port of Cádiz: but in 1503 its administration was given a permanent central organisation. This was the Casa de Contratación, or Board of Trade, housed in rooms in the alcázar of Seville. It consisted originally of a Factor, Treasurer and Secretary, who met daily and jointly disposed of all questions of shipping, supplies, trade, treasure and emigration. In 1510, after a dispute with the city, the Casa acquired its own magistrate; and once having attained judicial rights, all its officials were styled judges. In addition to its administrative duties, the Casa was also responsible for pilotage, and became a famous centre for nautical studies. Its first Pilot-Major was Vespucci, who was succeeded by Díaz de Solís and Cabot.

Until 1524 questions of Indian policy were settled by the crown and its secretaries. Bishop Rodríguez de Fonseca, who had specialised in these matters since the preparation of Columbus' second fleet, managed all correspondence with the royal governors from 1508, merely referring questions of justice to the Council of Castile. But in the general reconstruction undertaken by Charles American affairs were placed under a separate body, the Supreme Royal Council of the Indies, to which the Board of Trade in Seville was subordinated. The Council now subjected the Board to fairly regular examinations and intervened in its frequent disputes with the public authorities of Seville.

The creative work of the Council of the Indies consisted in the establishment of a new code of laws for a New World. The application of the laws of Castile to America became progressively more difficult as the settlers extended their control over large native populations, more susceptible than the Moriscos of being converted, and, it seemed, woven into a Spanish pattern of society. Thus the *repartimiento*, or division of conquered land and property which had been practised during the reconquest, gave way to the *encomienda* or 'trust', under which the Indian inhabitants were required to work for the conqueror who held their land, but were protected, indoctrinated and paid for work in excess of their tribute. In a society where money-values had been unknown, this system inevitably gave rise to grave and general abuses. In 1512 the Laws of Burgos had clarified what must and must not be expected of the Indians, but it was even then too late to apply these exacting regulations conceived in the detached and legalistic atmosphere of Castile to a society already very differently constituted. A long struggle for the welfare of the Indians was carried on by Bartolomé de las Casas, a landowner who in 1510 had become the first priest to be ordained in the New World. His attacks on the encomienda system led to the introduction of Negroes, who were regarded as naturally servile, into the New World, and also to attempts to stimulate Spanish peasant emigration, in the hope of producing a free mestizo society. But these experiments failed, and Las Casas fell back on the idea of a reform of the legal system, embodied in the New Laws of the Indies, promulgated in 1542. This would have limited the duration of existing encomiendas and prohibited the concession of new ones. It provoked such opposition that the Viceroy of Mexico was obliged to suspend it, while in Peru the settlers took up arms against the royal authorities. Las Casas himself returned to Europe and devoted himself to the composition of tracts on the abuses of the conquerors; his charges were in part well founded, but the general picture he drew of Spanish America was so black and his statistics so exaggerated that when translated and circulated among the nations of Europe they gave a devastating picture of Spanish colonisation which was extensively used by Spain's enemies. The encomienda system was gradually brought to an end; but in the mining areas of Peru and Mexico the substitution of forced labour by drafts, so that all the male population was required to work a spell in the mines, produced similar, if different, abuses and evasions.

4. SPAIN IN THE SIXTEENTH CENTURY

After the upheaval of the 'comunidades', Spanish domestic history disappears in a profusion of incidents in Italy, Germany, the Netherlands, France, Mediterranean Africa and America. Imperialism raised a superstructure of interests above and beyond the Spanish state; and even when it had been removed, its legacy of pretensions and taxation continued to overburden the minds

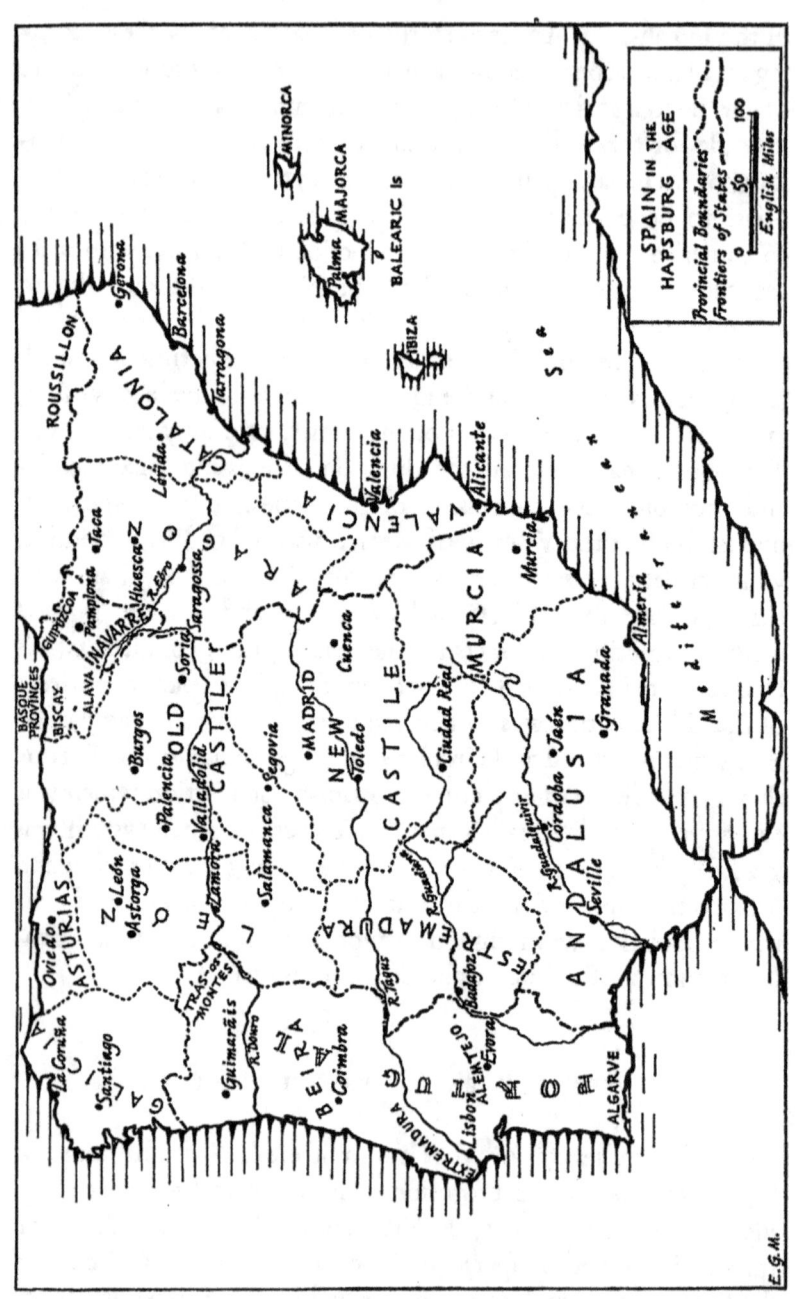

and lives of succeeding generations. For Charles, successively Archduke, King and Emperor, Spain was the intermediate reality between two illusions: the exorbitant pretensions of his house and the unrealisable hope of a universal state. Whether he was seeking to embrace the whole of Christendom or striving to hold together a crumbling inheritance, success or failure depended on Spain: '*je ne puis estre soubstenu sinon de mes royaulmes d'Espaigne*', he told his brother. After the revolt of Castile, he attempted to adapt Spain to his most pressing needs, reforming the system of Councils so as to strengthen those of war and finance, as in Burgundy, and reshaping the class system of Castile to form an imperial nobility. But since he was invariably distracted by larger issues and must always study Castilian prejudices, such changes were not pressed home or rigorously enforced. So that he might attend to imperial matters his advisers recommended that all Spanish affairs which did not involve war or finance should be reduced to a routine that could be performed by an official with a seal: an excess of new laws would reflect on the competence of his predecessors and was to be avoided. Similarly, such domestic questions as the indoctrination or expulsion of the Moriscos, in which any decision might deplete the imperial treasury or aggrieve the great landowners, were evaded. Thus if the empire brought immense changes in the outlook of Castilians, it also left many mediaeval situations unaltered; and both Charles' reluctance to settle political questions and his constant demands for money tended to entrench his Spanish subjects behind their traditional rights and usages.

Philip II's outlook was, by contrast, intensely Castilian: his very birth was a pledge by his father that Spanish interests would not be neglected. Owing to the Emperor's long absences, he was educated by his pious Portuguese mother and taught little about the wider world: even the advice Charles wrote down for him was concerned with persons rather than with policies. In his first regency, as a mere boy, Philip, guided by Cardinal Tavera, then President of Castile, was well grounded in the duties of a Spanish ruler, the conservation and expansion of the faith and of royal authority and the dispensation of justice. He learnt to regard himself as the fountain-head of all equity and wisdom, under God, and conceived it his duty to carry his authority to every corner of his kingdom, thus perfecting the work of Isabella. Already on his first visit to the Netherlands his rigid views were well known; and before his second visit news of his intention to resuscitate the Inquisition preceded him, and confirmed his reputation as an autocrat.

But in Castile the ruler's authority was far from absolute. On his accession he was required to swear to obey all the laws and customs of his realms, and to make no fundamental change without consulting them. In Charles' time the constant need for money made it impossible for the crown to force its authority on cortes and when on two occasions he endeavoured to obtain consent to a universal tax, he was conspicuously defeated: in the end a change of system was negotiated town by town, but never promulgated as a general law. At first Philip, who could ask for new taxation as a Spaniard and not as an international institution, still met with similar opposition; but in the course of time the weight of his central government became much greater. The crown's very power derived in part from the assumption that its actions were reasonable: 'in France people tolerate such things since the king rules rather as a despot than as a natural lord and follows his whim rather than reason', it was believed. Philip had few whims; but he gradually acquired a peculiar monopoly of reasonableness bordering on omniscience. His dislike of opposition led him steadily to reduce the area of regional and individual rights and privileges. In case of necessity a higher 'reason of state' was held to justify unconstitutional actions, but grave Spaniards resented this 'new doctrine'. Even when it was reduced to an appearance, legality remained the over-riding preoccupation in Philip's state.

As in the days of Ferdinand and Isabella, the monarch governed through a group of councils to which the organs of administration, justice and finance were subordinated. The downthrust of royal authority met the upthrust of popular representation in the municipality, where the king's nominee, the corregidor, sat with elected alcaldes and regidores, and in cortes, at which a limited number of towns presented proposals for redress. Although the picture appears to be one of autocracy, the peculiar decentralisation of royal power through the corregidors had arisen from the need for the crown to protect municipal government from abuses, and by means of this extended regalism the crown could impose itself in widely separated cities and areas of strongly marked geographical and social differentiation which have never found any adequate way of representing themselves in a single parliament or cortes.

Between the monarch and his Councils stood the royal secretaries. Since the death of Gattinara, Charles had resolved never to give himself to a single minister and recommended his son to follow his example. But while Charles had attended his Council of State and relied on such men as Cobos and the elder Granvelle to conduct his financial affairs or diplomatic negotiations, Philip, by parental counsel and a natural instinct to sever himself from men of more forceful character than his own, withdrew from personal contact with the Councils and dealt with them by written communications. Because of this, he was scarcely approachable except through his secretaries, who usually reflected his own timeless industriousness.

Of the dozen or so Councils, some dealt with the affairs of certain kingdoms, Aragon, the Indies, Italy (from 1555), Portugal (from 1582) and briefly, Flanders; others with special departments, Finance, the Inquisition, the Military Orders, the Cruzada. Above them all stood the Councils of State and of Castile. The first of these was the ancient *curia* of the Kings of Castile, and consequently by tradition a preserve of the nobility, the mediaeval warlords; since their tutelage had been thrown off, it had no official president and no regular sessions, but was summoned at the royal pleasure as a whole or in part. Charles introduced foreigners to it and treated it as his privy council for imperial affairs, but under Philip it was promptly Castilianised and turned into a purely consultative body composed of retired viceroys and other elder statesmen: when reinforced by military experts it continued to serve as a Council of War.

The effective control of domestic affairs had passed to the Royal

Council of Castile, reconstituted in 1480 with a predominance of jurists representing not only Castile, but the lower Councils as well. Its chairman, the 'President of Castile', enjoyed special dignity, and under Charles was invariably an ecclesiastic, the great nobility being excluded on principle: Philip, however, appointed a former viceroy, a nobleman, several clerics and the energetic jurist Espinosa (1565–72). This body was at once the supreme political cabinet and the highest court of appeal in the land. In 1575 one important branch of this Council's work, questions of appointments and patronage, was put under the 'chamber of Castile'. But it was only in the last year of Philip's reign that the Council was divided into two 'salas' which sat separately, thus establishing the distinction between the administrative cabinet and the supreme court of appeal.

In the Council of Aragon, the vice-chancellor and 'regents' were natives of the three eastern kingdoms, whose interests they represented in the Council of Castile through a delegation. The regents of Aragon were all jurists, and were carefully precluded from making political decisions, so that the tradition of Aragonese sovereignty was slowly stifled. This process is most clearly seen in the affairs of Italy. The Spanish interest in Sicily and Naples was of Aragonese origin; but Charles had possessed himself of Milan in his imperial capacity and delivered it to Philip as heir to Castile. In 1554, when Philip married Mary Tudor, he was also invested with the crown of Naples, and a year later, on his father's abdication, with that of Sicily. Thus the whole Aragonese interest in Italy was gradually lifted out of the control of the eastern kingdom and centralised in the crown, and the encroachment was completed by the formation of a Council of Italy, an act which did not pass unchallenged in the cortes of Catalonia.

A third Council of general importance was that of the Inquisition. This body, despite its religious function, was controlled by the crown, and now threatened to become a means for assuring the allegiance of all Spaniards to one king and one church; it was in fact the only direct instrument of royal justice in the semi-autonomous kingdoms of Aragon. At first the eastern kingdoms had had a separate Inquisitor-General; and the assimilation of the office with that of Castile was much resented. But even papal representations against the enlargement of the Inquisition's jurisdiction were unavailing, and Philip never ceased to favour this useful body, with its ten regional inquisitions and its twenty thousand familiars, who enjoyed privileges and a small salary in return for reporting offences against the faith. If as a 'thought-police' (in a state which had no other) its efficiency was moderate, as a source of sinecures it remained unrivalled.

Of the remaining Councils, the chief were those of Finance and the Indies, through which the crown collected at least a portion of the revenues paid to it. In the days of Ferdinand and Isabella the finances of the state were still controlled by the Mayor-domo or Great Chamberlain through a court of accounts and a finance office. This honeypot was too strong an attraction for the nobility, and already in 1517 Charles appointed a Secretary for Finance, the Andalusian Francisco de los Cobos, who for thirty years was his chief financial officer. On his return from the north, Charles instituted the Council of Finance, modelled on that of Burgundy, through which he hoped to centralise all receipts and authorise all payments. It began to function early in 1523 under Count Henry of Nassau-Dillenburg, but it was soon Castilianised and from 1529 onwards Cobos was its moving spirit. Although the aristocracy was successfully excluded in favour of bureaucrats, whose peculations were on a more modest scale, it proved quite impossible to harness expenditure to revenue, partly because of the resistance of interested or privileged parties and partly because of the soaring rate of extraordinary expenditure. From the time of Charles' imperial coronation receipts bore no relation to charges, and the function of the Council was to conceal the disastrous disequilibrium by pledging everything that was pledgeable. During the period of his wars with Francis I Charles' revenues were in theory rather greater than those of his rival, though in practice inefficiency in collection and arrears made him the poorer of the two. From 1550 he was borrowing from two to four million ducats a year, and had pawned his revenues for several years ahead: arrears of debt averaged about two million ducats and interest-rates were approaching fifty per cent: these material difficulties form the background of Charles' physical and nervous collapse. He himself proposed to oblige his creditors to accept a reduction in their claims, but the Finance Council refused to permit a scheme which they thought would finally ruin his credit.

Philip II refused to repudiate his father's debts, but was twice obliged to suspend payments in order to force his bankers to accept more favourable terms. He appointed a Factor-General with theoretical powers to receive all monies; but, like many reforms, this was never achieved. The Council of the Indies resisted the intrusion of that of Finance and their dual control of the Board of Trade in Seville merely led to confusion. In 1593 Finance sought to prevent the Indies from making any disbursement without previous sanction; after protests from Seville a ruling was obtained that urgent expenditure might be incurred, provided that it was at once reported. Four years later a further attempt met with no greater success. Moreover, certain finances escaped these two bodies, since the minor Councils of the Military Orders and the Cruzada dealt with concessions granted by the papacy from the revenues of the church. There was no real system of intercommunication between the Councils, and questions affecting more than one or raising problems of jurisdiction could only be settled by reference to the crown.

The men who governed Spain in the sixteenth century were predominantly jurists. This class virtually monopolised the Councils of Castile, Aragon, the Indies and Finance. Most of them were trained in the universities of Valladolid, Salamanca and Alcalá de Henares, and they had usually served for a term in the provincial courts or municipalities. Entry to the Council of Castile was rarely gained by anyone who had not served for a long period in one of the lower councils. Thus the effective control of the state lay in the hands of a relatively small body of men, perhaps less than a thousand during the two reigns, who were drawn mainly from the middle classes of Old Castile or Leon, educated in a uniform Romanist discipline, and subjected to a lengthy but rather narrow administrative experience.

In 1501 the Inquisition attempted to prevent the descendants of converted Jews or Muslims from entering the Councils, and there ensued a long contest between partisans of a pure Castilianism and those who held more liberal views. *Conversos* had held high office in Aragon and had been conspicuous in furthering the policy of unification under John II: in Castile, too, they had enjoyed great influence with Isabella. In Charles' time there were still some New Christians in the Council of Castile and more in Aragon; but after Paul IV had wildly denounced all Spaniards as 'Jews and schismatics' discrimination increased. When Philip's tutor, Cardinal Silíceo, was appointed to the diocese of Toledo, he forbade the admission of converts to the priesthood, and the struggle continued, with Jesuits and Dominicans taking opposite sides, during the rest of the reign.

The old nobility, whose leaders had for so long distinguished themselves by their destructive feuds and their ambitions to control or corrupt their ruler, had no recognisable cohesion when Charles came to the throne. In order perhaps to render their divisions permanent, he selected twenty-five members of twenty families and elevated them as great, '*grandes*'.[1] These were chosen rather to exalt the power of the crown than for any special distinction of antiquity or wealth: others attained the dignity from time to time, and by the end of the century the number of grandees had risen to about ninety. Members of the great families served the crown as generals, diplomats or viceroys: however, Charles never lost his mistrust of them and warned his son that Alba might try to establish a protectorate over the crown. Philip was careful to avoid intimacy with him or his rivals, and until the end of the century most, though not all, of the great names had to be content with only unimportant posts at court.

In fact a great social displacement had occurred. Old Castile regarded itself as of 'pure' stock, thus inheriting the tradition of those northern Visigoths who had resisted assimilation by intermarriage with the semitised Hispano-Romans of the south. In this attitude Castile distinguished itself from the Galaico-Portuguese and Aragonese areas during most of the Reconquest; but its supposed purity had been compromised after the capture of

[1] i.e. greater than the 'títulos del reino'.

Toledo in New Castile, and hopelessly lost in Andalusia. The ancient families of the north remained relatively modest, while their offshoots ruled over vast tracts of central and southern Spain and greatly eclipsed them in wealth and individual influence. But, unlike the peasant stock of Castile, they were no longer 'pure': so little so that when the disappointed author of the *Tizón de la Nobleza* began to examine genealogies he was able to allege that all the great families of Spain were tainted with Jewish blood.

But it was not beyond the power of Old Castile to produce a new dominating caste. She had supplied her early counts with 'peasant-knights' and still gave Cisneros *caballeros pardos*. She had moreover provided the class of jurists on whom the mantle of political power had fallen. The war of the comuneros accelerated the process of social cleavage; and throughout the sixteenth century the new caste of 'hidalgos' dominated Spain. This word had of old been loosely applied to all nobles; but it was now limited to the 'squirearchy', who differed in standing from the peasants, but could not claim antiquity of family. There was at first a formal hidalgo class, but entry was never closed, and by the end of the sixteenth century it had come rather to represent a set of principles and a way of life. If Charles could create the thirteen soldiers who stood by Pizarro 'hidalgos', he could also elevate many others for smaller services, even by subscription to the *juros*, or entailable bonds.[1] By the middle of Charles' reign virtually all members of the Councils and most procurators to cortes and corregidores, alcaldes and regidores were hidalgos. In some regions as much as a fifth of the population laid claim to *hidalguía*, and in Guipúzcoa the whole population boldly asserted it.

[1] The *juros* derived from the mediaeval practice by which the crown assigned revenues or annuities in payment of services rendered or in return for military obligations. These were collected by the beneficiary from an assigned source, so that the treasury received only the balance after these deductions had been made. But the word *juros* was also applied to the interest paid on state borrowings or bonds. When the crown required ready money, it would receive capital subscriptions, promising to pay a fixed rate of interest, up to seven per cent. *Hidalguía* was the bait offered by a desperate treasury for investments of this kind. Philip II still hesitated to countenance the outright sale of *hidalguía*, which only came into its own in the seventeenth century.

By the end of the century Castilian hidalguía had become a state of mind. The hidalgo was a catholic and a royalist, he had never worked with his hands, and abhorred trade and industry, which he consigned to Jews, Moriscos, foreigners and plebeians. His income was often as meagre as his pride was great. He might own a small and neglected property (as did the most famous hidalgo of all), but he more probably lived on state bonds, fixed rents (*censos*), or a small salary, preferably drawn from the king or a sinecure appointment. He was therefore the first to suffer from the constant depreciation of money values. But he had inherited the peasant virtues of sobriety, patience, courage, piety and respect for authority; and drew a firm line between them and the semitic vices of acquisitiveness, activity and change: others might live for to-morrow: he was content to live for to-day and eternity. But the hidalgo was not only the knight-errant of literature: he was also the soldier and the functionary on whom the Castilian state depended; his was the voice of command in a hundred battles, of decision in a thousand administrative matters, and of morality and tradition in a million sermons and lawsuits.

Like the social order of sixteenth-century Castile, the great development of the Spanish church was an adaptation of forces created by the reconquest to the needs of imperialism. It is hardly true that the mediaeval Castilians were an especially spiritual people; yet they made religion a militant social activity and came gradually to identify the act of reconquering Spain with the intention to rechristianise it. Above all, the Castilian church had been reinvigorated by Isabella and Cisneros, whose reforms succeeded precisely where the church was weakest in the rest of Europe, among the regulars and in theological education. Spanish Franciscans and Dominicans established new standards of idealism and morality, and there was therefore no strong impulse towards a 'reformation'. Because of its crusading pretensions, the Spanish crown acquired the military Orders, made its church 'national' by means of the Inquisition, and seized a large proportion of the ecclesiastical revenues. The royal patronage which reserved the right of appointing prelates to the crown was interpreted to mean that it would almost invariably appoint Spaniards. It achieved almost as much as Henry VIII while professing perfect orthodoxy. The Spanish church was at once active, administrative and contemplative. In America the missionary led the same hazardous life as the soldier and explorer. The secular cleric, trained in civil and ecclesiastical law, alternately administered a see and sat on a royal council. The contemplative, unrestrained by obstacles of formal theology, fought the doubts of converts and the backslidings of worldlings. These three aspects of Spanish religion found special expression in the Jesuits, the Inquisition and a great mystical movement. The Society of Jesus, founded by a Basque hidalgo and soldier, St Ignatius of Loyola, at Montmartre in 1534, applied military discipline to religion. In Spain this army of salvation was long regarded as an enthusiasm, and even the conversion of a Valencian duke, St Francis Borja, did not quite allay Charles' dislike of it. Because of its universal outlook, Philip preferred it as a missionary body, and sided with the Spanish clergy in resisting its claim to enter the pulpit and confessional, but its very independence of the crown and Inquisition recommended it to Rome.

Philip's Inquisition was a more general and drastic institution than Sixtus IV had ever intended. Although Dominican in origins, its very existence implied the failure of conversion by reason and exhortation, and the need to produce an atmosphere of 'sincerity' through intimidation. Almost inevitably the Inquisition appealed to the worst type of bureaucrat, who coveted the exercise of power without final responsibility under the pretext of serving morality.

The third of these movements, Spanish mysticism, belongs especially to the new converts. Blessed John of Avila, the 'Apostle of Andalusia'; Fray Luis, the Morisco of Granada; St John of the Cross; Santa Teresa, the conversa of Avila, all these were missionaries of the spirit who sought to rise above the rational system of indoctrination which had long been practised with small success.

These religious manifestations were certainly assisted by the great material wealth of the Castilian church and by fiscal policies which diverted men and women and money into the more accessible of the two privileged classes. The scale of this wealth is difficult to assess. Marineo Sículo, who spent a lifetime in Spain, thought that the wealth of the country was equally divided between the crown, the nobles and the church, though he advances no proof of the statement. The church undoubtedly contributed large sums to the state: in 1519 Leo X awarded Charles a tithe of the income of the clergy: this was raised to a quarter in 1532, and in 1539 the first-fruits of all benefices for a year were added. On several occasions Charles desired to convert the property of the church to his military projects against the Turks, hoping to be allowed to seize half the plate in Spain, and finally accepting half a million ducats: when later he wrote from Germany asking Philip to effect a seizure, the Council refused to assist. Philip, for his part, claimed as permanent every concession once made by Rome, and twenty years later Pius V was convinced that there was nothing to choose between him and his father. The *cruzada*, the revenues of the Orders, and forced loans placed perhaps a third of the church's income in the hands of the King.

The crown's main revenues were derived from its towns, and throughout the century the cortes of Castile were convoked at short intervals. As early as 1520 the towns had taken the view that the nobility and clergy, being exempt from tribute, did not form part of cortes, and they were no longer called. In 1527 Charles convened all three classes in the hope that they would pay for a great campaign to save Hungary, but the ancient idea that Castile's crusading obligations were limited to the Peninsula and Africa prevailed, and the nobility in particular were prepared to fight, but not to pay taxes. In 1538 Charles again called a group of nobles and all the prelates simultaneously with the cortes of the towns in the hope of securing common consent to the new tax, the *sisa*; but the nobility remained obdurate, and as there was some danger that the three classes would unite, Charles readily agreed that only the meeting of the towns constituted cortes.

These still consisted of the traditional eighteen 'villas de cortes', each of which appointed two procurators, now drawn from the hidalgo class. They repeatedly claimed from the Emperor preferential attention for Spanish affairs, and pointed to the neglect of justice owing to his long absences: they also frequently criticised the waste and 'inefficiency' of the methods of collecting taxes. But they rarely commented on his wider policies or put forward detailed plans for a consistent economic or financial policy.

Philip also called the Castilian cortes frequently, and pondered long over their complaints (sometimes leaving them a year or more without an answer). He was almost as anxious as his father to receive a large and prompt service, but he resented criticism and feared to make concessions which might seem to support local privileges. Perhaps because of this, he strengthened the system of corregidores, whose duties were now extended and defined. Through these officials he hoped to forestall the raising of complaints and even to stimulate the payment of services. In theory, the elected officials of a municipality were not bound to vote with the corregidor, and they could always appeal directly to the crown. In fact, the corregidor could decide what was to be discussed at council-meetings and held a strong advantage over the elected members. The paper-loving King imagined that his favourite device of the 'residencia', the inspection of an outgoing official's work and financial situation on relinquishing office, was sufficient to guarantee the rectitude of his representatives. Neither in Spain nor in its overseas possessions could administration and justice proceed rapidly. Communications from Madrid or Toledo to Seville or Barcelona usually took three or four days; those to the Netherlands ten; and to Naples or Milan a fortnight, while a message to the remoter parts of America might require nine months to reach its destination. A certain cumbrousness in the Spanish state was therefore inevitable.

To turn from the government to the governed, sixteenth-century Castile had a population of about six and a quarter millions, or three-quarters of the total population of Spain. It seems probable that the figure was less at the beginning of the century and greater in its middle decade. A perceptible decline occurred between 1560 and 1590, due partly to emigration to America, partly to the increasingly high rate of celibacy, and partly to military and other losses.

As in mediaeval times, the north remained the area of small towns and large villages, or in the humid Atlantic belt, of a dispersed rural population, while Andalusia[1] was the region of large cities and extremes of wealth. In 1530 the largest town in northern Castile was Valladolid, where Ferdinand and Isabella had resided and set up their administration (1530, 38,000; 1594, 34,000).[2] The Emperor, however, preferred the 'imperial' city of Toledo in New Castile (1530, 32,000; 1594, 55,000); despite the offence thus given to its rival, the Old Castilian capital of Burgos. In 1561 Philip established his court almost between the two Castiles at the town where Charles had kept the King of France captive. In those days Madrid had been no more than a large village, but when in 1564 Philip began to build the Escorial as a mausoleum for his father, a palace and a monastery, its pre-eminence seemed assured, and by the end of the century it had already outgrown Valladolid. As courtiers, place-hunters, functionaries and purveyors flocked to it, the lanes of new mansions behind the alcazar were extended by building warrens of tenements. The new capital remained exclusively a court-city, lacking any industries or even agricultural wealth of its own.

No other town in northern Castile exceeded 30,000. Salamanca, the university city and centre of southern Leon, rose from 15 to 30,000; Segovia from 13 to 28,000: and Burgos, Avila and Alcalá de Henares grew proportionately. Medina del Campo, the scene of the greatest fair in Spain, had been the third city of Castile in 1530, but it later dwindled to relative unimportance. Galicia, falling to isolation as the new nationalism deprived the old pilgrimage of its general fame, had now no large towns: although Santiago,

[1] The domains of Castile included Old Castile, New Castile (the kingdom of Toledo), Leon, Asturias, Galicia, the Basque Provinces, Extremadura, Andalusia and Murcia, none of which now had autonomous organs of government. But Castilians were essentially the inhabitants of Old and New Castile, and of their conquests in Andalusia: thus a defeated rebel, Don Alfonso Fernández Coronel of Aguilar in Andalusia, bitterly remarked: 'This is Castile, that makes men and breaks them.'

[2] The mediaeval court of Castile had been highly peripatetic. Isabella set up her audiencia at Valladolid and installed her archives in the nearby castle of Simancas: she had intended to make a new capital at Granada.

Vigo and Orense all exceeded 5,000 inhabitants in 1530, they fell to 3,000 or less by 1594.

The general growth of the Castilian towns was accompanied by a steady decrease of the rural population. Since 1480 the Castilian peasant had been freed of any lingering feudal ties, and he readily moved to the towns or was recruited for the army. To fifteenth-century travellers life in rural Castile had seemed strange and primitive, and even in the middle of the sixteenth the dress and customs of the peasants were noticeably mediaeval: it is not difficult to understand the attraction of the small but rapidly-changing towns and of military life with its prospect of wealth and power. Already in the previous century the peasant had been weaned from agriculture by the steady spread of sheep-farming. This industry was encouraged by the nobility, which possessed great tracts of uncultivated land, and protected by the crown through the Mesta, the sheep-farmers' guild. At first produced for export, Spanish wool fed a growing domestic textile industry in the first half of the century; but by its middle years Spanish textiles had already been outproduced and underpriced, and the vast flocks of the Mesta had begun to decrease.

Beyond the thinly populated expanses of the lower meseta, from which the military Orders drew their main wealth, lay Andalusia, now enriched by the concentration of American trade at Seville. Only at the beginning of the century had this city begun to lose its oriental appearance as houses were turned 'outwards' with windows on the streets: its large and heterogeneous population reached 45,000 in 1530 and 90,000 in 1594, and it thus remained by far the largest town in the Peninsula. It was followed by Granada, Córdoba (1530, 38,000), Jaén, Baeza and Ubeda, the last three all woollen-centres which expanded rapidly with the American trade.

In many ways the economy of sixteenth-century Castile remained a collection of loosely linked localisms. In much of the north rural society was remote and agricultural methods had changed little since pre-Roman times. To some extent its isolation was retrogressive: Galicia had had its own international relations in the great days of the pilgrim-route, but these had now dwindled to a mild dependence on imported grain. In Castile the import of booty and tribute from the south had once been a major industry, but from the fourteenth century its main trade was directed northwards. As English wool came to be absorbed by a national industry, the Flemish market had turned to Spain and drew heavily on Castile for its raw materials, and half the Castilian clip was exported. This trade was centred in Burgos and was conducted through the ports of Laredo and Bilbao.

From the early years of the sixteenth century there was also a rapid growth in the textile industry of northern Spain. Its centre was at Segovia, which had manufactured cloth for the court of Henry IV and reached the height of its prosperity between 1530 and 1550: in its hey-day it had fifty guilds, or twice as many as Valladolid.[1] Woollens were also manufactured in other towns of northern Castile, Aragon (Saragossa and Jaca), and Catalonia. But after the middle of the century this prosperity was already passing. Castile was still one of the least industrialised countries in Europe, and its industries had scarcely begun to rise when they were crushed under the double pressure of the Emperor's taxation and the competition of foreign producers and even of new woollen centres in Andalusia.

The influence of the New World on the vivid graph of the Castilian economy was direct and disastrous, though the volume of American treasure brought to Spain is often exaggerated. During the period 1503–60 the average annual receipts of bullion by the crown were about 220,000 ducats, while registered private imports averaged some 350,000 ducats, of which the crown received one fifth. In addition there were unascertainable, but large, entries of contraband bullion. As compared with the total revenues of the Castilian crown these sums were considerable but not overwhelming: they fell far short of paying for Charles' costly campaigns in Europe, or even of the dowry of his Empress (900,000 ducats, of which about half was actually received). But they were sufficient to influence the austere economy of Castile,

---

[1] Guild organisation remained relatively weak in Castile. In Andalusia Seville had sixty guilds and Granada forty; but Barcelona had seventy-one guilds in the fifteenth century and ninety-four in the sixteenth.

and the practice of encumbering them for several years ahead ensured that they had the greatest possible inflationary effect: during the course of the century prices were quadrupled, the increase originating in Seville and spreading outwards.

As news spread of the fantastic wealth won by the fortunate 'first conquerors' in the New World, many adventurous Castilians emigrated: new settlements proliferated throughout the Americas and there was an urgent demand for textiles and such goods as wine and oil, for which prices far above those prevailing in Castile were paid. At the end of Charles' reign his Castilian subjects urged forcible measures to stop the effects of the boom. They desired that exports to America be prohibited: if Americans wanted cloth, let them make their own, not buy up the produce of Castile: let none be permitted to manufacture expensive textiles such as the new-rich Americans demanded, but only homely woollens that Castilians could afford: above all, let prices be fixed. The desire to defend the old Castilian sobriety was strong. But such restrictive policies were unenforceable, and the general rise of prices favoured new woollen centres in Andalusia and especially foreign goods produced under more competitive conditions. Probably as early as 1560 the effects of depopulation began to be felt, and already in 1573 cortes were plaintively recalling the good old days when everyone in the woollen towns and the villages round them was busy. The Castilian silk industry suffered a similar decline, hastened by sumptuary laws and, in the case of Granada, by civil strife and the removal of the Moriscos.

The crisis does in fact indicate the underlying schism in the Spanish state. Castile, still stolidly agrarian and mediaeval in occupation and outlook, persisted in seeking to restore the old stable economy of the just price and to maintain the laws against usury. In the south, with its ancient commercial traditions and its large Jewish population, these convictions were less strongly held, and the Emperor's straits and his engagements to his bankers forced him to take the less strict view: when early in his reign his government attempted to bring an action for usury against his bankers, he intervened and the case was dropped. But he did not pursue any consistent policy, wavering between the exhortations of cortes and the exigencies of the moment: by attempting to maintain a gold-backed currency and to operate a system of price-control, Spain lost both coin and commerce. Far-sighted Spaniards were far from blind to these dangers, even before the French converso Jean Bodin described them in 1568. But from the beginning of his reign the Emperor of Europe had no real control over his own, or Spain's, fortunes.

The three realms of Aragon were, like Spain itself, one when viewed from without, but separate in the eyes of one another. All were represented in the Council of Aragon at court; but each was governed separately by a viceroy who, until the cortes of Tarazona, must be of the royal family or of native birth. All enjoyed the 'liberties of Aragon', which preserved their cortes, their traditional systems of justice, military service, currency and taxation, and expressly prohibited the entry of 'foreign' (i.e. Castilian) troops, save in the case of foreign war, and functionaries, and safeguarded the natives from deportation, secret trial or imprisonment, or torture, except if accused of forgery.

The cortes of the three realms usually met simultaneously as the General Cortes of Aragon at the small town of Monzón; but the three bodies deliberated separately, put forward different grievances and might adopt different attitudes on questions of service. Thus in 1528 the Aragonese voted Charles 200,000 Barcelonese pounds; the Valencians 100,000; and the Catalans, being aggrieved, nothing: thereafter the total service was usually 600,000 pounds. The crown's other revenues in Aragon included the three masterships (*maestrazgos*) and rather exceeded the value of the service.[1]

The separation of the realms of Aragon from Castile was complete: Catalan merchants had consuls to govern their communities

---

[1] The population of the three realms of Aragon was probably about a million and a quarter. During the century that of Aragon proper rose from 260,000 to 355,000, and that of Valencia from 273,000 to an estimated 487,000 (1610): Catalonia had 323,000 in 1553. The growth of Valencia, and in part that of Aragon, was probably due to the influx of refugees from Granada: Catalonia, though it had many converted Jews, had few Muslims.

in Andalusia precisely as in other foreign countries. In Catalonia this feeling of independence was intensified by a different language and a church as national as that of Castile. To the Emperor, as 'King of Kings', the pretensions of the Aragonese monarchy were annoying but not intolerable; but Philip, by birth, training and conviction a Castilian, could not envisage himself as separately King of Aragon and insisted on regarding the eastern realm as a 'viceroyalty', not a kingdom.

IX

THE LATER HAPSBURGS

PHILIP II was survived, not by numerous heirs as the Emperor had hoped, but by only one son, born in 1578, a decade after the death of Don Carlos.[1] Because of his poor health, the prince was spared a rigorous upbringing: when he was nineteen a report prepared for his father revealed that he got up late, took no healthy exercise, showed no interest in society and ought to be married. Although he was then introduced to the work of the royal councils, he displayed only indifference towards his responsibilities, and his father must have felt, as he is reported to have said to Moura, that God had given him many kingdoms, but no son fit to rule over them, adding, 'Ah, Don Cristóbal, I fear he will let them govern him!'

The kingdoms were indeed immense. For the first time all the realms of the Peninsula, Castile, Portugal, Navarre, Aragon, Catalonia and Valencia, had done homage to a single heir. Despite the defection of Holland and Zealand, Philip III was the real master of Flanders, and Artois and the Franche-Comté; and by his control of Milan he could almost encircle France and at the same time keep contact with his cousins in Austria. His hegemony over central Italy was assured by the *presidi* on the coast of Tuscany, and in the south he was King of Naples and Sicily and

---

[1] Philip spent much of his reign in mourning: seventeen members of his family died during his lifetime. He was four times married, to Maria of Portugal, mother of Don Carlos; to Mary Tudor; to Isabel of Valois, mother of Isabel Clara Eugenia and Catalina Micaela; and to his niece Anna of Austria, mother of Ferdinand, Carlos Lorenzo, Diego (who all died young), Philip III and Maria.

master of Sardinia. In North Africa he dominated Oran, Ceuta, Tangier and the Canaries, and as King of Portugal he ruled Guinea, Angola and the way-stations of Moçambique, as well as the Cape Verdes and Madeira. In America, the Spanish possessions were intact from California to Cape Horn, and with the acquisition of Portuguese Brazil they embraced the whole of the southern sub-continent. In Asia, Spain possessed the Philippines, from which she tapped the trade of China; and though the Dutch were now forcing the Portuguese out of the Spice Islands and would soon hold the upper hand in the Indian Ocean, Philip III nevertheless concluded an alliance with the Shah of Persia and thus threatened his Turkish enemies from the rear. Less than a generation had passed since the union of the two Peninsular empires, and to contemporaries they presented an appearance of vast wealth and immense power.

Philip II had sought to leave his son a heritage of peace. He had liquidated his French adventure with the Treaty of Vervins, and negotiated a settlement in the Netherlands which gave the Flemings an appearance of sovereignty: only with England was no approximation possible while her throne was occupied by Elizabeth.

It had been Philip's hope that such experienced statesmen of the old school as Moura and Idiáquez would show his son how to turn these advantages to account; but the day after his death, Philip III handed over the conduct of affairs to Francisco Gómez de Sandoval y Rojas, fourth Marquis of Denia and soon to become Duke of Lerma. The favourite, a grandson of St. Francis Borja, was a suave and courtly nobleman of fifty: he had established his ascendancy during the young king's childhood and was to keep it for twenty years.

Lerma was at once the representative and the rival of his class. After the long subordination of the aristocracy, it was perhaps inevitable that a grandee should seize power: Philip II is said to have been warned of Lerma's influence over his son and to have made him Viceroy of Valencia in order to remove him. The Denias were Castilianised Valencians, and Lerma pursued the Philippine policy of centralisation, which he was presently to further by obtaining a virtual abdication of the rights of the Valencian cortes and by the expulsion of the Valencian Moriscos. But if these actions and his pursuit of external peace were in line with the old King's desires, his fantastic self-aggrandisement certainly was not. Since the death of the ducal saint, his family had become somewhat straitened, and Lerma now amply redressed their fortunes: he created his uncles Archbishop of Toledo and President of Portugal, his son Duke of Uceda, his grandson Count of Ampudia, and his brothers-in-law Viceroys of Naples and Peru. His incessant purchases of towns and estates aroused bitter protests and even revolts among their apprehensive inhabitants. But flagrant peculation was not rare among seventeenth-century favourites, and it was still possible to believe that the ostentation of Lerma and his set and the splendid entertainments with which he beguiled the listless King were a proof of greatness.

In the Netherlands, the efforts of Alexander Farnese to restore Spanish power had been interrupted by his two incursions into France: on his death four successive governors in as many years made little progress. In 1596 the Archduke Albert was appointed governor, and since England and France had recognised the sovereignty of the Northern Provinces, Philip II decided to grant independence to Flanders, marrying the Archduke to his daughter Isabel-Clara-Eugenia and bestowing the contentious heritage on them. The concession was more apparent than real, since they depended on Spanish and Italian troops; and Philip carefully reserved the reversion to his own son in case Albert and Isabel should leave no heirs. The new dispensation was at once tested by a resumption of the war in which the protestants won the battle of the Dunes in 1600. It now became necessary to move fresh troops from Italy to the north, and by good fortune, the brothers Spinola, members of the great Genoese family, volunteered for the struggle. In 1604 Ostend was won after a siege lasting three years, one of the famous contests of the age, and it was even possible to take Dutch territory north of the Rhine. On the strength of these two successes Lerma instructed Spinola to obtain a peace or long truce with the Dutch 'without seeming to desire it', and after negotiations lasting two years, peace was concluded at Bergen-op-Zoom. It was disguised as a nine-year truce in order to spare Spain from openly acknowledging the rebels as equals: nevertheless, the independence of the United Provinces was admitted and they were granted freedom of trade with Spain, and, with obscure limitations, even in the New World. Dutch and English naval successes had rendered Spanish communications with the Netherlands precarious and impelled Spain to seek an end to the war. But peace left the mouth of the Scheldt in Dutch hands and exposed the port of Antwerp and the whole of the south, the 'Obedient Provinces', to a gradual impoverishment.

Meanwhile, the war with England was also brought to an end. Essex' raid on Cádiz in 1596 had gone unavenged, but Lerma gathered a second and smaller Armada, which was dispersed by storm in 1601. In the following year he resumed the policy of active assistance to the Irish patriots, raising thirty-three ships to support the Earl of Tyrone's rising. The enterprise was to have been favoured by the Spanish Archbishop of Dublin, but the invaders failed to concert their plans: the Spanish force was dispersed by storm, and only 3,500 men under Don Juan de Aguila were able to land at Kinsale: other contingents were cut off in Baltimore and Castlehaven. O'Sullivan could not relieve Kinsale, and the garrison finally surrendered and was repatriated, being accompanied to Spain by a band of Irish leaders.

The failure was soon followed by the death of Queen Elizabeth and the accession of James I. The peaceful change of dynasty showed that there was no hope of a spontaneous movement in favour of a catholic sovereign, and Spain therefore treated with the new ruler. Although the French proposed an alliance which would have perpetuated the Spanish war, James preferred to make peace in London in 1604 and sent his admiral to Valladolid to ratify it in the following year. The settlement was popular in Spain, where it was expected that the silver-fleets would now cross the Atlantic unimpeded by English corsairs.

The phase of pacification was completed by an alliance with France. The widow of Henry IV, Marie de Medici, readily accepted the Pope's suggestion that the two royal houses should enter into a new matrimonial alliance which might serve as a basis for the defence of Christianity against the Turks, and in 1612 Prince Philip (IV) of Spain was betrothed to Isabel of Bourbon and Louis XIII to Ana of Austria: the brides, each of whom renounced any claim to the throne of her own country, were exchanged in 1615.

The possibility that Henry IV would resume the Franco-Turkish alliance and at the same time provoke a rebellion of the Spanish Moriscos revived the old question of Peninsular unification. By reason of his birth and his short tenure of the viceroyalty, Lerma was well equipped to pursue in Valencia the policy of centralisation which Philip II had applied in Aragon. In 1604 he largely undermined the Valencian cortes, and five years later he curbed the power of the Valencian lords by removing their Morisco serfs. The question of a general expulsion of the Moriscos was not new. It had been discussed by the Council of State in Lisbon in 1580, but Philip II had then hesitated to stir up trouble and nothing had been done: since the Moriscos were in theory Christians, they could not be expelled so long as any hope remained of inducing them to practise the faith that had been thrust upon them. Some years later disorders in Aragon gave rise to fears of Moroccan or French intrigues among the Morisco population, and the question was viewed as a matter of defence; but again no step was taken.

With the opening of the new reign, the picture changed. In 1602 the Archbishop of Valencia, who had striven to convert them for more than thirty years, finally decided that the task was impossible, and asked the King for their expulsion. This admission of spiritual defeat led to the summoning of a new junta in which the prelates of Valencia, the viceroy and others all recommended the same course. The victims attempted to purchase a postponement, but their offers were rejected, and in April 1609 the Council of State decided to proceed with a general expulsion, beginning with Valencia. In order to avoid the risk of war, veteran tercios were brought from Italy to cordon off the kingdom and the viceroy called up its militia. On September 22nd, he published an

K

edict that the Moriscos were to depart within three days: six per cent of the adults might remain to explain their husbandry to the Old Christians who would take over their land; the rest were to be embarked for Algiers, Tunis and Oran, taking with them only what they could carry. The first party to be removed came from the estate of Lerma's kinsman and rival, the Duke of Gandía, who, like other Valencian noblemen, escorted his peasants to the ports: one of them, the Duke of Maqueda, accompanied his to Oran. When in January 1610 the decrees of expulsion were issued for Andalusia and Murcia, they were much less rigorously enforced, while the Castilian Moriscos were permitted to remain. The banished, who were Muslims and 'foreigners' in Spain, were treated as Christians and Spaniards in Morocco, and many were murdered on their arrival.

The number of Moriscos reported to have been expelled was just under 102,000, but this total may be not quite complete. No certain statistics exist of the number of Moriscos in Spain at this time, and in many regions they were not now clearly distinguishable from the rest of the population. The proportion of expulsions is scarcely sufficient to have 'caused' the decadence of Spain. But statistics which suggest that the expulsion had little or no effect on the Spanish economy are not altogether convincing. Lerma desired to break the power of the Valencian nobles, and he probably succeeded in ruining some of their estates and in driving Moriscos in other parts of Spain away from the land: thus in 1626 a procurator from Granada assured cortes that there were plenty of Moors in Andalusia, but that none of them were willing to tend cattle or to work in the fields, where there was a notable shortage of labour. If therefore the 'expulsion' did not deprive Spain of all her most skilled and industrious cultivators, nevertheless, like the transfers during the war of the Alpujarras, it removed many of them from the places in which they could be most useful and hastened the process of depopulation.

The decline of Spain which occurred during the reign of Philip III springs directly from the incapacity of the monarch, who had hitherto alone kept the balance between the nobility, the church and the third of the state that was described as 'royal' or 'popular'.

The social discipline maintained with difficulty by Philip II now decayed, and as the country grew poorer corruption, sinecurism, evasion of taxation and idleness were magnified, and as they grew, further weakened the real authority of the crown. The favourite's own self-indulgence spread rapidly among his intimates. His page, Rodrigo Calderón, rose to be Marquis of Siete Iglesias, acquired an extraordinary fortune, and was finally arrested, and executed in the next reign. His secretary, Pedro Franqueza, Count of Villalonga and Villafranqueza, also flourished prodigiously until he was arrested, ordered to reimburse what he had stolen, and condemned to life-imprisonment. When his own fall became imminent, Lerma was created a cardinal and so raised above the hazards of investigation. The reign was prolific in new titles of nobility and in the disposal of honours, offices, privileges and lands. Officials were no longer chosen for their ability or character, but appointed by recommendation or purchase. In order to raise ready money the crown pressed the sale of offices to its logical conclusion, disposing not only of expectations, but creating appointments for sale. Many who had enriched themselves were ready to pay high prices for offices carrying relatively small salaries but they did not expect to exert themselves in the offices they had acquired, and the crown was left encumbered with obligations and officials.[1] While the state assumed ever-increasing liabilities, its resources dwindled. Imports of American silver had reached their highest level during the last years of Philip II, and fell by about a third in the period 1601–5, recovering after 1606, and declining steadily after 1611: by the middle of the century they amounted to less than a tenth of those of the peak years. All receipts had been spent before they arrived, and even at the beginning of the reign silver coin had virtually disappeared: in 1601 orders were given for an inventory to be made of private and church plate, but the proposal for a seizure was abandoned. Instead the government fell back on the device of debasement, which Philip II had refused to sanction. The bronze coinage was doubled in face-value in 1603

---

[1] The creation of monopolies for gunpowder, playing cards, quicksilver, pepper, etc., was followed by the appointment of special courts with judges and other officials to enforce them.

and five years later Philip accepted a special service from cortes in return for a promise not to repeat the process. But the state of his finances was such that he twice had to obtain release from his undertaking. Heavy loads of copper were now required for even small transactions, and every sort of expedient from alchemy to meatless days was propounded.

However, it would be unwise to take too literally either the complaints or the remedies put forward in a bureaucratic capital which delighted in ostentation, gossip and hyperbole and had no power to mend matters. The fall in the receipts of bullion was partly offset by an expansion of trade in American agricultural products, which now far exceeded silver in total value. Cortes continued to meet, and if in 1607 the two procurators chosen by lot to represent the capital turned out as if by magic to be Lerma and Calderón, there were still at the end of the reign outspoken representatives who could tell the King what was amiss. Their first criticism was that the crown had recklessly dissipated its wealth by providing favours for useless dependents: as a result revenues were earmarked four years ahead, and soldiers deserted because they were not paid. The collection of taxes was so corrupt and inefficient that the cost sometimes exceeded the amount gathered, while the burden was driving more and more people to found chaplaincies or entrust their property to ecclesiastics in their family: it seemed possible that most of the country would soon pass out of the royal domain into that of the church. Moreover contests of jurisdiction gave rise to endless lawsuits on which the graduates of the universities existed. Philip was urged to appoint suitable men as corregidores and to reduce their power to dispose of municipal offices; to prohibit luxuries by sumptuary laws; to ban the entry of manufactured goods; to forbid notaries to convey properties to the church without previous sanction; and to prevent the decline of agriculture through depopulation.

Since the peace with the United Provinces, Spain had tacitly surrendered Portuguese interests in the east to the Dutch. The result, far from satiating the commercial ambitions of that small nation, was merely to whet its appetite for colonial expansion and to suggest designs for a general invasion of the overseas monopoly claimed by the two Peninsular states. In Spain itself imports increased and Spanish industry was further depleted. Not only did the Dutch carry Spanish goods, but as domestic industries failed, Spanish ships came to depend on imported timber, tar and sail-cloth. The manufacture of arms and textiles dwindled, and the guild system fell into decay: as early as 1619 the Council of Castile was urged to prevent the collapse of industry, but no effective measures were taken, and the once busy towns of Segovia and Toledo lapsed into inactivity. Rural depopulation was ascribed partly to the departure of the nobility and gentry for Madrid, and partly to the 'millones', or communal taxes, which remained fixed even if the population decreased, so that the survivors fled to avoid insupportable burdens.

Searching as these self-criticisms are, it must be remembered that some of the abuses they indicate had always existed in one form or another. Most Spaniards remained patient and robust; and they believed in the fundamental greatness of their monarchy. Since 1615, however, they were threatened by a renewal of the two great struggles of the preceding century, the wars of religion and the competition between the Hapsburgs and France: and although they were to avoid the opening stages of the Thirty Years War, they were finally drawn into long and ruinous conflicts with Holland, France and England. The first brushes took place in Italy, where the hegemony of Spain was challenged by the Duke of Savoy in alliance with the Republic of Venice. Since the beginning of the century Spain had sought to strengthen the links between Milan and Austria by occupying and fortifying the Valtelline, and this advance threatened to encircle the Venetian territories. On the death of the Duke of Mantua, Savoy claimed and occupied the small marquisate of Montferrat, and the Spanish viceroys in Milan fought a desultory war which was ended by the peace of Pavia in 1617, when Louis XIII as mediator restored the disputed town to Mantua. Thereafter the Venetians extended their friendship from France to the United Provinces, with which they concluded a formal alliance. The reappearance of Venice as an enemy caused the Spanish authorities in Italy to seek revenge in the famous 'conspiracy of Venice'. At this time Spanish Italy was controlled by the Marquis of Villafranca, Viceroy of Milan, and the Duke of Osuna, who as Viceroy of Naples commanded a powerful naval force, with which he supported the Slav corsairs, the Uscocks, in their struggle against the Venetians in the Adriatic. These two, in collaboration with the Marquis of Bedmar, the Spanish Ambassador in Venice, appear to have plotted to overthrow the republic on Ascension day 1618 by means of a coup d'état, but the signory had wind of the troubles and promptly hanged a group of agitators: both Bedmar and Osuna denied all knowledge of the intrigue.

Lerma was now seventy, and found himself confronted by the ambitions of a new generation. His first rival was his own son, the Duke of Uceda, who became the leader of a clique which included Don Gaspar de Guzmán, Count of Olivares, the favourite of the heir to the throne, and Fr Aliaga, the King's confessor. In 1618 this group persuaded Philip to dismiss Lerma, and to permit the arrest and trial of Rodrigo Calderón.

Shortly before, Philip had at length opened his eyes to the state of his kingdom and asked the Council of Castile to propose remedies: these were to reduce taxation, which was held to be responsible for the depopulation of Castile, to cut the frivolous scattering of '*mercedes*', to curtail the wasteful expenditure of the royal household, to limit the number of tax-collectors, priests and monasteries, and to assist the farmer and peasant. But Uceda achieved very little towards undoing the harm caused by his father; and when shortly after visiting Portugal in 1619, the King suffered the first attack of the disease of which he was to die a year later, it was already too late to redeem the wasted years.

The new king, Philip IV (1621-65), was a promising and good-natured boy of sixteen. When Uceda enquired who was to do business with him, he at once designated the uncle of Olivares, the venerable Don Baltasar de Zúñiga. Olivares had patiently established a personal ascendancy, fought hard to keep it and worked with Uceda for the overthrow of his father: he now had the satisfaction of dismissing his recent ally with a triumphant: 'All is mine!' From that moment for twenty years Olivares tended the source of his power like a tender plant, handing Philip his shirt in the morning, his guns in the afternoon, and his papers in the evening.

There could scarcely have been a greater contrast than that between the fair, milky Hapsburg youth and the swarthy, bullet-headed, domineering *valido*, twenty years his senior. Olivares' father, a nobleman from Seville, had been Philip II's ambassador in Rome; he had treated the Pope with a certain truculence, and nourished a grudge for not having been made a grandee. His younger son, already grandly attended, had studied at Salamanca and been voted rector by the students. Once appointed to the prince's household, he had never faltered in his chosen ambition, and exercised his authority with all the intensity of an Alvaro de Luna. There is no proof that he corrupted Philip IV as a youth; his own private life, apart from his lust for power, became impeccably respectable. Yet he certainly did nothing to prevent an impressionable boy from growing into an eager, if conscience-stricken, voluptuary, whose small sense of duty was overwhelmed by his minister's passion to rule.

The new favourite rapidly disbanded the clients and hangers-on of the preceding 'situation'. Uceda was placed under arrest and Lerma forbidden to return to Madrid: Calderón, already tried and hoping for a pardon, was soon executed. Olivares advanced members of his own family, achieving the coveted grandeeship for himself and bestowing it on several relations. But his main object was not wealth, and he felt only contempt for the great nobility which had stood by while Lerma despoiled the state. He intended to restore Spain to her imperial greatness, and to resume the policies of Philip II where they had been abandoned. A civilian with an itch to command and a dictator with no head for finance, his main weapon was his extraordinary self-confidence, which was translated into a characteristic diplomacy of aggressive procrastination.

In foreign affairs Olivares inherited peace with England and the United Provinces and an insecure accommodation with France. In the last year of Philip III Spain had intervened in the northern struggle when she expelled the Calvinists from the Valtelline in order to assure her communications with Austria. But her moment of decision arrived in 1621, when the Archduke Albert died in Flanders and the nine-year truce with the United Provinces expired. Although the Archduchess survived for twelve years, the future of the Spanish Netherlands depended on Spain's willingness to defend them, and the Council of State in Madrid resolved that the burden must be shouldered and the war resumed. In 1622 Spinola invaded the disputed Duchy of Julich, and the conflict spread from the Low Countries, where Richelieu supported the Dutch, to the Valtelline and to America. Within three months of the ending of the truce the Dutch had formed the West India Company which raided Spanish shipping and in 1624 seized Bahia in Brazil: although it was driven out by a strong Spanish-Portuguese expedition in the following year, it later established itself firmly in the rich sugar-producing area of Pernambuco: Dutch Brazil was the first major intrusion into the Peninsular New World.

In Flanders Spinola took Breda in 1625 after a lengthy siege, and this success was soon followed by the death of his adversary, Maurice of Nassau. In the Valtelline, the Pope strove to bring Spain and France to terms, and although agreement was momentarily reached, the former refused to dismantle her fortifications, and when the struggle was renewed the French were able to restore the valleys to their Swiss Calvinist allies by the treaty of 1626. Spinola, who had advised against the resumption of the war, now recommended the conclusion of a long truce with the United Provinces, if possible for thirty years; but Olivares again overruled him.

The war was indeed popular in Madrid. Olivares' first measures had included the setting up of a Junta for the Reform of Customs (1622) with powers to investigate all fortunes acquired during the past thirty years. The prospect of bringing back Castilian simplicity by sumptuary laws and military discipline by dictatorship was a stirring one. Peace, not war, seemed to be Spain's enemy: for the years of truce were associated with Lerma's extravagances and the vast economic gains achieved by the Dutch. Moreover, a French Cardinal leading a coalition of protestants formed an attractive enemy; nobility, churchmen and private persons promptly came forward with donations for the cause. . .

In London the Spanish Ambassador, Gondomar, had long entertained James I with the prospect of a closer alliance in order to keep England permanently free of French influence. The King was tempted: he had married his daughter to the protestant Elector-Palatine of Bavaria, whose territories were invaded by the Emperor in 1621, and conceived the hope that a marriage in Spain might become the means of restoring his son-in-law and raising himself as arbiter between the two religious factions. So, suddenly in March, 1623, his heir appeared incognito in Madrid to snatch glimpses of a Spanish infanta, while Buckingham wooed Olivares. But a protestant marriage was now almost inconceivable in Spain, and the minister impeded a dispensation and at the same time alleged the difficulty of obtaining it: in June, James, chagrined by the failure of the adventure, called his 'dear Baby' home.

This romantic episode, which might have formed the thread of one of those comedias on which the people of Madrid doted, confirmed them in their no less romantic conviction that they were still the greatest power in the world. Buckingham allowed his resentment against Olivares' bad faith to drive him into an alliance with the Dutch, and in 1625 Sir Edward Cecil's fleet delivered an ill-conceived attack on Cádiz, while Spain supported Richelieu's intervention against England.

As Spain wavered on the brink of a new war, Olivares had been forced to give serious thought to her condition. Already in 1621 he had warned Philip that the key to her problems was financial: it would take years to repair the damage caused in the previous reign, and favours must be strictly limited to those who performed services. But four years later the will to enforce economies had already weakened, and Olivares decided that the only possible course was to achieve political and fiscal uniformity throughout the Peninsula.

'Let Your Majesty consider,' he advised, 'that the most important business of your monarchy is to become King of Spain. I mean not merely to be King of Portugal, Aragon and Valencia and

Count of Barcelona, but to work and plan with silent and secret counsel to reduce these ... to the style and laws of Castile, with no distinction: if you achieve this Your Majesty will be the greatest king on earth.' The choice was whether Spain should be a centralised and imperial state able by discipline to compensate for her lack of physical resources, or a federal monarchy in which the welfare of the parts was more important than the power of the whole. Castilians had no doubt that the first policy was the right one, and Olivares noted three ways of achieving it: first, to favour the leaders of the non-Castilian realms by bringing them to Madrid and appointing them to offices, or arranging Castilian marriages for them so that they would forget their ties of birth; second, to negotiate, with the backing of a large army; and third, 'not so justified, but the most efficacious', to stir up some riot or disturbance and use this as a pretext to bring in troops and introduce the laws of Castile 'as in a new conquest' (1625). These views illustrate clearly the Spanish view of the irrevocability of local privileges: moreover, all three methods convey the implication that the non-Castilians were unalterably reluctant to receive the laws of Castile: they must be bribed, coerced or tricked into union. The fixed intention to 'bestow' Castilian laws precluded any idea of a greater unity to which all might contribute through constitutional growth. Nor does Olivares seem to have been disposed to study the situation: he admitted that he did not know how many titles there were in the eastern kingdoms and added 'nor does it matter'. And to ignorance was wedded a preposterous pretension of secrecy: Philip should execute his plan 'without declaring it'.

But Olivares' intentions were no secret. In 1626 Philip met the cortes of Aragon at Barbastro, and was finally accorded service after swearing to observe the fueros. But in Barcelona his attempts to cultivate the Catalans failed completely, and feeling against him and his favourite ran so high that they were obliged to leave the city secretly. Even the Valencians, who were summoned to Monzón, protested against being called out of their own kingdom and resisted the grant of a service as long as they dared. Far from desiring to share the privileges, sacrifices and mismanagement of

Castile, the eastern kingdoms clung jealously to their remaining rights, and their alarms were shared by the Portuguese and even by the Basques. In 1625 the Portuguese collaborated fully in the 'Expedition of the Vassals' for the recovery of Bahia from the Dutch: six years later, it was impossible to raise men and money in Lisbon even for the defence of Brazil. At the same time an attempt to establish a salt-monopoly in contravention of the local fueros provoked a riot in Biscay which threatened to degenerate into a social war.

From 1627 onwards Spain found herself involved in a series of foreign wars which, if at first unimportant, were none the less costly and exhausting. When the Duke of Mantua died, the Duke of Savoy proposed to Olivares that they should seize and divide Montferrat while Richelieu was occupied with the Huguenots. In the following year the French had recovered and were ready to strike back, and Olivares hastily made peace with England, but failed to hold Savoy: by 1631 he was prepared to conclude an unfavourable treaty with France. But the death of the Archduchess Isabel-Clara-Eugenia (1633) put an end to the fiction of autonomy in the Netherlands, and it became necessary to find a successor. Olivares had admitted that 'if the states of Flanders could be left without a master when the Infanta dies, that would be best, but as it cannot be, Your Majesty must keep them'. It was finally decided to send the king's brother, the Cardinal-Infante Ferdinand, who proved an able soldier and in 1634 won the great victory of Nördlingen against the Swedes and Germans. This was the signal for both France and Spain to join in the Thirty Years War. Hitherto, Richelieu had plotted with the German protestants to weaken the Netherlands and break through the chain of territories by which the Hapsburgs encircled France; but he now precipitated a general struggle in which he hoped to overrun Flanders and sever the Hapsburg chain in Italy. Although Spain was defeated in the Valtelline, the Cardinal-Infante crossed Picardy and in 1636 threatened to enter Paris. For a moment fortune smiled. Parma was conquered and the Valtelline regained, while Richelieu's attempt to enter Spain at Fuenterrabía and Roussillon met with little success. France too was groaning under the Cardinal's taxation, and she seemed to be almost more exhausted than her enemy.

But the last chance of making a favourable bargain was missed, and in the following three years Spanish affairs took a disastrous turn. The decision lay no longer with armies in the field but in the will and endurance of the nation as a whole. Now, in the midst of the war, Olivares demanded new contributions from Portugal and Catalonia and simultaneously the surrender of their autonomy. In Portugal the application of these taxes led to small riots in 1637; and Olivares was reminded that if the governor, the Duchess of Mantua, should die or retire, it would be necessary to send another member of the royal family or appoint a Portuguese. But the royal house was lamentably small, and few Portuguese could be trusted to collaborate. A nobleman, the Count of Linhares, was invited to Madrid, loaded with presents and offered the viceroyalty of Brazil and the lieutenant-governorship of Portugal under the Duchess. But as reports of disturbances continued, Olivares sent detachments of Castilian troops to impose order, and summoned a group of Portuguese nobles and prelates to Madrid to discuss unification.

In 1639 Richelieu, whose agents were active in both Lisbon and Barcelona, made a determined attack on Roussillon, and his troops took the town of Salses. It was recovered shortly after, largely by Catalan levies, but their success merely stimulated the Principality to resist Olivares when he ordered 'foreign' contingents to be billetted in Catalonia and Catalan troops to serve in Italy. The billetted troops had not been paid, and they proceeded to live off the Catalan countryside. The Viceroy, Santa Coloma, warned Olivares that he should either appease the Catalans by ending billetting, or else send more troops to hold them down. Santa Coloma, though himself a Catalan, was a 'centralist' and a disciplinarian; and when the Generalitat asked him to intervene to uphold the fueros he promptly arrested the petitioners. This outrage against the magistrates was followed by more attacks on the troops; and on June 7, when the itinerant harvesters, the 'Segadors', resorted to Barcelona for the festivity of Corpus Christi, they fell on the Castilian guard and attacked the

Viceroy's house. The municipality recommended Santa Coloma to take refuge in a Genoese ship in the port. At first he refused, and when he did decide, it was too late: he was murdered as he waited on the strand for a boat, and the mob attacked the houses of the authorities and released their arrested magistrates.

When news of the 'Bloody Corpus' reached Madrid Catalan advisers urged Olivares to withdraw the 'foreign' troops. Instead he arrested a Catalan deputation, called an assembly of ministers, and read them a 'discharge of the royal conscience' which was in effect a declaration of war on Catalonia. The Catalans sent to Aragon, Valencia, Navarre, Portugal and France in quest of help. Louis XIII at once recognised Catalonia as an independent republic under his protection; and on December 1st, a Portuguese revolution led to the overthrow of the Duchess of Mantua and the restoration of independence. Lisbon was freed in the course of a morning and the crown was offered to the Duke of Braganza, who, as John IV, became the founder of a new dynasty.

Philip had lost, it was said, two kingdoms in one week. Olivares buoyantly congratulated his master on having gained them, since in theory both rebellions would lead to the suppression of all local rights and the introduction of Castilian uniformity on which he had set his mind. But his policy had already failed. He appointed an Andalusian, the Marquis of Los Vélez, to be Viceroy of Catalonia; but the Castilian forces were defeated by the Catalans at Montjuich and forced to retire to Tarragona, while a French army moved into Barcelona. Efforts to end the Portuguese Restoration were no more successful; and in Andalusia—part of 'Castile' itself—the Duke of Medina Sidonia, brother to the new Queen of Portugal, entered into an ill-considered conspiracy to make himself king with foreign aid. The plot was discovered and his distant kinship with Olivares alone saved his life. Meanwhile, Seville was seized with alarm and prices doubled in the space of a year.

In 1642 Louis XIII joined the French army before Perpignan, and Philip, whom Olivares had hitherto kept in Madrid, insisted on departing for the front. On the way he was able to meet the Duchess of Mantua and learn from her lips how Portugal had been lost. The year had been a disastrous one: the Spanish army in Roussillon was dispersed and Perpignan capitulated: the cortes-town of Monzón fell, and though Tortosa at the mouth of the Ebro was held, the royal army led by the Marquis of Leganés was routed before Lérida. Philip returned woefully to Madrid to prepare for the defence of Aragon in the following spring.

Olivares' own optimism was at last exhausted, and other voices began to reach the King. His French Queen, long disregarded, had striven to raise troops during his absence and now urged him to dismiss his favourite. At length Olivares himself asked to be relieved; and Philip, reluctantly, gave him permission to retire in January 1643. Although he was later placed under restraint at Toro, his enemies were not able to persuade Philip to bring him to trial: he died in 1645.

The gloomy campaign which brought Olivares down was followed by the deaths of Richelieu and of Louis XIII and the accession to the throne of France of Louis XIV, a child of five and half a Spaniard. The enemy now seemed not quite so formidable. Philip announced his intention of governing without a favourite, of forsaking dissipation and of devoting himself entirely to the welfare of his people. On his way to the front he had stayed at Agreda and met the abbess of the convent of the Immaculate Conception, Mother María Coronel, with whom he began to correspond, confessing his weaknesses to her and seeking consolation and good counsel. Her influence helped him to resist some of the temptations that beset him, and her advice ranged from moral questions to the very conduct of the war. But even with the aid of the nun and of his Queen, Philip could not stand permanently alone, and began to confide much of his work to Don Luis de Haro, a nephew of Olivares, who guided Spain's affairs until his death in 1661.

In Catalonia the royal army, now commanded by a Portuguese general, Felipe da Silva, recovered Monzón and Lérida in 1644, but owing to jealousies, he was removed, and a new French onslaught led by d'Harcourt recovered several Catalan towns.

The struggle continued with varying fortunes: if the Castilians failed by plot and assault to recover Barcelona, and lost Tortosa, the French could not retake Lérida. A spirit of stalemate set in over the front, and for the Catalans the novelty of a French viceroy began to lose its charms. In Portugal the danger had seemed less urgent, and John IV had had time to establish himself and conclude an alliance with Charles I of England: in 1644 the Portuguese won the victory of Montijo and thereafter held the Castilians on the defensive.

The collapse of 1640 now began to have its repercussions in Europe. In the north the victorious Infante Ferdinand had died at Brussels in 1641, and the command had passed to the Portuguese soldier and writer, Dom Francisco Manuel de Melo. In May 1643 he laid siege to Rocroy, which was relieved by the younger Condé, and in a hard-fought battle the veteran Spanish tercios, long regarded as almost invincible, at last went down in a disastrous defeat. In the following years the Spaniards were to abandon Gravelines, Courtrai, Dunkirk and other places, and to suffer a further reverse when Condé took their artillery and baggage at Lens in 1647. In Sicily, still the granary of the Spanish Mediterranean, the Viceroy, Los Vélez, laid on new taxes and attempted to control the sale of bread. The populace rebelled and forced him to take refuge aboard a galley, whence he negotiated a settlement (1646). In Milan, Prince Thomas of Savoy abandoned the Spanish side and took service with Mazarin. In Naples the imposition of taxes on food set off the rising of the fisherman Masaniello (April 1647): the Viceroy, the Duke of Arcos, was besieged in his castle, and although a Spanish fleet commanded by Don John of Austria arrived in the harbour the citizens resisted his bombardment. A French force appeared to stir up Angevin sentiment, and part of the Neapolitan nobility recognised the Duke of Guise as heir to the ancient claim, but he was at length taken prisoner and the kingdom pacified.

Meanwhile in Madrid death had removed Philip's loyal Queen (October 1644) and his son, Don Baltasar Carlos (October 1646): his heir was now an eight-year old daughter, María Teresa. These blows dispirited him, and he was with difficulty persuaded to marry again. His new bride was his fifteen-year-old niece Mariana of Austria, a match which, if it symbolised the solidarity

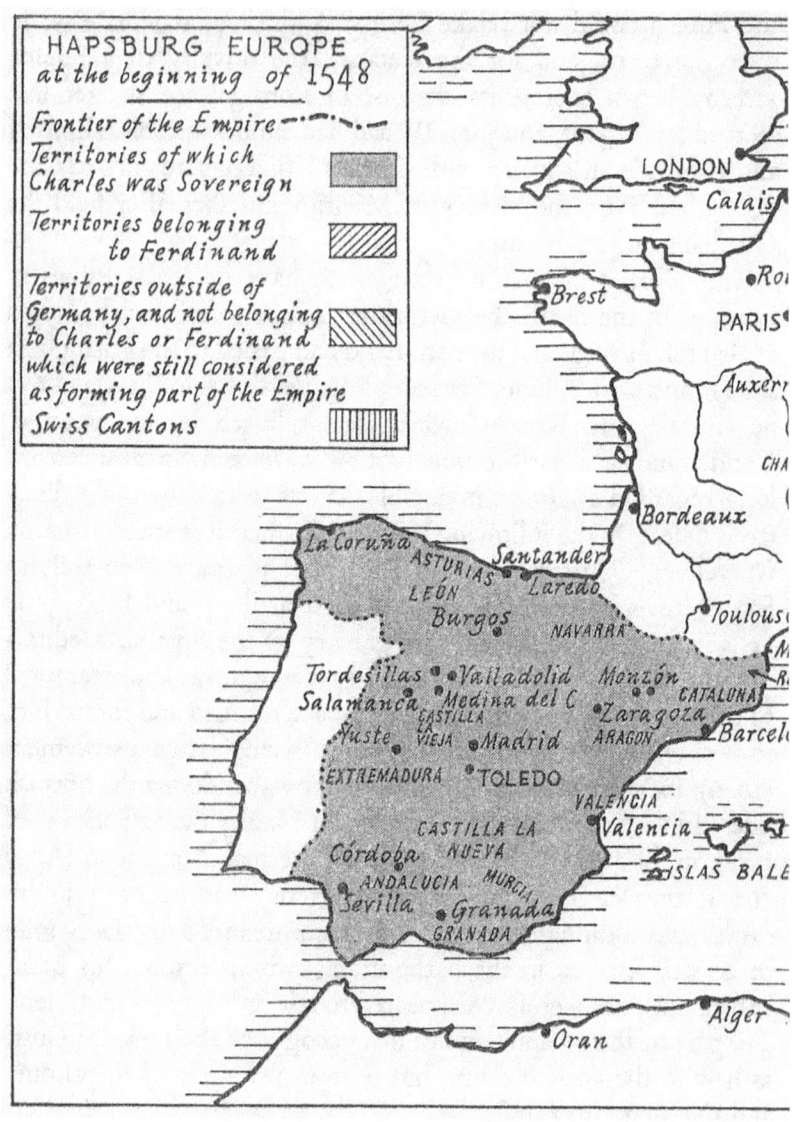

of the House of Austria, also hastened its ruin, for its only fruit was the degenerate Charles II.

Already in 1645 negotiations had been begun to put an end to the Thirty Years War, and they were to lead to the treaties of Westphalia of 1648, by which the Emperor made peace with the French and both Hapsburg branches recognised the independence of the United Provinces. Spain and France remained at war: Mazarin had demanded that Philip should abandon the Netherlands in return for the evacuation of Catalonia, and these exorbitant terms revealed his design to dominate the Low Countries and gave the Dutch and Spaniards a common interest against him.

There followed a respite. In France, Mazarin's efforts to extend his power and level the nobility provoked civil war; and several of his generals, including Condé and Turenne, passed into the service of Spain. In 1652 Barcelona was reconquered after a long siege, and Philip restored the privileges of the Catalans, thus reversing Olivares' policy. In England, too, the execution of Charles I had seemed to remove an enemy: Philip's ambassador lodged no protest against the regicide, and commercial and practical interests at first prevailed over other considerations. But this mutual toleration could not long continue. Charles I had restored the Anglo-Portuguese alliance in 1642, and the Portuguese now sought its renewal from Cromwell, and the defenders of the 'Portugal trade' in Parliament eventually won the day. The first envoy of the Commonwealth to Madrid was murdered by royalist refugees and his secretary received scant courtesy from the Spanish authorities, while protestant merchants complained constantly of the interference of the Inquisition. The restored monarchy of Portugal had offered good terms to the Dutch and was obliged to extend them to the English, while Spain still refused to admit English merchants to her American colonies or to relax the rigours of her religious police. In 1654 the Anglo-Portuguese alliance was revived, and in the same year Cromwell concluded a treaty with Mazarin against Spain. Blake was ordered to seize the Spanish treasure-fleet without a declaration of war, while Penn and Venables took Jamaica. This conquest was at once the first permanent loss of Spanish territory and the first step in the colonial expansion of England.

The intervention of the English republic completed the collapse of Spain. In 1656 and 1657 two treasure-fleets were lost, and in 1658 Turenne won the battle of the Dunes against Don Juan José and Condé. Dunkirk itself capitulated and all Flanders was exposed. Already in 1656 an agent of Mazarin had secretly opened negotiations in Madrid, but only after the birth of an heir to the Spanish throne at the end of 1657 could Philip think seriously of a dynastic alliance. Even now, the Austrian faction which surrounded Queen Mariana in Madrid did its best to prevent the conclusion of peace, offering a new alliance and even the despatch of troops to Flanders. But in June 1659 Haro met Mazarin at the frontier and in October the French formally requested the hand of Philip's daughter for Louis XIV. By the treaty of the Pyrenees Spain accepted the loss of Artois and part of French-speaking Flanders: Catalonia remained with her, but Roussillon became part of France. Despite the territorial surrender, the treaty was fervently celebrated in Madrid, and Haro received the ill-omened title of 'Prince of the Peace'.

Spain remained at war with Portugal, and Philip's first thought in the six years that remained to him was to reannex the neighbouring kingdom. He had obtained a French undertaking not to intervene in its affairs and all mention of it was omitted from the treaty of the Pyrenees. Nevertheless, Louis XIV helped to recruit troops for Portugal; and when Charles II was restored to the English throne, he resumed the Portuguese connection and consolidated it by marrying Catherine of Braganza.

Since the Portuguese Restoration Philip had conducted intermittent campaigns against the Braganzas without success. Plans for an invasion to coincide with the Peace of the Pyrenees failed ignominiously. Attacks down the Tagus valley were blunted by the frontier fortifications of Elvas, and incursions from Galicia had no better result. Don Juan José was given command of an army of 20,000 in 1661, but he was now faced by Marshal Schomberg with foreign reinforcements. Although Evora was taken in 1663, the Portuguese fought back to win the victory of

Ameixial, followed by that of Montes Claros two years later: in the first, Don Juan José was routed as he withdrew into Spain, and in the second his successor, Caracena, lost half his army.

These had been years of disillusionment for Philip. In 1661 his heir, Philip-Prosper, died; and although another son was born to him in the same year, it became clear that a long minority must follow. On the death of Haro, no single minister could command the allegiance of the court, and Philip divided the administration between the Count of Castrillo, Haro's uncle, the Duke of Medina de las Torres, and the Inquisitor-General, each of whom submitted business to him in turn. But no change was made in the system of government and appointments, and no measures were taken to revive industry or agriculture. The crown continued to sell offices for sums which could scarcely be recovered unless by corruption. It was not unusual for several persons to have purchased expectations, and these 'futurarios' must look forward to long years of waiting and perhaps in the end find the office they had bought bestowed on someone else. This peculiar confusion of the present with the future made the possibility of financial reform more remote than ever. In 1654 Philip told the cortes of Castile that he had received only 3 million of a service of 10 million ducats, and only 8 or 9 million, out of total revenues of 18 million ducats, while his debts amounted to 120 million. A general impoverishment had occurred during the course of the reign. On Philip's accession a fairly large class of nobles, churchmen and officials still enjoyed considerable wealth, even if at the expense of the treasury and the tribute-payers. At his death, a few great incomes were left: but many of the nobility had been rendered bankrupt by demands for contributions and the once powerful hidalgo caste had been reduced by service in the wars, emigration, celibacy and profligacy. Even in Olivares' time it was ceasing to supply leaders: there were 'no heads', he had declared in a moment of exasperation. Once more, however, it is necessary to temper the traditional view of Spanish decadence. Wealth and display still existed in Madrid. Haro, his kinsmen and a number of nobles and courtiers possessed great riches: many other Spaniards talked large and wore fine clothes, and if they did not toil or economise, this was because industry was discredited and constant devaluations had shown the futility of saving. Most of the crafts and trades of the capital were exercised by Frenchmen, who were said to number 40,000: they would scarcely have come to Madrid if the whole country had been submerged in poverty.

When Philip IV died in September 1665, his heir was a child of five, so feeble that he had only recently been weaned from a succession of fourteen wet-nurses. At nine he was still unable to read, but thereafter he made some progress despite recurrent fevers and sicknesses. For all his physical degeneracy, he survived till the age of thirty-nine and was twice married. His mind seems to have been clear if limited, and his character kindly. Philip IV had appointed his widow Mariana regent and had also named a council which included his son by the actress Isabel Calderón, Don Juan José. In this prince the last remnants of Hapsburg sanity were united to a certain plebeian toughness; and although his conduct of the war in Portugal had not been conspicuously successful, his pretensions to leadership were not altogether unfounded. When relieved of his command, he put forward a demand to be recognised as an infante of Spain and to be appointed first minister; but the Queen feared that he intended to usurp the regency and to make himself successor to the throne, and therefore sought his return to the front. She herself had little experience of affairs, and turned for guidance to her confessor, Fr Nithard, an earnest German Jesuit, who was promoted Inquisitor-General and brought into the Council on the death of the old Archbishop of Toledo.

In 1667 Louis XIV took advantage of the minority to seize part of the Spanish Netherlands on the trivial pretext of a local form of inheritance. Spain was quite unable to oppose him, and England, Holland and Sweden formed an alliance and thrust their mediation upon him. The ensuing peace of Aix-la-Chapelle (May 1668) restored Franche-Comté to Spain, but left France with the system of fortresses from Charleroi to Douai and Lille through which she could open a breach in the midst of the Spanish Netherlands and command the mouth of the Scheldt. It was now no longer possible for the Spaniards to threaten Paris from their Belgian frontier. A few weeks earlier peace had been made with Portugal, whose independence was at last recognised. But Spanish pride had only been swallowed by two foreigners, Mariana and Nithard, who were bitterly criticised for these treaties.

Don Juan José, who had been sent by the Queen to reside at his priory at Consuegra, became the leader of the opposition, demanding the dismissal of Nithard and advancing on the capital at the head of a band of several hundred armed adherents. The first of the *pronunciamientos* was tacitly supported by the Council of Castile. But when finally Nithard left Spain for Rome, to become Spanish ambassador and later Cardinal, Mariana again refused to admit Don Juan José, and he still hesitated to seize power. She first appointed him Governor of the Netherlands, and when he refused this undesirable duty, sent him to Saragossa as Vicar-General of Aragon and Catalonia. He had at the time of his advance on the capital prepared a political programme which was clandestinely distributed: like many such documents, it denounced familiar abuses—the burden of taxation, the concession of favours, the weakness of the army and the maladministration of justice,—but its only positive suggestion was the formation of an advisory committee of experienced ministers. However, his object appears to have been to rally opinion in the east and south against the governing class of Madrid: the Queen offered to call cortes (that is, to sound the opinion of Castile), but this he refused. The knowledge that he stood for lower taxes recommended him to the populace of the capital, and the Queen and Council of Castile feared a popular rising in his favour. It was therefore decided to organise a new regiment of the Guard, which, being fitted out with the large hats introduced by Schomberg, was christened 'la Chamberga'.

The Queen had also accepted Don Juan José's proposal for a committee, the Junta of Reliefs, which issued a number of orders before lapsing into inactivity. The Council of Finance accepted a few modest reforms, the collection of the taxes on meat, wine, oil and vinegar (the 'millions') by one body instead of four, the unification of the additional alcabalas at four per cent, instead of four separate additions of one per cent, and the suppression of certain offices as they fell vacant. The Junta abolished the sale of hereditary offices (but only in small towns) and cancelled a number of offices purchased since 1630. After this the urge for reform quickly abated.

In Saragossa Don Juan José won some popularity by persecuting the Viceroy, the Count of Aranda, who was regarded as a centralist and an enemy of the fueros. He fled to Madrid, and the Queen retorted by cutting off Don Juan José's pay and again appointing him Governor of Flanders. He pretended illness and attempted to build himself a following in Aragon, but his position was an equivocal one, and everything he attempted could be frustrated by some convenient privilege. Meanwhile, his adherents in Madrid began to lose confidence in his star.

The Queen's efforts to rule without a favourite had proved unsuccessful. By 1672 the ministers left by Philip IV had almost all been removed, and she turned to a new adviser, Fernando de Valenzuela, who had won her confidence from a modest position in her household. Valenzuela was a pushful and clever young Andalusian, with some of Lerma's cupidity and a little of Olivares' resolution: the nobility, who were to accuse him of fantastic peculation when he fell, readily pocketed their pride and received favours from him while he was in power. His policy was a simple one, to please as many people as possible. He provided bread and bullfights during two years of bad harvests and near-famine, and at the same time revived the popular sumptuary legislation against the wearing of gold and brocade. Since the Chamberga was regarded as an offence to Castilian loyalism, he dressed it in the same uniform as the other guards. As the Queen desired to share in the universal quest for wealth, he showed her how to obtain rewards for making appointments; and when in November 1674 it was decided to give Charles II his own household, he chose its officers from the highest of the nobility, Medinaceli, Albuquerque and the Admiral: no Spanish prince had ever been better attended. Valenzuela himself remained governor of El Pardo, where the young King resided.

When Charles reached the age of fourteen in 1675, the Queen

and her favourite prolonged the regency: and disappointed courtiers again appealed to Don Juan José. Although the Queen made him Viceroy of Naples, he lingered in Spain, and on November 1, the King called the Cardinal of Aragon, and stated that he would assume power and arrest Valenzuela. Don Juan José appeared and was cheered in the streets; but he was not yet victorious. Mariana descended upon her son, who obediently signed a written order that his half-brother should go to Italy. A meeting of the Councils of State and of Castile decided that the King should sign decrees himself, that Don Juan José should go to Italy, and also that Valenzuela should leave Madrid. But neither of the rivals left the country. Valenzuela spent a month or two as Governor of Granada, and then returned, dissolved the royal council and established himself in the King's own chambers. Thus ensconced, he obtained an order that all the Councils except Castile were to transact business with him. But Castile and the grandees petitioned Charles for his removal, and when he doubled the Chamberga, brought in cavalry and armed the palace servants, they demanded his arrest. Don Juan José advanced from Saragossa, and Valenzuela fled, to be captured, tried, deprived of his property and deported to the Philippines: he ended his picaresque career by being thrown from a horse in Mexico.

Despite the opposition of part of the Council, Don Juan José was now able to take power, installing himself in the King's rooms and forcing the Queen-mother and her friends to leave Madrid. For all his dashing manner, his conduct of affairs was disappointing. Since the peace of Aix-la-Chapelle, with which the Emperor, England and Holland sought to restrain the aggressive power of France, Louis XIV had attempted to buy the Spanish Netherlands, or to exchange them for Roussillon and Cerdagne. These offers had been rejected, and Spain allied with Holland while France was joined by England. In 1672 Louis XIV again invaded the Low Countries, and the Emperor and Spain joined the Dutch: in reply Louis turned his armies against the Franche-Comté, where the Spanish garrisons were soon overrun. This campaign, concluded in 1674, finally broke Spanish communications between Milan and Flanders and ended the encirclement of

France first achieved by Charles V nearly a century and a half before. The war was then transferred to the Pyrenees, where the French won Puigcerdá and Figueras, and to Sicily. Once more Spain was exhausted, and the threat of a new invasion of Catalonia forced Don Juan José to accept the peace of Nimwegen, by which he gave up Franche-Comté, but received compensation in Flanders.

Although the peace was duly celebrated in Madrid, it exposed Don Juan José to the very criticisms he had once levelled against Nithard. National pride could not achieve victories, but it was readily directed against any concession to Spain's enemies. Two parties were now taking shape, one of which formed round Don Juan José, and favoured a settlement with France, while the other, led by Mariana, stood by the Austrian connection. The chief issue between them was the young King's marriage, and in 1679 the favourite finally decided on a French match and the betrothal was celebrated in Paris. But within a month he had fallen ill and died; and the Queen-mother returned to Charles' side and awaited him in Madrid when he brought back his bride, Louis XIV's niece, María-Luisa of Orleans, in 1680.

The appointment of a new valido was a matter of such difficulty that the secretary of 'Despacho Universal', Eguía, proposed that no first minister should be designated: however, Charles finally appointed the Duke of Medinaceli, a moderate supporter of the late favourite. With a feeble king and a divided court he could do little to produce those emotional and social changes that were needed to revive the Spanish state. The new Great Junta of Finance was at once lost in a profusion of detail, and his proposal for a unified budget so alarmed the old Council that it was promptly forgotten. The penury of the crown continued. Private bullion arriving with the Indies fleet was regularly impounded, and one of the aggrieved, the Elector of Brandenburg, retorted by seizing Spanish ships at Ostend. In July 1680, the palace staff in Madrid, which had not been paid for over a year, went on strike. A merchant who demanded a reduction of taxes was murdered. Reform had become impossible, for the weight of custom, privilege and debt had produced something near inertia. The orders of a degenerate king and an amiable favourite were respected, but ignored.

It was still on questions of foreign policy that ministers rose or fell. In 1683 Louis XIV had impatiently seized Courtrai and Dixmude, and Spain again declared war. In the following year Catalonia was entered and Gerona besieged, while the Spanish garrison in Luxemburg found itself forced to surrender. In August, 1684, by the treaty of Ratisbon, Louis received Strasbourg for twenty years and Spain accepted the loss of Luxemburg. A few months later Medinaceli was persuaded to share his responsibilities with the Count of Oropesa, only to be dismissed soon after.

Oropesa governed the tottering empire from 1685 until 1691. He attempted to reform the royal household, which consumed nearly half Spain's revenues, and once more prohibited the import of luxuries. The air was again full of hopeful schemes, but neither King nor minister had the power to enforce them against the tangle of privileges which assured the welfare of the fortunate: Spanish individualism, that immense reservoir of social energy, was now dedicated solely to the task of conserving particular rights.

Meanwhile, French military might had reached its peak; and to oppose it the Emperor, Spain and Sweden formed the Confederation of Augsburg, to which James II of England and Holland later adhered. Louis XIV spared no effort to undo the alliance, and in 1688 war became inevitable as his enemy William III succeeded to the throne of England. In the following year the French Queen of Spain died; her wild and extravagant nature had achieved nothing in her husband's sombre court, and she made no attempt to compete with her Austrian mother-in-law, who now arranged for Charles to marry Ana of Neuburg, a sister of the Empress. This match, if it crowned Oropesa's system of alliances, dashed Louis XIV's ambitions and provoked him to declare war once again. The French took Mons in the north, entered Savoy and the Milanese, and made a small advance into Catalonia.

Meanwhile, in Madrid the Austrian party was in the ascendant. The new Queen was governed by her confessor and her rapacious companion, Baroness Berlepsch; and in 1691 she secured the dismissal of the moderate Oropesa and the nomination of a ministry subservient to the Austrian cause, the Dukes of Pastrana (who died in 1693) and Montalto, Marquis of Villafranca and Counts of Melgar and Aguilar. Against them the so-called Seven Just Men attempted to persuade Charles to conclude a separate peace with Louis XIV, but their efforts had no result. In 1693 the French forced their way into central Catalonia, taking Gerona and Palamós, and their general Noailles assumed the title of Viceroy. Aragon became alarmed and urged that the King should go to the front. The subject was debated by the Council of State, and Charles listened to the discussion from behind a screen: he was, it was said, heard running to his Queen delightedly shouting: 'We don't have to go to Aragon!'

In 1696 Louis XIV ordered his generals to take Barcelona, which was occupied by Vendôme in August of the following year. It had become clear that Charles would have no succession by his second wife, and Louis therefore adroitly negotiated the generous peace of Rijswick: Catalonia was evacuated and the Spanish possessions in Flanders were restored as at the peace of Nimwegen. More was now to be achieved by diplomacy than by war.

Apart from the unfortunate Charles, Philip IV had left two daughters: Maria-Teresa, who had married Louis XIV, but had expressly forfeited all claim to the Spanish throne, and Margarita-Teresa, who had married the Emperor Leopold I, renouncing her personal rights: her claim was deemed to have passed through her daughter, the wife of the Elector of Bavaria, to her grandson Joseph-Ferdinand, born in 1692. This succession was supported in Madrid by the Queen-mother and some of the ministers, notably Oropesa, and in September 1696 Charles made a will in favour of this child. But on Mariana's death the Emperor sent a veteran ambassador, Count von Harrach, to Spain to build up a party in favour of his son, the Archduke Charles, who at least was of an age to defend his claim: since Spaniards were united in their desire to preserve the integrity of their territory, it was capable of commanding general support. But the Emperor also had his ambitions, and he now demanded the cession of the

Milanese. This, combined with the particular unpopularity of the Queen and her clique, enabled Louis XIV to intervene in Madrid. Having restored what he had won from Spain without any equivalent compensation, he sent the Marquis d'Harcourt to try conclusions with von Harrach.

D'Harcourt found the Austrian party well entrenched: Catalonia and Milan were governed by Germans and the Viceroy of Naples favoured the Emperor, but the rift at court between supporters of the infant Joseph-Ferdinand and those of the Archduke was deepening. A quarrel between Countess Berlepsch and von Harrach gave d'Harcourt the opportunity to approach the Queen and to win over Cardinal Portocarrero, thereafter the stoutest partisan of the French connection. Soon after, von Harrach rashly returned to Austria, leaving his inexperienced son to take his place.

Louis XIV offered to secure Spanish independence by authorising the Dauphin to transmit his 'rights' to whichever of his sons Spain might select. He brushed aside the renunciation his wife had made with an allusion to his responsibilities to God, and emphasised the realities of the situation by a declaration that if the Spaniards would not make the choice between one or the other of his grandsons, he would press the Dauphin's claim by force of arms. His attitude was well calculated to shake the double Austrian claim: the threat of force made the Bavarian infant a poor candidate, while the offer of a choice, however illusory, was more attractive than the imposition of the Archduke.

But in Europe the possible increase of French power inspired much alarm: William III in particular feared a union of the two crowns. In order to prevent a general alignment of the maritime powers and Austria, Louis put forward a proposal for the partition of Spain. He would be satisfied with the Two Sicilies, Tuscany and the Spanish Basque Country for himself; the Archduke Charles might take the Milanese, and the little Bavarian prince should receive what was left (August 1698). The Emperor received this suggestion with indignation and reiterated his son's claim. It was now clear that the choice of either the Archduke or a French prince would mean war, and the Spanish court therefore inclined to the Bavarian Prince. But scarcely had the jurists of Spain and Italy given their verdicts in his favour when he died in February 1699. Faced with a direct competition between the Austrian and French heirs, the smaller powers, and especially England, were as alarmed by the prospect of a reconstitution of the empire of Charles V as by the Bourbon hegemony, and Louis appeased them with new partition agreements which assured them that France would not annex Spain or the Spanish New World.

But the final decision rested with Charles II himself. At the end of 1698 he had prepared a will bequeathing his possessions to the Prince of Bavaria: now each side sought to cajole or bewilder him into deciding for it. His Queen upheld the Austrian cause, but the French made ever-increasing inroads: the court was venal, and while the penurious Austrians had long drawn subsidies from Spain, the Bourbons were able to pay handsome douceurs. Even those who hoped that peace would cure Spain's miseries could not ignore the proofs of French military power. As a last bid, the Austrian party persuaded the wretched King that the fits from which he suffered were the work of demons and persuaded him to receive the attentions of a German exorcist, Mauro Tenda. But a rival specialist in this treatment, Froilán Díaz, who had the advantage of being a Spaniard, turned out to have Bourbon sympathies; and it was left to Cardinal Portocarrero to exorcise the exorcists by establishing himself in the King's chamber to prevent the entry of political hobgoblins.

Finally, Charles' fear of death was even more directly exploited. He was taken to the Escorial and shown the sepulchres of his Austrian predecessors and his French wife. At this final stage the decision came not from the reasoning of an unbalanced king, but out of the bosom of the church itself. The traditional church, and especially the Inquisition, had done all it could in the Austrian cause: Charles' confessor and the Inquisitor-General had raised their demons. But the Cardinal and the Pope were won over to the Bourbons, the first from conviction or interest, and the second lest the empire should recover Naples and restore its control over the Roman states.

Charles was finally convinced that it would be a mortal sin to leave his throne to the Emperor, and on October 2, 1700 he signed a new testament in which he recognised that Maria-Teresa had renounced her claim only to avoid the union of Spain with France and that as this contingency no longer threatened, her repudiation had lost its validity. A month later, on November 1st, he died.

X

THE BOURBON RÉGIME

AT Versailles Louis XIV presented his young grandson, Philip, Duke of Anjou, to his court as the new King of Spain, and the day of the Hapsburgs was done. When the first of the old dynasty had arrived two centuries before, Spain had been scarcely more than a name and an aspiration. Under the Hapsburgs Castile had unified the Peninsula, acquired the vastest empire yet known, and produced what was properly thought of as a 'system'. Since the death of Charles V no one had regarded the royal house as alien: like the church, it was inextricably associated with the fortunes of the state, and Hapsburg royalism had been the very essence of Castilian society, the ultimate guarantor of the rights of individuals and localities and the necessary symbol of a national unity that had never existed outside it. If at first the pathetic figure of Charles II sufficed to hold the Hapsburg system together, his Austrian mother and wife did not. Cortes, which had continued to meet under Philip IV, were no longer convoked; the national literature, intensely social and royalist, withered away: the Inquisition, once the sword of the state, had grown too heavy for the feeble monarch to wield. To Frenchmen who came in with the Bourbons the country seemed strangely passive and inert: '*un corps mort qui ne se défend point*', wrote Fénelon. Yet if the political body was corrupt and its mind exhausted, the social body, inured to privations, was still robust. 'Low as Spain is, there is no nation can so soon retrieve itself', observed an Englishman.

Philip V was a mild, docile youth of seventeen. His grandfather had exhorted him to be a good Spaniard, but never to forget his

French birth. The warning was hardly necessary. Unlike the Hapsburgs, the Bourbons long remained foreigners among their new subjects; if Charles V had sent out Spaniards to conquer the world, the Bourbons were to attempt to bring Europe into Spain. Philip himself yearned for France. A few months after his accession he was married to a girl of thirteen, María-Luisa of Savoy, and became excessively uxorious, but neither she nor the King of France could stir him to industry. His grandfather had not intended that he should display much independence; but even he became alarmed at Philip's indolence. In middle life he was driven by nostalgia rather than ambition to abdicate the crown of Spain in the hope of succeeding Louis XIV. He was disappointed, resumed his reign, and in later years sank into incurable melancholy.

On his arrival in Spain Philip was well supplied with French advisers, who despite their mutual jealousies and assumptions of superiority over the Spaniards slowly replaced the old 'system' by the new 'régime'. The Spanish administration continued to function through the traditional councils: their presidents, headed by the 'President of Castile', constituted a form of cabinet, the *Universal Despacho*, whose secretary transacted business with the sovereign. In view of Philip's lack of experience and of Spanish, this procedure had to be modified, and the secretary gave way to a triumvirate, consisting of Cardinal Portocarrero, regarded as the Spaniard most responsible for the change of dynasty, the President of Castile, and the French Ambassador, d'Harcourt. Madrid had thus no secrets from Versailles.

Outside formal matters of policy the great influence was that of Mme de la Trémouille, Princesse des Ursins (Orsini), the widow of a Spanish grandee and an Italian nobleman, who as *camarera-mayor* to the queen exerted a complete ascendancy over both her and her husband. But the wall of Spanish traditionalism was difficult to breach. The grandees, distinguished by a variety of menial functions, monopolised the offices of the royal household: Mme des Ursins (whose accounts are frequently exaggerated) describes the scuffle in church when the Count of Priego presumed to move the royal chair nearer to the prayer-desk, a function of the Duke of Osuna. The rivalries of the nobility had been stimulated to such a point that they themselves confessed that if the King or Queen were put to nurse they would rather see the nurse rule than one of their equals; but this jealous negativism also impeded the entry of French practices. Every office-holder vigorously stuck to his rights and patronage: all were agreed in reserving office to Castilians and excluding other Spaniards, who were still 'foreigners'. Since most places had been sold for several lives, the King had few favours to bestow. He could not even pay his household regularly, and many of his troops habitually begged their bread. Because of Castilian exclusivism the other regions saw to it that their liability for taxation was never exceeded. The church was wealthy in plate and land, but loth to relieve the shortage of bullion. The enjoyment of the veneration which Spaniards professed towards their sovereigns seemed to the French a poor substitute for real authority.

Philip had scarcely grown accustomed to his crown when it became the pretext for a general war. This was a resumption of the struggle for hegemony between France and Austria, but it was also the first of the great wars of modern Europe, fought not only to resolve ancient dynastic rivalries, but also to maintain a necessary equilibrium between nations. Despite Louis XIV's undertaking that the thrones of France and Spain should never be joined, the Bourbonising of Spain opened wide the gates of Italy and threatened the Mediterranean interests of Austria. When the Emperor Leopold decided to fight for his son's claim to the Spanish throne, he was joined by England and Holland in the Grand Alliance; and in 1701 Prince Eugene of Savoy crossed the Alps and defeated the French in the Milanese. In the following year Philip V took a Spanish army to Italy, and the Alliance retorted by preparing for the Archduke Charles to invade Spain. It was at first intended to seize Cádiz and so to wrest the American trade from French control and provoke a rebellion in Andalusia. But Sir George Rooke and his Anglo-Dutch force failed to take the town, and although he sank or captured the Spanish treasure-galleons at Vigo, it was still necessary for the allies to secure a strong base for a land-war. Thus in 1703 Portugal joined the Grand Alliance, and the Archduke landed at Lisbon.

Philip now returned from Italy, but he was unable to prevent the English from seizing Gibraltar in 1704. Soon after, Catalonia declared for the Archduke and resolutely adhered to his cause even after the European war was over. In October 1705 the Archduke entered Barcelona as 'Charles III', and by the following year Philip's situation seemed desperate. The armies of the Alliance had advanced from Portugal and approached Madrid, though they left it to occupy Murcia, thus rejoining their fleet and consolidating the eastern provinces held by the Hapsburgs. Lake took Alicante, Majorca and Ibiza. In the north Ramillies spelt the end of Spanish domination in Flanders; and in Italy the battle of Turin lost her the Milanese. The French alliance could not prevent the Archduke from entering Madrid, while Philip and his court retired to Burgos.

But Castile and western Spain, which had hitherto shown no great enthusiasm for the new dynasty, now recovered, stirred partly by active French help and partly by the realisation that Charles had committed himself to the dismemberment of Spain; the defection of Catalonia and the news that Portugal had been promised Galicia and part of Extremadura, and England and Holland had reserved shares in Spanish America roused Castilian resistance. Charles received no welcome in Madrid, and withdrew with his allies to Valencia. The Bourbon armies, now commanded by Berwick, repulsed them at Almansa in April 1707, and recovered much of eastern Spain.

But the Bourbons lost Sardinia and Minorca; and in Africa Oran, held by Spain since the days of Cisneros, was seized by the Muslims. In a final effort the Anglo-Austrian armies won the victories of Almenara and Saragossa and again entered Madrid in September 1710; but the whole of the court and nobility evacuated the capital. The Bourbon armies still held Old Castile, and by the victories of Brihuega and Villaviciosa (December 1710) they regained control of Madrid and of all central Spain. Soon only Catalonia and the Balearics held out. Barcelona, still invoking its treaty with England, finally capitulated after a heroic siege on September 11, 1714. But despite this extraordinary feat of endurance, the character of the struggle had already changed four years earlier, when the Archduke succeeded to the Austrian throne. The smaller powers desired a restoration of Hapsburg imperialism even less than an extension of Bourbon hegemony. In England, the Whigs were overthrown, and a Tory government made a sudden change of face: Holland, Portugal, Savoy and Prussia all successively sought peace, first with France at Utrecht (1713) and then with Spain at Rastadt (1714-5). Only Spain and the empire remained nominally at war.

For Spain the struggle had been disastrous. For the first time since the reconquest a foreign enemy had marched across Castile. The remains of the Burgundian heritage in Flanders had been surrendered to the Emperor, as well as the Milanese, Naples and Sardinia, Sicily had gone to the Duke of Savoy; England held Gibraltar and Minorca, and by wresting the *asiento* or slave-trade monopoly from the French, opened a breach in the economic system of the New World. Little more than a decade of Bourbon rule had proved infinitely more costly than a whole century of Hapsburg 'decadence', for all its futile monarchs, predatory favourites and administrative torpor. That such concessions had to be accepted was due in part to the attitude of Louis XIV, who alternately protested to Philip the great services he was rendering Spain and planned to bring the struggle to an end at her expense.

So acute was the crisis that Philip V was not only enabled, but forced, to apply the measures of centralisation desired by Olivares. The association of Catalonia, Valencia and part of Aragon with the King's enemies provided the classical pretext for the suppression of their privileges and the extension of the powers of the central government. In 1707 the fueros of Aragon and Valencia were swept away. In Aragon the Castilian municipality with its corregidor and regidores was implanted everywhere, while in Catalonia twelve cities were given corregidores, and in Barcelona the ancient Concell de Cent and Diputació were replaced by manageable juntas. The Catalan nobility were deprived of their few grandeeships and remained 'agraviados', victims of injustice. The eastern realms ceased to be regarded as 'kingdoms' with their own laws, and the office of Viceroy, which seemed to invest its holder with quasi-regal attributes, was swept away. In its stead the

Bourbons appointed Captains-general, who, if they too exercised military and civil powers, were clearly servants of the crown and agents of the central government. Their first function was to preside over the audiencias set up in Saragossa, Valencia, Barcelona and Palma de Mallorca in imitation of the royal tribunals of Valladolid and Granada. The same official was later introduced into Castile, bringing with him a new form of military autocracy.

Little difficulty was encountered in the suppression of the various cortes. Even during the reign of Charles II the Castilian cortes had ceased to meet, though Don Juan José, seeking the favour of the Aragonese, had taken the King to Saragossa to receive the oath there. With the imposition of a general law and uniform system of taxation, regular meetings of cortes lost their purpose, and almost their only function was to recognise the heir to the crown. In 1702 while Philip was in Italy his young Queen had summoned cortes in Aragon in the hope of raising money, but had found the representatives disobliging. Consequently in 1709 the Aragonese and Valencians were called to Madrid, and in 1724 the Catalans also came to the capital. Only in loyalist Navarre, where cortes resembled a general junta like those which managed the affairs of the Basque provinces, were the ancient prerogatives respected. The realms of Spain were at last represented in a single body, but one which had now scarcely more than symbolic value. The French connection had thus produced two apparently conflicting, if logical, results, external disintegration and internal integration.

But if the centralising aspirations of the Bourbons coincided with those of the Castilians up to this point, it proved easier to alter names and appearances than the essence of things. The proposed abolition of the Basque fueros was soon abandoned, and even after the publication of the 'New Plan' which laid down the outlines of centralist policy in 1716, Catalonia was left with her commercial law, her currency, taxation and military service. In Castile, the war had divided the old nobility, part of which was now in exile or disgrace. The Council of Castile had greatly increased its jurisdiction, though in doing so it had lost its sense of corporate unity: the remaining Councils began to give way to a departmental system with secretaries for State, Marine and the Indies, Finance and War. But these changes were perhaps more apparent than real: there was constant resistance to all real reforms, and Frenchmen who had been surprised at the lack of 'opposition' and had noted the absence of financial interests, the docility of the Madrid press, the ignorance of Spanish ladies and the quiescence of literature (the publication of books had almost stopped during the doubtful years of the war), now began to understand the nature of that apparent passivity.

Perhaps the most difficult and necessary reforms were those of finance. Philip V had received the services of a French economist, Orry, who wrestled against stiff resistance to establish a uniform system of taxation: he fought so hard that even a compatriot thought that he would 'either be hanged or become a great man'. The extinction of the *juros*, the public debt of the Hapsburgs, ruined moderate fortunes without repairing those of the crown. By 1707 the royal revenues barely exceeded half a million pounds, or a third of the cost of the war, and the imposition of a loan on the church was resisted by most of the clergy. It was only in December 1713, when the war was almost over, that the system of taxation was reformed by a decree which divided the whole of Spain into provinces for the farming of internal revenues and customs. When Orry and his Spanish collaborator Macanaz placed before the Council of Castile a plan for the spoliation of the church, it was condemned as heretical by the Inquisition; and although the members of both Councils who were opposed to Gallican principles were dismissed and Cardinal del Giudice disgraced for his opposition, it was not long before Orry himself was overthrown.

In 1714 the young Queen María-Luisa died. Through her Mme des Ursins had exercised complete domination over the King; and when she disappeared, the royal widower, the victim of abnormal sensuality and unusual propriety, grew so melancholy that even the female eminence recognised the need for a new queen. Fr Alberoni, a mellifluous Parmesan who had arrived in Spain with Vendôme for the war and had stayed as representative of his native state, lost no time in recommending a compatriot,

Elizabeth Farnese, niece and stepdaughter of the reigning Duke, whom he represented as a 'good-natured Lombard girl, devoid of temper, all heart. . . .' The match was made, and the Lombard maiden travelled into Spain by way of Bayonne and Pamplona. When Mme des Ursins appeared to welcome her, the new Queen instantly ordered a conveniently posted guard to 'arrest the madwoman' and had her bundled away in a waiting coach. The episode had been carefully planned by the ingenious Parmesan, who now became the formulator of Spanish policy. It was a defeat for Gallicanism. Alberoni's coup was directed against 'this lady' who 'had contrived to be the despot, removing everyone else from the King's side, fostering in him a horrible mistrust of his vassals, and maintaining herself in authority by placing the government of the monarchy in the hands of two men, Orry and Macanaz, without ability, without knowledge, devoid of law, faith and honour. . . .'

That an obscure Italian priest should have gained control of the destinies of Spain was in itself surprising: Castilian royalists had accepted a Bourbon king and fought for him, but after the War of the Succession it was no longer possible to be enthusiastic for the French connection, especially when the might of Louis XIV was broken and his place taken by an infant grandson and a rackety regent. Yet no other alliance seemed possible: Austria occupied Spain's European heritage and England held Gibraltar and Minorca. In the confusion that followed the civil war no Spaniard was yet able or willing to set a course for the new dynasty; and the vacancy was filled by the agent of the Dukes of Parma, who traced their descent to a bastard daughter of Charles V and a bastard son of Pope Paul III.

The new 'nurse' was in no hurry to assume control of affairs. He must first educate the simple Lombard girl, who was more interested in Italian sweetmeats than in affairs of State. In his view Spain should reconstitute her naval power so that she might stand up to Great Britain in the asiento question and regain Gibraltar and Minorca. He realised that such a recovery would require several years; but the Parmesan Queen and her family were impatient, and insisted on taking advantage of a minor incident to occupy

Sardinia and later Sicily (1717). Alberoni was unwisely drawn into the Duchess of Maine's intrigue to make Philip V regent of France, and succeeded in alienating the French government and perturbing the remaining guarantors of the settlement of Utrecht. The English were especially alarmed by Spanish naval policy; and Byng was instructed to destroy her new fleet even while Stanhope negotiated in Madrid (1718). Alberoni's only friends were now Russia and Sweden and the Stuarts. In 1719 James 'III' was welcomed in Spain and an invasion of Scotland with the aid of Peter the Great projected. In reply, the Hanoverian English landed at Vigo and the French occupied the Basque Provinces. The Duke of Parma warned his niece that Alberoni had become impossible, and she at once disowned and dismissed him.

Philip was obliged to return Sardinia and Sicily to Savoy and the Empire, and adhered to the Quadruple Alliance which guaranteed the peace of Utrecht. His only gain was the reservation of the Duchies of Parma, Piacenza and Tuscany for his son by Elizabeth Farnese. The Emperor still deferred acknowledging him as King of Spain, and negotiations at Cambrai threatened to become interminable. Philip therefore resumed the French alliance with a double betrothal: his heir Luis would marry Luisa-Isabel of Orleans and the young Louis XV was betrothed to a daughter of Elizabeth Farnese. His Queen's pretensions could not conceal the fact that Philip's reign had failed in its main object, to save Spain from partition, and an incurable melancholy now preyed upon his mind.

He longed for Versailles: even La Granja, the first of those Bourbon palaces which were sighs for the indulgent comfort of France and Italy, did not relieve his nostalgia. The foolish plot of the Duchess of Maine had given him the idea that he might yet succeed not merely to the regency, but even to the throne of France, if, as seemed possible, the sickly Louis XV should die. The guarantee of Utrecht that the crowns of Spain and France should never be united stood in his way; but in February 1724 he removed this obstacle by abdicating the throne of Spain and retiring in assumed disillusionment to San Ildefonso. In fact, his young son, Luis I, governed only in name, and when he died in

August of the same year Philip, now more genuinely disillusioned, resumed his reign.

Luis had shown himself a bright if unstudious boy, and his young French wife was so wild that Spanish gossip proclaimed her mad. Nevertheless, some courtiers had pinned their expectations on the young couple, and Philip's resumption led to divisions. His ministers were temporarily overshadowed by the flamboyant Baron Ripperdá. This Dutch colonel had been employed as a trade expert at Utrecht and by Alberoni as a financial adviser. He had embraced catholicism, received charge of a factory at Guadalajara, and been made general superintendent of manufactures. But he aimed higher, and was given his chance in 1725, when the French abruptly returned the Spanish princess so that Louis XV might marry Maria Leczinska. This insult infuriated both Elizabeth Farnese and the populace of Madrid, where French residents feared a general massacre. All relations with the senior Bourbon branch were broken off, and Spain first approached England, then concluded a double marriage with Portugal, and finally performed a complete volte-face by entering an alliance with Austria. Europe was realigned, and as of old Spain and the Empire faced France and England.

With this change Ripperdá prospered amazingly. Having negotiated the Austrian treaty and promised Vienna impossible subsidies, he returned to Madrid, where he developed Alberoni's naval and mercantilist policy in an even more exaggerated form. He dismissed functionaries, suspended payments, raised the price of gold, concentrated an army in Galicia, and prepared to invade England while assuring Stanhope that he meant peace. Even when Philip was disillusioned and arrested the 'romancing Dutchman' he was allowed to retire with a generous, if unpaid, pension, and ended his days by going to Morocco and embracing Islam in Tetuán, where his remains are still revered.

The succession of foreign vizirs was now interrupted, and the most influential minister was Patiño, a man of wide experience who had collaborated with Alberoni in the restoration of the navy and assumed active control of various departments, thus becoming the first of the 'universal ministers' through whom the Bourbons preferred to rule. In contrast to the Hapsburg favourites, who acquired power by virtue of their intimacy with the monarchs, Patiño and his successors were schooled in the departments of state before being entrusted with office; and although there was never any doubt that reforms should appear to emanate from the ruler, the concept of promotion to the highest authority established a new relationship between the crown and its subjects.

But the new dynasty was above all the product of foreign policy, and in this field it still proved difficult to find firm ground. Spain's frontier was no longer a fortress-province two days' march from Paris, but in Andalusia and the Balearics. Alberoni had realised that if Spain were to recover Gibraltar and Minorca she must equip a strong fleet, but he had too soon exposed her new resources to attack. Ripperdá, in attempting to set up a war for the English succession, proposed to win a Scotch Gibraltar with only five ships of the line, and staked all on the resumption of the Austrian alliance. This would have canalised the trade of America through the Austrian-controlled ports of Ostend and Trieste, in return for imperial support in bringing about the recovery of Gibraltar. But the Emperor, whose only heir was a young daughter, Maria-Theresa, desired to run no risks; and in 1727 Spain alone mobilised a land army for an unsuccessful siege of the lost stronghold. The exorbitance of the Emperor cooled Spanish ardour, and the English wished only for peace to preserve their advantages. Consequently, after prolonged intrigues and bickerings at the Congress of Soissons, the French took the opportunity to separate both Spain and England from the swollen Empire, and the three powers signed the treaty of Seville of 1729, which enabled Spain to place garrisons in the Italian territories reserved for the Farnese heir, and guaranteed English commercial privileges. The problem of Gibraltar and Minorca was passed over in silence. But when the Duke of Parma died in 1731 the Emperor occupied the disputed territories, and in order to avoid war, England and Spain negotiated a new treaty of Vienna, by which Austria recognised the Spanish Farnese as Duke of Parma. In the same year Elizabeth's son occupied his duchy, and Spanish troops returned to Italy escorted by English ships.

L*

Philip had meanwhile become a chronic hypochondriac, spending whole days in bed and giving midnight audiences, or avoiding his ministers altogether. In order to frustrate his furtive attempts to abdicate, the Queen kept him away from the Council of Castile until her Italian aspirations were satisfied. Once the danger of a new war had been averted, the troops that had been assembled were sent against Oran, which surrendered to the Duke of Montemar in 1732. In the following year, while the French were disputing the Polish succession with the Hapsburgs, a tempting opportunity occurred to recover Naples and Sicily under cover of a resumption of the Bourbon alliance. In November the first Family Compact was concluded in Madrid, and in the following spring Charles of Parma occupied Naples and shortly after took Sicily. By a new treaty of Vienna (1736) the Empire recognised these gains in exchange for the relinquishment of Parma.

The credit for this revival belongs in no small degree to Patiño, who had understood better than his predecessors that reforms could not revive Spain, but that once her pulse were quickened she might accept changes. Patiño held the offices of Minister for Marine and the Indies and of Finance: he had worked with Alberoni and, like him, hoped to concentrate trade at Cádiz, intending to remove the Ostend company to Trieste in order to conserve the central European market. To restore commerce and counter the attacks of freebooters, he planned to establish monopolist trading-companies which would contribute to defence: thus the Guipúzcoa Company was launched to market cocoa from Venezuela and eighteenth-century Spain acquired a notable taste for chocolate. A Havana company, launched in 1740, did not prosper, and a Catalan company with privileges in Santo Domingo was finally ruined by war with England, while a Philippine company projected in 1733 became active only fifty years later, when it brought in the Chinese silks from which mantones 'of Manila' were made.

But Spain was no longer in full control over her American possessions. England, following the example of Holland, had devoted herself to securing commercial advantages from her. Already in Charles II's day Spain had conceded freedom of commerce and navigation at places where the English had previously traded, but she claimed the right to license and search all ships in American waters, and disputes continued to arise until the end of the century. With the War of the Spanish Succession the Bourbons attempted to assert a Franco-Spanish monopoly of American trade which the English vigorously resisted; and at Utrecht England obtained the right hitherto held by France, to introduce 4,800 Negroes a year to the Spanish colonies. This contract, the 'asiento', was at once itself a valuable concession and a pretext for clandestine commerce; and the Spanish government did its best to limit it in execution, constantly appealing to the right of search and countering abuses with violence. But since a renewal of open war might lead to the expulsion of the logwood and mahogany-cutters who had settled in the Honduras, the English government concentrated on demands for compensation for Spanish attacks. These were whittled down by the Spaniards, and the dispute turned on the legality of the right of search. When at last, in December 1739, war was declared, England was stirred by concern for Captain Jenkins' ear, alleged to have been barbarously severed eight years earlier and now produced from a box, while Spain (where eighteenth-century sensibility had not yet sunk so deep) published the shocking incident of an English captain who had cut off the nose and ears of a Spanish captive and forced him to eat them, thus destroying the evidence of his brutality.

The war began with Admiral Vernon's capture of Puerto Bello, the Caribbean terminus of the transatlantic sea-route and for long the main importing centre of the New World. But news of the attack stirred Spain to vigorous action. All English residents were required to leave the country, and the importation of English manufactures was made punishable by death. Privateers, aided by the French, were sent against English merchantmen, and numerous captures made. When Vernon assaulted Cartagena with a strong advantage in numbers, he was beaten off by American troops and failed equally in an attempt to take Santiago in Cuba.

But in 1740 the colonial war gave way to a renewal of European strife. The Emperor Charles VI died, leaving the Hapsburg throne to his daughter Maria Theresa. Although her succession had been guaranteed by the powers, the occasion was too tempting to miss. While Frederick of Prussia seized Silesia, Philip put forward a general claim as heir to the Empire under cover of which he hoped to recover the Milanese. Consequently Spanish troops were landed at Genoa. But England and Savoy remained in the Austrian camp, and an English fleet summarily prevented Charles of Naples from intervening, a humiliation he never forgot. Although the Family Compact was resumed by the treaty of Versailles in 1743, under which Spain stood to recover Milan, Parma, Gibraltar and Minorca, and Philip V was able at last to enter Milan as a conqueror, his triumph was short-lived: in 1745 France and Spain were defeated at Trebbia, and Philip was forced to withdraw. A month later he died of apoplexy, and the crown passed to his fourth and eldest surviving son by Maria-Luisa of Savoy, Ferdinand VI (1746–1759).

The new ruler had been Prince of Asturias since the death of Luis and had been married to the Portuguese princess Barbara of Braganza in 1729. His bellicose stepmother had kept'him in the background during her lifetime, and Ferdinand desired only harmony. He and his wife were united and childless: their single passion was music, and their favourite the singer Farinelli, whose very sterility placed a limit to his ambitions. The removal from the stage of Elizabeth Farnese ended Spain's wider ambitions in Italy: Portugal, which had given her her new Queen, desired only that she should remain as she was.

Philip's last ministers had been pupils of Patiño, Campillo, who died in 1743, and Zenon Somodevilla, Marquis of La Ensenada, the first member of the great nobility to appear as a Bourbon minister. Ensenada, who had taken the French part in restoring the Family Compact and had supported the Italian war, had some of the qualities of the old validos. His influence was counterbalanced by that of José de Carvajal y Lancáster, who inclined towards an 'English' policy, but there was little risk that either minister would violate the desires of their timid and peaceable master. The treaty of Aix put an end to the European conflict in April 1748. By it Ferdinand's half-brother Philip received recognition as Duke of Parma; and Spain engaged in no more wars for the rest of the reign.

These were years of tranquillity, but also of recuperation. While the court disported itself in the toy 'fleet of the Tagus', the decorative barges which cruised among the gardens of Aranjuez, a genuine navy was being constructed in the yards of El Ferrol, Cádiz and Cartagena, and new regiments, raised in the once autonomous realms, were added to the army. The crown was both enhanced and nationalised. The succession of a French-speaking king had spelt the end of the particular culture of the Hapsburgs: in the so-called Golden Century the theatre especially had become the vehicle whereby the Spanish mind paid its court with sentiments of impeccable royalism. Now the Bourbons took charge of the very instrument of expression. Philip's mayor-domo, the Marquis of Villena, had founded the Royal Academy of the Language, which published its famous dictionary 'of authorities' in 1739.[1] A Royal Academy of History was founded in 1738, and that of Noble Arts (later of San Fernando) in 1744. These institutions had perhaps no active political purpose, but they expressed the secular universalism which was the ideal of the new dynasty. The same impulse led to the founding of a royal College for the education of nobles and the revival of domestic arts under royal protection. But the grafting of French manners on Spanish matter was a slow process. The art of the old dynasty had reached it height with Velázquez, who from his palace-studio dominated the Hapsburg world with a dispassionate mastery never achieved by Olivares. His successors at court fell into a myopic literalism much concerned with details of court dress. The new house brought in foreign painters to exalt it in monstrous and embarrassing apotheoses, and it was only in the last quarter of the century that Goya broke through the bonds of conventional academicism. In the domestic arts the uncompromising forms preferred by Spaniards married awkwardly with the more

---

[1] In Barcelona the Academy of Buenas Letras was founded in 1729 and received the royal title in 1759: its Catalan Dictionary was undertaken to save the language from extinction after the teaching of Castilian had been made compulsory in Catalan schools.

graceful style of eighteenth-century Europe, and in pottery the neolithic shapes of unbroken Spanish tradition underlay new and often incongruous decorations. Until the second half of the century Spanish everyday dress remained incorrigibly Hapsburgian. Nor was it possible rapidly to alter the old system of agriculture. Under an imperial monarchy the nobility had forsaken their estates for residence at court or service abroad and few displayed any interest in agricultural improvement. In the eighteenth century the countrypeople were so imbued with conservatism that any change in rural methods was viewed with superstitious hostility. In 1746 the first of the economic societies, the 'Sociedad Económica de Amigos del País', was founded in the Basque Provinces, and the spread of these associations, usually of small proprietors, gradually revived interest in the land.

The new régime had also to make adjustments with the Spanish church, whose defence of religious orthodoxy was paralleled by its attachment to its temporalities. The Hapsburgs had only scratched the surface of the problem of mortmain, and while the Spanish state was sinking into poverty and inertia, the churches of the south were bedecking themselves with the most prodigal baroque. The changes proposed by Orry and Macanaz were defeated, but taxes were levied on ecclesiastics and the crown limited the number of priests ordained, and although the Spanish Bourbons reached a concordat with Rome in 1737 by which they recognised the general immunities of the church, the peculiar interpenetration of church and state which had been characteristic of Hapsburg Spain disappeared. The Inquisition had been the sword of the Hapsburg state, and the papacy did not complain as the Bourbons slowly sheathed it. A more profound difficulty lay between the crown and the Jesuits, who, as defenders of universalism, were strongly opposed to the secularisation of culture and education. In France Bourbon regalism was followed by the rationalist 'enlightenment' spread with the aid of freemasonry. In Spain an English lodge had been founded as early as 1727, but from the middle of the century Spanish masonry was predominantly French. After the papal condemnation Ferdinand VI prohibited it in 1751, but in the following reign it was closely associated with the regalist ministers, and the Count of Aranda was the head of a Spanish grand orient. Meanwhile, in 1753 Ferdinand VI concluded a new concordat by which Benedict XIV recognised his right to appoint prelates in Spain and the Indies with the reservation of fifty-two benefices, and conceded the right of the crown to receive the revenues of vacant sees.

At this time, England and France competed for influence at the Spanish court. In 1750 the question of English interests in America was settled. The English now renounced the slave-trade and undertook to pay Ferdinand compensation for the South Sea Company, receiving in return the right to trade in agreed places on terms of equality with Spaniards. This led to a French counter-attack, with claims in the West Indies and for the 'ancient limits' of Acadia in North America. When Carvajal, the mainstay of the 'English' party, died in April 1754, the French looked forward to the return of Ensenada and the consequent restoration of the Family Pact. But before the hesitant monarch could decide, his chamberlain, the Duke of Huéscar, later of Alba, persuaded him to appoint Ricardo Wall, an Irish expatriate born at Nantes who had served in the Spanish army. The new minister maintained good relations with England, but the expectation that he would limit the growth of the Spanish navy was not fulfilled: he avoided responsibility for the Marine department, which was managed by an ally of Ensenada.

When in 1756 Anglo-French rivalry for ascendancy in northern Europe led to the Seven Years War, the Franco-Austrians attempted to win Spain from her neutrality by offering the recovery of Gibraltar and Minorca as inducements. But Ferdinand was firmly wedded to peace, and when the French sent a force from Toulon to besiege Minorca, its loss caused the fall of Newcastle, the rise of Pitt, and the exemplary execution of Byng, but did not move Spain out of her neutrality. When France offered it as an inducement for her to enter the war, the English countered by proposing the return of Gibraltar if she would continue to stand aside. But by now Spanish neutrality was assured: Barbara died in 1758, and Ferdinand lapsed into a maniac melancholy, sometimes sitting motionless on a stool (once for eighteen hours) sometimes lying in bed and throwing dishes at the servants. Finally, after a continuous illness of ten months, he died, 'childless', it was said, 'but with a numerous offspring of patriotic virtues'.

Ferdinand's half-brother and successor, Charles III (1759–1788), was that eldest son of Elizabeth Farnese who had been Duke of Parma and King of Naples. He had the air of rusticity that Alberoni had praised in his mother, some of whose spirit he had inherited. His qualities were not outstanding, but he had avoided the stultifying upbringing reserved for Spanish heirs, and had broadened his tastes and interests in Italy. He was married to Maria-Amalia of Saxony and had six children, of whom the eldest was mad; the second, Charles, became Prince of the Asturias, and the third, Ferdinand, King of the Two Sicilies.

Charles III landed at Barcelona in October 1759, and reached Madrid in December. He retained the services of Ferdinand's ministers, but entrusted the responsibility for finance to a Neapolitan, the Marquis of Squillace (hispanised as Esquilache). Charles' Queen belonged to an anti-French house, and he at first preserved neutrality; but after her death in 1760, he allowed the Family Pact to be renewed. There were mounting complaints against English misdeeds in America and he himself did not forget the English ultimatum delivered to him during his early years in Naples: he therefore proposed that the Pact should be applied to the mutual preservation of the overseas possessions of France and Spain. Choiseul at once exploited this opening, urging that Spain insist on the elimination of English settlements on the logwood coast, and on reparations, and announcing the renewal of the Pact in August 1761. Spain had expected that the agreement would remain secret in order to avoid the danger of immediate hostilities: Britain too had no wish to add to her enemies and deferred recalling her Ambassador, but in January 1762 Lord Bristol left Madrid and war was declared. France and Spain entered into an offensive and defensive alliance and invited Portugal to join them. But Pombal, though he desired to limit the privileges of the English in Portugal, had no wish to sacrifice the Anglo-Portuguese connection, and declared neutrality. A Franco-Spanish force attempted to invade Portugal and occupied Almeida near the frontier, while Spain seized the Brazilian colony of Sacramento on the River Plate. In reply the English occupied Havana (August 1762), several of the West Indian Islands, and Manila in the Philippines. Spain's entry into the war had been just late enough to share in France's defeat, and by the treaty of Paris (1763) she surrendered St Vincent, Tobago and Grenada, Florida, and the right to cut logwood in the Honduras: in compensation she received from France New Orleans and western Louisiana.

The quarrel with Portugal about the Sacramento colony had unexpected repercussions. The settlement faced the Spanish port of Buenos Aires with which it drove a flourishing contraband trade, mainly in English goods. It also adjoined the Jesuit reductions of Paraguay, where the missionaries protected the Guarani Indians against the incursions of the Brazilian 'bandeirantes' of São Paulo. In 1759 the Spanish-Portuguese treaty of Madrid had returned Sacramento to Portugal, and the Jesuits, suffering new depredations, opposed the settlement and applauded the re-entry of the Spaniards in 1761. But with the peace of 1763 Sacramento was again restored to Portugal. The Jesuits once more protested; and their opposition was to be made one of the pretexts for their expulsion.

Not only the Bourbon courts, but the Braganzas were now determined to wrest control of education from the Society. As the spirit of rationalism spread, the Jesuit exploitation of the great Lisbon earthquake seemed not only superstitious but treasonable, since the belief that the cataclysm was a punishment or judgement reflected on the actions of a beneficent monarch. The Jesuits, poised between the regular, secular and lay conditions, were exceptionally sensitive to the opening rift between church and state; and the Bourbons, no less jealous of their authority, loaded all manner of charges against them, of which perhaps the deepest and truest was that of 'seeking universal domination'.

In Spain the mysterious struggle between the two parties came to a head with the popular riots of 1766. Since the resignation of Wall, Squillace had been joined by another Italian, Grimaldi. Both were intent on reform and determined to break the forces of tradition. There followed a stream of legislation of a social and sumptuary nature: Spaniards were accustomed to decrees against display and applauded them, but not that they should be enforced. Squillace was accused of profiteering by negotiating with the monopolies for the supply of bread and oil to the city: such tales were habitually invented in cases where they were not true. In January 1766 a royal order forbade public officials to wear the round chambergo hat and long cape that still recalled the Hapsburg regime, and in March the order was extended to the whole populace, and officials with shears stood ready to trim offenders. Eighteenth-century Spaniards were no less tenacious of their customs and costumes than sixteenth century Moriscos. The royal edicts were defaced; the houses of the two Italians were stoned, and disturbances lasted for ten days during which the royal guards were intimidated by the mob. At length Charles suspended the decree and dismissed Squillace. He himself retired to Aranjuez, so distressed that he resolved never to reside in Madrid again, and some advisers suggested that he should remove his capital to Valencia or Seville. But a minister of unusual determination now appeared. This was the Count of Aranda, a convinced encyclopedist and a leading freemason, who is said to have turned the populace against the Hapsburgian cloak and hat by making it the uniform of the public executioner.

In December the cocked hat and coat had won the day, and Charles returned to his capital. An extraordinary Council attributed the blame for the rising to the 'hand of a religious body', and in January 1767 the main charges against the Jesuits were recapitulated by the minister Campomanes. In April the Society was expelled from Spain and its members rudely deported to the Papal States. The ministers of the Catholic courts then began to demand its total extinction. Clement XIII resisted for some years, but in 1773 the Count of Floridablanca finally succeeded in extracting the necessary brief. Meanwhile Aranda had confided his designs on the Inquisition to Voltaire, whose *Dictionnaire Philosophique* (1769) claimed that Aranda 'a été béni de l'Europe entière en rognant les griffes et en limant les dents du monstre:

mais il respire encore. . . .' This premature congratulation helped to bring Aranda down.

His collaborator, Pablo de Olavide, had philosophised in Paris, and produced a plan for the reform of the University of Seville, which was applied at Salamanca in 1771. He was then entrusted with a scheme for settling six thousand colonists in the Sierra Morena. The colonists would be Flemish and German catholics, but no monasteries would be allowed. The plan was a useful one, since the villages would be situated near the main road from Andalusia to Madrid, which was infested with bandits, but Olavide fell foul of the Inquisition, was accused of heresy, imprisoned, deprived of his possessions and condemned to eight years' reclusion, which he avoided by fleeing to France; he remained twenty years in exile (1778–98).

The failure of the Walloon guards to cope with the riots of 1766 had alarmed Charles, and there followed an extensive reform of the army. In 1768 new Ordinances were introduced and the establishment was fixed at forty regiments of infantry and twenty-two of cavalry: a quarter of the infantry were Irish, Walloons, Swiss or Italians, while the royal guard was divided into Walloons and Spaniards. An Irishman, Alexander O'Reilly, introduced the Prussian system with the aid of French officers. Meanwhile, the municipal levies were reorganised as provincial militia.

The Bourbons were still far from achieving any real sense of identification with the Spanish people. The old vehement royalism, which took pride in the fact that the Hapsburgs needed no guard, had given way to an unimpassioned acceptance. Castilians had proudly been vassals of the Hapsburgs, aware of their own and the crown's mutual obligations. They viewed without affection their new condition of subjects, which they shared with non-Castilian Spaniards. Alienated from the profoundest of Castilian institutions, the Inquisition, the Jesuits, cortes, the traditionalist theatre, the dynasty possessed no emperor, conqueror or justicer, and sought self-aggrandisement in the new titles it created: the bringer of the Act of Guarantee from Naples in 1737 had been made Marquis of the Guarantee, and the escort who accompanied Charles III and his family to Spain was created

Marquis of the Royal Transport. It again relied on foreign or foreign-influenced advisers, the 'afrancesados'. From the time of Squillace and Aranda, frenchification in greater or less degree was the object of all ministers. By the end of the century it had permeated the court aristocracy. Meanwhile, the Bourbon ruler attempted to make contact with his people. At the beginning of his reign Charles III sought to loosen the oligarchy which controlled the municipalities. In 1760 these were placed under the direct supervision of the Council of Castile, and six years later an attempt was made to ensure the appointment of non-nobles and even peasants to local offices. Two new offices were created, the '*diputados del común*', whose function was to facilitate the distribution of goods and prevent corruption in the supply of foodstuffs, and the '*síndico personero*', who represented the municipality in legal questions. The new officers were to be chosen by '*compromisarios*' elected from each parish, and persons of all ranks were eligible. How successful these innovations were is uncertain. In some areas, such as the Basque Provinces, where local government was not corrupt, the new procedure was regarded as a slight by the regidores: elsewhere, even the right of direct appeal to the Council of Castile was probably insufficient to check ancient abuses. By the end of the reign, the reformers had fallen back on a strengthening of the power of the 'corregidor', who now became the instrument of an interventionist central authority, no longer with the attributes of a royal judge, but rather a technical functionary for the application of reforms.

As the Family Pact was cemented and the ministers of the enlightenment pursued their objects, Spain's foreign policy was drawn closely into line with that of France and directed mainly against Great Britain. The Treaty of 1763 had left her without Gibraltar, Minorca and Florida, and she was further aggrieved by the steady flow of uncustomed goods into the rising viceroyalty of Buenos Aires. In 1770 the British occupation of the Falkland Islands presaged an unwelcome extension of foreign interests in the area. A Spanish expedition was sent to dislodge the settlers, and both Charles III and Choiseul were prepared for war. But Louis XV refused to become involved and dismissed his minister;

and Aranda, closely committed to the French alliance, fell shortly afterwards.

In North Africa the Bourbons had resumed the traditional struggle in 1732, but after the conquest of Oran there had been only occasional clashes with the Barbary corsairs. Melilla had been occupied since 1496 and Ceuta had remained in Spanish hands after the Portuguese restoration. In 1767 a treaty was signed with the Sultan of Morocco which granted trading concessions to Spain; but this was repudiated seven years later, when Moroccans and Algerians made an alliance for the recapture of these places. The Moroccan attacks on Ceuta and Melilla failed, and as the Algerians remained inactive, the Sultan proposed to revenge himself by changing sides. Grimaldi organised a large expedition under O'Reilly against Algiers in 1775, but it failed and the minister resigned. Some years later Algiers was bombarded by the Spanish navy, and its ruler, like those of Morocco and Tunis, accepted terms, agreed to the opening of consulates, and admitted freedom of worship for Spanish traders and residents.

In America both France and Spain hesitated to disturb the peace because of the strength of British sea-power; but in 1776 the revolt of the English colonies offered both countries the opportunity to avenge themselves for their defeat in the Seven Years War. Spain first sought to recover the Sacramento colony and sent troops into southern Brazil to avenge Portuguese expansion in the old Jesuit territories. When the King of Portugal died and the all-powerful Pombal fell, his successor, Maria I, concluded the treaty of San Ildefonso by which Sacramento again passed into Spanish hands, together with the islands of Fernando Po and Annobón in the Gulf of Guinea (March 1778). France now recognised the United States and pressed Spain to make war on Great Britain. But Charles, mindful of his belated and costly intervention in the Seven Years War, hesitated and proposed mediation, though on terms which the English could not accept. Finally in April 1779, he concluded a secret alliance with France, under which he hoped to recover Gibraltar, Minorca and Florida and to force the logwood-cutters out of the Honduras. News of British defeats at the hands of the American colonists and of plans for surprise attacks on the Philippines finally drove him to abandon neutrality, and in June he declared war.

At this time the Spanish fleet was strong, while the war in America had weakened Britain and the Spanish treaty with Portugal almost neutralised the Anglo-Portuguese Alliance. The French plan was for a joint landing in England, and the Spanish fleet under Luis de Córdoba united with the French and swept the Channel only to be dispersed by bad weather. However, the transport of English troops to America was interrupted, and the American war consequently shortened.

Spain for her part assisted the colonists in Mississippi and Florida, and disputed the right of search now claimed by Great Britain. But her main object was to recover Gibraltar, which was blockaded in 1779, but relieved in the following year when Rodney defeated Lángara off Cádiz. When the siege was resumed, a French engineer brought up ten floating batteries with 220 cannon mounted on them: they were destroyed, and Lord Howe was again able to relieve the garrison. Within the terms of contemporary warfare, the Rock was shown to be impregnable. Meanwhile, the English, less confident of their ability to hold Minorca, had offered it to Russia in exchange for a permanent alliance, but the Tsarina had refused to be drawn: in August 1781 Crillon led a successful expedition against it and the garrison of San Felipe surrendered in February 1782.

In the following November Great Britain was forced to accept the independence of the United States, and she was now ready to negotiate peace with her European rivals. At Versailles in 1783 she accepted the loss of Minorca and Florida, but retained her rights on the logwood coast and recovered the Bahamas. As to Gibraltar, Great Britain set the price for its surrender at the return of all Spanish conquests in the late war, including Florida, and the cession of Puerto Rico or other areas in the Antilles: Aranda, who was left to make the final decision, found the price too high.

The close of Charles III's reign saw at last a new structure rising out of the old Hapsburg ruins, though it was still scarcely half built. The visitor to Madrid in the middle of the century was struck by the antique appearance of what he saw: architecture, dress and customs were still substantially those of the last century. The court itself was an island. But from about 1760 newer tastes began to prevail. Peace brought public works and economic development, a steady rise of prices, and a general prosperity. The institutions founded in previous reigns for the encouragement of art and culture now commenced to bear fruit. A new learning began to contemplate Spanish history with a certain detachment. The poem of the Cid and many other manuscripts were unearthed and printed. The theatre, which had long languished, found the contrast between old and new customs a fruitful subject for a minor genre. In architecture the luxuriant southern baroque, which had reached as far north as Madrid, now gave way to a new Spanish style, Castilian in its sobriety, yet French in its rationalism, the Neo-Classical. In painting the discernment of Charles III brought forward artists of a finer quality: royal apotheoses, painted with more politeness than truth, went out of fashion; and if the illustrations of Goya and Bayeu represent a Spanish society that scarcely existed, they nonetheless indicate an aspiration towards a new and general standard of good taste.

When Charles died in December 1788, he was succeeded by his second son, Charles IV, a simple fellow of forty with a taste for clocks and, later, embroidery. Born in Naples, he had arrived in Spain as a youth, and he was dominated by his Italian Queen, María-Luisa of Parma, by whom he had three sons and several daughters. He retained the services of his father's chief minister, José Moñino, Count of Floridablanca. This Murcian lawyer, a member of the rising professional bourgeoisie, stood for a jealous regalism that constantly asserted the prerogatives of the crown, a Jansenist attitude towards religion based on respect for the individual conscience and the independence of civil authority, an absolutist government without reference to cortes, a foreign policy closely moulded to the Family Pact, and a paternalistic view of society in which the monarch was the patron of culture, the sponsor of commerce and the reviver of agriculture.

But Charles IV had hardly occupied the throne for six months when the French States-General began to defy Louis XVI, the nominal head of his house and his ally. Charles, and most of Spain with him, was horrified when the French deputies refused to be dissolved and proclaimed themselves a National Assembly. Three months later the Spanish cortes assembled in Madrid to take the oath of allegiance to Charles' heir, and instead of being dissolved immediately they were asked to revoke the Salic law, introduced into Spain by Philip V: however, no pragmatic was issued and the point was later to become the pretext for a long-contested civil war.

Despite his anxiety about the affairs of France, Floridablanca hoped to maintain the Family Pact, for the balance of power in America depended on the French alliance. He nevertheless took elaborate precautions to prevent the entry of revolutionary contagion: all newspapers except the official gazette were suppressed, and an oath of loyalty was extracted from foreign residents in Spain, most of whom were Frenchmen. Meanwhile, he made somewhat impractical efforts in Paris to defend Louis' authority, refusing to admit the existence of the constitution without an assurance that the King had accepted it of his own free-will. His stickling provoked the French government without helping the French King; and Floridablanca seems not to have told Charles of the exact state of affairs: the Queen of Portugal, who was informed, was driven out of her mind by the news.

Floridablanca's hesitations led to his fall in February 1792. His successor was the inveterate Francophile Aranda, who set the French alliance above the Family Compact. Spain now stood aside from the Austrian and Prussian attempt to save Louis and when the French armies had defeated the invaders, the National Assembly boldly forced her to choose between peace or war. The Spanish ministers were divided between their attachment to the French alliance and their loyalty to monarchism. Spain was unequipped to carry on a land-war with France or a sea-war with England; and her best hope was therefore to establish a neutral block with Portugal, based on the kinship of the Spanish Bourbons and the Braganzas. But while Aranda struggled with the French ambassador, the King and Queen took fright, dismissed him and gave his place to Manuel Godoy, a guards-officer of twenty-five, who had been made lieutenant-general of the army, Duke of Alcudia, a grandee and a member of the Council of State.

These distinctions had been thrust upon him since Charles and María-Luisa had come to distrust the professional Francophiles who had filled the ministries, and hoped by elevating an ambitious, if inexperienced, member of the provincial nobility to have a favourite who owed everything to them and would therefore be implicitly loyal. His first task was to save Louis XVI and avoid war with France. His only weapon was bribery, and he failed to influence the vote in the Convention. In March 1793 France declared war on the Spanish Bourbons and prepared to invade Catalonia.

In Spain the aristocracy, the church and the people were in favour of a war against the latest enormity of their ancient rival. An alliance was made with Great Britain, and three armies were put into the field. In 1793 Caro took Hendaye, while Ricardos occupied the Roussillon and entered Perpignan. But at Toulon the Anglo-Spanish attempt to relieve the French royalists came to grief, and in 1794 the French armies reconquered Roussillon and crossed the frontier at Figueras and on the Basque border. The following campaign brought them forward in a sweep to the Ebro, and Madrid itself was threatened. The Spanish armies were broken, and Godoy had no choice but to make an immediate peace. In July 1795 the French undertook to evacuate Spain in return for the surrender of the Spanish half of the island of Santo Domingo.

These terms were relatively mild, for the French intended to use Godoy as a lever to force Portugal to give up her alliance with England and close her ports to British ships. He arranged a meeting between his master and the Portuguese Regent, but his moral suasion proved insufficient, and in August 1796 Spain entered into the treaty of San Ildefonso, by which Charles bound himself to France and placed his fleet at the service of the revolutionaries for their war against England. The war was begun two months later, and in February 1797 Admiral Jervis defeated the Spanish fleet off Cape St. Vincent, while Abercromby seized Trinidad.

Godoy had now surrendered possessions in the Spanish Antilles to both contestants. During the rest of 1797 he hesitated to admit French troops for the attack on Portugal; and for a time pressure was relaxed as Great Britain negotiated with the Directory. But in

1798 the new French government pressed him to drive the emigrés out of Spain and to attack Portugal. There was now good reason to resist, for in Italy the French-dominated Cisalpine Republic of Modena attacked Parma, and expelled its Duke, María-Luisa's brother, despite Spanish protests, while papal authority had been overthrown in Rome. For a moment, the French proposed to remove Godoy by establishing him as Grand Master of St John to rule Malta, but he refused the offer and the French pressed for his dismissal. The Spanish court was now divided by faction and intrigue as in the last days of the Hapsburg régime, and the tutor to the young Prince of the Asturias, Canon Escoiquiz, persuaded Charles to put Godoy aside. Power now passed to Saavedra and Jovellanos, men of the enlightenment, but of unsuspect patriotism: Saavedra accepted French demands for the expulsion of the emigrés: Godoy, though not in office, remained at court and continued to enjoy royal favour.

Napoleon was now engaged in his Egyptian campaign. His defeat in the Battle of the Nile (August 1798) and the liberation of Bourbon Naples encouraged Turkey, Russia and finally Austria to resist French exorbitance, but Charles and his ministers persistently tried to negotiate for peace, and when French troops drove his brother out of Naples, Charles abjectly requested that the kingdom should be granted to a Spanish prince. When the Directory collapsed and the victorious Napoleon presented himself in Paris in October 1799 and swept away the last vapours of popular republicanism, some Spaniards, including Escoiquiz, were persuaded that as the revolution was over and the threat to monarchy withdrawn it would now be possible to resume the French alliance.

But French policy towards Spain tightened. In 1800 a new treaty of San Ildefonso awarded María-Luisa's brother the title of King of Tuscany in return for the services of six Spanish warships and an undertaking by Spain to collaborate in forcing Portugal to repudiate the English connection. Spain now dared not oppose France by land or England by sea, and in order to keep up a precarious neutrality, her admiral Mazarredo tried to insist that his ships should be used only for the defence of Spain or the recovery of Minorca. But Napoleon had other uses for them. He sent his brother Lucien to Madrid to obtain the removal of Urquijo and Mazarredo, and Godoy again assumed power. In Europe, the peace of Luneville had broken up the coalition against France, and left Britain to resist alone, with Portugal as her only foothold on the continent. Consequently Napoleon brought full pressure to bear on Spain, and early in 1801 Godoy agreed to collaborate in the conquest of her neighbour and to place her fleet under French command. In May Spanish armies, reinforced with French contingents, entered Portugal and in the brief War of the Oranges forced her to close her ports: in return France and Spain would guarantee the integrity of her territory. It was a theatrical war and an unreal peace: having introduced French troops into the Peninsula, Napoleon sent reinforcements in order to stiffen his demands on Portugal.

He had now little to fear from Charles or Godoy, and readily abandoned Spain in the treaty of Amiens in March 1802. When the war was resumed a year later, he at once demanded that Spain should enter it and furnish 24,000 men and her fleet. Godoy protested and clung to a tortuous form of neutrality, agreeing to pay tribute of six million francs a month and to admit French cloths and other imports on favourable terms. By means of an ultimatum, Napoleon obliged Spain also to open her ports to French warships. After this success he attempted to force the same system upon Portugal, using Godoy as his instrument. As a result England began to treat Spain as an enemy and in October 1804 seized her treasure-fleet.

Now at last Spain abandoned any pretence of neutrality and declared war on England. Immediately afterwards the Emperor concluded a new treaty for the use of thirty Spanish warships, with which he intended to draw off Nelson's fleet and so break the blockade of Brest and El Ferrol. The French Mediterranean division sailed out of Toulon and entered Cádiz, but only six Spanish ships were ready to sail. A sortie to the Caribbean was carried out, but it did not relieve the blockade, and as the combined fleet returned to Cádiz, it was destroyed in the battle of Trafalgar.

This defeat forced Godoy to resume his policy of appeasement and evasion. As Napoleon prepared the attack on Prussia that was to end in the victory of Jena, Spain again sent her war contribution; but during the campaign Godoy launched an appeal to loyal Spaniards for collaboration in the national defence. This premature revelation of his underlying motives convinced Napoleon that Godoy and his master and mistress had served their purpose.

Thus while Charles was complacently awarding Godoy the title of Grand Admiral with the style of Supreme Highness, Napoleon's agents were again stirring up his enemies. The Emperor had an unconditional admirer in Canon Escoiquiz, whose charge, Prince Ferdinand, was now twenty-three. This youth was now persuaded to write to the conqueror to ask for a lady of his family in marriage: the letter was steeped in flattery of the Emperor and in malice towards the Queen and Godoy, and the French made good use of it.

But Napoleon had now extracted a Spanish contingent for use in Germany, and his main object was again to close the Portuguese ports. He therefore opened negotiations for the dismemberment of Portugal, which resulted in the treaty of Fontainebleau of October 27, 1807. Already a French army under Junot had crossed the Pyrenees and begun the long tramp to Lisbon. In theory María-Luisa's brother was to receive 'northern Lusitania' in compensation for the loss of Etruria, whilst Godoy would be Prince of the Algarve and Alemtejo: but whether Napoleon ever intended to honour his agreement is doubtful. At the end of October, Charles discovered his son's correspondence with the Emperor, including, it was said, a letter in which he proposed the murder of Godoy. The two parties were now in open conflict. Charles wrote a pitiable letter to Napoleon announcing his intention to depose his son, arrested the wretched youth and formally accused him of treason. But Godoy and the Queen now realised the extent to which they had been duped, and Ferdinand addressed letters of apology to his doting father and was forgiven.

A few weeks later the Portuguese royal family left Lisbon for Brazil, escorted by a British fleet, while Junot and his vanguard advanced down the Tagus and the French armies streamed across northern Spain, seizing the fortresses of Pamplona and Barcelona. In March 1808 Murat arrived in Burgos as lieutenant-general, and Napoleon demanded a new treaty which would reduce Spain to complete dependence. Godoy thought that Charles should reply by summoning Napoleon to abide by the existing treaty, and if necessary depart for Seville and sail for America. But as Murat advanced on the capital, there was growing consternation among the people, who now blamed Godoy for all the humiliations which had been put upon the monarchy. Stirred up by his enemies, the mob of Aranjuez sacked the favourite's house. Godoy himself was captured and maltreated, and only saved from death by Murat, who sent him to Bayonne. A few days later, Charles, who had clung too long to his adored Manuel, abdicated in favour of the Prince of the Asturias, Ferdinand VII, (March 19, 1808).

Ferdinand, however undeservingly, now found himself the idol of the Spanish people, who imagined his father and Godoy to have been the sole tools of French policy. While the populace in Madrid and other cities were exulting in the downfall of the supposed traitor, however, Murat was instructing Charles IV to protest against his son's disloyalty and to assert that his abdication had been extorted from him under threat of violence. Ferdinand still hoped for a dynastic alliance with the Emperor, while Murat revealed his own pretensions to rule Spain by a display of inordinate splendour. It was for the Emperor to decide. Apparently accepting the Marshal's account of his personal prestige in Madrid, he summoned Ferdinand to meet him at Bayonne, and the idol of Spain accepted without much hesitation. In fact, the Emperor had already offered the crown to his brother Louis, King of Holland, who refused it. Leaving a Junta to exercise power in Madrid, Ferdinand arrived in Bayonne at the end of April, only to find that Napoleon regarded him as an enemy and would offer him nothing better than the crown of Etruria. When he refused, his parents and Godoy were produced, and the unhappy family were left to wrangle. In the great crisis, the policy of the Spanish Bourbons had been at best tortuous and at worst supine. They now unashamedly went with the stream. When news came of the uprising of the Spanish people on May 2, 1808, Charles IV issued a proclamation informing the Spanish authorities that he had created Murat his lieutenant-general in Spain, while Ferdinand was prevailed upon to recognise his father once more. Having obtained this abdication, Napoleon had no difficulty in persuading Charles to surrender his crown. Early in June he proclaimed his brother Joseph Bonaparte King of Spain: the old king received a pension and his son was held in confinement in the castle of Valençay until the end of the war in 1814.

If history has been generous to Charles III, it has been harsh to his son. Charles' temperament inclined towards the easy-going pacifism of his uncle, Ferdinand VI. A man of simple piety, he found himself divided from the traditions of his subjects by the regalism of his house and his father's xenophilia. Faced with the rivalries and intrigues of the advanced party, who were bound together by mere intellectual attachments, he sought a valido who should be a loyal servant of the throne. Traditionalists and clericals of the old school were barred to him by the ideology of his house, and he lighted on Godoy, a product of the reformed Bourbon army, to whom he remained pathetically faithful. For all Charles' support, Godoy could not dominate the court or keep the heir to the throne out of the hands of his rivals. Lacking any real moral or physical power, he involved himself in sordid intrigues with Lucien Bonaparte in the poor hope of tricking the Emperor and matching the treachery of Talleyrand, who had contrived the Spanish coup. Napoleon, not Charles, sickened of him. But once French troops had entered Spain, the court was united in its detestation of him. In the explosion of Aranjuez, courtiers and mob thought only of avenging themselves on the valido and replacing the doting monarch with his son. When the necessary sacrifice had been made, the new holders of power were the group of admirers of Napoleon that had formed round Ferdinand. These dazzled collaborators, led by the pedagogue Escoiquiz, accompanied the prince to Bayonne, where they sublimated their infatuation in a Ciceronic protest. Even Charles was, Bourbonlike, more afraid of his own subjects than of Napoleon, and went to

Bayonne confidently believing that so great a hero was incapable of baseness.

As to Ferdinand, he was now under duress, and though he still pestered his captor for a bride from the imperial family, the news was circulated in Spain that he had given the word to resist and this was sufficient to revive the monarchical faith of the Spanish people: for six years he was a symbol of national resistance, 'the Desired'.

XI

LIBERALISM

IN Spain everything but the race regularly decays. Talleyrand had calculated the power of resistance of Charles IV's court as exactly as Louis XIV had judged the solidity of the Hapsburg throne. But in each case the final decision rested with the Spanish people. Talleyrand himself first marvelled at the success of his plan, then realised that it had been an irreparable error. In the War of the Succession both claimants had been foreigners, and the Bourbon had won because the Austrian had set the eastern and western realms against Castile and undertaken to partition the whole. Now, after a century of unification, the monarchy was more than ever the symbol of political authority. Spaniards soon forgot that the Bourbons were strangers, xenophiles, reformers, and remembered only that the sequestration of the crown by a foreigner touched their very existence.

The War of Independence began on May 2, 1808, when a French escort prepared to remove Ferdinand's younger brother, Francisco de Paula, from Madrid. As the weeping boy left the palace, a crowd pressed forward and cut the traces of the coaches, carrying him back to the balcony and applauding him. Murat's troops appeared in the streets and engaged in a hand-to-hand struggle with the palace-servants and guards and the crowd. A band of Spaniards headed by two officers, Daoiz and Velarde, entered the artillery-park, distributed arms and wheeled out cannon. Both leaders were soon killed and their followers dispersed: most of the Spanish army obeyed the orders of the Junta and remained in its barracks. Once the insurrection had failed, Murat set up a military court and established a reign of terror. Perhaps 150 Frenchmen had died: in addition to the Spaniards killed in the streets, several hundreds more fell before Murat's firing-squads.

This was perhaps Madrid's first introduction to military discipline. Brawls, disorders and food riots had not been unfamiliar, but the violence of the Spanish mob was either the result of sudden excitement or of popular earnestness: it often went unpunished and was never indiscriminately repressed. Murat, deluded by the sudden calm, informed Napoleon that the peace would not be disturbed again: 'the pill had been swallowed'.

The rising sufficed to decide the Emperor against letting any Bourbon return to Spain, and a month later he finally bestowed the crown on his brother Joseph, cloaking the transfer with an air of legality by convoking a form of cortes at Bayonne. This body was to consist of 150 Francophile Spaniards, of whom 91 (three-quarters of them members of the nobility and only eight from the towns) accepted the invitation, and debated and approved a draft constitution placed before them under French patronage. Joseph would have a senate of twenty-four members, nominated by himself, and a chamber of 162 deputies representing the three estates. In proof of their reforming intentions, the cortes of Bayonne abolished the use of torture, established freedom of conscience and reduced the entailed estates. On July 21 Joseph arrived in Spain: four days later, he was proclaimed King at Toledo.

But by now the news of the revolt in Madrid had spread far and wide. Murat, his own aspirations thwarted, began to see things in a truer perspective, and falling prudently ill, retired from Spain on May 22. Already the country was in a state of latent insurrection. The authorities, the Junta in Madrid and the captains-general in the provinces, remained passive, and it was left to the alcalde of the village of Móstoles near Madrid to summon the nation to rise. Municipal authorities successively denounced the invaders, and on May 23 Canon Llano Ponte summoned the whole province of Oviedo to take up arms and formed a junta which declared war on Napoleon and sent a delegation to England to ask for help. In Valencia another ecclesiastic launched a similar movement, and the French and their Spanish allies were massacred in the streets, while a priestly horde drove out Moncey's army. In Seville, news of the abdications in Bayonne touched off a rising of the people led by a group of the provincial nobility and the Archbishop and clergy: arms were distributed and a committee formed, which at once claimed to be the Supreme Junta for Spain and the Indies, a piece of Andalusian pretentiousness that was to give rise to many jealousies. By June the risings had spread to Extremadura and to Aragon, and in many places the governors appointed by Charles IV were ruthlessly assassinated: in Cádiz, where a French fleet was blockaded in the harbour by the English, the Francophile governor, assailed by infuriated monks, refused to confess and died crying 'Viva Francia!'

At this unpropitious moment Joseph was preparing to claim his throne. In Cuenca a French force sacked the town, despoiling the churches despite his protests. The Emperor thought that a display of force would soon set things right, and on July 14 Bessières won a conclusive victory over Blake and Cuesta at Medina de Ríoseco; but at the same time General Castaños, commander of San Roque, opposite Gibraltar, supported by Reding with his 'army of Granada', fell upon Dupont's corps and forced it to capitulate at Bailén. Some eighteen thousand French were taken prisoner, with 120 cannon as well as rifles and horses: the Spanish losses numbered less than a thousand killed and wounded. For Spaniards the Napoleonic legend was already half destroyed.

Joseph, newly arrived in Madrid, found the whole of southern Spain held by the insurgents and a great breach opening northwards to Madrid. He had no choice but to return to Bayonne. As he did so, Wellesley landed in Portugal, compelling Junot to sign the convention of Sintra and to evacuate the west. By the end of the summer the French held only the north-central quarter of the Peninsula, where Ney, with his headquarters at Logroño, awaited the arrival of the Emperor himself, who was preparing to advance with a massive army of six corps.

Meanwhile, the patchwork of local committees had so far overcome their differences as to recognise a single central Junta, which met at Aranjuez: its twenty-four members (later increased) included ex-ministers, nobles and regional delegates, under the presidency of the aged Floridablanca. Its deliberations were cut short by the news of Napoleon's attack. As the Emperor approached, the Junta retreated southwards. Floridablanca died on the journey, and his place was taken by Jovellanos, the Asturian advocate of a moderate and national liberalism. But the committee inevitably represented very diverse tendencies: it had already reinstated the Jesuits and appointed an Inquisitor-General, and it proposed to rally the nation behind it by convoking cortes, but the pressure of events made it necessary to defer any such assembly for more than a year and a half. The loss of Madrid dissipated the easy optimism which had followed Bailén; and having formally declared war on France on November 14th, a month before the occupation of the capital, the Junta concluded a treaty of alliance with Great Britain (January 14, 1809).

On December 4, Napoleon had entered Madrid, where he ordered the inhabitants to take an oath on the sacraments to his brother, abolished the Council of Castile and the Inquisition, and decreed a reduction in the number of monasteries and fiscal reforms. The capital seemed almost passive; and after raising a hotch-potch army, largely composed of foreigners, Napoleon recalled his brother to resume his interrupted reign, telling him: '*Vous serez mieux logé que moi*'. The Emperor himself went to drive Sir John Moore out of Galicia, but disturbed by news of stirrings in Austria and intrigues in Paris, he handed over the command to Soult and hastened back to France.

As he re-entered Paris, Joseph returned to Madrid, where he was received without enthusiasm or repugnance. He set himself to win the hearts of his subjects, hearing mass daily, attending the bullfight and rewarding his servants generously. His followers, the *afrancesados*, included aristocrats and functionaries, reformers and place-hunters: some of them, like Joseph himself, hoped to bestow a new administration on Spain, and they bravely swept away the old Councils, the old distinctions of rank, and the variety of local imposts and weights and measures. All monasteries were now closed, and secular *lycées* were given charge of education. The foreign tyranny achieved things that the boldest of Spaniards had scarcely envisaged. Yet an air of impermanence and insecurity prevailed: Joseph had still no control over his brother's armies, who continued to plunder, desecrate and be slaughtered by pious provincials, and though he had his own military ambitions, he was without experience or energy. He was surrounded by French careerists, and an air of provincial tragedy hung over his court: for all his amiable intentions, he could never be anything to Spaniards but *'Pepe Botellas'*, a drunken grenadier.

During 1809 Joseph reigned over most of northern and western Spain. Soult had carried Oporto, and Victor won Extremadura with his victory at Medellín in March, while Sebastiani entered La Mancha. The Emperor's first object was to drive the English out of Portugal, but in July Wellington advanced up the Tagus as far as Talavera, and successfully opposed Victor and only withdrew for lack of supplies as Soult approached. Joseph claimed a victory (though the Emperor knew that he had suffered a reverse), and he was further encouraged when in November Soult helped him to disperse the southern Spanish forces at Ocaña. He now decided to undertake the conquest of Andalusia, while the Emperor mounted his third invasion of Portugal. Thus in January 1810, Soult marched southwards upon Seville, and the Supreme Junta, no longer able to resist, retired to the Isle of the Lion at Cádiz, where it was separated from the mainland by salt-marshes. Here the government, supported by English sea-power, was as safe from the French as the Phoenicians had been from their Tartessian neighbours.

But for Joseph the Andalusian expedition was an almost bloodless victory. He was delighted by his success and by the apparent transigence of the Andalusians. Napoleon himself, intent on the English armies in the west, had seen no urgency for the campaign; and as Soult's army occupied the south, the French control of Castile and Leon grew increasingly precarious. Scarcely had Joseph written to his brother forecasting the imminent fall of Cádiz when the Emperor, who had learned to distrust all news from Spain, decided that the Peninsula could only be subjected by military government and decreed the dismemberment of the puppet kingdom: Catalonia and the area north of the Ebro would be annexed to France and the rest divided between the marshals, leaving Joseph in control only of Madrid and the centre. Thus over most of Spain political power passed to the army, Soult in Andalusia, Suchet in Aragon, Macdonald in Catalonia and Masséna in the west.

The decree of February, 1810 removed any real prestige Joseph might have acquired. His protests were again ignored, and he returned from his mild Andalusian triumphs to a Madrid where his receptions were avoided and his parades and bull-fights attended with cheerful scepticism. Soon even propaganda and largesse were impossible, for the dismemberment reduced Joseph's government to indigence. He thought of selling the expropriated monastic properties and dividing the proceeds with the populace, but this plan was vetoed in Paris. When in July, 1810, Louis Bonaparte was removed from the throne of Holland his own situation became almost intolerable.

Meanwhile, Spanish authority was concentrated at Cádiz. The Supreme Junta, recognised by England as the legitimate representative of Ferdinand VII and now styled the 'Council of Regency', had in its first stage in December 1808 authorised the arming of the people and legalised the 'cuadrillas' of irregulars, and in April 1809 it had recognised the civilian forces as a national militia. Popular leaders sprang up everywhere, and their armed bands cut off French detachments and foraging-parties, impeded communications, and forced the municipalities and alcaldes to disobey Joseph and the marshals.

In the winter of 1810-11, when there was a lull in the major war, theirs were almost the only operations: their picturesque heroes, fighting monks, bandits, desperadoes, justicers, peasant-generals and amateur kings revived the epic sense of Spanish life and gave a new political power to the provincial masses. The fame of their achievements, real and legendary, soon spread far and wide; and like those of all resistances, their tales grew in the telling.

The Junta itself had not achieved homogeneity during its stay in Seville. Its leader, Jovellanos, favoured moderate but far-reaching reforms: he and others like him now tended to look away from French models, corrupted by Napoleon's autocracy, and to seek inspiration from their English allies. But others, emboldened by the attitude of the church and the monks in defiance of the French, desired to restore traditional clericalism without diminution. When finally the Junta was able to summon cortes, the first tendency was in the ascendant. On September 24, 1810, a single body, the cortes of Cádiz, assembled and began to prepare a new Constitution in opposition to the French dispensation of Bayonne. The deputies consisted of representatives of the old cortes-towns, of new provincial juntas, and at least in theory, of the people, who were to have one member for each 50,000 inhabitants in Spain and one for each 100,000 Spaniards in America. The Frenchified aristocracy, which had predominated at Bayonne, was almost eliminated, and the majority of the deputies consisted of lawyers, priests, officers and provincial property-owners, members of the middle class which had neither been denationalised by the French alliance, nor yet remained unaffected, as did the masses, by European ideas.

As their deliberations proceeded, the reforming faction increased its preponderance, and the resulting Constitution of 1812 became the beacon of Spanish and southern European liberalism for half a century. By it the procurators did their duty to 'God, patria and king', swearing to maintain the catholic religion, the integrity of national territory and the laws of the land, and the throne of Ferdinand VII. But to these impeccable principles they added the joint sovereignty of king and people, the separation of powers, the submission of the king to the will of cortes on the question of his marriage and in the conclusion of treaties, equality of rights between Peninsular and American Spaniards, the total abolition of seigneurial privileges, the adoption of the elective principle in local government, the suppression of the Inquisition and the payment of taxes by the clergy: these matters, and extensions of them, were to keep Spaniards busy for the rest of the century. But for the moment they were scarcely more than an aspiration. During the whole of 1811 the members of the constituent cortes had the French armies constantly in sight on the mainland, and their King was a captive in France. Far from the crushing traditions of a bureaucratic capital and braced by the commercial air of a great seaport, they dreamed of an ideal Spain at once free from foreign domination and from ancient abuses.

Meanwhile, the English had advanced from central Portugal to the Spanish frontier, where Wellington won the battles of Fuentes de Oñoro and Albuera in May 1811. Badajoz remained in French hands, and early in 1812 French contingents occupied Valencia, which had been defended by the Irish Spaniard Blake. But in this year Napoleon was too deeply committed in Russia to reinforce Spain; and Wellington, after reducing Badajoz and Ciudad Rodrigo, advanced into Leon, and fought the crucial battle of Salamanca, where the Emperor had instructed Marmont to conquer or perish: the town could not be held, and the French forces again retreated. Joseph, in alarm, summoned Soult to abandon Andalusia, and himself retired to Valencia. Wellington at last entered Madrid on August 12, and in the midst of fervent rejoicings the Constitution of Cádiz was promulgated on the following day.

The capital had already undergone famine the winter before; and Wellington, finding himself checked at Burgos, was forced to return to Portugal, leaving the hungry meseta to its inhabitants and the French. On November 2, Joseph I made his last entry. Although the Emperor decided to establish his headquarters at Valladolid, Joseph now refused to leave Madrid, for fear of surrendering his last shred of independence. But in May news came of the English advance to Salamanca, and the guerrillero el Empecinado was already prowling in the neighbourhood of the capital. On May 23 the Intruder-King gave the order to evacuate, and four days later not a Frenchman remained. A month after, Wellington came up with Napoleon's armies at Vitoria and won the final victory of the war. Only the frontier forts in the Basque country and Navarre and Suchet's army in the east now held out, and in October the allies crossed the Bidassoa and entered France.

Meanwhile, the desired Ferdinand had remained in easy confinement at Valençay. The Count of Montijo had sought to make contact with him, and Napoleon had tested him with an effusive letter purporting to be written by George III: he chose to remain quietly in his place until in November, 1813 the Emperor was reminded of his existence and proposed an extraordinary undertaking. The Emperor was perturbed at the spread of anarchy in the Peninsula, encouraged by the English: it would be helpful if Ferdinand would return with a view to restoring the Franco-Spanish alliance and saving the monarchy and nobility. Ferdinand hesitated, but his old advisers Escoiquiz and San Carlos persuaded him to accept and he signed the treaty of Valençay on December 8, 1813.

This was the moment of crisis. The reformers of Cádiz were aware that the changes embodied in their Constitution were contingent on the essential question of authority. They had acted in Ferdinand's name but asserted the sovereignty of the people, and all that they had done depended on his acceptance of this new principle. The troubles of Spain were not the outcome of party rivalries within a constitution, but of a fundamental issue involving the position of the crown: liberalism in Spain meant not a party but a system.

That Ferdinand would not readily surrender his rights was soon evident. The government of Cádiz transferred itself to Madrid on January 5, 1814, and when his emissary San Carlos sought an understanding with them there, they promptly rejected the treaty of Valençay. Already in January 1811 they had decided that any act of the King's while he was under duress was void, and they had agreed to make no treaty except with English consent. Far from accepting San Carlos' proposals, they demanded that Ferdinand should not re-enter Spain until he had accepted the Constitution; they also forbade the return of his advisers and sought to lay down the exact circumstances of his resumption. These demands Ferdinand could afford to ignore. The people thought only of 'the Desired', whose re-enthronement was the very justification of all their sufferings and the symbol of their regained liberty. He entered Spain from Perpignan and repaired to Valencia, where a loyal army awaited him. On May 4th he issued a manifesto repudiating the Constitution and announcing his intention to abolish the liberal cortes.

In Madrid, the deputies vainly voted to make the reform of the Constitution a crime. A mob dragged the stone of liberty from the cortes building, and would have done as much with the deputies themselves had they not been placed under arrest. On May 13, 1814, Ferdinand and absolutism were restored in Madrid.

The repression continued for five years. Arbitrary arrests were now carried out not by the decrepit Inquisition, but by the more efficient police system introduced from revolutionary France. A legion of spies sought to penetrate the masonic lodges in which liberalism took refuge, and the men of 1812 were imprisoned, deported to Africa or executed. The persecution matched the savagery of the war. Ferdinand himself was by nature vindictive, and if he had not been ashamed to fawn on Napoleon, he had no mercy for those Spaniards who had shown a stronger spirit and had taken advantage of his sequestration to usurp his authority. He was not the first Bourbon to feel insecure in Spain, and he now readily abandoned reformers of all kinds, relying on the traditionalist aristocracy, the church and the officers of the old army, and endeavouring to bridge the gap that separated his house from the masses by cultivating bull-fighters and other popular figures, who formed his famous *camarilla*.[1]

But while the Bourbon monarchy now purged its past xenophilia and its abject adulation of Napoleon in an orgy of 'patriotic' repression, the Spanish people was itself divided between ancient usages and new principles. Over much of the country the events of the last decade had left only a general dislike of everything that was foreign and a passionate desire to be left alone. This was true

[1] The coursing of bulls from horse-back had been a pastime of the nobility since mediaeval times, and was particularly popular in the seventeenth century, when the municipalities celebrated royal and other festivities with demonstrations of skill by the local aristocracy. But it was not favoured by the Bourbons, who preferred more intellectual pursuits. Thus in the eighteenth century bull-fighting was taken over by the people, and the chief executant became the plebeian matador fighting on foot. However, the art of horsemanship was preserved by the formation of riding-societies, the Maestranzas, and these bodies also patronised the popular art of bull-fighting and built the earliest bull-rings. In the south the sporting aristocracy regularly consorted with the populace in its dissipations. But the Bourbon kings and their reforming ministers looked with disfavour on 'chulapería', and tried to cultivate the politer atmosphere of the fête-champêtre. Ferdinand's cult of plebeian traditionalism did not fail to strike the imagination of the masses.

of areas in the north which had known only the devastations of advancing and retreating armies. It was also largely true of Madrid, where the French occupation had ended in impoverishment and famine and the government of Cádiz had had no time to strike root. On arriving in Madrid the men of 1812 had themselves begun the classification and punishment of all Spaniards who had collaborated with Joseph (the *josefinos*), many of whom had already retired to exile in France: others were persecuted with the liberals of Cádiz.

Nevertheless, liberalism had implanted itself in Spanish minds, and could not now be eradicated. The period of reaction was punctuated by revolts—Mina at Pamplona in 1814, Porlier at Corunna in 1815, a plot in Madrid in 1816 and a rising in Catalonia in 1817. Most of these movements originated in the army, which now exercised unusual authority. The eighteenth-century Bourbons had replaced the old Viceroys (except in Navarre) with 'Captains-General', who were presidents of the judicial system and military commanders. The office had first been created to enforce Bourbon law in the realms of Aragon, but it was later extended, and by the end of the eighteenth century there were ten of these military governors. During the French wars the title was used without specific territorial connotation as a military rank (of which the first holder was Godoy), and with the suspension of civil administration Ferdinand had no hesitation in restoring this instrument of Bourbon domination. Thus the highest officers of the army obtained, in time of emergency, virtually dictatorial powers. But while the older officers trained under the last Bourbon reform were conservatives, the army also included many liberals, and its lodges and clubs were in many regions secure from absolutist spies and police. Moreover, the regular army had fought side by side with the guerrilleros, and many of its younger officers had served as irregulars: more than any other institution, therefore, the army represented the conflicting loyalties and aspirations of the Spanish people.

But if in Spain a weak and suspicious monarch, supported by reactionary generals and priests and a sorely-tried mob which knew as little of constitutionalism as it did of the real character of the Deseado, could attempt to obliterate the great upheaval, no such feat was possible in America. In 1806 an English force, subsequently disowned by Canning, had seized Buenos Aires, only to be defeated by Spanish and creole levies. This action had filled the native Americans with pride and self-confidence, and both the assembly at Bayonne and that of Cádiz included representatives of the colonies. But for six years, from 1808 to 1814, Spain had been unable to send troops to America, and the colonial leaders began to work actively for the overthrow of Spanish power, stimulated by the example of the English colonies in whose independence Spain herself had had a hand. The inhabitants of Buenos Aires now enjoyed the benefit of free trade with Great Britain, and came out for self-government in May 1810, refusing to accept the authority of Joseph Bonaparte and acknowledging Ferdinand VII. A month before, the council of Caracas had also assumed executive powers and summoned a congress, which in due course proclaimed the independence of the United States of Venezuela.

Meanwhile, forces from the River Plate, now no longer concealing their intention to seek full independence, moved against the seat of Spanish power in Peru. By 1814, when Ferdinand returned to Spain, the Americans were deeply engaged in the struggle against their viceroys and were determined never to surrender what they had won. In 1814 the Argentine Congress sent a mission to Spain to ask Ferdinand to grant independence or to appoint a constitutional king. Had he accepted the principle of popular sovereignty in Spain, he could scarcely have refused this request. But he had already committed himself to an absolutist restoration, and declined to make concessions to the Americans. In Venezuela the viceregal forces defeated Bolívar and recovered Caracas, and Ferdinand at once sent out reinforcements. But the movement for independence soon recovered its impetus. In 1816 the viceroyalty of La Plata transformed itself into the Confederated States of the River Plate, the future Argentine Republic, and the independence of Chile was completed at Maipú in 1818. In the following year New Granada (the future Colombia) and Venezuela united under a 'sovereign congress'; and Bolívar from the north and San Martín from the south prepared for the final assault on the citadel of Spanish authority at Lima.

The repression of liberalism in Spain thus coincided with the critical years in America. As the liberating movements converged upon Lima, it became a matter of urgency to reinforce the failing Spanish garrisons, and troops were concentrated in Cádiz and other ports. But on January, 1820, Rafael Riego, commanding an Asturian battalion, and Antonio Quiroga, colonel of the Royal Regiment, proclaimed the restoration of the Constitution of 1812 in the vicinity of Cádiz, and they were after some hesitation supported by troops at Corunna, El Ferrol, Saragossa and Barcelona. The sudden spread of the movement alarmed Ferdinand and his ministers, and at the beginning of March the King announced his willingness to accept the Constitution, publishing shortly afterwards a manifesto with the famous declaration: '*Marchemos francamente, y yo el primero, por la senda constitucional!*' Cortes were convoked for the following July: in the meanwhile a junta was formed which restored the liberal institutions existing at the time of Ferdinand's return, and the departments of state were entrusted to temperate constitutionalists led by Agustín Argüelles.

But Riego and the victims of the late persecution were in no mood for moderation, and the secret masonic lodges, now emerging into the open as patriotic societies, propounded the more advanced ideals of the French Revolution, swathed in resounding rhetoric. The government did not dare to suppress these enthusiastic assemblies, and it attempted instead to disband the army at Cádiz: when Riego indignantly rebuked it for its want of gratitude, it deprived him of the Captaincy-General of Galicia with which he had been rewarded. As a result, the debates in the new cortes were embittered and the constitutionalists divided into two factions, the 'moderados', who belonged in the main to the generation of 1812, and the 'exaltados' or extremists, consisting chiefly of new men. Meanwhile, the afrancesados were permitted to return to Spain, and the two liberal streams converged.

Because of the disruptions caused by the war and the loss of a great proportion of the American trade the government incurred a heavy deficit, established at 572 million reales in 1820. The liberal remedy was the ancient one of appropriation from the church. The Inquisition, the traditional watch-dog of church property, had been abolished by both Joseph and the liberals of Cádiz, but revived by the conservatives of 1814, only to be again suppressed in 1820. The monastic orders, whose dissolution by Napoleon had swollen the guerrillero bands with fighting monks, had also recovered their possessions in 1814; but the liberals now again proposed to abolish them, to prohibit the foundation of new monasteries, and to offer a reward to every monk who secularised himself. These measures led to a protest by the nuncio and the withdrawal from Madrid of Ferdinand: when he returned, the mob rudely reviled him, and he bitterly complained that his ministers had exposed him to indignity and resumed contact with the provincial absolutists, whose guerrillas were already in the field in Navarre, Aragon and Catalonia.

The country was now divided between two systems. The point at issue between them was the character to be assumed by an only too impressionable King. It was now well known that during the war of independence Ferdinand had sat quietly at Napoleon's feet and that the fervently patriotic letters bearing his rubric which had circulated among the juntas were forgeries. His own inclinations were conservative, but he would go the way of the strongest. For the liberals therefore it was an urgent matter to consolidate their seizure of power. They were no longer a small minority, but their adherents consisted mainly of the populace of the large towns and ports, who were most accessible to propaganda and change, and especially those of the south, which had suffered least, accommodated itself to both French and English influences, and felt a certain proprietorship in the Constitution of Cádiz. The rural population of the north, where local self-expression was strong and attachment to the church vigorous, remained anti-liberal.

The key to the full control of Spain lay in the question of local administration. If the people was to be sovereign, it must somehow elect cortes and there must be some basis for representation.

Under the Hapsburgs this had never existed, since Castile alone had claimed to deal with affairs of state and so to 'govern' all Spain, while the eastern realms had managed their own domestic affairs. The Bourbons had established a measure of administrative uniformity. Castile had been divided into twenty-four provinces, while each of the eastern realms and the Basque states was also treated as a 'province'. This arrangement was perfectly conventional and it respected the ancient fueros, but valuable as it may have been for fiscal purposes, it provided no basis for political representation since it placed each of the small towns of Castile on terms of equality with each of the parts of the kingdom of Aragon. Charles III had desired to replace this system by a division into uniform provinces each of thirty leagues, but so radical a change threatened such a mass of privileges that it was shelved. In 1812 the reformers of Cádiz were obliged to adopt the provincial system as a basis for elections, which must perforce be indirect: the male citizens of each parish would choose 'compromisarios', and the 'compromisarios' of each partido (the subdivision of the province) would choose electors: a provincial assembly of electors would finally appoint the deputy or deputies for the province.

This system, though it made allowance for inequalities in the size of the provinces, still required a degree of uniformity in local administration, and this in turn gave unusual importance to the ministry of the interior, which was to become the centre of political patronage for the rest of the century. In 1812 this ministry was set up as 'Gobernación', taking the place of the ancient Council of Castile. It disappeared in 1814 and was promptly restored in 1820. Early in 1822, the foundation of the new centralised administrative, political and fiscal system was laid, when Spain was divided into fifty-two provinces. At the moment, this was a mere paper victory for the liberals, for all the privileged areas of the north were already up in arms in the name of the King, and even in Madrid there were violent demonstrations for and against constitutional monarchy. The tension increased when news was received of the creation of a Council of Regency at Urgel in the Catalan Pyrenees, where the Marquis of Mataflorida, supported by the French Bourbons, was preparing the way for a conservative reaction. Ferdinand VII now urged the crowned heads of Europe to save him from the tyranny of liberalism, and at the Congress of Verona, Austria, Prussia, Russia and France concluded a secret treaty for the restoration of order in the Peninsula. Their demands were rejected by the liberal minister San Miguel; and in April 1823 Louis XVIII's nephew, the Duke of Angoulême, began the invasion of Spain with his 'hundred thousand Frenchmen calling on the name of St. Louis'. As they advanced, the Spanish liberals vainly appointed Riego Commander-in-Chief and retreated to the south, carrying the King with them. Their armies were brushed aside, and in September the cortes retreated to their birthplace at Cádiz, there to expire, turning the captive Ferdinand VII over to his deliverers.

The acts of the second liberal dispensation were at once annulled, and for seven years Spain was again ruled by an 'absolute' king. Ferdinand's first minister was Canon Victor Sáez, whose repression was so brutal that even Louis XVIII and the Tsar were alarmed, and on their protest he was removed. His successors divided into two opposing tendencies, the court-party who regarded the crown as the natural source of secular reform and stood for a return to the enlightened despotism of Charles III, and the 'Traditionalists' or Apostolicals, who associated eighteenth century reform with revolution and looked back to the Hapsburg system with its interpenetration of church and state. The most conspicuous of the first group, Francisco Zea Bermúdez, made a brief attempt to restore the Bourbon régime of enlightenment in 1824: even when he failed and was dismissed in October 1825, the financial reformers Xavier de Burgos and López Ballesteros pressed for the central control of public funds and the creation of a ministry of the interior, while the traditionalists stood by the ancient Council of Castile. Between these two groups, the minister of Justice, Tadeo Calomarde, attempted to steer his inconstant and vengeful master.

The principal instrument of reaction in the country at large was the Royalist Volunteers, launched in 1823 by the Regency of Urgell. This conservative militia, subsidised at first by the French and later paid for out of municipal funds, had been organised on a local basis. In 1825 it successfully resisted the attempt of the government to subject it to the Ministry of War, and only in the following year did it accept an Inspector-General personally responsible to Ferdinand. But the leaders of the traditionalist faction looked now rather to Ferdinand's brother, Don Carlos Isidro, a pious prince who was dominated by his Portuguese wife. Since Ferdinand was childless from his three marriages, Don Carlos was his heir, and from him the Apostolical party confidently expected a return to full traditionalism. But in August 1827 the Catalans rose in revolt against the central government. Ferdinand despatched the Count of España to repress the movement, which he did with the greatest severity, hanging many of its leaders, and causing one of those implicated, the Archbishop of Tarragona, to confess to Ferdinand that Don Carlos had been a party to the plot. From this moment Ferdinand was filled with distrust of his brother and inclined towards the reforming faction.

Since the succession of Don Carlos would have led to the immediate triumph of the extreme reactionaries, the 'enlightened' ministers persuaded Ferdinand to contract a fourth marriage, this time with his sprightly niece, María-Cristina of Naples, who arrived in Madrid in December 1829 and presented him with a daughter, the future Isabella II, in November 1830. Even before her birth, this child had become the symbol of resistance to the Apostolic movement, and in March Ferdinand had sought to remove any possible doubt that a female might succeed by publishing a pragmatic which formally abrogated the Salic law. In view of the example of Isabella I it might be thought that there could be no hesitation on this point. But the 'traditionalists' insisted that the Bourbon dynasty had implanted the French system of succession in the male line: to this it was replied that Charles IV had abrogated the Salic law at the cortes of 1789, though his decision was only now published and reaffirmed.

The future was evidently with the liberals, and their day was brought nearer by the French Revolution of July, which caused the government to close the universities to avoid the meeting of 'restless young people'. The exiles were already beginning to return. The crisis was reached in September 1832 when Ferdinand fell ill and seemed to be on the point of death. Calomarde at once summoned the Council of Ministers, then headed by the Count of Alcudia, and it was agreed to appoint the young Queen regent and to invite Don Carlos to associate himself with the regency and betrothe his son to Isabella. But Don Carlos refused to enter the regency or to accept the marriage: he knew, he said, that God would call him to account if he let the crown go to one who had no just right to it. Alcudia was inclined to accept his demands, and a decree was drawn up withdrawing the pragmatic and virtually presenting the throne to the King's brother: the Queen herself weakly consented to the spoliation of her daughter's rights.

According to the traditional version, the legitimate succession was saved by María-Cristina's sister Luisa-Carlota, who arrived post-haste from the south and boxed Calomarde's ears. In fact, the change was probably forced by liberal disturbances in the capital, and the intervention of the Minister of War, Zambrano, who had been absent in Madrid at the moment of the palace crisis. By the end of the month Ferdinand had recovered. Alcudia was made Ambassador to Russia and Calomarde was exiled. Zambrano, the proponent of the female succession, became head of the royal guard, while Zea Bermúdez, the leader of the 'despotic' liberals, was summoned to become Minister of State, and the other ministries passed to discreet constitutionalists. Thus liberalism made its third and final entry into Spain.[1]

Ferdinand survived for a year. During this time Zea reopened the universities, which had been closed for almost two years, and published an amnesty: the way appeared to lay open for a complete reconciliation between the enlightened absolutists and the moderate constitutionalists, both of whom looked forward to an age of boundless progress under an infant queen. As to the traditionalists, they were responsible for a series of plots and scares; and although Don Carlos had asserted his loyalty to Ferdinand as

[1] None of the old ministers were persecuted or incurred special hatred except Calomarde: he had been the instrument of a vindictive monarch, and had persecuted liberals after 1820 and apostolicals in 1827. But his gravest fault lay in having failed to uphold Isabella at the moment of crisis.

long as the King lived, he and his wife were dismissed to Portugal in March 1833, whence they issued a protest when the oath was taken to Isabella three months later. On September 29th, Ferdinand died, and the crown passed to his daughter, who was nearly three years old.

María-Cristina had been duly appointed regent, and she was assisted by a council which included respected conservatives such as General Castaños, now Duke of Bailén. Zea Bermúdez remained first minister and prepared a manifesto in which the regent declared her belief in absolute monarchy: 'the best form of government for a country is that to which it is accustomed'. This statement disappointed the liberals and failed to conciliate the Carlists. In vain did Zea offer on the one hand to uphold religion and the 'fundamental laws' of the monarchy 'without admitting dangerous innovations' and on the other to introduce 'those administrative reforms which alone can bring prosperity and happiness'. Within four days of Ferdinand's death a provincial postmaster had proclaimed Don Carlos at Talavera and the fire of traditionalism was running through the Basque Provinces, Navarre, Old Castile, Aragon, Catalonia and Valencia. Zea ordered the disbandment of the Royalist Volunteers, and sought to appease the liberals by establishing branches of the Ministry of Fomento throughout the country and restoring the liberal division into provinces, now numbering forty-nine. These steps did not silence the liberal clamour for a convocation of cortes, and when the demand was supported by a group of generals Zea gave way, and Martínez de la Rosa, a deputy of 1812, though now much sobered, took power in January 1834.

A solution for the vexed question of royal authority had now been found in the 'octroyée' constitution, and under the new ministry the regent granted a Royal Statute modelled on the French *Charte*. It provided for cortes of two chambers, but reserved to the crown the right to summon and dismiss them and also to determine the subject of debate: these limitations fell far short of the desires of the extremists.

Meanwhile, the Carlist movement had developed into a civil war. The conflict between absolutists and constitutionalists was not limited to Spain. Portugal was divided between Dona Maria da Glória, daughter of Dom Pedro, the constitutionalist ex-Emperor of Brazil, and his younger brother Dom Miguel, who upheld absolutism, while in France the Duchess of Berry (though a sister to María-Cristina) led the opposition to Louis-Philippe. England and France had already given support to the Portuguese constitutionalists, and Palmerston now proposed a general pact, the Quadruple Alliance, under which both powers undertook to sustain the young Queens of the Peninsula against their wicked uncles (April 1834). This was soon followed by the capitulation of the Portuguese absolutists and the departure of Dom Miguel for exile. Don Carlos was offered a pension and a home in England; but he left Portugal without accepting any commitments and in London his presence was taken so lightly that he had no difficulty in leaving his lodgings and, guided by a French adventurer, reached the Basque hills: here, aided by loans from legitimists and speculators, he was able to hold out for four years, despite the exertions of successive governments in Madrid.

He found an improvised administration, strongly influenced by the Apostolicals, and a peasant army organised by a brilliant officer, Zumalacarregui. The special interest of the Basques lay in the preservation of their precious fueros, which had so far escaped the centralising grasp of Bourbons, Bonapartes and liberals. These included the payment of an agreed contribution to Madrid instead of taxation, exemption from military service, and an administrative autonomy so complete that the Spanish frontier lay, for purposes of excise, not at the Pyrenees but on the Ebro. In these rolling hills the church was closely identified with the inhabitants and possessed no large estates, and the anti-clericalism which had spread from the south to Madrid was neither understood nor desired.

The war was an expensive one. The Cristinist armies could not penetrate the Carlist fastnesses, and were frayed by minor actions or driven to desert by lack of pay and food. Zumalacarregui himself died in the Carlist siege of Bilbao, and in 1836 the city would have fallen but for the enterprise of the Cristinist General Espartero. By now part of Aragon and Catalonia were controlled by the Carlist guerrilleros under the command of Cabrera. But Don Carlos could not take the city of Bilbao; and when at last in September 1837 he made his long-deferred advance on Madrid, he traversed the northern meseta, circled round the capital, and hesitated whether to attack or await reinforcements. As he did so, the populace of the city was armed and prepared to resist. Don Carlos had perhaps hoped for a negotiated settlement, but none was possible and he decided to retreat.

The morale of the Carlist forces now rapidly declined. One of their leaders, General Maroto, arrested his four colleagues and had them shot. Don Carlos, caught by surprise, gave him the supreme command; and he began secret negotiations with Espartero, with whom he had served in Peru. When at last Don Carlos assembled his men and asked them what they wished to do, they all shouted for Maroto; and on August 31, 1839, the war was ended with an embrace and the Convention of Vergara. The Carlist officers were offered admission into the Cristinist army, while Don Carlos himself retired to France. Cabrera, who had remained free in the east, gave up the struggle in July 1840.

In Madrid the romantic monarchism of Martínez de la Rosa had failed to withstand the stress of war. The public debt rose rapidly with each campaign; already in 1834 it had been decided to sell the common lands, and in the following year the disposal of national property was resumed: a wholesale spoliation of the church could not long be deferred. As the war continued, extremism and demogogy were intensified. The creation of a National Guard, imitated from France, released regular troops for the war, but it also greatly increased the power of the populace. In a riot in Madrid the Captain-General was murdered in a parley with the rebels and the government did not dare to impose discipline. Soon after, an outbreak of cholera gave rise to wild rumours that the monks had poisoned the water: as a result mobs raided the monasteries and eighty religious were murdered on July 17, 1834.

Martínez had made minor inroads on ecclesiastical privileges, such as the abolition of the 'voto de Santiago' and other tributes, but faced with the impossibility of financing the war, he had prepared to turn to England and France for loans rather than seize the property of the church. This policy led to his fall, and in June 1835 he was replaced by his Minister of Finance, the Count of Toreno, who at once abolished the Society of Jesus and all monasteries with less than twelve members. This was the signal for violent attacks on religious houses, especially in the eastern cities of Barcelona, Saragossa, Valencia and Murcia, which demanded constituent cortes and a Supreme Junta.

Toreno's resources were soon exhausted; but the hero of the hour was Juan Alvarez Mendizábal, a Jew from Cádiz who had set up as a banker in London, and having financed the constitutionalist campaign in Portugal, enjoyed a prodigious reputation as a man of expedients. He saw that the confiscation of church property might pay for the war, and that its redistribution could be made the basis of a landowning middle-class pledged to constitutionalism, and, he hoped, able to hold a balance between recklessness and reaction. Fortified by new cortes, in which he had an overwhelming majority, Mendizábal issued the decrees of February 19 and March 8, 1836, which extinguished the religious orders and confiscated their property. Only those bodies devoted to education and the care of the sick were exempted. Great facilities were given to purchasers, both to raise ready money and for political reasons: many irregularities took place, and sudden fortunes were acquired, yet the war dragged on.

Mendizábal's political skill did not match his financial reputation, and he was quickly replaced by a moderate, Istúriz, who dissolved cortes and asked for a French intervention to end the war. The withdrawal from extremism was favoured by the regent, who had secretly married an upstanding young guardsman called Muñoz: for a moment it was feared that a new Godoy had arrived, but the Queen's husband was content with the title of Duke of Riánsares, some commercial transactions and the large family María-Cristina surreptitiously bore him. Istúriz now undertook to revise the statute and strengthen her prerogatives. But his request for a dissolution led to violent demonstrations among the disgruntled exaltados or 'progressists', as they now called themselves. In Andalusia and the east there was agitation for the

Constitution of 1812; and on August 12, 1836, a group of sergeants at La Granja, where the royal family was passing the summer, demanded to be admitted to the regent's drawing-room, and insisted that she should dismiss Istúriz and bring back the liberal Constitution, to which, after some expostulation, she agreed.

From this curious revolution there issued a progressist government led by José Maria Calatrava, an Extremaduran veteran of 1812, who (like Istúriz) had been among the 'exaltados' in 1820 and had drawn up the liberal criminal code. He now restored the municipal law of 1823 and the liberty of the press. He created an 'intendency' for the treasury in each province, seized the church's plate, sequestered the temporalities of absent bishops, and confiscated the property of private persons known to be Carlists. Meanwhile the Constitution of 1812 was replaced by that of 1837. This, instead of recognising catholicism as the only religion of Spaniards, merely assured them of freedom of worship and acknowledged the obligation of the state to support the catholic cult. This change coincided with Don Carlos' advance on Madrid, and if it stimulated anti-clerical extremists to resist, it also caused the moderado officers of the Cristinist army to protest. The pronunciamiento of Pozuelo de Aravaca forced Calatrava's resignation.

Espartero now pursued the Carlists back to the north. Both they and the progressists had shot their bolt. The funds seized from the church enabled the new moderado government, led by the Count of Ofalia, to build up a fresh army which was held in reserve in Andalusia to contain the revolutionary fervour of the southern cities. Its commander was General Narváez, the future moderado leader and dictator, a native of the Granadine town of Loja and a member of the conservative land-owning class. The existence of Narváez's army aroused the jealousy of Espartero, the most successful of the Cristinist generals, who gravitated towards the progressists.

It was now clear that the control of Spain would go to the general who could end the war. Espartero had realised this, and in his negotiations with Maroto he accepted two conditions:

respect for the Basque fueros and immunity for the Carlist officers, those who were willing to recognise Isabella II being admitted into the national army. The surrender of Vergara on these terms (April 31, 1839) left only the Apostolical or extremist clerical faction of the Carlists unappeased. Nevertheless, the survival of local autonomies was in contradiction to the centralising policy of liberalism, and the progressists strenuously opposed a government bill to confirm the Basque privileges pending negotiations with the provincial leaders and forced the addition of a phrase to safeguard the 'constitutional unity of the monarchy'. The ministry dissolved cortes and produced a moderado majority, while the progressists kept up a violent campaign of opposition. But the political issue was further complicated by a personal conflict: Espartero, annoyed by the independence of the politicians and the rise of Narváez, who now appeared as the strongest of the moderado ministers, demanded that his officers should be rewarded according to his own recommendations and forced the resignation of his rival. Immediately after, the moderados produced their own bill for municipal government. It fell back on the Bourbon solution of reform from above, reserving to the crown the right to appoint alcaldes in provincial capitals, and to the provincial authorities that of appointing those of smaller places. This measure, which conferred enormous powers on the provincial 'political chief', hereafter the pivot of the Spanish political system, was pressed through despite progressist protests that it violated the Constitution of 1837.

Neither solution offered any direct hope for the Basques. The political struggle was for the control of the cities, where the moderado law would cancel the effect of the popular majority in favour of the progressists. Espartero's prestige as the vanquisher of Carlism and upholder of the constitutional rights of Isabella II was now thrown into the balance against his rival generals, the regent and her moderado friends. In June 1840 she and her daughters travelled to Saragossa to review his victorious troops. She duly offered him power, but the 'Duke of Victory', as he now became, refused to accept without an undertaking that the moderado municipal law would not receive the royal assent.

When the regent declined this condition, he celebrated a triumphal entry into Barcelona, where he was sure of the military authorities and of the sympathy of the populace, and repeated his demand. María-Cristina retorted by giving her sanction to the contentious law, but signs of unrest alarmed her into giving way. The progressists had begun to rise in Madrid, and the movement spread rapidly through the country: everywhere popular juntas supported Espartero, who still insisted that María-Cristina should rescind the municipal law and publicly place the blame for the crisis on the moderados. She refused, and on October 12th resigned the regency and left Spain.

The progressists now swept into power, and new cortes decided by a small majority to appoint a single regent instead of a triple regency, and by a large one that it should be the glorious Duke of Victory. The young Queen, now ten, was placed under the tutorship of the venerable Argüelles. The moderado municipal law was abolished, while political offenders of the left were pardoned and the constitutionalist officers amply rewarded. But Espartero divided power between the small group of soldiers who had risen with him (the 'ayacuchos') and those progressists who had voted for the single regency ('the unitarians'). In Catalonia there was mounting resistance by the industrialists to his free-trade policy, and when the eastern provinces set up their own juntas, he ordered them to be dissolved. Barcelona disobeyed, and he had the city recklessly bombarded in December 1842.

This action lost him the support of many of the progressists. Already in 1841 a group of moderado officers had attempted a counter-coup and had even forced their way into the palace to seize the Queen: but the rising was overcome without serious difficulty and three of its leaders were executed. In May 1843 a Catalan progressist, General Prim, led a movement against Espartero, and he was soon joined by Generals Narváez and O'Donnell. In July Espartero made his way to Cádiz and embarked for England, while a new government accorded him the distinction of 'national execration'.

The autumn of 1843 saw not only the displacement of the Duke of Victory, but also the overthrow of the progressists, on whose radical policy the war had been won. They had carried forward the struggle by stirring up anti-clericalism for both political and fiscal motives; but although by the end of the war the urban masses had been turned against monasticism, the plundering of ecclesiastical property had had little effect on the great burden of debt. The exaltados had now no more to offer. Even Mendizábal's brief return to office in 1843 contributed nothing: progressism faltered, and its extreme wing crumbled into republicanism. Its true object, the 'sovereignty of the people', had become inconvenient. During the struggle authority was wielded neither by the people, nor by the regent; governments were not created by cortes, but cortes by governments, and the first care of each new ministry was to assure itself of a majority by asking the regent for a dissolution. Once the war was over, liberal theory required the application of a genuine municipal law and real suffrage. But there were numerous obstacles to this. Controlled elections offered the politicians a convenient escape from opposition. The two branches of the 'great liberal family' favoured different constitutional procedures, and if each acted as opposition under the other's system when forced to do so, neither would the moderados administer a system of popular sovereignty, nor the progressists return to the octroyé Statute.

Espartero was briefly succeeded by a coalition, which avoided the difficult question of the regency by declaring Isabella of age on her thirteenth birthday. But when she summoned the progressist Olózaga to form the first cabinet of her majority, he ended the coalition, and the moderados retaliated by a slanderous campaign in which he was accused of obtaining the Queen's signature by force. She dismissed him, and in May 1843 delivered the reins of government to the redoubtable Narváez: the moderados were to hold power for a decade.

They at once began to prepare a new Constitution, promulgated in 1845. It made away with 'national sovereignty' and gave the Queen power to appoint all the members of the upper house and to decide the question of her marriage without reference to cortes. At the same time, the sale of church property was halted and provision was made for the payment of the clergy by the state in compensation for the ecclesiastical revenues that had been seized.

On the question of religion the new constitution adopted a position midway between those of 1812 and 1837. In 1812, catholicism had been declared 'the sole religion' of Spaniards: in 1837, it was defined as merely 'the religion Spaniards profess'. It now became 'the religion of the Spanish nation', which the state was committed to maintain, though others might still exist. On this basis a concordat was negotiated, though it could not be ratified until 1851. As had been foreseen, the spoliation of church property had created a liberal vested interest which was by no means confined to the progressists: the question of the legal and spiritual situation of the new capitalists was as difficult as that of the secularised monastics. Since the end of the war some conservatives had hoped for a dynastic reconciliation, to be brought about by the marriage of Isabella to the son of Don Carlos, the Count of Montemolín, known as 'Charles VI'. This had been the idea of Alcudia on Isabella's accession, but Don Carlos still intransigently insisted that his son should be in effect King of Spain, and the negotiations again failed.

Isabella herself was generous and impulsive but, despite the efforts of the worthy Argüelles, lacking in character and instruction. Her sister and heir, Luisa-Fernanda, was nearly two years her junior. With the rise of the moderados, their mother had returned from exile (1844), and since she now enjoyed power without responsibility, made the life of the ministers more difficult than ever. Palace intrigues brought three changes of government in the spring of 1846, and although power finally passed to Istúriz, who enjoyed María-Cristina's confidence, it was clear that her influence could only be checked by the marriage of the Queen. But this subject raised many difficulties. France saw in it the opportunity to renew the Bourbon pact, while Great Britain hoped to counter reactionary and corrupt influences by presenting a Coburg. In September 1845, at Eu, each power agreed to withdraw its candidate, leaving the field to a Neapolitan Bourbon, the Carlist, and the two sons of Francisco de Paula, the scared boy whom the Madrid mob had tried to rescue from the French on

May 2, 1808: Francisco de Asís, Duke of Cádiz, pious, unintelligent and reputedly impotent, and Henry, Duke of Seville, of progressist sympathies. Palmerston, newly succeeding Aberdeen, again put forward the Coburg, but on being reminded of the agreement of Eu, declared in favour of the Duke of Seville. In reply, Guizot abandoned the entente, and at once concluded a double match: Isabella would marry her cousin of Cádiz and her sister Louis-Philippe's fifth son, the Duke of Montpensier. The double wedding was celebrated on October 10, 1846. However, a French succession did not follow: an impotent husband was no check to Isabella's generous nature, and she was to present Francisco de Asís with no fewer than nine children.

The affair of the Spanish marriages was to weaken the Anglo-French partnership and indirectly to cost Louis-Philippe his throne in the stormy year of 1848. It also caused the Carlists to restate their claims and almost brought about a renewal of the struggle: there was unrest in the Basque provinces and Cabrera returned to Catalonia, but open war was averted. With the recognition of Isabella by Rome Carlism was deprived of one of its strongest supports, and a religious settlement could not be long delayed. The intransigent Gregory XVI was succeeded by Pius IX; and when he was forced to leave Rome in the upheaval of 1848, the Madrid government responded to his appeals and sent a small force to Gaeta for his protection. Meanwhile, the fall of the French monarchy reverberated in Spain. Narváez took dictatorial powers to suppress the progressists in Madrid, Barcelona and other capitals, and forced the withdrawal of the British minister, Bulwer, on account of his sympathies for the opposition.

Meanwhile, the revival of clericalism began to have its effect at court. Isabella had at first shown a marked predilection for generals, and especially for the handsome Serrano, whom Narváez abruptly packed off to Granada; but she now came under the influence of a miracle-working nun, Sor Patrocinio. During the Carlist war, this lady had been afflicted with stigmata, and had been condemned as an impostor. She used her powers to persuade the Queen to refound convents, since by the concordat two orders 'and one other', unspecified, but generally understood to be the Jesuits, were to be readmitted to Spain. Similar influences were brought to bear on the King-Consort, whose confessor succeeded in overthrowing Narváez for a day in October 1849.

By now the moderado movement was itself dividing. The continued dominance of Narváez and other soldiers irked the civilians. The country, though reviving from the exhaustion of the war, was crowded with generals and crippled with debt. Spain was lagging far behind in those material advances which were altering the pattern of nineteenth-century Europe, and it was time for financiers and entrepreneurs to relieve generals and politicians of some of their burdens and privileges. Although new cortes were elected in 1850 with a contrived majority, the insistence of the Minister of Finance, Bravo Murillo, on achieving economies and publishing, for the first time, the national accounts, forced Narváez to resign. But Bravo's reforms included a virtual suspension of political life, while Narváez's removal provoked a swelling demand for genuine elections from the progressists. There followed a succession of short-lived ministries. As nineteenth-century capitalism established itself in Madrid the normal appetite for safe places and sinecures was whetted by new opportunities. The redistribution of property had produced an eager speculative class captained by the financier Salamanca, whose name is borne by a suburb of Madrid. The entry of foreign capital, especially from France, further stimulated economic progress, while for the politicians, the construction of the first railways offered rich opportunities for peculation. In these matters the Queen-Mother and her husband were generally believed to have a special interest.

In 1853 the Count of San Luis, the president of the council of ministers, attempted to appease his rivals by showering favours on them in an attempt to cover up the scandalous disposal of railway contracts. Outvoted, he suspended cortes, arrested his most prominent adversaries, and deported several of the generals. The exercise of arbitrary powers to support a stale and corrupt government led to a series of revolts which began in Saragossa in February 1854. In June O'Donnell made a pronunciamiento: opposing forces led by the Minister of War advanced to Vicálvaro, where the two parties fought an indecisive battle. A second revolutionary appeal fell flat; and it was only on July 7, when O'Donnell issued a manifesto defining his aims, that the progressists rallied to him. On July 17 the government resigned, and the mob attacked the residences of María-Cristina, Salamanca and others who were alleged to have feathered their nests. When a popular junta set itself up in Madrid, and there were demands for a change of dynasty, Isabella appealed to Espartero to save her, and at the end of the month the Duke of Victory formed a new government with O'Donnell.

The upheaval of 1854, which for a moment seemed likely to overthrow the throne, instead gave it a new lease of life. The Queen-Mother departed for Portugal, the railway-concessions were annulled, and cortes dissolved. Moderate progressists, led by Olózaga, and progressive moderados, led by González Bravo, launched a manifesto for a Liberal Union. The first experiences of the new régime were unpromising. The reform of the royal household, rendered necessary by the irresponsibility of the Queen and the intrigues of her familiars, was only carried through after many protests. Once more it was decided to change the constitution, but the discussions were protracted, and the reform that took shape under the aegis of Espartero became increasingly progressist in character: national sovereignty, an elected senate, a national militia, were all reversions to the régime of 1837. In July 1856 O'Donnell, in concert with the Queen, led a coup against Espartero and his partisans: the left-wing progressists and democrats attempted to fight back, but after a tense struggle in Madrid, Saragossa, Barcelona and other cities, the central government prevailed. O'Donnell suspended the new constitution (which was never promulgated) and restored that of 1845, modified by an Additional Act.

The coup of July 1856 was the work of O'Donnell and Isabella. The general was anxious to be free of Espartero and of the national militia, the revival of which gave the extreme progressists a strong instrument against the ministry. The Queen, for her part, was alarmed at the progressist intention to admit a limited freedom of private worship and to resume the sale of church property. Although her fears on the first point were assuaged by the return to the Constitution of 1845, the treasury still needed funds, and proceeded with a bill for the disposal of church property. When it was presented to her, she at first refused to imperil her soul by signing it; but despite the efforts of nun and nuncio, she was at last prevailed upon to give it her assent. The nuncio at once left the country, and there were again sporadic Carlist risings led by Cabrera in Catalonia. Isabella, despite her undertakings to O'Donnell, suddenly replaced him by Narváez (October 12, 1856); and the moderado leader completed the return to the conservatism of 1845, enforcing once more the hierarchical local government law and reviving the practice of entailment for the benefit of grandees and hereditary seats in the Senate.

Narváez's government fell a year later, in October 1857; in June 1858 O'Donnell returned to power and the Liberal Union governed the country for almost five years. It now found a solution to the long-standing problem of church property. The Pope no longer insisted on the return of land that had already been sold, and agreed that that still held by the state should be paid for in bonds bearing interest at three per cent. The government thus received temporary financial relief which was reflected in fictitious budgetary surpluses: in fact the disposal of the church lands had merely saddled the state with the obligation to maintain the clergy and enriched a new landowning class, while the large numbers of poor formerly succoured by the monasteries took to begging at church-doors and in the streets. These operations, like the speculation in new enterprises, tended to concentrate prosperity in Madrid, which presented a lively and active appearance in marked contrast with the run-down provincial towns of the north.

O'Donnell also embarked on the traditional foreign policy of war against the infidel. In 1857 the murder of Spanish missionaries in Cochin-China had been followed by a small Franco-Spanish punitive expedition. When in August 1859 Berbers attacked a Spanish guard-post in Morocco, O'Donnell delivered an ultimatum and landed an army near Ceuta. It cleared the mountains behind the southern Pillar of Hercules, marched to Río Martín, where it was reinforced by sea, and fought the battle of Tetuán on February 2, 1860. Finally the engagement of Wad-Ras opened the road to Tangier (March 23), and the sultan accepted O'Donnell's terms. Spain received a small strip of territory, a guarantee of a neutral zone, and an indemnity of ten million dollars payable from the customs-dues of Tetuán, which was temporarily occupied.

The resumption of the crusade against Islam was followed by two interventions in the affairs of the former American colonies. The Mexican liberals, no less impoverished than those of Spain, had, like them, laid hands on the property of the church, but also on that of foreign investors. Napoleon III, linked to Spain by marriage, persuaded O'Donnell to join him in an expedition to recover European capital and prestige in Mexico, and at the end of 1861 General Prim landed at Vera Cruz with a force of 6,000 men as part of an Anglo-Spanish contingent. But when Napoleon revealed his intention to win a throne for the Austrian Archduke Maximilian, both allies withdrew their support, and while the French launched the Archduke on his tragic adventure, Prim and his men retired to Cuba, which, with Puerto Rico, remained the only Spanish possession in the New World. Also in 1861, the Dominican Republic, threatened by its neighbour Haiti, declared itself re-incorporated in the Spanish monarchy, only to reassert its independence four years later. Finally, in December 1865, Spain found herself involved in a quarrel with Peru, which joined Chile in an alliance against her: both governments declared war, and the Spanish admiral Méndez Núñez led an expedition against Callao. Peace was restored by the mediation of the United States in 1871.

These small engagements reflect the opportunist nature of O'Donnell's government, which achieved a short period of stability for the throne. In November 1857, the wayward Queen had presented the nation with an heir, the future Alfonso XII, whose paternity was attributed to a Catalan colonel, and she had won some popularity as her armies resumed the imperial tradition. But her erratic interventions in political affairs hastened the disintegration of the Liberal Union. She had supported Prim's withdrawal from Mexico although O'Donnell had opposed it, and when the minister asked for a dissolution of cortes she pressed for the dismissal of two of his ministers and he resigned (March 1863).

Although the Liberal Union had been in some ways the most effective government Spain had enjoyed since the beginning of the century, it had not provided a firm basis for an enduring representative system. Even when the anti-constitutional Carlists were set aside, the two main divisions of what was euphemistically called 'the great liberal family' held opposing views about the political structure of the state. At first each had eliminated the other on achieving power, and in consequence had divided into factions and produced its own opposition. The Liberal Union had been a centre party, a fusion of the more collaborative spirits of the two wings, held together partly by the authority of O'Donnell and partly by the external pressure of extreme conservatives and advanced democrats. For all its liberal professions, its actions had been conservative: it had exercised power under the moderado Constitution, had disbanded the national militia, and had made war on the Mexican liberals. On the religious question, it had been distinctly conciliatory.

The need for a regular alternation of parties had long been recognised, and in the crisis of 1863 the progressist leaders urged the Queen to appoint ministers pledged to this policy. But when finally the Marquis of Miraflores was entrusted with the formation of a cabinet in March 1863, he dissolved cortes and sought to enforce the limitations on the electorate favoured by the moderates. As a result, the progressists ordered their followers to boycott the elections, and only one of their members appeared in the following cortes.

The progressists were by now convinced that palace influences, the so-called 'traditional obstacles', were permanently opposed to them. Their leader, Olózaga, had already stated this view, and in May 1864 it was supported by a successful general, Prim, at a public demonstration. But Prim's attempts to raise the flag of rebellion proved unsuccessful, and in September Isabella again entrusted power to Narváez, who governed dictatorially until the following June. From this time, the parties of the left became progressively more hostile to the Queen, though only the Democrats formally advocated republicanism. In view of the state of public finances, the government sought a remedy by selling crown properties, proposing to assign three-quarters of the proceeds to the treasury and a quarter to the Queen. While this scheme, 'the gesture', evoked loud official applause for Isabella's patriotism, the republican press condemned it as a seizure of public property. The author of this view was Emilio Castelar, then a professor in the University of Madrid, and the government demanded his dismissal and even removed the rector for refusing to comply. Student demonstrations were violently repressed by the Civil Guard and army: in the 'hecatomb' of Saint Daniel's Night (April 10, 1865), nine youths were reported to have been killed and a hundred wounded. Narváez's government was bitterly criticised, and he was soon after dismissed.

To succeed him, Isabella called on O'Donnell, who made serious but unavailing efforts to reconcile the progressists. They refused to be associated with his government; and his attempts to woo Prim, his recognition of the new Italian monarchy and his offer to broaden the electorate all failed to strike a response. With the progressists it was now an article of propaganda that their policies could never succeed under the existing ruler.

Prim's comings and goings, in exile or in disguise, appealed to the imagination of the younger generation, and after he had made unsuccessful pronouncements on the Portuguese frontier and in Barcelona, O'Donnell declared a state of siege and suspended the constitutional guarantees. The progressists now returned to the tactics they had used successfully thirty years before by recruiting most of the sergeants in the Spanish army. On June 22, 1866 the artillery sergeants at San Gil in Madrid rose and seized the barracks. O'Donnell called out the loyal troops, and received the support of most of the leading generals, including Narváez and Serrano, who rapidly repressed the rebels and executed sixty-eight of their leaders.

Isabella was again alarmed for the safety of her throne; and when O'Donnell insisted on strengthening his hold on the Senate, she opposed him and called on Narváez to form a government. Most of the prominent liberals were now in exile: the progressists, who were opposed to Isabella and the influences of her palace, but did not yet repudiate the Bourbon dynasty, rallied at Ostend, while the republicans, led by Pi y Margall and Castelar, formed a centre in Paris. Only in June 1867 did all the opposition parties agree to leave the question of the régime to be decided by a popular vote or by a popularly elected National Assembly. In December Prim and Sagasta interviewed the veteran Carlist Cabrera in London, but their proposal that the traditionalist pretender should constitutionalise himself was again rejected.

Meanwhile, Narváez had informed cortes of his programme and immediately obtained a dissolution. Governing by decree, he attempted to defend the throne by establishing a Rural Guard to control the provinces, modifying the existing municipal law and reorganising the universities. By now the conservative system had become little else than a military dictatorship. A group of senators and deputies prepared a petition to the Queen for the re-opening of cortes, and Narváez retorted by consigning his old rival and late ally, Serrano, to Majorca. When finally new cortes gathered at the end of March 1867 Narváez's decrees were sanctioned over the protests of a small minority, consisting mainly of members of the Liberal Union. But this body was now enfeebled and split, and the death of O'Donnell in November removed any hope that it might become the means of reuniting liberals around the throne. Its more advanced wing joined the progressists and democrats to form the movement of 'liberal conciliation', hoping to settle the dynastic issue by replacing Isabella by her sister, the Duchess of Montpensier.

At the beginning of 1868 Isabella's tottering throne was maintained entirely by the moderado rump and the small group of political generals who had controlled Spain since the end of the civil war. Her sheet-anchor was Narváez, who held that 'Spain is full of scoundrels' and that therefore 'to govern is to resist'. When he died in April 1868, the throne was undefended and the moderados divided. The new minister, González Bravo, vainly appealed for cohesion and the maintenance of order. Even Serrano, now nominal leader of the Liberal Union, and his cohort of generals favoured a new ruler, and were accordingly banished from the capital, while the Montpensiers were asked to leave the country. When finally Isabella departed to take the waters on the north coast, the conspirators gathered at Gibraltar, and Prim warned Admiral Topete in Cádiz of what was afoot. On September 18th they, with Serrano and Primo de Rivera, published a revolutionary manifesto and set up a provisional government. Most of the towns of the south and east responded to the liberal call, while government forces marched from the capital to Córdoba to defend the approaches to the meseta. They tried to bar the way to the insurgents at Alcolea with its bridge over the Guadalquivir, but their commander was wounded and withdrew. The people of Madrid at once rose, and a revolutionary junta declared Isabella deposed. She retired into France, delivered a protest from Pau and established herself in Paris.

The revolution was directed against Isabella as a queen. Twenty years before, she had been popular among the Spanish people, and she would again be rapturously welcomed when she returned to Madrid for her son's wedding. If she was now discredited, this was due less to her favourites and her inconsequential treatment of her ministers than to the progressist conviction that she had allowed her spiritual advisers to shut the door against liberalism, and that this had caused her mismanagement of cortes and her excessive reliance on Narváez's dictatorship. But having once more expelled the Jesuits, the revolutionary party found little to agree on. Admiral Topete had supposed that the object of the movement was to place Isabella's sister on the throne, for the Montpensiers were popular in the south; but in Madrid a republican junta had already established itself in the Ministry of the Interior, and when Prim and his colleagues entered the capital at the end of October, they declared their own preference for constitutional monarchy, but their willingness to abide by the decision of the people. Constituent cortes were called for February 1869.

This body consisted of 214 Monarchists and 55 Republicans. However, the defeated moderados were not represented, so that monarchical opinion was limited to Unionists and progressists, while the Democrats, who had now adopted federalism as a remedy for Spanish ills, had convinced themselves that the application of this theory was more important than the question of régime. The discussion on the religious issue also produced very conflicting views. Anticlericalism was again in the ascendant, and Castelar spoke for the separation of church and state and the secularisation of teaching. Finally the assembly declared for religious liberty and for a monarchy in which the ruler's powers would be limited to the choice of a prime minister and the right of veto. An oath of allegiance would be required of all public officials, and would be extended to the prelates.

The new formulation of liberal principles was naturally opposed by the Carlists: and when Serrano was elected regent and Prim President of the Council of Ministers, the republicans, who looked upon the former as a doubtful ally and were disappointed by Prim's failure to support the abolition of the monarchy, denounced the new régime as a military dictatorship. Meanwhile, the makers of the new Constitution were in search of a chrysalis for their royal coccoon. The Unionists urged the candidature of the Montpensiers, while the progressists favoured a new house free from Bourbon attachments. One of the opponents of Montpensier was the radical Duke of Seville, brother of the late King-Consort, who was challenged to a duel by Montpensier and shot dead. The incident deprived both participants of the throne, for the survivor was tried, and condemned to banishment and to pay a fine to his victim's heir: he was later returned to cortes as deputy for Cádiz.

Those who favoured a new dynasty looked towards a German prince or to the former King-Consort of Portugal. Prim even proposed the name of Espartero, but the aged Duke of Victory refused the distinction. The most acceptable German, Leopold of Hohenzollern-Sigmaringen, was strongly opposed by Napoleon III, who feared that the accession of a Prussian officer would lead to the encirclement of France as in the days of the Hapsburg hegemony. Napoleon had been well disposed towards Isabella II, and his Spanish wife was to some extent involved in Peninsular affairs. He had moreover recently failed to place his Austrian protégé on the Mexican throne and seen Bismarck's Germany defeat Austria in the short campaign of Sadowa. But instead of requesting Prim not to proceed with the German candidature, he demanded that the Prussian King should forbid it, and when William III complied, pressed for further assurances. The Kaiser refused to receive his ambassador, and he incontinently declared war. Within a few weeks the French armies had been crushed at Sedan and the French empire had ceased to exist: in January 1871 the new German empire was proclaimed at Versailles. For the second time in a quarter of a century a Spanish dynastic problem had been the means of overturning a French régime.

The sudden reappearance of revolutionary forces in France and the emergence of the Second Republic gave heart to the Spanish extremists and made the selection of a king a matter of some urgency. Prim could now turn only to Italy. The house of Savoy was admired by Spanish liberals for its anti-clericalism. The King of Italy's third son, Amadeo, Duke of Aosta, was ready to accept the Spanish crown, provided that none of the powers objected: none did, and in November 1870 cortes voted him into the vacant throne. He received 191 votes, to 64 for a federal republic, 22 for Montpensier, 8 for Espartero, 2 for Alfonso (XII), 1 for the Duchess of Montpensier, and 19 blanks: this vote was, however, hardly a measure of Spanish monarchism, since the Carlists (to whom the House of Savoy was anathema) and moderados were not represented.

On the first day of 1871 the young Amadeo arrived in Spain, confident that the vote of the cortes reflected the real desires of the Spanish people and hopeful that in some obscure way the ancient association between Spain and Italy might be revived. He also relied on the powerful support of Prim. But on reaching Cartagena he learned that the kingmaker had been murdered four days earlier as he left cortes. No one was clearly incriminated, although a dossier of 18,000 pages, a monument of Spanish encyclopaedism, was compiled.

Amadeo's reign lasted just two years. Prim, who had exercised great authority among the progressists, might have established him; but Serrano had spent too long in the Bourbon camp and still inspired distrust as Isabella's 'handsome general'. By the end of

1871 the liberal centre had again split. Its two leaders were Sagasta and Zorrilla: the first of these, receiving the mantle of O'Donnell, was to become the great master of fusionism, the 'old shepherd' of the unruly liberal flock, whose own ideas and principles were never too precise or rigid, while Zorrilla represented the more dogmatic left-wing progressists and also commanded the confidence of the republicans. The crown naturally inclined towards Sagasta, who governed till May 1872, when he was assailed with accusations of corruption, and forced to resign.

Meanwhile, the Carlists had held a council in London in July 1868, as a result of which the new pretender assumed the title of 'Duke of Madrid'.[1] On the fall of Isabella, she and González Bravo were disposed to recognise the traditionalist claim, and in 1869 some two dozen traditionalist deputies were elected to the Constituent Cortes. When the Spanish crown was offered to the anti-clerical dynasty of Savoy, many catholics rallied to the cause, and in the election of 1871 González Bravo's brother-in-law led a group of seventy-nine Carlist deputies. But this minority was blotted out in the next election, and in the spring of 1872 a new Carlist war began. Charles 'VII' crossed the frontier, denouncing the foreign King, and summoned his followers to rise. For a time much of the north adhered to the pretender, though his forces were never formidable. Eventually, Serrano, who had been entrusted with the task of suppressing the rebels, granted them mild terms at Amorebeitia (May 24).

Amadeo now offered Serrano power, but on his appearance in cortes the parties of the left vehemently condemned his moderation

[1] The original traditionalist claimant Charles 'V' survived until 1855: his widow, the Princess of Beira, long held court at the Loredan palace in Venice. His elder son, Charles 'VI', Count of Montemolín, who failed to marry Isabella or to win support in the adventure of San Carlos de la Rápita (1860), died at Trieste in 1861. His second son, Don Juan, professed liberal ideas, and finally ceded his claim to his heir, Charles 'VII', Duke of Madrid, in October 1868.

A speech at the council of London (July 1868) simplified the issue in the following words: 'we are Carlists, because we are catholics, and if it were possible that the triumph of Carlism should not mean the triumph of catholic truth, we should not be Carlists.'

towards the Carlists, and he asked the King to authorise him to declare a state of siege. Amadeo, aware that Narváez's dictatorial system had cost Isabella her throne, refused to depart from the constitution. Serrano duly resigned, and the crown had no choice but to call on Zorrilla. As a result new elections were held and eighty-three republicans were returned. At the end of the year Amadeo was finally divided from his ministers and cortes by a question of military discipline, which, though apparently trivial, placed him in an impossible situation. Zorrilla had decided to advance General Hidalgo, an artilleryman who had taken the part of the rebels in the progressist 'sergeants' revolt' of 1866. His elevation was evidently a political one; and the rest of the artillery officers protested by resigning their commissions, to which Zorrilla retorted by promoting the sergeants to take their places. Behind this act of ludicrous intransigence lay the wider question of the separation of the army from political life: the generation of generals who had attained vast political influence by saving constitutionalism in the Carlist war was now tapering away; and their successors, unable to enter politics under such advantageous circumstances, preferred to regard the army as a professional body pledged to the existing régime. The progressists for their part, traditionally opposed to the professional officers and favourable to a citizen's militia, still profoundly distrusted an institution which had lent itself to so many pronunciamientos. Amadeo consequently signed the decree which promoted the artillery sergeants, and presented his own abdication in February 1873, leaving the Spaniards to their own oblique dissidences, secure in the knowledge that he had never tried to impose himself on 'the national will as represented in cortes'. The same cortes at once transfigured itself into a National Assembly and proclaimed a Republic under the presidency of Don Estanislao Figueras. It was a republic imposed neither by popular suffrage nor by force of arms, but by sheer weight of oratory—'a conspiracy of society, nature and history', as Castelar defined it. Not even the National Assembly was republican by origin; but having eliminated the Bourbons and almost every other available royal line, the majority had no course left but to adopt the principles of the minority.

These principles spread, however, with surprising rapidity. Republicanism had existed in Spain for almost a quarter of a century, but it had hitherto made no notable progress, partly because many Spaniards were inveterately loyal to the crown and partly because its general policies were not strikingly different from those of the monarchist parties. But in the last years of Isabella II it had adopted the federal idea, largely through the impassioned advocacy of Castelar and Pi y Margall; and in the peculiar vacuum left by the withdrawal of Amadeo, this thesis met with almost no opposition. Its attraction lay in its radical attitude towards the religious problem and its extremely traditional treatment of regionalism. For federation reversed the centralising policy adopted by the Bourbon reformers and every successive constitutional regime, and returned to the ancient system of provincial autonomy. It found particularly ready acceptance in Catalonia, where most of the population was opposed to the progressive centralisation of Madrid. On the overthrow of Isabella, the federalists had formed a series of regional pacts, covering (1) Aragon, Catalonia and Valencia; (2) Andalusia, Extremadura and Murcia; (3) the two Castiles; (4) the Basque Provinces, and (5) Galicia and Asturias: these were to be coalesced in a national pact, which would form the basis of the federal democratic republic and might lead to an Iberian union with Portugal: the 'autonomy of hierarchies' would enable each region to govern itself. The federalists had counted on the support of the Catalan Prim, and turned sharply against him when he committed himself to monarchism: as a result of their demonstrations, a state of siege had been declared and their deputies had walked out of cortes.

But when elections for a new Constituent Assembly were held in May 1873, the monarchists abstained, and a federal form of government was adopted by 218 votes to 2. The reformers produced a constitution which divided Spain into fifteen states, each of which was entitled to maintain an armed force, impose taxation and raise its own loans. Even before this could come into effect, the regional zealots had taken affairs into their own hands. In Barcelona the Diputació proclaimed a 'Catalan State' on March 9,

1873, and the eastern provinces promptly took steps to divide themselves from the economic problems of the rest of Spain by erecting their own customs-barriers.

During the summer, the southern cities of Málaga, Seville, Granada, Cádiz and Murcia declared themselves to be 'cantons', and as soon as they received financial independence, began to exact forced loans from the leading tax-payers, to issue bonds and to strike money, while the central government found its revenues sharply diminished and its credit non-existent.

This feverish disintegration derived from a blind assumption that the rising power of the United States was the direct result of federal decentralisation, a delusion which was to produce similar, though less catastrophic, results in Brazil sixteen years later. The general sense of chaos was heightened by violent attacks on the church and army, and the murder of officers and priests. Such local constitutions as that of Granada declared the church to be independent of the state, abolished ecclesiastical titles and prohibited the external display of worship.

In Madrid, Figueras abruptly abandoned the republican government and retired to France, while Pi y Margall, the unfortunate author of the disintegration, was prime minister for a month, when he made way for Salmerón, who in turn was replaced by Castelar. Salmerón favoured a unitary republic and despatched General Pavía to Andalusia: by the autumn all the cantons there had been easily reduced. In the east Martínez Campos bombarded and captured Valencia. But in Murcia, where the cantonalists had been joined by the men of the naval and military base at Cartagena, the rebels held firm, making their own money, bombarding government-held Alicante and, after a brush with the warship *Friedrich Karl*, declaring war on Germany. The rebel fleet was finally delivered to the British navy and interned at Gibraltar, but the canton of Cartagena continued to resist until the collapse of the republic.

Cuba too was in open revolt, and when the Spanish authorities there seized a United States vessel, the *Verginius*, and shot fifty-seven rebels who were on board, there was immediate danger of war with the archetype of federal republics. Finally Castelar restored the *Verginius* and agreed to pay compensation. But the suppression of the cantons was still opposed by many of their representatives in cortes; and Pavía, who believed that the only solution lay in military dictatorship, insisted that the deputies should be dismissed. When cortes reassembled in January 1874, Castelar proposed the restoration of relations with Rome and was promptly outvoted. Before a successor could be appointed, Pavía consulted the Captains-General and demanded that cortes should disperse. It retorted by declaring him an outlaw, and Castelar announced his intention to die at his post. But when in the small hours troops began to file into the building, the deputies left in groups by the side-doors, and even Castelar was at last persuaded to go.

It is perhaps surprising that although Spain seemed to be on the point of collapse in 1873, Spaniards have regarded not it, but the loss of the final shreds of empire in 1898 as the nadir of their fortunes, the 'Disaster'. The first crisis, which was the direct result of their own intransigence and folly, provoked a rapid return to reason and self-discipline and banished some of the excesses and illusions of romantic liberalism. To the progressists Isabella had become the 'impossible lady', and the adjective was symptomatic of Spanish politics: the Carlists had washed their hands of constitutionalism, the army stood aside from Amadeo and the republic, the Catalans repudiated centralisation, and the municipalities of the south renounced any form of discipline at all. Unlimited freedom quickly proved intolerable, and the pieces were put together again. Reformers now began to busy themselves with the problems of education and agriculture; and even Castelar, emerging from his oratorical dream-world, became the apostle of 'possibilism'.

Since the crown had been abolished, the church separated, and cortes reduced to a mere rump, the only effective institution of the state was again the army. Pavía therefore gathered the Captains-General, and they entrusted power to Serrano, who suppressed the constitution and cortes, and announced that political life would not be resumed until order had been restored. The canton of Cartagena now collapsed, and the most direct threat to the régime came from the Carlists, who still held most of the Basque Provinces and had laid siege to the liberal city of Bilbao. In February a relieving force was defeated, and although Serrano himself led a series of onslaughts, the Carlist lines held firm, and it was only in May that he was able to enter the city. His comrade, Concha, was defeated and killed at Montemuro in June, and the war spread to Castile and even Andalusia. But the Carlists failed to take Irún or Pamplona and in 1875 they were defeated in the centre and in Catalonia: their Basque armies finally gave in at the beginning of 1876.

The partisans of a Bourbon restoration had calmly bided their time. On December 1st, 1874, Isabella's son, Alfonso, then a cadet at Sandhurst, issued a manifesto in which he professed his faith in the hereditary monarchy, declaring himself a good catholic and true liberal. At the end of the month General Martínez Campos pronounced for him at Sagunto; and his mentor, Cánovas del Castillo, received the reins of government from the liberal conciliator, Sagasta. In January 1885 Alfonso made his entry into Madrid, and soon after the veteran Carlist leader Cabrera recognised him and most of Don Carlos' loyalists went into exile in France.

Cánovas now established the form of government that was to see the century out, a moderate oligarchy skilfully disguised as parliamentary liberalism. He had long meditated on the causes of Spanish 'decadence' and the possibility of introducing the admired institutions of Great Britain. He had been careful not to precipitate the restoration; and Alfonso XII, unlike his mother, could be said not to have fought fellow-Spaniards for his throne. Cánovas' state would be catholic, though no one was to be molested for his religious beliefs: the implicit admission of freedom of worship aroused objections in Rome, but the form of words was voted with large majorities in both houses. As to the army, which had deposed Isabella and Amadeo and ended the republic, Cánovas intended that it should be taken out of the field of politics and severely professionalised, being encouraged to regard itself as the guarantor of the crown, which became once more the symbol of national unity: the rising of General Villacampo, who vainly attempted to restore the republic in 1886, was the last of the military pronunciamientos of the old style.

Against this traditionalist background Cánovas desired to set a parliamentary legislature based on a smoothly functioning two-party system. As the rotation of parties could not be produced naturally, it must be arranged by the political leaders. This would mean a continuation of the system of contrived elections, but since the national will had never genuinely made itself felt through the ballot, the price was a necessary one. Only parties which supported the crown would be allowed legal existence: and some Carlists and republicans were ready to make their peace with the new régime. The government was enabled to defend itself by suspending constitutional guarantees without reference to cortes, a right not conferred by the constitutions of 1812, 1837, 1845, 1856 and 1869. Thus neither public opinion, nor the deputies, nor a pronunciamiento could prevent a government from enforcing its policy.

The machinery of cortes was manipulated by the Minister of the Interior or 'Gobernación', through the network of 'political chiefs', now sanctioned by long custom. Under the system perfected by Romero Robledo, the minister could decide the composition of cortes by agreement with the provincial party leaders, settling the list of members to be returned and allocating whatever representation was thought expedient to the opposition, often about a quarter. Those who sat in cortes were thus essentially representatives of local cliques or bosses (the 'caciques') and their main function in Madrid was to defend these interests: since all local patronage from the highest officials downwards was controlled by this system no politician ever dreamed of abolishing it.

In launching his new system Cánovas had the distinct advantage that all the old leaders were gone. Narváez, O'Donnell and Prim were dead. Serrano died before he could recover from his republican escapade. Espartero was forgotten. Cánovas' followers were essentially the heirs of the old Liberal Union: he himself had been O'Donnell's confidential collaborator in 1854. This group had inherited the mantle of the old Moderados and now called itself the Conservative-Liberal party. For an opposition leader, Cánovas naturally looked among the former progressists many of whom had tucked away their Phrygian bonnets. Zorrilla refused to collaborate, and went into exile as an impenitent republican, but Sagasta, more transigent, agreed to lead the 'fusionist' opposition, which was to receive power in 1881: when, four years later, Alfonso XII died of tuberculosis, leaving an unborn heir, the future Alfonso XIII, the peaceful rotation of the parties was formalised in the so-called 'Pact of El Pardo', and the regency of the Austrian Queen-Mother was attended by none of the usual difficulties.

Despite its admirable façade, Cánovas' system remained essentially artificial. Although he could command large majorities in cortes, it was common knowledge that in his army the officers outnumbered the men. Nor did he succeed in swelling the ranks. To his right there were only the extreme Moderados and the Carlists. For the former the country at large felt little affection, regarding them as mere egoistic capitalists. As to the Carlists, they remained consistently opposed to liberalism in all its forms; even after the reconciliation with Rome many preferred to remain outside the political system, while in the Basque provinces Cánovas was still regarded as the 'assassin of the fueros'.

In contrast to Cánovas' small and closely controlled body, the new liberal party led by Sagasta consisted of a variety of groups including catholics and anti-clericals, free-traders and protectionists, and supporters and opponents of universal suffrage. None of the half-dozen leaders of the main groups could dominate the party as a whole, and only Sagasta, by his extraordinary talent for manipulation, could hold the block together: even he, when in office, was obliged to allow his ministers something approaching autonomy in their respective spheres. The diversity of the liberals was soon increased by their association with the penitent republicans. Since its failure the anti-dynastic movement had split into three: those reconciled to the monarchy and led by Castelar, who demanded electoral reform and universal suffrage, a middle group under Salmerón, which returned to cortes in 1886, and the irreconcilables under Ruiz Zorrilla, who still longed for a glorious revolution.

All that the liberal factions had in common was a belief that some exclusive political solution was the ultimate key to power, and a general disinclination to undertake any real reform. Little was done for education or justice. Even the army was small and inefficient in relation to its cost. The public debt was repeatedly consolidated, yet its service constantly increased. As in the sixteenth century, the only social concern of politicians was to keep prices down for fear of arousing discontent in the large towns. When in 1889 Don Claudio Moyano sought to launch a movement to restrict imports and to protect the Spanish peasant, the plan was generally condemned in Madrid as a mere attempt to buy votes, a new form of 'caciquismo'. Only in Catalonia did it evoke some response: there the industrialists had long demanded a policy of high tariffs, and their interests now coincided with those of the country-people, who, having vainly supported Carlism in defence of their ancient privileges, found themselves thrown back on their own resources. In 1888 the Catalan regional League petitioned the regent for Catalan cortes, with a regional treasury and army, according to the 'indefeasible rights of the Catalan nation'; but the very mention of such pretensions only infuriated the politicians of Madrid. Over much of southern and eastern Spain the rural masses, now completely excluded from political life, began to look towards the anarchists: seen in retrospect, that general abdication of responsibilities which had produced the anarchy of 1873 seemed the most desirable form of government. When in 1890 Castelar's demand for universal suffrage was accepted and passed into law, both bourgeois republicans and such workers' candidates as were considered moderate were allowed to present themselves; but except in Castile, where orthodox socialism had made some headway, the workers were now disillusioned by the class-restrictions imposed by the governments of the restoration. They had learned to do without the church and crown, and they could easily do without politicians. In 1892 there were anarchist risings in Andalusia and Catalonia, and bands of peasants who attacked Jerez cried: 'Death to the bourgeoisie!' The bourgeoisie, absorbed in their own affairs and in the amiable artificiality of the political world of Madrid, scarcely noticed that the liberal cries they themselves had once uttered had now assumed a more menacing sound.

But the restored monarchy received its rudest shock from without. Alfonso XII, had married his cousin, the daughter of the Montpensiers, in 1878: it had been a popular match, but the bride died only five months later; and the earnest cadet turned into a reckless roué, whose amours were picturesque, indiscreet and popular. After Cánovas' careful tutelage, he found Sagasta less exacting, and was allowed both to ruin his own health and to create to some extent conditions of foreign policy. Since the beginning of the century Spain had been influenced by French and English ideas: only the Carlists had kept up the traditional Austrian connection. But the disaster of 1870 had lowered French prestige; and Cánovas, who regarded France and the rest of the Latin world as tainted with decadence, saw in Prussian military power as in English commercial enterprise evidence of the northern virtues. Alfonso's second marriage, to the Archduchess María-Cristina of Hapsburg-Lorraine, had little direct political significance in 1879, but it proved that Carlism no longer monopolised the Austrian connection. Soon after, Alfonso visited Munich and Vienna, where he was received by Franz-Joseph, and Hamburg, where the Kaiser displayed his armies to him and made him a colonel in the Uhlans: when he returned by way of Paris, there were demonstrations against him and the French President was obliged to present his apologies.

Since the Mexican adventure, Spain had played little direct part in the affairs of Europe. But the partition of Africa served to remind her of her own imperial interests, to revive her resentment against Great Britain for holding Gibraltar, to arouse jealousy against France for her expansion into Algeria and Morocco, and to evoke a certain admiration for the successes of Germany. In 1880 a conference in Madrid regulated Franco-Spanish claims to 'protect' Morocco, but without establishing any real cordiality: when Muslim rebels killed Spanish farmers in Oran, the question of indemnity caused some tension with France. These affairs were small enough, but the heritage of Isabella I still seemed nearer and dearer than the Sulu Islands, claimed by Germany in 1881-5, or the Carolines, where German pretensions caused a brief commotion in 1885: in the latter case the Pope arbitrated and Spanish rights were eventually sold to Germany in 1898.

But the final blow to Spanish imperialism was dealt by the United States. Spain still possessed Cuba, Puerto Rico and the Philippine Islands. Cuba had acquired special importance in the eyes of the United States during the Civil War; and three years after the victory of the North an insurrection broke out in the island with the object of seeking independence from Spain and the abolition of slavery. In 1869 Grant threatened to recognise the rebels as belligerents and proposed to buy Cuba from Spain, but his advisers were unwilling to risk a war, and even in the midst of the federal disintegration of 1873 Spain would not consider relinquishing her valuable colony. Thus the *Verginius* incident was settled and the struggle continued until 1878, when General Martínez Campos concluded the peace of Zanjón, by which Cuba obtained a degree of self-government already conceded to Puerto Rico. Until 1895 an uneasy peace reigned in the island, but the attempts of the Cuban deputies in Madrid to obtain administrative reforms and to free the island from the tariffs imposed by the Catalan industrialists were heavily defeated. In 1895 the patriot Martí resumed the struggle, and although he was killed in a skirmish, the insurrection spread rapidly, and the governor Martínez Campos, the pacifier of 1878, asked to be relieved. He was replaced by General Weyler, who amply justified his reputation for severity. His conduct of the war was condemned by President McKinley, and the United States now granted the Cuban leaders the status of belligerents.

In 1897 Cánovas was murdered by an Italian anarchist and power passed to Sagasta, who hoped to placate the United States by granting Cuba autonomy, recalling Weyler and announcing an amnesty. But these concessions were lost on American opinion. Early in 1898 the battleship *Maine* was despatched to Havana to safeguard American interests, only to explode in the harbour with the loss of 266 men. The United States popular press lashed opinion into a frenzy and while Americans believed that the explosion was caused externally by a mine, Spaniards held that it was internal. But the facts had become irrelevant: despite the efforts of the Pope and others, American opinion could not be calmed. McKinley demanded an armistice and the release of the imprisoned patriots. This was equivalent to the surrender of the island, and the Spanish government would not accept it. On April 11, 1898, the President sought powers to force the issue, and Congress declared Cuba independent. In reply the Spanish government sent its Atlantic fleet under Admiral Cervera to Cuba to do battle against hopeless odds. He was blockaded at Santiago, and when shelled by the Americans sailed out and lost all his fleet in the ensuing combat. A second fleet in the Philippines was destroyed by Commodore Dewey, and Manila surrendered on August 12th. American troops had already occupied Cuba in concert with the insurgents.

Sagasta had now no choice but to sue for peace. McKinley demanded the evacuation of Cuba and the cession of Puerto Rico to the United States as an indemnity: Manila would also remain in American hands. When negotiations opened the points for discussion were reduced to the question of the Cuban debt and the future of the Philippines. Although the Spaniards pointed out that Manila had been taken after the end of hostilities, their objections were overruled, and a payment of 20 million dollars was received for the sovereignty of the Philippines.

XII

SPAIN AND THE SOCIAL AGE

THE immediate effects of Spain's 'Disaster' were less striking than those of the disintegration of 1868–73. The Austrian regent was by no means popular, but there was no anti-dynastic upheaval. The army did not attempt to seize power, though its pride and prestige were sorely wounded. National bankruptcy, which seemed imminent, was avoided. The Liberal government which had accepted defeat did not at once fall, and even when it did, soon returned to power, still led by Sagasta. It was only much later that the famous 'generation of '98', stirred by the emotions of the defeat, made its varied voices heard. The most eminent thinker of the moment produced a purely practical plan for national regeneration: the resettlement of the land, the revival of agriculture, new roads and cheaper transport, a reform of taxation, the introduction of compulsory military service, the extension of education and the imposition of a strong social discipline. His analysis of Spain's economic problems has hardly been bettered, and for fifty years governments have to a greater or less degree followed his recommendations.

Yet the very imperturbability of the political apparatus proved its insensitiveness to Spain's real thoughts. During the whole of the nineteenth century Spaniards had debated the problem of authority and society. 'Absolutism' was no longer tolerable, except in the privileged north, where it had never existed. The exercise of 'national sovereignty' had proved impracticable, and the conservative liberals who had held power since the middle of the century had excluded the masses by means of a restricted electorate and other devices. The long controversy about the source of

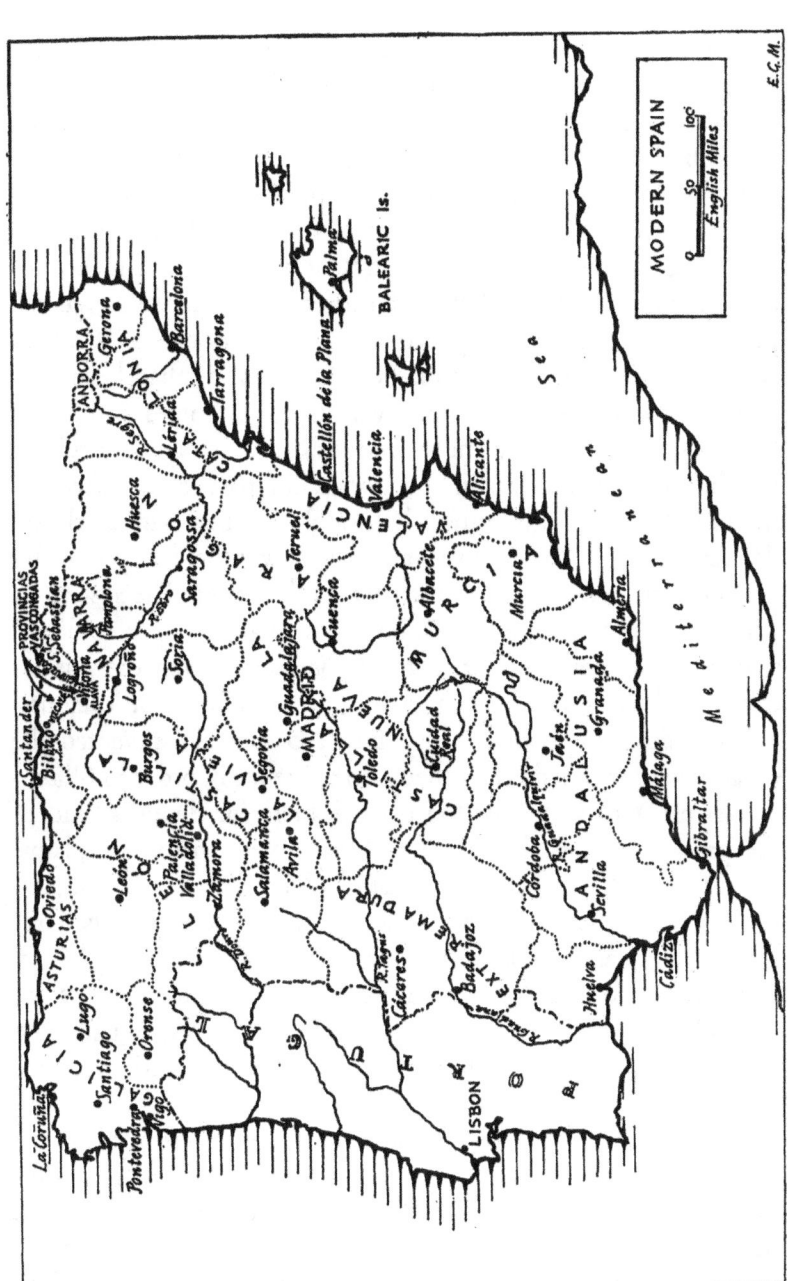

power had ended in the elimination of both poles, the superstitious queen and the uninstructed populace. In his restoration Cánovas had carefully placed the contentious interests outside the political arena. The powers of the crown were limited: the army became the upholder of the existing order; the church was removed from politics; and the masses were excluded by means of a limited electorate and a strict application of the law of association. This left the field to a professional political class composed of orators, lawyers, journalists and functionaries. While in contemporary France the want of political parties had been supplied by factions supporting the various royal houses which had briefly held the throne, now outnumbered by an amorphous republican block, in Spain the two main parties corresponded broadly to the English model, though neither had a clearly defined political programme and each was held together by personal attachments rather than by its doctrines. The system of patronage, moreover, had become an essential part of the political structure. Members of cortes could dispose of even the highest offices in the provincial bureaucracy, and local bosses or 'caciques' assured the election of the deputies. No one had invented the great machine: it had been called into existence in order to fill two complementary needs: of the party leaders for deputies, and of the party members for sinecures. There were many complaints against the system, but no one, least of all in cortes, ever attempted to abolish it. Even Sagasta, though his followers included reformers of many kinds, disbelieved in 'reform' in any political sense. Like the conventional theatre of the seventeenth century, cortes had become the place for patriotic platitudes, and the first requisite in a Spanish statesman was a high standard of public oratory.

The survival of Cánovas' Restoration clearly depended on the collaboration of the leaders of both sides, without which rotativism would collapse. Both sides spoke of 'new masses' and approved of 'universal suffrage', but neither intended that the narrow electorate imposed in 1876 should be unduly expanded. Each desired the general support of labour, but the men of the restoration had succeeded better in restoring conservative institutions such as the army and the church than in remaking liberalism, and they regarded labour as another corporate interest rather than as a political force.

The history of the decade from the death of Sagasta in 1903 to the assassination of Canalejas in 1913 is that of the decline and collapse of the two-party system, whose leaders failed to adjust it to conflicting social interests. The most difficult of the new problems was that of Catalonia. The eighteenth-century Bourbons had attempted to associate the revival of Spanish industry with an exclusive or protectionist colonial policy. As a result the American colonies, and especially the merchants of the poorer province of La Plata, which had long enjoyed the benefits of contraband goods, reacted strongly in favour of free trade. This policy was also advocated in Spain itself by the liberals of Cádiz, and in general by the politicians of the first half of the nineteenth century, whose chief concern was to placate the urban masses. But Bourbon industrial policy, though it achieved only moderate success in most of Spain, brought a period of rapid if belated industrial growth to Catalonia, which increasingly pressed the central government for protection. The Catalans successfully resisted Espartero's free-trade policy, and in the second half of the century their contribution to the treasury of an impoverished government was so important that their demands could not be ignored. Already in 1873 Catalonia had demanded her own economic system; and after the final collapse of the Carlist movement in 1876 even such traditionalist leaders as the Bishop of Vich began to assume a 'regional' attitude which was by no means incompatible with the demands of the liberal bourgeoisie. From Prim, the Catalan soldier who had overthrown the Bourbon centralist monarchy, and Pi y Margall, who had attempted to federalise the Peninsula, Catalan thought moved on to Amirall whose book *Lo Catalanisme* (1886) vindicated the Principality's claim to an 'independent' history, and the authors of the '*Bases de Manresa*,' who in 1892 drew up a general programme for all sections of regional opinion. But since the collapse of the First Republic, autonomist ideas were under a cloud, and these theorists still possessed only a small following. It was left to the Cuban war to unite and intensify Catalan feeling.

The Catalan industrialists had acquired great interests in the remaining Spanish colonies, where an effective tariff-system was in operation; and one of the strongest influences against concessions to the Cuban patriots had come from the Catalan deputies in Madrid. Moreover, Catalonia was both critical of the conduct of the war and jealous of any concession of autonomy when it was denied to herself. When finally the colonies were lost, the Cuban and Philippine markets passed to the United States, and the central government sought to pay for its military defeat by raising taxes on commerce and industry. The post-war budget aroused opposition everywhere, but in Catalonia it produced intense resentment against Madrid. In his Conservative government of 1900-1, Silvela included moderate Catalans, but he was forced to resign by the general hostility to his proposals, and in 1901 the Catalan Lliga fought the election on the issue of regional autonomy and scored an overwhelming victory. This was not only a real judgement on the Cuban war, but also a breakdown in the system of controlled elections.

The sense of frustration and resistance was by no means confined to Catalonia, but in the rest of Spain there was no adequate outlet for this feeling; and when the liberals resumed power their first thought was to mend the break in the political machine. Sagasta therefore made an alliance with the cacique of the Barcelona slums, Alejandro Lerroux, the 'Emperor of the Paralelo', a radical republican noted for his virulent anti-clericalism, and with his help won Barcelona in 1903, only to lose it to the Lliga in 1905 when, after Sagasta's death, the new leaders withdrew from the alliance.

The Spanish labour movement which thus began to acquire political influence was by no means unified. In the previous century Spanish liberalism had been essentially a middle-class movement, though in view of the small size of the bourgeoisie its progressist wing had always readily accepted the collaboration of the urban artisans, who formed the backbone of the national guard or militia. But in rural areas liberalism had had a different effect: while the country-people of the north were active Conservatives and Carlists, the landless peasants of the south and east found themselves abandoned. Here seasonal poverty was endemic, and in bad times labourers depended on the charity of monasteries, which used much of their incomes to supply quantities of food to those in want. Although English travellers of the eighteenth century are frequently critical of the maintenance of able-bodied men by ecclesiastical charity, they never attempt to explain how this population was to find work. The assumption that if the church were dispossessed a revival of economic activity would follow was quite unjustified. With the seizure of monastic property this relief ceased, and the proceeds were devoured by the government. The new landlords saw no reason to be encumbered with the poor; and when life became intolerable peasants would congregate in the small towns to protest. After 1840 these peasant risings were not uncommon: that of 1857 was savagely repressed by Narváez, while four years later O'Donnell more moderately dispersed a force of ten thousand at Narváez's birthplace of Loja. In much of Andalusia chronic rural unemployment was unrelieved by the presence of any sort of industry; but in the east the expansion of Barcelona had spread to Valencia, where the urban proletariat of the Catalan towns merged into the impoverished peasantry of the south. In 1868 the anarchist philosopher Bakunin, who had observed similar societies in Naples, sent his disciple Fanelli to Spain, and his teachings were warmly received in Mediterranean Spain. Two years later a small anarchist congress met in Barcelona, and in 1873 an anarchist schoolteacher organised a strike at Alcoy to demand the eight-hour day. But after the collapse of the federal Republic, Serrano suppressed anarchism, and for several years it was only heard of in the form of secret associations such as the Black Hand, formed spasmodically to intimidate landlords.

The right of association was restored by Sagasta in 1881. In the meantime, a small socialist party had been formed by a Madrid printer, Pablo Iglesias. It progressed slowly, since its sphere of action was largely confined to Iglesias' own trade. Although it repudiated the bourgeois parties, neither Sagasta nor Cánovas was blind to the possible influence of this disciplined movement, whose ethics derived from the old Castilian puritanism. When Sagasta adopted Castelar's policy of 'universal suffrage', the conservatives were faced with the choice of abandoning their narrow oligarchical ground or seeing their rivals forge ahead: they therefore offered concessions to organised labour, and Iglesias established his 'centres of labour' and introduced the celebration of Labour Day. But it was only with the loss of the colonies that his rejection of the old parties took on a new meaning and socialist membership sharply increased.

Anarchism now reappeared in Catalonia, where in 1891 its new campaign against the established order took the form of bomb-outrages. The government's reply was to create a special police force, euphemistically called the Social Brigade, for the repression of industrial strife. But in Catalonia the repression of anarchism was directed by the military authorities, and it was in reply to the ruthlessness of the Captain-General, Weyler, that an anarchist assassinated Cánovas in 1897. Sorel's doctrine of moral regeneration through violence succeeded particularly well in the harsh atmosphere of Catalan industry, and when in 1902 the French anarcho-syndicalist organisation was re-formed with a view to uniting all workers in a single strictly disciplined body pledged to renounce political action and resort to the strike weapon, there was an immediate response in Spain. In 1902 a general strike was declared in Barcelona, while spasmodic anarchist strikes occurred in Andalusia for several years.

In 1902 the regent had resigned in favour of her son Alfonso XIII, then aged sixteen; and in the following year Sagasta, the surviving founder of rotativism, died. Both dynastic parties now lost their cohesion. Cánovas' mantle had been divided between two conservative contenders, Silvela and Maura. Silvela, a distinguished and dignified statesman, had successfully presided over the consolidation of the war-debt, but his temperament did not incline him towards new social policies. In 1903 he frankly declared that he had lost faith in a country which did not desire a fleet, an army or education: 'it is only interested in material reforms, is only inspired by the progress of agriculture, industry, commerce and public works. This is the reality and it may be right, but in order to direct public affairs I needed the country to have an army, a navy, a foreign policy. . . .' His successor, Antonio Maura, felt the same desire to uphold dignity: he realised the need for an overhaul of the political machine, and hoped to rally the indifferent middle-classes and the former Carlists, few of whom had followed their leaders into the constitutionalist camp at the Restoration. But when he insisted on relaxing the control of elections, his party at once lost forty seats. The political bosses were alarmed and the King was perturbed at the small republican advance, yet it appeared to have no effect on the bourgeoisie which Maura had hoped to shock. His mild attitude towards regional aspirations, adopted in the hope of reconciling the Carlists, merely fortified the Catalans in their pretensions.

The removal of Sagasta had left the 'great liberal family' without a shepherd. Its various sections at first resolved themselves into two groups, one of which followed the veteran Montero Ríos, while the others adhered to Segismundo Moret, who was defeated by a small margin in the contest for the leadership. Scarcely had Montero Ríos assumed his responsibilities when his government found itself confronted with a new aspect of the Catalan imbroglio. When two Barcelona newspapers published cartoons offensive to the army, a group of officers forced their way into the editorial offices and smashed the equipment. The Catalans, always sensitive to the presence of Castilian forces, protested; but the Captain-General was determined to uphold the honour of the army and refused to discipline the culprits, assuming the leadership of the protesting officers and receiving the support of his colleagues. Some liberals wished to placate Catalan opinion by removing several of the most outspoken Captains-General, but the Minister of War declined to take any such step, and the government finally took refuge in a suspension of the constitutional guarantees. This action split the party: and Moret formed a new government, which passed the 'Law of Jurisdictions', by which all offences against the army or patriotic feeling were referred to military courts (March 1906). This solution inevitably aggrieved the Catalans and deepened their quarrel with the army.

Moret himself was an Anglophile and a free-trader, and it was during his term of office that Alfonso XIII married an English princess, Victoria Eugenia of Battenburg. This was the first Anglo-Spanish royal match since that of Philip and Mary, and the first marriage of an English princess in Spain since the Middle Ages. The wedding almost ended in a regicide, for a Catalan anarchist hurled a bomb at the royal carriage as it passed (May 1906).

But the new influence in Spanish political life came instead from France, where the Second Republic had moved from laicism to anti-clericalism. In 1882 it had made all public instruction laic, and four years later had forbidden the clergy to teach in state schools, withdrawing the right to educate from the prohibited orders, the Jesuits. For some years this legislation was not fully enforced, but in 1901 the growth of the religious congregations was halted on the pretext that the formation of societies exempt from the economic laws of the state was offensive: three years later all teaching by the congregations was prohibited.

'When France sneezes, Spain cries "Jesus!".' Whereas Montero Ríos had followed a policy similar to that of the conservatives under which rotativism could continue to function, Moret considered that his variegated party could be held together only by striking out on a line of its own. In a speech from the throne he announced that this would include electoral reform, social legislation, and the settlement of the question of the religious orders. In the press, however, it was freely stated that he intended to raise the controversial issues of freedom of worship and civil marriage; and these questions were anathema to the Conservatives. Since the Restoration had banished religious questions from politics, the Spanish church had recovered its old wealth, while the anti-clericalism of the French Republic had caused the French church to place its investments in Spain and had driven many regulars and Jesuits across the frontier. The laws which limited the number of orders were disregarded, and Spain now possessed more regulars than in the great days of the sixteenth century.

Meanwhile, Moret had failed to hold the Liberal party together, and power passed back to Maura, who held elections early in 1907. They were conducted by a Murcian politician, Juan de la Cierva, who provided a conservative 'majority' of 253 and reduced the liberals to 74. All the Catalan groups, including Carlists and Republicans, had now united under Francisco Cambó, the leader of the middle-class regionalists, and this block, the Solidaridad, won all but three of the forty-four Catalan seats. Their success brought demands for the withdrawal of the Law of Jurisdictions, the maintenance of Catalan civil law, and the creation of a regional organisation with its own funds for education and public works. But Maura's sympathy for devolution was rooted in his desire to conciliate the traditionalists, and he now dashed the hopes of Catalan extremists by declaring that Catalonia would receive only such reforms as the central government might authorise and that there would never be any concession of sovereignty. There followed a campaign to split the Solidaridad. La Cierva introduced a new law of local administration calculated to appease the right-wing Catalan Lliga, and a bill against terrorism which rendered anarchist centres and newspapers illegal, and laid down a minimum sentence of three years for propagandists. While the Conservatives thus sought an alliance with the Catalan right and repressed the left, the Madrid Liberals made an active alliance with the Catalan radicals and republicans, as a result of which Lerroux wrested Barcelona from the regionalists in the elections of 1908. Thus the conventional alignment was for a moment restored, though in order to hold Catalan support the Liberals had been forced to go outside the narrow 'dynastic' limits set by Cánovas.

In the decade that had elapsed since the Disaster, Spain had remained on the edge of European affairs. Her chief overseas interest was now Morocco, where she held a group of five garrison towns. During the period of Anglo-French rivalry, Great Britain had opposed French expansion in North Africa and had preferred the presence of Spain in the area facing Gibraltar. In 1902 the French had come to an agreement with Sagasta by which northern and western Morocco, including Fez, would be reserved to Spain, while France would make the rest her sphere of influence. The proposed treaty had not been referred to Great Britain; and when Sagasta fell, the Conservatives refused to sign it, partly on this ground, and partly because the occupation of the poorest and most hostile area of west Africa then seemed scarcely feasible.

But with the establishment of the Anglo-French entente and the restriction of British interests in Morocco, France and Spain were at liberty to negotiate freely, and a secret treaty was concluded for an eventual partition. Its terms became known however, and in 1905 the Kaiser descended precipitately on Tangier, forcing the meeting of the powers at the Conference of Algeciras (1906). In the following year Maura declared that Spain could not afford to see the area between the Muluya river and the Atlantic coast beyond Tangier fall into foreign hands; and although this area was greatly reduced as compared with that secretly offered by France in 1902, the claim was generally approved in Spain.

When in 1909 Spanish troops became involved in a clash with Berber tribes in the Riff and the commander called for reinforcements, the Ministry of War at once ordered the Catalan reservists to report for duty. This decision, with its evident political implications, provoked a general strike and a sudden explosion of popular violence in Barcelona. In the 'Tragic Week' a score of churches and thirty-four convents were sacked and burnt, and only after many workers had been shot in the streets or executed was calm restored. One of the victims was a militant anarchist, Francisco Ferrer, whose fate caused a general outcry throughout Europe. Maura and his cabinet had agreed not to intervene in the case, but when Ferrer was executed on October 13, 1909, the vehemence of international feeling was such that the King asked for his resignation: almost ten years were to pass before he was again summoned to form a government.

The events of 1909 discredited not only Maura, but the conservative party. The socialists, radicals and other republicans had registered a loud protest against the Moroccan war and forced a change of government. As a result, their faith in political action was restored, and in the elections of 1910 two socialists, one of them Iglesias himself, were for the first time elected to cortes. From now until 1917 the Spanish socialist movement spread more rapidly.

But inevitably the burden of government now rested with the Liberals. Moret had lost credit as a result of his alliance with the anti-dynastic groups, and the leadership passed to José Canalejas, whose prestige was generally recognised. A majority was contrived for him by his lieutenant Romanones, an apt pupil of Sagasta, and he proceeded to negotiate a settlement of the Catalan question on the basis of regional control of education and public works. This limited devolution was accompanied by the recognition of the right of the Catalan deputies and senators to meet as a regional group, a power conceded by the Law of Mancomunidades, finally passed in 1913.

In the labour question Canalejas sought a similar compromise. The admission of socialists to municipal government and even to cortes had warded off the immediate danger of revolution. But a lasting alliance with the anti-dynastic parties, such as Moret had proposed to risk, was not possible, and Canalejas offered appeasement by again emphasising the anti-clerical tradition of liberalism. In view of the newly acquired power of a church more intent on canonries than sainthood, Canalejas prepared once more to do battle with the Vatican by insisting that the Law of Congregations, which limited the number of regular clergy, should be enforced, and that the catholic monopoly of public worship be ended. The Vatican protested and the clergy organised demonstrations throughout the country, while in the north Carlists began to talk of their claimant James 'III', though since he had never set foot in Spain and the church was now associated with the existing order, this threat was scarcely real. But Canalejas' anti-clericalism did not suffice to win over the anti-dynastic parties. In 1912 the railway unions, now claiming 127,000 members, staged a strike which he ended by mobilising the strikers under military law, a measure adopted by Briand in France in 1910. The strike was effectively broken, but Canalejas ceased to enjoy the confidence of the workers, and in November 1912 he was assassinated by an anarchist while browsing in a bookstore in Madrid.

With Maura excluded from office and Canalejas dead, the two dynastic parties ceased to play their customary role. Maura had expected to be recalled in 1912, but when the King summoned another liberal, Romanones, he realised that the crown was prepared to end the rotativist system rather than recall him to office and accordingly resigned the leadership of his party, which passed to Eduardo Dato. Although rotativism was restored, the simple alternation of two conventionally equated groups was no longer possible. The Liberals had admitted the parties of the left, even though they were republican, and could therefore claim to be more representative of public opinion than the Conservatives. Even the latter, when it was their turn to stage an election, readily admitted democrats and republicans to cortes in order to split the Liberal minority. Thus the Conservative cortes of 1914 included 239 government deputies, 82 Liberals, 28 Democrats (republicans reconciled to the monarchy), 19 Republicans, 11 Reformists, 12 Catalan Regionalists, and 4 Traditionalists. Already the two-party system of the Restoration had given way to a sheaf of parties, and rotativism was destined to be replaced by government by coalition.

Meanwhile, the anticipated partition of Morocco had led to the abrupt French seizure of Fez. Spain must now decide whether or not to occupy the zone reserved for her, and in 1911 Canalejas entered into negotiations for a further definition of the spheres of influence and the building of a railway from Tangier to Fez. At the outbreak of the European war, Spain's main overseas interest therefore called for a degree of collaboration with France. In 1913 Alfonso XIII and Romanones met the French President at Cartagena and declared their agreement on matters of foreign policy: Spain had however refused to admit the passage of French troops through her territory to Africa in case of war; and when in 1914 the Conservatives returned to power Dato pledged himself to neutrality, prohibiting any campaign in favour of Spanish intervention.

Nevertheless, 'static neutrality' covered a wide range of opinions. In general, the Spanish right, with its autocratic tradition, inclined towards the Central Powers, while the liberals favoured France and Great Britain. The Carlists, or 'Jaimists' as they now were, adhered to the Austrian tradition, though their pretender had served in the Russian army and had allied sympathies.

To their leader, Vázquez de Mella, an allied defeat would imply the recovery of Gibraltar; and many aristocrats and ecclesiastics looked for an ebbing of the great tide of liberalism, associating, as they did, English and French influence with the weakening of their own privileges. Monarchists of the constitutionalist tradition and the bourgeois republicans of the left generally supported the allies. For the socialists, the war, like the Spanish campaign in Morocco, was in theory a struggle of imperialistic capitalists in which all workers should remain neutral; but Spanish labour leaders realised that only an allied victory was likely to produce the conditions they desired. Meanwhile, the sale of cereals and other agricultural produce rapidly enriched Spanish merchants and landowners, while the interruption of the export trade of the belligerents enabled her to borrow part of their overseas markets, especially in Latin America. The result of these and other transactions was to liquidate the national debt accumulated since 1898 and to raise the gold reserve from £23 million to £89 million. In these circumstances neutralism seemed assured.

In 1917, however, the German blockade, accompanied by a vigorous propaganda campaign, resulted in the fall of the Liberal government, and the general rise in prices, aggravated by wartime profiteering, was followed by the most serious labour disturbances Spain had yet known. In March 1917 the labour republicans again staged a general strike, and their leaders were arrested. This incident marked the failure of the liberal policy of limited co-operation with the anti-dynastic groups; and the army, which since the Restoration had been identified with the existing order, now again began to raise its voice. In the past, it had often had its officers' associations, one of which had played an important part in the crisis of King Amadeo. These juntas had been restored in 1910, and although their immediate purpose was to protect the interests of the officer class, they now also demanded political reforms. They had not at this stage any clear policy of their own, but they were drawn into the political arena partly by their desire to defend the throne, partly by the effect of inflation on their own interests, and partly by their old rivalry with the Catalans and the anti-military anarchists. It was clear that any reform dictated by the army would not benefit Catalan opinion, and the Catalan deputies, ranging from the regionalist banker Cambó to the republican demagogue Lerroux, at once demanded a special session of cortes and a constitutional assembly. When the government refused to comply, fifteen senators and sixty-three deputies anticipated a possible military coup by assembling in Barcelona. The central government declared this and other 'renovationist' assemblies revolutionary and dissolved them.

Meanwhile, the military leaders had held discussions with the government of García Prieto, which failed to satisfy them and resigned. The army's candidate for political power was Maura, still remembered as the represser of the disturbances in Barcelona in 1909. But even he was unwilling to bind himself to a purely military régime, and after the King had sounded the views of the dynastic parties, he called upon Dato. But scarcely had the Renovation movement shot its bolt when the workers' organisations again declared a general strike and the socialist General Union of Labour (UGT) and the anarchist National Confederation (CNT) demanded a 'socialist democratic republic'. The movement was headed by all the most prominent workers' leaders and was put down by the army without great difficulty except in Asturias, where the miners resisted. But the country was put on a war-footing for two months, and the labour leaders found themselves no longer in cortes, but in prison, where they received the improbable sentence of 'perpetual reclusion'. Their demands, presented in terms which admitted no compromise, conveyed the threat of a social revolution such as was to sweep Russia a few months later.

When the state of emergency ended in October, the military leaders again pressed for political changes. Dato resigned and neither party was willing to supply a puppet prime minister. The only solution was therefore a 'government of concentration' or general coalition, including all the monarchist leaders. The army's candidate in the new ministry was the former right-hand of Maura, La Cierva, who held the Ministry of War. When he presented the military reforms demanded by the army, the

Catalans withdrew and the heterogeneous ministry almost collapsed, while the success of the army's trade-unions encouraged other public servants to demand the right of association: this La Cierva proposed to forbid. In March 1918 all the monarchist leaders, Maura, Dato, Romanones, García Prieto, Cambó and others, formed a new coalition, the 'national government', and it seemed for a moment that some settlement might be found.

But the war, with its opportunities for profit and its legacy of inflation, had depressed the old liberal classes. Modest property-owners, retired officers and functionaries and other pensioners were reduced to poverty, while the new-rich, the war profiteers, only demanded that politicians or the army should prevent 'disorder'. Meanwhile, the European post-war situation itself suggested extreme solutions. The division of the Austrian empire on a basis of linguistic and racial self-determinism inspired the Mancomunidad to demand a parliament with executive power for Catalonia; this caused a government crisis and led to the withdrawal of the Catalan deputies in December 1918. At the same time, the Spanish workers deduced from the success of the Russian revolution that they could achieve the same result for themselves by violence. The anarchists resumed the struggle for the millennial revolution, and Barcelona became more than ever notorious for the recklessness of its political underworld. The wave of revolutionary passion was intensified by the collapse of the war-time industrial boom, and during the winter of 1919–20 social protest was scarcely distinguishable from gang warfare: strikes and hunger bred spiritual exaltation and physical violence in a society of mystical gunmen and picaresque martyrs, and since most of the syndicalist leaders were under arrest, negotiation was almost impossible.

In April 1919 the King entrusted power to Maura and La Cierva, who again arranged elections and imposed military law in Barcelona. But their attempts to shield the throne, pass a budget and impose order on the workers merely increased the social agitation of Barcelona, which raged throughout 1920. Their failure temporarily silenced the military leaders, and in March 1920 power passed back to Dato. But this mildly conciliatory step was followed by demands from the employers for the dissolution of the CNT, which had already been declared illegal, and when the captain-general of Catalonia, General Martínez Anido, instituted a new repression, Dato himself was murdered by an anarchist in Madrid. The King now recalled Maura, who included in his cabinet La Cierva, Cambó, and Vázquez de Mella: this was the first time a Carlist had appeared in a constitutional government, and Vázquez made no secret of his belief that the only answer to the dictatorship of the proletariat was dictatorship of the army. The great conflict of the Spanish nineteenth century had reached its *reductio ad absurdum*.

The crown was now dependent on the army and on a thin segment of right-wing opinion, which seemed likely to carry it into the dead-end of military government. The Liberals therefore hesitated to identify themselves too closely with the régime, or to lose touch with the bourgeois Republicans, many of whom had graduated to the left through their own ranks. In the social ferment of the post-war world the issue of the régime had been taken over from the bourgeois republicans and adopted by the 'new masses'. Yet the experience of Portugal showed that republicanism itself was not the fundamental issue: there rotativism had collapsed and the monarchy had been overthrown in 1910, and the war had brought even graver economic disruption than in Spain; and the republican parties succeeded one another in a series of short-lived governments, constantly shaken by strikes and acts of violence.

But in July 1921 Spain was faced with a catastrophic diversion. Since the demarcation of the Spanish zone of Morocco a decade before, the army had been engaged in an intermittent 'pacification' of the tribesmen of the Riff. Apart from some mineral deposits, Spanish Morocco had no resources to justify intensive economic development such as the French were able to apply in their more fertile protectorate. Its occupation was difficult and costly, and had remained military in character. In 1921 two forces were preparing to reduce the qabilas of the Riff, one with headquarters in the capital, Tetuán, and the other based on Melilla. The second force, consisting of nearly 26,000 men, was commanded by General Silvestre who had planned a coastal advance to the east, but was checked by a small reverse at Abarran. After consultation with the commander in Tetuán, General Berenguer, it was agreed that the operation should be halted until the Moors in the western zone had surrendered. But while General Silvestre's force relaxed, the Moorish commander 'Abdu'l-Karim quietly concentrated his forces in the eastern sector, and on July 19 surrounded the post of Igueriban. Next day General Silvestre asked for reinforcements, and without reporting the critical state of his front, decided to advance with all the forces at his command. On reaching Annual, however, he abandoned his original plan to hold it and began to withdraw towards the coast. As he did so his army was routed: it proved impossible to make more than brief stands between the front and Melilla, and by the middle of August the Moors were almost within sight of the city. The total Spanish losses were nearly fifteen thousand men, as well as great quantities of machine-guns and equipment: Silvestre himself committed suicide. This new military disaster intensified the Spanish crisis. Although General Berenguer soon recovered most of the territory that had been lost, the army became unpopular and hypersensitive, and the opponents of the régime, believing it to be on the verge of collapse, redoubled their efforts. The King again summoned Maura and La Cierva, and the latter pressed through a decree by which the military juntas, now known as 'informative commissions', were at last subordinated to the Ministry of War. But popular feeling against the army was still strong, and the enquiry into responsibilities was charged with political perils. A military commission had already been set up, but the politicians of the left demanded that it should be replaced by a civil court with the widest possible terms of reference. It was meanwhile put about, and widely believed, that the King had expressly ordered Silvestre's advance and that the whole war in Morocco was prolonged by the politicians for sinister reasons. The question of the enquiry brought down the government, and in December 1922 García Prieto formed a 'concentration of the left'. The dynastic parties were now demoralised, and when the new government formed its majority in April 1923, more than a third of the members were returned unopposed. The political careerists had already lost faith in the régime of 1876, and terrorism was again intensified: one of those assassinated was the Cardinal-Archbishop of Saragossa. The army again pressed for a sterner policy of repression, but the government refused to comply. In September 1923 the garrison in Barcelona revolted, and it was promptly joined by others throughout the country. The civilian government had no choice but to submit and on September 13th a military ministry was formed by the Captain-General of Barcelona, General Miguel Primo de Rivera.

General Primo de Rivera was a member of a land-owning and soldiering family of Jerez, an eloquent and demonstrative Andalusian aristocrat with no special convictions and no special programme, unless to restore order and uphold the monarchy, army and church. Like many soldiers, he had little use for the politicians. He himself began by emphasising the temporary nature of his government and as an expedient, his military Directory was welcomed.

No one had lifted a finger to save the parliamentary régime, or to protest against the suspension of the Constitution of 1876 and of civil rights, but when a deputation of politicians waited on the King to remind him that the Constitution required a convocation of cortes before the end of the year, they were dismissed without an answer. The crown was thus associated with the extra-legal character of the government, and the Directory became a dictatorship.

Primo de Rivera's first measures were designed to stifle political agitation. In Catalonia, the Mancomunidad was suppressed and all autonomist propaganda was prohibited: while the dictatorship continued there was to be no question of Catalan autonomy. It was generally supposed that the chief object of the coup was to prevent the publication of the report on the disaster of Annual: these papers conveniently disappeared. The press was subjected to a strict military censorship, and the terrorist campaign, deprived of any immediate purpose and of publicity, sank into obscurity.

The dictator's most popular achievement was the ending of the Moroccan war. When 'Abdu'l-Karim carried his attacks into

French territory, Primo de Rivera joined with General Pétain in a combined operation, and himself landed at Alhucemas, capturing the Moroccan headquarters in October 1925: 'Abdu'l-Karim surrendered to the French in the following year, and the whole area was rapidly pacified. Meanwhile, the question of Tangier was formally settled: the French claim to precedence was accepted by the powers, and Spain was constrained to play second fiddle in an international administration. She had desired that Tangier, with its large Spanish population, should become the capital of her zone; and having raised the issue at Geneva and failed to obtain either a revision of the statute of Tangier or a permanent seat in the League Council, she withdrew from the League in September 1926.

The dictator also achieved a temporary settlement of the labour question. Now that both politicians and workers' leaders were debarred from the pursuit of political power and the ministries were safely occupied by senior officers and public order was maintained by the army, there was no difficulty in setting up the framework of a social state free from the hazards of numerical democracy. The model for this had been established by Mussolini, and Primo de Rivera appointed local committees of five employers and five workers under the chairmanship of a government official to settle conditions of work and draw up collective contracts. In each trade or industry these local committees were responsible to a national council, on which labour and employers were again equally represented. Ultimately these were to be constituted into twenty-seven corporations covering all sectors of economic life. Like Italian corporativism, the Spanish system was an adaptation of catholic social doctrine, and its initiation was followed by a growth of relations between the two countries. In 1923 Alfonso XIII visited Rome and discussed a plan for co-ordinating Spanish and Italian bases in the western Mediterranean, and in 1926 an Italo-Spanish treaty of friendship was concluded.

Nevertheless, Spain did not follow Italy into fascism. Primo de Rivera was an Andalusian aristocrat, and he possessed neither the doctrinal fervour nor the hypnotic bumptiousness that captivated Italians. The Spanish workers were prepared, since they must, to take what advantages the dictatorship offered them, but they did not march behind it, while Primo de Rivera's object was not to create a monolith of labour, but to encourage the socialists, who were in the main Castilians and men of discipline, and play them off against the anarchists, whom he regarded as infected with Catalan separatism and anti-national. As an expedient, this policy was successful, and the pacification of industry was followed by a period of economic expansion, during which new roads and railways were built and an atmosphere of modest prosperity was restored.

Until the end of 1925 the dictatorship remained an extra-legal institution, and the dictator hoped that his achievements would suffice to discredit the old politicians or convert them into adherents. These hopes were not realised, and he therefore founded a new party, the Patriotic Union, controlled by the leader of the military juntas, and in September 1927 instituted an Assembly of 350 persons appointed on a corporative basis and including nominees of provincial governors, bureaucrats and representatives of commerce, labour and agriculture. This body was to prepare a new constitutional system which would be submitted to a plebiscite so that elections might be held in 1931.

But the Assembly had neither independence nor legislative power, and the promised constitution, with its consequent elections or referendum, never took shape. Confident in the apparent success of his Moroccan and labour policies, the dictator ignored almost constant expressions of disapproval, muffled as they were by censorship and police activity. The thinkers of '1898' had inculcated the lessons of sobriety and honesty, and emphasised the influences of ignorance and obscurantism in the old political system. Now, a generation later, their pupils were critical of the three supports of the old order, church, army and crown, and resented the dictator's clumsy attempts to impede the free expression of opinion: his jocular addresses to the nation and his assertion that his régime was 'illegal, but patriotic' irritated his hearers. In Catalonia, which was subjected to a repressive anti-regionalist policy, the left-wing leader, Colonel Macià, vainly attempted to restore 'national independence' by invading the Principality from

France. Anarchism began to revive, and there were frequent skirmishes between workers and the police. Even the army was by no means unanimous: in 1925, at the age of eighty-six, General Weyler attempted his first pronunciamiento, and in 1929 the artillery, disgruntled by interferences in its traditional system of promotion, joined in a revolt led by a former conservative minister. His acquittal by a court-martial made it plain that the dictator had forfeited the confidence of the army. His fate was sealed by the failure of his economic policy. The programme of expansion was only continued at the cost of mounting budgetary deficits, and it was now threatened by the world depression. It became increasingly difficult to hold labour neutral and to defend the peseta. In January 1930 the Finance minister, Sr Calvo Sotelo, resigned, and after a final and unsuccessful attempt to rally the captains-general behind him, Primo de Rivera was dismissed in February and retired to Paris, where he died a month later.

His successor was General Berenguer, now head of the King's military household, whose mission was to prepare the way for a return to constitutional government. The transition was a difficult one, for if Primo de Rivera had been thrust forward as the choice of the army, Berenguer appeared as the King's dictator. The Constitution of 1876 had been in suspense for six and a half years. There was no hope of restoring rotativism, and the old party system was disrupted: the Patriotic Union had struck no roots. While General Berenguer and the monarchist politicians were deliberating, the anti-dynastic parties, bourgeois republicans, Catalan leftists and socialists, entered a formal coalition in the Pact of San Sebastián (August 1930). All three agreed to work for the overthrow of the monarchy, and the Central Revolutionary Committee engaged itself to grant autonomy to Catalonia.

General Berenguer relaxed the censorship and reopened the universities; and as the repression was lifted a wave of strikes followed. In December two young officers led a revolt in the garrison at Jaca. Their advance on Saragossa was easily repulsed, and they themselves were executed. There was a parallel rising at the Madrid air-base, and the Revolutionary Committee issued a republican manifesto, as the result of which its members were arrested on a charge of sedition. The republic now had its martyrs, and the government was faced with the double necessity to hold elections and to prosecute its enemies. When General Berenguer at length announced the summoning of cortes under the old Constitution, a storm of protest was aroused and he resigned (February 14, 1931). His successor, Romanones, formed a ministry which included the old political leaders, La Cierva and García Prieto, and tried to negotiate a compromise. In order to avoid the issue of the régime, the government would hold a constituent election for certain specified amendments to the Constitution of 1876. But when Romanones offered this solution to the leader of the Revolutionary Committee, Sr Alcalá Zamora, formerly his lieutenant in a monarchist cabinet and now under arrest, he received the reply that the Committee would accept nothing short of constituent cortes. A new government was formed under the leadership of Admiral J. B. Aznar, and municipal elections were called for April, those for cortes being deferred. Thus the municipal elections became a test of the question of the régime. Meanwhile, the trial of the Jaca insurgents and of the Revolutionary Committee (which boldly demanded that the public prosecutor should prove the legality of the dictatorship) kept the issue well before the public eye.

The critical elections took place on April 12, 1931. Their full results were not published, but any design to falsify the returns was quickly abandoned and the Minister of War at once informed the Captains-General that the anti-dynastic parties had won large majorities in all the principal cities. The heavy republican vote in Madrid, Barcelona, Valencia and other towns, cancelled monarchical majorities in rural areas. Since the inception of constitutionalism, the consent of the towns had been sufficient to govern the country. The cabinet at once began negotiations for the transmission of power, and Alfonso XIII left Madrid, though without signing a formal act of abdication. On April 14th, the republican leaders, already constituted as a shadow government, occupied the departments of state.

The moment was one of general enthusiasm. The passion for

sobriety, instruction and social improvement promised a new atmosphere in national affairs. Spanish intellectuals proposed to banish military pomposity and clerical obscurantism with the weapons of pacifism and rationalism. The new republicans were intensely conscious of Spain and of Spanish problems, but hostile to traditional institutions. Most of the intellectual leaders of the day, Ortega y Gasset, Unamuno, Marañón, Altamira, Pérez de Ayala, Cossío, welcomed the republic: and writers and professors readily accepted diplomatic posts under the new régime, or more generously strove to remedy the shortcomings of an inadequate educational system.

But the moral and intellectual leaders, though their influence was great, did not govern Spain. Those who received power in 1931 were the dispossessed constitutionalists of 1923; Alcalá Zamora and Miguel Maura had been liberal ministers under the monarchy and were now Prime Minister and Minister of the Interior: Alejandro Lerroux had graduated from mob radicalism in Barcelona to liberal conformity in Madrid. To them were added such militant intellectuals as Fernando de los Ríos, a socialist professor from Granada and nephew of the educator Giner de los Ríos, Manuel Azaña, a civil servant and man of letters, and Marcelino Domingo, a former schoolmaster who now became Minister of Education. To their left, the socialist labour movement was represented by Francisco Largo Caballero, who had succeeded the veteran Pablo Iglesias as leader of the UGT, and Indalecio Prieto, whose Basque socialism was less doctrinal and exclusive. The Castilian socialist movement had, with the aid of Primo de Rivera's corporative machinery, now achieved a solid organisation: the two anarchist bodies, the National Confederation of Labour (CNT) and the smaller Iberian Anarchist Federation (FAI) continued to disbelieve in formal government, but actively to bring forward the millennial workers' state by dint of strikes. But the republicanism of 1931 was in the main still a bourgeois creed descended from that of 1873. Disillusioned with federalism and divided from the American model by the Disaster, it had inclined to French influences: where the French pattern did not apply, as in the land question, there were those who sought guidance from Russia. But neither parties nor programmes were yet clearly defined. The new government at first intended to defer all major legislation until after the election of constituent cortes. But within a week it had declared for religious toleration and the secularisation of cemeteries, and these tendencies had been condemned in a pastoral by Cardinal Segura of Seville, who urged Catholics to resist the 'enemies of Jesus Christ'. In the middle of May a wave of active anticlericalism swept across the country, and about a sixth of the convents and religious schools in Madrid were burnt or sacked. The anti-militarist government made no use of the army to enforce discipline. It did however remedy the gap in its own defences by organising a new police-force, the Assault Guards, as the guardians of republican order.

When on June 28 elections were held for the constituent cortes, the results revealed that the new Republican parties were weaker, and the Socialists stronger, than had been supposed: no Monarchists presented themselves. The right-wing Republicans led by Alcalá Zamora and Miguel Maura won only 20 seats; the Radical centre of Lerroux, 98; Azaña's Republican Action, 30; the Radical Socialists of Domingo and Alvaro de Albornoz, 56; and the Socialists of Largo and Prieto, 114. This proof of the strength of the left exposed the government to strong pressure from labour, and already in July there were jubilant strikes, and the anarcho-syndicalists seized Seville and governed it for ten days. A draft constitution had been drawn up by the provisional government, and it was debated from July to December. Under the Constitution of 1931 Spain became a 'democratic republic of workers of all classes'. It had no official religion and renounced war as an instrument of national policy. It guaranteed freedom and equality before the law to its citizens. They would be represented by one deputy for each 50,000 inhabitants in each province, sitting in a single chamber.[1] The pledge to Catalonia was redeemed by a clause which would give any group of provinces the right to submit to the central government proposals for

---

[1] A proposal for a second chamber was dropped: it would have consisted of four groups each of sixty members, representing respectively the workers, employers, liberal professions, and universities and religious bodies.

a statute, though federations of autonomous provinces were prohibited.

The most immediately contentious part of the Constitution was that concerning religion. There was to be freedom of conscience, and the state would cease to subsidise the church at the end of two years. Civil marriage and divorce were introduced, and all education was secular and inspired by 'ideals of human solidarity'. The law governing the religious orders would be strictly enforced. A strong impulse was given to the debate on this subject by Azaña, who boldly asserted that Spain had 'ceased to be catholic', and that the security of the republic required that the Jesuits be expelled. The article was at length approved by 178 votes to 59. Two catholic ministers, Alcalá Zamora and Maura, at once resigned; three others were absent from the session, as were the Basque deputies. Azaña's leading speech assured him of the succession, and soon after Alcalá Zamora was conveniently elevated to be the first president of the Second Republic.

The apparently mild and literary ex-civil servant had already established his toughness; as Minister of War he had extracted an oath of loyalty from all officers, and had reduced their strength from 25,000 to 9,000. He readily pledged himself to the anti-clerical programme, autonomy for Catalonia and the redistribution of land. Having thus identified the republic with his own left-wing programme, he acquired with the Law for the Defence of the Republic powers to suppress publications, forbid meetings, close associations, and arrest, fine or exile all those deemed guilty of acts against the state, despite the guarantees of freedom, the right of assembly, and the prohibition against confiscation embodied in the Constitution itself. For the same reason, the former king was arraigned in cortes and condemned to banishment for life on a charge of 'high treason'.

The need for a robust social discipline as a climate for reform had often been recognised. This was particularly necessary in order to achieve a redistribution of the land, in which a reforming government would meet with the opposition of landowners, many of whom were themselves heirs of the liberal spoliation of the nineteenth century, and could not count on the forbearance of the peasants, with their anarchist tendencies. An incident at Castilblanco in Extremadura had illustrated the desperate intensity with which illiterate peasants held their anarchist principles and the need for a strong central authority. The provisional government had already outlined a plan for the breaking up of large estates, and in 1932 the Agrarian Law was debated and passed. It provided for the expropriation of properties exceeding a given area in the lower meseta and Andalusia, and offered compensation in government bonds (not fully negotiable) based on the value declared for taxation: owners of entailed estates would receive compensation only for recent improvements. The law was a severe one, and it overlooked many difficulties of application: it aroused the hostility of the landowners and the hopes of the rural labourer, and its failure would inevitably precipitate a new wave of anarchism.

But perhaps the most disturbing question for Castilians was that of Catalan autonomy. Immediately after the elections, the leader of the Catalan left, Lluis Companys, had declared a Catalan state as the first of the 'Federation of Iberian Republics'. This far exceeded the question of regional autonomy, and after discussions with Madrid republicans agreement was reached on the extent of the devolution which Catalonia should enjoy and the procedure to be followed. A 'statute' was approved by referendum in the Catalan provinces and submitted to cortes. It was debated between May and September 1932, and finally pressed through by Azaña. There were good reasons for Castilian hesitation in ratifying it. The federal republic of 1873, which had brought Catalonia a glimpse of independence, had brought only anarchy to the rest of Spain, and Castilians looked back on the experience with repugnance. As Companys' first declaration had shown, the idea of 'Iberian Federalism' was still cherished by some Catalans, who hoped to make it palatable in Castile by insinuating that it might lead to the reincorporation of Portugal: since the Portuguese had no interest at all in sacrificing their independence, the argument was disingenuous, and could scarcely conceal the fact that a renascence of federalism must weaken the central government. When the statute which created the 'Generalitat' was granted, Catalans rejoiced that 'before long the other peoples of Spain would have their statutes'; the Basque Provinces voted for autonomy in June 1932, the Galicians produced a draft in December. Meanwhile, the Navarrese decided not to join the Basque autonomous area, and a regional assembly held in Andalusia in February 1933 failed to reach agreement. But these events aroused great opposition to the government and united many sectors of opinion that had hitherto remained divided. Although the Constitution prohibited the autonomous states from collaborating against the central government, this important restriction was hard to define and still harder to enforce, and the use of the autonomies to defy the central government, and the consequent fear of a deliberate disintegration, was a major cause of civil conflict.

By the middle of 1932 many moderate republicans had begun to feel that the régime they had was not the régime they had desired. In August General Sanjurjo, who as director of the Civil Guard, had maintained an attitude of neutrality on the fall of the monarchy, rebelled in Seville. His rising was promptly put down, and he was condemned to death, reprieved and released in the amnesty of 1934. Although his movement touched off a series of disturbances in Andalusia, its effect was to rally the supporters of the régime, and the government was able to present its laws for the control of the religious orders with relatively little opposition. It was followed by the final approval of the Catalan statute and the Agrarian Law.

This last now introduced a form of collectivism derived from the Russian model of 1923, and it was followed by widespread unrest among peasant anarchists. When a group of village reformers attempted to defy the world in the tiny hamlet of Casas Viejas, near Medina Sidonia, and killed two Civil Guards, orders were given for a rigorous punishment which was brutally carried out. A political campaign developed from the incident, and Azaña's truculence in dealing with his critics, together with much discontent in rural areas, brought a sharp decline in support for the government in the municipal elections of April 1933.

From these results it now appeared that the country was fairly equally divided between right, centre and left. Although the law restricting the religious orders was passed by a large majority in cortes, there were frequent demonstrations by university students, some of whom joined the new fascist movement, the Phalanx, founded by José Antonio Primo de Rivera, the son of the former dictator. Waves of strikes in support of the government kept the country in a turmoil, and finally in November the government resigned and the constituent cortes were dissolved.

In the elections of November 1933 the monarchist parties returned to the fray and women exercised the vote for the first time. As a result, the parties of the right won 207 seats, an advance of 165: those of the centre made a small gain with 167; and those of the left were reduced to 99, a loss of 192. The new right-wing block included 43 Traditionalists and Monarchists and 62 members of the catholic Popular Action party, led by Sr J. M. Gil Robles, who believed that it was possible to build up a catholic régime within the framework of the constitution. Although he and other right-wing groups formed a coalition, the CEDA, they did not possess an absolute majority, and the president therefore entrusted Lerroux with the task of forming a government of the centre. The heavy swing from the left was taken as a repudiation of Azaña's law to secularise education and of the Agrarian Law, and when expropriations of land were stopped the anarcho-syndicalists revolted in various parts of the country, and a state of emergency was imposed.

Having annulled the contentious legislation of the left-wing regime, the Lerroux government fell in March 1934. A peculiar responsibility rested with the president of the Republic. Under the constitution his powers resembled those of the monarch whose former palace was now his office: his business was to sanction legislation, choose the head of the government, and if necessary dissolve cortes. But since under the Constitution of 1876 the dissolution had usually been pressed on the monarch in order that the government might win a majority, the creators of the Republican constitution had permitted the president to dissolve cortes only twice during his six-year term of office: if he was thought to have authorised the second dissolution without good cause, he might be subjected to an enquiry and even deposed. In making this law the fathers of the Republic had clearly overestimated the stability of their governments, and had failed to foresee the deadlock which would result from a system of three blocks, instead of two.

Alcalá Zamora had resigned as Prime Minister after voting against his own government on the anti-clerical clause of the Constitution, and on being elected to the presidency he had been promptly presented with similar legislation for his signature. He had shown his own feelings by deferring his assent until the last possible moment and had then signed: this action, however constitutional, was resented by the right, while the left was no less hostile to him and sought to prevent him from granting power to the right-wing block by constant strikes, as a result of which the anarcho-syndicalist centres were shut. The centre and right government now presented a bill for the amnesty of all those convicted of political offences under the left-wing Republic, including the first active enemy of the régime, General Sanjurjo. This bill gave rise to impassioned debates. When it was passed, Alcalá Zamora again gave his signature, but published a statement of his disapproval. Neither quite responsible, as a minister, nor irresponsible, as a monarch, he was under the cross-fire of both parties for having associated himself against his conscience with the anti-clericalism of the left and the 'anti-Republican' amnesty of the right.

The minority government of the centre could, with the support of the right, undo the work of the left, but it could not initiate any policy of its own. On Lerroux's fall the leader of the right expected to be called; but either because the president distrusted Sr Gil Robles, or because he feared the effect of a right-wing government in an excited country, he would go no further than appoint a series of coalitions in which the CEDA and, ultimately, Sr Gil Robles, were represented.

This conflict was heightened by the opposition of Catalonia and the Basque Provinces to the reversal of the left-wing programme. The Basques, still in quest of their statute, held elections for delegates to assess their contribution to the central treasury, but these elections were declared illegal by the Madrid government, and the alcaldes of the Basque towns were accordingly arrested. Meanwhile, as Madrid moved to the right, Catalonia veered to the left. Since the central government's Agrarian Law, though still in the statute-book, was in suspense, the Catalans voted their own 'Ley de Cultivos', which was rejected by the Supreme Court (the 'Tribunal of Guarantees') on the ground that the matter lay outside the jurisdiction of the Generalitat. The deputies of the Catalan left and those of the Basques walked out of cortes, and in Barcelona the Catalan president ignored the Supreme Court and ratified the law. There followed a long deadlock, and a period of extreme excitement. In Catalonia Companys threatened that if Madrid could not create the 'Hispanic ideal', Catalonia would establish its own nationality; and Azaña praised the Catalan left as the 'only republican power' in Spain. These were revolutionary utterances, and in September the Basque deputies resigned and set up with the Catalans just such an inter-regional understanding as the Constitution proscribed. Socialists and anarchists added their mite with the now familiar general strike.

As the tension increased, the right-wing leaders in cortes again demanded power and forced the government to resign. Alcalá Zamora still refused to precipitate a conflict by appointing Gil Robles, and again called upon Lerroux. There followed two rebellions, one in Catalonia and the other in Asturias. In Barcelona, Companys proclaimed the independence of the Catalan state as part of the 'Federal Spanish Republic', declaring that 'monarchist and fascist forces' had betrayed the Republic and that all 'authentic republicans' had risen in arms. This was untrue. When Companys called upon the Captain-General, a Catalan, to rally to his new republic, he was met with a refusal.

But in Oviedo, a real revolution had begun. For three days there was intense fighting in the city as army columns faced a force of some six thousand miners armed with machine-guns, tanks and dynamite bombs: some fourteen hundred lives were lost, and nearly three thousand persons were wounded. By the end of October, the prisons were full, and those under arrest included Azaña, alleged to be involved in Companys' attempted coup, and Largo Caballero.

The destruction and loss of life in Asturias sobered Spain for a time. Companys (on whose behalf it was argued that to pronounce for a federal instead of a unitary republic could not be treason) was sentenced to thirty years' imprisonment, and Azaña was released. A score of death-sentences was passed, but when the parties of the right insisted on their execution, while those of the centre were for reprieve, there followed a new government crisis. Gil Robles again failed either to win power or to force an election and Lerroux formed a new minority government. Meanwhile, Catalan autonomy was only saved when Cambó, the veteran leader of the Lliga, persuaded Madrid that Catalonia as a whole was not to blame for Companys' rebellion. The statute was then merely suspended, and the central government appointed a Governor-general as president of the Generalitat.

In 1931 provision had been made for a review of the Constitution after four years; and early in 1935 the president expressed the view that this might include a modification of the Catalan statute and the abrogation of the clause which secularised all education. Various degrees of modification were proposed by the parties of the right and centre, but Azaña, whose stock had risen rapidly since his exoneration from responsibility in the Catalan affair, threatened that if cortes should attempt to alter the Constitution in any way, he would no longer enjoin moderation on his supporters. This threat paralysed the parties of the centre, which were now also shaken by a financial scandal involving several associates of Lerroux. After the sixth cabinet crisis in less than a year, the president called upon Sr M. Portela Valladares, lately Governor-general in Catalonia, who was defeated within a fortnight. He then suspended cortes, and at length decided to exercise his prerogative and granted a second dissolution. He appointed February 16, 1936 as the day for the new elections.

Two years of government by inadequate minorities had wasted the prestige of the centre parties, long condemned to purely negative policies. The right-wing block now came face to face with the left-wing Popular Front, formed in imitation of the new French coalition. Azaña had emerged from his eclipse as the strongest politician in Spain, and in the autumn of 1935 he had demanded a combination of forces of the left. It was not difficult to find a programme: the defence of the Constitution of 1931, the resumption of the agrarian and educational reforms, an amnesty for the political offenders as sweeping as that pushed through by the right, and the reinstatement of all officials dismissed as 'incompatible' by the late government. The Popular Front now won 256 seats, an advance of 157, while the centre dropped to 52, and the parties of the right remained stable. The poll numbered about nine millions, of which 48·7 per cent were claimed for the Popular Front, and 46·2 for the right, leaving about 5 per cent for the centre. As in 1931 the cities showed large left-wing majorities and the largest party was again the Socialists. The amnesty was granted; Companys returned to the presidency of the Catalan Generalitat, and a new wave of church-burning occurred, while in the south peasants who had waited two years for land began to occupy it in anticipation of agrarian reform. But if for the bourgeois parties, the 'revolution' had now been accomplished, for their allies it still lay ahead, whether it was the spontaneous and centreless anarchist millennium or the coordinated but problematic conquest of political power of the socialists.

In Madrid the Popular Front first turned upon the President. On the pretext that he had dissolved cortes unjustifiably, Alcalá Zamora was removed, and Azaña was elected into his place. But although the strong man of 1931 intended to take power with him to the National Palace and duly entrusted a less prominent member of his own party with the task of forming a government, the situation soon passed beyond his control. Even Azaña could not endow the presidency with political power, and the government became less and less able to impose order or justice. Successive amnesties appeared to authorise political crime, and on June 16 Gil Robles stated that more than fifteen hundred persons had been killed or wounded in political conflicts since the elections, and that there had been no less than 340 'general strikes'. The climax was reached on July 12 when a fascist band murdered an Assault Guard: on the following day a group of his companions removed the right-wing politician Calvo Sotelo from his house and deposited his body at a suburban cemetery. A few days later the army replied with a pronunciamiento.

The catastrophe of the Second Republic acquired a special significance for a European and American generation brought up in the liberal tradition and in the illusion that a pacific internationalism could ensure a new age of peace. Its faith in liberal conservatism had been shaken by the inadequacy of governments of the right and centre in facing the world's economic crisis, and it therefore inclined to socialist internationalism. But the extravagances of German socialism and the success of Italian aggression in Abyssinia had suddenly exposed the precariousness of a European order secured, but no longer upheld, by American aid. The 'sanctions' with which the League of Nations had tried to check or castigate Italy were still awaiting withdrawal as the Spanish crisis burst. European liberals had no difficulty in identifying themselves with the republic whose ideals had been proclaimed to the world five years earlier. Their fears were soon justified as Italy began to supply aircraft to the rebels, and having assured herself of the passivity of the Non-Intervention Committee of which she formed part, undertook with increasing boldness to guarantee their victory. Germany, too, seized the opportunity to support what appeared to be the anti-French party, and it was on the anvil of the Spanish war that the Italo-German 'Axis' was forged.

In Spain itself the European alignment was scarcely a matter of direct interest until 1936. Since 1808 Spanish politics had had a revolutionary tone, and major changes had always been made on the tide of an upheaval which had usually called forth its corrective reaction. The rebellion of July 1936 was a pronunciamiento intended to check the career of the Second Republic as Pavía had checked the First, and its motives were the same: the belief that public order was in danger and that it was the function of the army to prevent anarchy and enforce social discipline.

The republic now plunged into war was no longer the republic of 1931, and there were many who had decided that it had gone astray, 'no era esto'. The turning-point appears to have been the rebellion of 1934 in which the parties of the left placed their politics outside the system they had erected. The Spanish labour movement, whether anarchist or socialist, had traditionally repudiated bourgeois parliamentary government: the socialists had held seats in cortes until 1917, but they had then suddenly declared for a workers' revolution. In the confusion of the following three years they had sent a delegation to Russia, the majority of which opposed association with the Soviet international, though a minority broke away to form the Spanish Communist Party in 1923. This was repressed during the dictatorship and played no very prominent part in Spanish political life until the formation of the Popular Front, when it was represented for the first time in cortes with fifteen deputies and set itself the task of building a bridge between the rival socialist and anarchist movements in order to press forward the revolution by both legal and extra-legal action. There was however fairly strong opposition to infiltration in the socialist movement, whose leader, Largo Caballero, had expressly repudiated the seizure of power by violence in 1930. But by remaining outside the Popular Front cabinet he now seemed disposed to hedge; and while the bourgeois republicans were left with the task of putting into operation the legislation suspended during the government of the right, the workers' parties consolidated their victory by a rapid development of their militias, which, if they recalled the popular National Guard of the nineteenth century, differed from it in that they were not under political control.

These militias now formed the backbone of the republic's defence, and it was due to them that the army was not able to make a clean sweep. The military leaders in Madrid and Barcelona were captured and shot, and General Sanjurjo was killed in an air accident as he flew back from exile in Lisbon. The revolt succeeded in Old Castile, where General Mola met with small resistance, in Saragossa, Seville and Morocco, where General Franco, whom the republican government had sent as captain-general to the Canaries, arrived to take charge of the army's main depot, and, as it transpired, to lead the movement.

Within a few days all Spain was divided into two camps. The areas loyal to the government comprised Catalonia, Valencia, Murcia and eastern Andalusia, the whole of the centre including La Mancha, New Castile and Extremadura, and in the north the Asturias and the Basque Provinces. This left the insurgents with most of the north from Galicia to Aragon, western Andalusia and Morocco: they also held Toledo as a military island in republican territory. At sea the naval base at Cartagena remained with the government, though many of the officers had been murdered, while that of El Ferrol, near Corunna, soon fell to the insurgents. A small number of officers, together with part of the Civil Guard and most of the republican Assault Guard adhered to the government, but by far the greater part of its forces was composed of improvised brigades of militiamen.

The territorial division was formed rapidly and almost instinctively, and it corresponds approximately with that of 1872–3, when the central government was defied successively by the Carlist north and the federalist south and east. In its essence the schism also recalls the pre-Roman division of Indo-European and post-Tartessian Spain with their differing conceptions of the use and tenure of the land and their contrasting views of society. But these ancient subnational realities assumed political forms only in response to modern impulses, and it is easy to misread the relationship between the two.[1]

---

[1] In the north the Basques, who had preserved their fueros intact for many generations, were deprived of them by nineteenth-century liberalism, and after long campaigning as extreme conservatives at last snatched a brief independence in alliance with the left-wing republic, while their Navarrese cousins rejected the political autonomy of the republic, and received administrative and fiscal privileges from the nationalists: these divergent attitudes recall the flexibility of the ancient *behetrias*, though the actual alignment is modern. The oppositionism of southern and eastern Spain is more complex: in the south the popularity of anarchism suggests not a superabundance, but a deficiency of local institutions, and the relevance of Bakunin's doctrine was that it taught a landless peasantry that violence was the only remedy against an unjust social order. The immediate background of southern anarchism is the frustration of

The first object of the insurgents was to join their three zones by obtaining command of the straits and forcing a passage through western Extremadura: this was achieved by the capture of Badajoz on August 15th. In the following month they sealed off the Basque Provinces from France by occupying Irún and San Sebastián.

Meanwhile, in Madrid a new government had been formed under Largo Caballero, who included such prominent socialists as Prieto, Negrín and Alvarez del Vayo. This change was accompanied by a rapid growth of aid from Russia and the organisation of the International Brigade, which rallied to the defence of Madrid in October and permitted the republicans to hold a line just west and south of the city. Here the converging rebel columns were halted on the outskirts, despite General Mola's boast that a 'fifth column' would emerge from within the capital. Meanwhile, the republican government established itself in Valencia.

Before the end of July Italian military seaplanes were being supplied from Sardinia to Morocco, while Italian forces secured the Balearics and established a naval and air-base at Palma. On August 1st France proposed a general policy of non-intervention and a committee was set up in London, which if it showed that the European powers desired that the conflict should not at once spread, sadly failed to justify its title. In November Germany and Italy recognised General Franco's government and intimated that they would insist on its victory. Meanwhile, Negrín had delivered most of Spain's gold reserves, amounting to about fifty-one metric tons, to Russia in payment for arms and services. France feared further humiliations at the hands of Italy, and attempted without visibly committing herself to build up the resistance of the Valencian government, while Great Britain, sharing neither

liberalism, and behind that lies the new feudalism of the reconquest, which accounts for the creation of conditions which anarchism was designed to remedy from Extremadura to Valencia. In Catalonia ancient autonomy survived until the nineteenth century, when it was transformed by an economic and cultural revival and became not only antiquarian and conservative but contemporary and 'progressive'. The significance of Catalan feeling lies precisely in the fact that it is not confined to questions of traditional jurisdiction, but extends to matters of economic and social policy that affect the whole Spanish state.

these fears nor commitments, sought a 'gentlemen's agreement' with Italy for the preservation of the *status quo* in the Mediterranean. Early in 1937 Italian troops landed in southern Spain and took part in the capture of Málaga in February, though they were soon to suffer a spectacular reverse at Guadalajara. German and Italian ships were now patrolling the Mediterranean coast of Spain, and when in May Republican aircraft attacked an Italian vessel and the German cruiser *Deutschland*, Hitler ordered the bombardment of Almería, and both powers withdrew temporarily from the Non-Intervention Committee, but continued openly to sabotage its objects and to delay the withdrawal of their 'volunteers'. In August the sinking of ships by thinly disguised Italian submarines as far afield as Turkey led to the Noyon Conference, after which Great Britain and France took over the patrolling of the Mediterranean.

Meanwhile, General Mola's armies had reduced northern Spain. In October 1936 the republican government had granted the Basques autonomy, and they had elected their own president and set up a government. But although this measure was expected to unite the catholic and fuerist country-people with socialist opinion in the towns, the outer lines of Basque defence quickly fell, and with them Durango and the armament-centre of Eibar. In June 1937 the 'Iron Ring' with which Bilbao had girded itself was pierced, and the city fell. In August a short campaign reduced Santander, and in October the whole of the Asturias was occupied. Although small groups of guerrillas remained in the mountains, effective resistance was at an end, and the Basque government took refuge in Catalonia.

The front now ran from the middle of the Pyrenees southward to Teruel, where it turned west to the Guadarramas, skirted Madrid, bellied out towards Extremadura, and cut back across the southern meseta to reach the sea at Motril south of Granada. This line of a thousand miles divided Spain approximately in half, and at the end of 1937 the Valencian government won its most striking victory by taking Teruel.

The very prolongation of the struggle had increased the commitments of Germany and Italy. By now the Spanish insurgents owed Italy some 4,500 million lire and Germany about two-thirds as much. As Mussolini remarked, 'we wish to be paid and must be paid,' and the two countries could be sure of this only if Spain were brought within their system. Mussolini intended to occupy the Balearics as long as possible, and to bring Spain into the Anti-Comintern Pact: he had, however, noticed that many Spaniards who supported the Nationalists were opposed to the development of fascist influences.

Meanwhile, Largo Caballero, with Russian aid, had turned the improvised militias of 1936 into a more professional and better-trained 'new army'.

With the relief of Madrid and the arrival of Russian arms and advisers, the hitherto small Communist party rapidly expanded and infiltrated the army with its political commissars. It professed to stand for the winning of the war and the postponement of the revolution, since Russia feared to alienate the western powers. But it also strove unremittingly to achieve control over the masses, and its 'chekas' ruthlessly persecuted the anarchist 'uncontrollables'. A short crisis in May 1937 in Barcelona ended in the subjection of the anarchists and the entry of centralist troops. Largo himself was opposed to the oppression of the anarchists and to any fusion of socialists and communists, and a communist-inspired campaign forced his resignation. He was replaced by the more malleable Negrín, while the right-wing socialist Prieto became Minister of War. In November the central government moved to Barcelona.

The following year, 1938, saw the republican cause reduced from improbability of success to the verge of collapse. In March the insurgent armies recovered Teruel and advanced down the Ebro valley to the Catalan frontier, taking Lérida on April 3rd, and soon after reaching the sea and dividing the republican zone in two. As nationalist forces entered Catalonia, General Franco proclaimed the end of the Catalan state and the restoration of a centralised administration. As a result, the Catalans, who had hitherto scarcely stirred out of their own territory, made a successful defence of Tortosa, and there followed another long period of stalemate. The Republicans were now unable to find arms, and faced with the prospect of defeat. On May 1st they had made tentative soundings for peace, and at the end of the summer Negrín put forward 'Thirteen Points', which included demands for a plebiscite, regional autonomy, a non-political army, agrarian reform and a guarantee of the rights of labour. These proposals were so unrealistic that rumours spread that Negrín would make way for a less intransigent leader; but no change took place, and at Christmas the nationalist forces resumed their onslaught on Catalonia, entering Barcelona on January 26, 1939. All idea of a resolute defence of the Catalan capital was abandoned, and the republican armies withdrew to the French frontier: about a quarter of a million refugees entered France.

The republican cortes, meeting at Figueras on the frontier, reduced Negrín's thirteen demands to a simple request for liberty. It was ignored, and the government withdrew into France. Azaña remained there to finish the war in exile, but Negrín and his ministers flew back to Valencia, whence they returned to Madrid. There the military situation was without hope and the inhabitants almost foodless. General Miaja, who had conducted the defence for more than two years, advised surrender: only the communists were for continued resistance. At the end of February Great Britain and France recognised the nationalist government, and Azaña resigned the presidency of the republic. Negrín attempted to constitute himself commander of the republican forces, but all parties except the communists entered a National Council of Defence under General Miaja and Sr Julián Besteiro, a veteran socialist. Negrín then departed for France, and the communists whom he had promoted fought a short but bitter battle against the rest of the republican army: after three days of bloodshed, they surrendered on March 12th.

The Council of Defence had already made contact with the nationalist headquarters at Burgos. The only terms that could be obtained were permission for those republicans who wished to leave to do so at once: for the rest, surrender was unconditional. On March 28th the nationalist forces entered the capital and by the following day all the provincial cities were in their hands and the war was over.

The military pronunciamiento was anti-red, but in July 1936 it had no precise colour of its own. Generals Sanjurjo, Mola and Franco had served under the dictatorship and under the republic: none were doctrinaire monarchists. They turned their backs on the Second Republic and its internationalism, anti-militarism, secularism, equalitarianism, socialism and proletarianism: they received the support of the catholic republicans of the right and the monarchists, but granted political power to neither of these groups, and reverted instead to traditionalism. This movement was without a pretender of its own and had recognised Alfonso XIII as King, but its political aspirations were summarised in the testament of Charles 'VII' and its social doctrines were those of the encyclicals of Leo XIII. The only part of Spain where these ideas were widely accepted was Navarre, which in 1932 had dissociated itself from the Basque demand for autonomy, and instead received it from the nationalists. Its Carlist requetés joined the nationalist movement, and by the end of the war many young catholics had assumed the characteristic red beret: traditionalism was again a political force, and its leader, the Count of Rodezno, had become a member of the Burgos government.

But the Traditionalist Communion was still the faith of a few and could scarcely win the masses, particularly the urban and industrial population recently impregnated with socialism and anarchism. Before the war two movements had appeared with the object of establishing control over organised labour and dividing it from the left-wing internationals: these were the Spanish Phalanx, founded in 1933 by José Antonio Primo de Rivera, who had been shot in prison at Alicante in 1936, and the National-Socialist Juntas of Offence, launched by Onésimo Redondo. Neither body had commanded more than a small following at the outbreak of the war, and General Franco was able to amalgamate them with the Carlist current under the cumbrous title of the Spanish Phalanx of Traditionalism and of the Offensive National-Socialist Committees (F.E.T. y de las J.O.N.S.). The single party was created by a decree of April 19, 1937, and by the following August an amalgamated programme was produced.

There were however, many possibilities of conflict in this diversified movement of unity. In particular the conservative forces of the nationalist régime were fervently catholic, while the parent of the Phalanx, Fascism, was secularist, and its aunt, National-Socialism, was anti-Christian. Although most dioceses accepted the convention by which the founder's portrait was stamped on the walls of each church, Cardinal Segura refused to permit this defacement in Seville. Nor did the army look kindly on the single party, and it was necessary to establish a separate section for officers. Even when it had found a programme, the Phalanx was not given political power. On the contrary, six months later General Franco set up a cabinet. He himself was its President, and its Vice-president was a Traditionalist, General Count Jordana, who took charge of foreign affairs. The Ministry of the Interior was given to Sr R. Serrano Súñer, General Franco's brother-in-law, and an ardent Phalangist since the previous year: the remaining ministries were divided between the two groups. At the close of the war there was thus a double state, one controlled by the middle-class conservatives, and the other ebulliently demagogic and 'social'. The two would ultimately merge as labour accepted the catholic doctrine of hierarchy, and General Franco would preside over the process in his four-fold capacity of Head of State, Generalissimo, Caudillo of the Party, and Chief of Government. Behind this multiplicity of roles the form of the state remained obscure. Traditionalists by definition favoured the restoration of the monarchy, while the Phalanx regarded this as a retrogressive step towards the bourgeois and liberal state which they had rejected. General Franco, for his part, referred guardedly to a possible restoration, though he made it clear that this might be a long way ahead.

Within the state, traditionalism predicated a religious monopoly of education, but because of its long association with the Basque fueros it favoured localism, and Charles 'VII' had promised devolution in the eastern realms within 'the whole and indivisible patria'. Phalangism was essentially centralist and uniformist. Thus while Navarre received administrative autonomy from the nationalist state, neither Basques nor Catalans could hope for concessions from it. In foreign policy, the testament of Charles 'VII' drawn up in 1897 enjoined the recovery of Gibraltar, union with Portugal, hegemony over Morocco and confederation with the former American colonies, under the device of 'integrity, honour and greatness'. These ideas were now transmuted into a 'will to empire' with special reference to Gibraltar and Morocco, and a desire to incorporate Latin America in a new cultural sphere of 'Hispanity'.

Only five months elapsed between the capture of Madrid and the outbreak of the European war. During this period two factors combined to give the Phalanx an ascendancy over the traditionalists; the state of dependency on the Axis powers and the need to assimilate large numbers of republican prisoners of war in order to normalise daily life. Spain had no formal alliance with either Italy or Germany: secret treaties with Italy, signed in November 1936, and with Germany, signed in March 1937 and revised in 1939, provided for consultation and benevolent neutrality in case of war. Each party engaged to enter into no alliance directed against the other, and the Italo-Spanish treaty ensured that in case of war the neutral party should assist the belligerent with supplies and the use of her ports and transports. In addition to these treaties Spain had adhered to the anti-Comintern pact in March 1939. Except among extreme Phalangists relations with Italy were much closer than with Germany: when a 'cultural' agreement was concluded with Germany in January 1939 catholic opinion successfully resisted its ratification.

Meanwhile, Spain had finished the war deeply in debt to both Italy and Germany, and without gold or foreign currency to pay for her immediate needs. Germany had demanded an important role in Spain's reconstruction as part of her reward and two of General Goering's trading corporations busily acquired Spanish minerals, hides and ores. While part of the economy was thus committed to Germany, the debt to Italy was scaled down to 50 million lire, to be paid between 1942 and 1967. Spain was urgently in need of cotton to keep the industries of Catalonia at work and of wheat and petroleum, and on May 19th she obtained a dollar credit for the purchase of cotton.

But in the middle of 1939, with the approach of war, the pressure of the Axis enabled the Phalangists to defeat the traditionalists, most of whom left the cabinet. The Foreign Minister General Jordana, who in the spring had given assurances that Spain harboured no designs against Gibraltar, was replaced, and Spain's relations with the Axis were managed by Serrano Súñer, the titular Minister of the Interior and controller of the Press: in June he told Ciano that Spain intended to recover Gibraltar and settle accounts with France in Morocco, but that two or three years of peace were essential to her. Only ten days after the cabinet change, there came news of Germany's pact with Russia (August 22nd), followed by the invasion of Catholic Poland.

In 1940 the German invasion of the Low Countries and France brought Hitler's troops to the Pyrenees. There were many reasons why this should arouse General Franco's natural caution: to condone an invasion was not only to court the fate of Godoy, but to invite a new rebellion by the many thousands of republicans not yet converted from 'Marxist materialism' or 'liberal capitalism' to the new system of National Syndicalism. Moreover, the sorely strained Spanish economy was likely to collapse if Britain cut off its supplies from overseas. As Italy joined the war, raising shrill cries of 'Corsica, Tunisia, Nice', Spain passed from neutrality to 'non-belligerency' and the Phalangists demanded Gibraltar, Morocco, Tangier and Oran. In June Spain occupied Tangier 'provisionally', and Britain accepted an intrusion which at least forestalled Italy or Germany. For the rest of 1940 the Spanish government tried to secure advantages from Germany with the least possible risk to itself.

But with the fall of France these aspirations no longer interested Hitler, for whom it was much more important to win over his defeated enemy and to avoid scaring her colonies into joining the resistance movement. When General Franco asked Mussolini to support his claims, he was told that unless Spain entered the war, he could not expect a share of the spoils. At this time a disastrous harvest had further reduced Spain's bread ration and her industry was almost paralysed by shortage of raw materials. In September Serrano visited Hitler and assured him that Spain would fight provided that her supplies could be guaranteed, but Hitler refused any undertaking unless a date for her entry into the war were fixed. A meeting between General Franco and Hitler at Hendaye produced no more concrete result.

Italy's disastrous attack on Greece changed the Mediterranean scene. Hitler now desired to close the straits, and proposals for the conquest of Gibraltar were discussed. But Serrano enlarged on Spain's economic difficulties and urged Hitler to give preference to Suez. In December Hitler suddenly informed the Spanish government that he wished German troops to pass through Spain in January 1941, but a few days later the German command discontinued preparations for the assault on Gibraltar: Hitler was now convinced of Spain's 'disloyalty' and gave up his attempts to bring her into the war.

In the early months of 1941, the great crisis seemed to be passing. Spain's avoidance of famine was due not to the Axis, but to the moderation of the British blockade. Moreover, the death of Alfonso XIII in Rome provoked a mild monarchist reaction as older Spaniards remembered the easy neutrality of 1914–8. When in May Serrano delivered a bellicose speech, the control of the press was taken out of his hands, though on the protest of the Germans it was quickly restored. But the German invasion of Russia now removed all immediate danger of a trespass into Spain and replaced the Spanish-German relationship on its former anti-comintern basis. General Franco publicly supported the German attack and sent a force of some seventeen thousand 'volunteers', the Blue Division, for service on the Russian front. In Madrid there were Phalangist demonstrations against Russia's allies, and General Franco prophesied an Axis victory.

But despite Serrano's Germanophile speeches, Spain still depended on the Atlantic sea-ways for essential imports, and for her Hitler's much advertised European self-sufficiency was never more than a boast. With the entry of the United States into the war, there was no longer any prospect of the cessation of the economic blockade, while the Council of Hispanity, launched in 1941 with the object of drawing the American republics into a Spanish 'cultural' and neutral block, failed to prevent them from adhering to the United States. In July 1942 the revival of cortes with the representation of the Phalanx, the National Syndicalists, provincial delegates, and others showed that the single party was not identical with the Spanish state, and in September Serrano was at last dismissed, and General Jordana returned to manage Spain's foreign affairs.

As the allies launched their offensive in North Africa, the Axis and its friends made a last attempt to prevent Spain from returning to neutrality, but General Jordana was now on firm ground and carried the day.

At this stage Spain echoed the hopes of the Vatican for a negotiated peace, on the grounds that Germany should be spared defeat in order to serve as a bulwark against communism. This 'peace offensive' was taken up with such vigour that Germany asked for it to be moderated lest it should be thought to emanate from her. It also offered the Allies the opportunity to remonstrate against the unneutral activities of the Spanish government in admitting German agents to Tangier, supplying German submarines, allowing the Phalanx to further German propaganda and maintaining the Blue Division in Russia. On October 1, 1943 General Franco referred to Spain's position as neutrality, not 'non-belligerency', and the Blue Division was withdrawn.

As the war drew to a close, it was inevitable the the victors should pass some form of judgement on his equivocations. In May 1944 Mr Churchill thanked him for not having intervened in the war and looked forward to an improvement in Anglo-Spanish relations: although this compliment was appreciated, it was followed by a counter-remonstrance to the Allied complaints of July 1943, in which General Franco expressed his resentment of the criticisms of the British wireless and press, and after some delay Mr Churchill replied with an account of some of the obstacles in the way of a closer understanding, and in particular of the persistent hostility of the Phalanx. Shortly afterwards Mr Roosevelt thought that there would be no place in the new world order for governments founded on Fascist principles, and at the San Francisco conference, Mexico, which had befriended large numbers of republican exiles, proposed the exclusion of régimes set up with the aid of the armed forces of the defeated powers. In May 1945 General Franco replied by defending the Christian and national merits of his own form of democracy and denying that his government was a dictatorship or that the Phalanx wielded political power: it was, he declared, an 'instrument of national unification'. In accordance with this new view, the party minister disappeared from the cabinet and allocations for party funds from the budget, whilst its national council was reduced from a hundred members to fifty. Several Phalangists remained in the government, and the party continued to control the syndicalist labour movement and the provincial political organisation, and in almost every province the civil governor or 'political chief' was also head of the Phalanx. Nevertheless, within the light of recent Spanish history, the concession was a real one, and it invited the victorious powers to accept the distinction between the Spanish government and the party. Were the western powers pressing for the régime to evolve or for it to commit suicide? The answer to this question soon became a political issue outside Spain. In France a wave of indignation against the execution by General Franco of a Spanish terrorist who had also been a prominent resistance fighter caused the Minister for Foreign Affairs to break off relations with Spain and to propose that the Spanish problem should be placed before the Security Council. Both Britain and the United States thought that the charter of the United Nations should not be used to cloak a form of intervention in the domestic affairs of a foreign state, but the three powers nevertheless issued a declaration of support for some form of interim government in Spain which might prepare for the holding of free elections (March 1946).

How this interim government might come into being was not revealed. General Franco had again declared himself a monarchist, but when four hundred and fifty prominent Spaniards addressed an open letter to the Bourbon claimant, John III, who had recently set up his court at Estoril, a number of the leaders were deprived of their seats in cortes, exiled or fined. Meanwhile, the republican government in exile, now headed by Sr J. Giral, awaited events in Paris and claimed to speak for an underground Alliance of Democratic Forces which embraced Republicans, Socialists and members of the workers' organisations, the UGT and CNT, in Spain. But partly because of Giral's acceptance of communist support and partly because of difficulties of adjustment between exiles and republicans in Spain, the shadow-government in Paris faded into obscurity, and in 1947 forfeited the support of the workers' movements.

Although the French proposal to lay the Spanish question before the Security Council had been withdrawn, the idea was at once appropriated by Poland, and in June 1946 a committee of five decided that the Spanish régime was not a danger, but a 'potential danger' to peace, and recommended the recall of ambassadors until such time as internal political freedom was restored. This caused General Franco no serious difficulty, and his propagandists depicted it as the result of communist intrigue. The United Nations turned its attention to other matters: in May 1949 a motion to restore freedom of action in opening diplomatic relations with Spain was passed, but not by the necessary two-thirds majority, and it was only in November 1950 that a similar motion was carried and the 'Spanish question' finally disappeared from the agenda.

After his brush with his fellow-monarchists in 1946, General Franco slowly prepared to define his position, and in March 1947 he announced a Law of Succession, which was accepted by a large majority in a referendum three months later: this was the first vote taken in Spain since 1936, and all those who had at any time been held under political arrest were excluded from it. The purport of the Law of Succession was to declare Spain a kingdom and a 'catholic and social' state: it left General Franco to decide when and in whose favour the monarchy should be restored and laid down that the King should accept the basic legislation of the existing régime—the Spanish 'Bill of Rights' (Fuero de los Españoles), the labour charter and the statute of cortes. The pretender at once rejected the law, pointing out that the monarchy could not be bound to an arbitrary régime or to 'fundamental laws' which were not observed. The leaders of the liberal and traditionalist monarchists, the Duke of Alba and Count of Rodezno, supported this repudiation. When in 1948 General

Franco assumed powers to grant grandeeships and titles the nobility again protested; but with few exceptions the monarchists failed to make any impression on public opinion, and the rigid censorship prevented them from calling General Franco's bluff.

Since he had found it expedient to play down the Phalanx, he had brought forward dissident monarchists of the catholic action movement, opening negotiations with the Vatican for a concordat to replace the existing *modus vivendi*, and had made life easier for the army, which in 1946 and 1947 still received forty per cent of the Spanish budget. But after the pretender's refusal to accept the Phalangist heritage and an unexpected and uncordial interview between him and the Caudillo in August 1948, the tide once more ran in favour of the Phalanx, and its secretary-general again appeared in the political scene and became a minister in the government. As the opposition parties in exile, ranging from the old catholic republican right of Gil Robles to the socialists and workers' groups (but excluding the communists) reached a 'statement of agreement', the régime made a tentative approach to the fundamental issue by holding a form of municipal elections. One third of the seats on the municipal councils was to be elective by heads of families: the remainder continued to be nominated by the syndicates or appointed by the civil governor, while the alcaldes of all towns with a population of ten thousand were appointed by the ministry of the interior and those of all smaller places by the civil governor. Given the rigid control of the press and all forms of information, the patriotic clatter of the Phalanx and the tradition of caciquismo in many parts of Spain, the elections had no real significance: cortes, consisting of appointed and ex-officio members, met for formal sessions to pass the government's laws, and so contentious a measure as the bill which empowered General Franco to grant titles was approved with only one opposition vote.

AFTERWORD

On beginning this History, I attempted to write a foreword, but the provisional 'conclusions' from which I started have now been either eliminated or incorporated in the text. I have left the interpretation of Spanish history to a separate study and not in general sought to forestall the reader's own judgments, but it is perhaps necessary to suggest lines on which older appreciations might be amended.

The nineteenth century, preoccupied with the theme of national history, concerned itself with the fortunes of the Spanish imperial state, accepting the foreshortening of European history that followed the Reformation. More recently, the absolute view of European nations has been modified, and by examining their origins historians have acquired a more organic vision of the preceding ages. If the nineteenth century saw Spain's greatness solely in terms of unity, and attributed even her decline to excessive conformism, the twentieth has turned to the Middle Ages and seen the opposite aspect of diversity. Some writers have sought to explain Spain's peculiarities entirely in terms of her experience of Islam, and their views have not gone unchallenged. It is quite impossible to ignore the millenium that runs from the landing of Ṭariq to the last prosecutions of Spanish Islamizers in the eighteenth century: to minimize the Islamic contribution because of the fewness of the Arab settlers is to slip into the error of racialism. Yet the mere fact of the conquest is not enough to 'explain' Spanish history. Not only Spain but other European lands have been washed by the high tides of Islam, and physically, if not spiritually, 'Roman' Spain and Muslim Spain are one. Spain's 'difference' lies first in her attempt to create an Islamic world of her own and secondly in the extremes of mutual attraction and repulsion that occurred while the two great religions of the Middle Ages confronted one another on her soil.

But the very extremism of Spanish history calls for longer perspectives, no longer limited by narrow concepts of culture and race. History is not 'culture', but the sum of human experience, the cause and effect of culture, which is in turn the cause and effect of race.

The essential condition of Spanish life is the semi-continental form of the Peninsula, an arena with two gates, that of the Pyrenean north left ajar by nature, but capable of being blocked by man, and that of the south barred by nature, but opened by man. The aboriginal polarity of the Peninsula was elaborated as successive peoples dominated the land and identified themselves with it, and the differentiation was increased with the arrival in the south and east of 'Almerians', Carthaginians, Romans, Arabs and Magribians, and in the north of successive waves of Indo-Europeans. The latest of these movements was the great Reconquest, which may be dated from the invention of the tomb of St. James, the prophet of the Leonese monarchy, an anti-Muhammad whose Mecca was in Galicia.

The Reconquest forged in the north a faith as undebateable as that of Islam, a speech as lapidary as classical Arab and a customary law as inflexible as the Koran. Its consequence was the political suppression and cultural subjugation of the southern extreme. But this process was accompanied by a differentiation of the northern conquerors according to their social traditions and their approach to the problems of expansion and resettlement. Thus the ancient polarity, cosmic, geographical, imperial and theological, was succeeded by a new east-west axis, legal, political, cultural and national, and it is on this framework that the existing duality of the Peninsula rests.

The Spain of modern times is of course no longer a semi-continent[1] but a nation. When on the threshold of our own age the rulers of Castile and Aragon first claimed to be kings of 'Spain', the ruler of Portugal protested against the arrogation. The history of Aragon, no less than that of Portugal, illustrates the difference between the 'Spanish' state and the social realities on which it rests. All nations are artificial creations, but the historical Spain, as distinct from the geographic, is more evidently the product of human effort and resolution, and therefore more problematic, than most. Not a few observers have remarked upon the apparent weakness of Peninsular institutions, and some have deduced an inherent inaptitude for social organization. But this lack is scarcely noticeable in the Middle Ages, and it becomes decisive only in the nineteenth century when institutional growth was proliferating most vigorously elsewhere. This was the period immediately following the great upheaval in which the American colonies had been detached and the traditional church had been deprived of its authority, and it seems clear that these two enterprises had hitherto absorbed the greater part of Spain's creative powers. Empire and religion were powerful masters, and their claims left little room for the intermediate and lesser loyalties that have constituted the main strength of the bourgeois state. The very grandiloquence of the Spanish nineteenth century refers back to an older mode of thought in which abstractions had real value, and it is for this reason that Spanish politicians vainly but indefatigably sought absolutes in a system that had come into existence to replace or relativize them. The Spanish nineteenth century might well say with Don Quixote "Dios lo remedie; que todo este mundo es máquinas y trazas, contrarias unas de otras."

Idealism is a form of thought that courts disillusionment and incurs tragedy. But it is also one in which nobility and dignity are not divorced from common actions, and the high object of social organization is not convenience, but justice.

[1] The word Spain appears to have been originally a purely geographical expression, while the other European states take their names from peoples or heroes. Thus England and France are the lands dominated by the Angles and the Franks, but Spaniards are Spaniards because they live in Spain.

INDEX

ABARRAN, 419
'Abbadids, rulers of Seville, 120, 121, 122, 123, 124, 125
'Abbas ibn Firnas, 76
'Abbasids, caliphs of Damascus, 70, 71 f., 76
Abbevillians, 16, 17, 20
Abdera, Adra, 30, 31
'Abdu'llah, Emir of Córdoba, 78, 84, 91; last Zirid K. of Granada, 107, 122, 124
'Abdu'l-'Aziz, governor of al-Andalus, 66, 67
'Abdu'l-Karim, 419, 420, 421
'Abdu'l-Malik, son of Almanzor, 88
'Abdu'r-Rahman I, Emir of Córdoba, 71; II, 73, 74, 75, 76, 77; III, caliph, 84 f., 94, 95
absolutism, Bourbon, 323, 324; restored, 361, 367, 370, 371, 402
Abu 'Abdu'llah, Boabdil, 192, 193, 194
Abu'l-Hasan, Mulay Hasan, 173, 192, 193
Abu'l-Walid Isma'il, 159
Abu Ya'qub, 125
academies, 333
Acadia, 335
Additional Act, 1856, 381
Admiral of Castile, 171, 172, 173
adoptionism, 79, 80
Adra, 30, 47
Adrian of Utrecht, Pope Adrian VI, 208, 209, 210, 212, 214, 216, 217
Afonso I Henriques, K. of Portugal, 110, 115; V, 173, 176, 188

afrancesados (Frenchified), 340, 345, 355, 358, 364
ibn al-Aftas, of Badajoz, 120
Agila, 55
Aglabids, 86
Agmat, 124
Agrarian Law, 1931, 428, 429, 430, 432
Aguila, Juan de, 288
Aisha, Q. of Granada, 192, 193
Aix-la-Chapelle, 309, 312
Akhila, 63, 65
Akra Leuké, Alicante, 32
Alalia, 30, 31
Alans, 51, 52
Alarcos, battle of, 117, 126
Alaric II, 55
Alava, 82, 156
Alba, Dukes of, 187; 221, 227, 232, 237, 239, 240, 246, 247, 273
Albaicín (Granada), 193
Albelda, battle of, 78, 83
Alberoni, Fr., later Cardinal, 325, 326, 327, 328, 329
Albert, Archduke, 287, 296
Albuquerque, Juan Alfonso de, 144, 145, 170
Albornoz, Alvaro de, 426
alcabala, sales-tax, tribute, 208, 209, 239
Alcáçovas, treaty of the, 188
Alcalá Zamora, Aniceto, 424, 425, 426, 427, 431, 432, 433
Alcántara, 246
Alcántara, Military Order of, 115, 189
Alcazarquivir, battle of, 245, 246
Alcolea, 387

453

Aledo, 107, 108, 124
Alexander VI Borgia, 196, 198; A. Farnese, 240, 252, 253, 287
Alexandria, 73; Council of, 49
Alfonso, I, K. of Asturias, 69, 70, 79; II, 79, 80; III, the Great, of Leon, 83, 91, 92, 93, 94; V, 99; VI, of Leon and Castile, 103, 105, 106, 107, 108, 109, 110, 122, 123, 136; VII, Raimúndez, 110, 111, 112, 113, 124, 136; VIII, of Castile, 113, 117, 118, 126, 137; IX, of Leon, 114, 116, 117, 118, 128; X, 'el Sabio', 130, 133, 137, 138, 139, 140, 141, 143, 151; XI, 141, 142, 143, 144, 145, 159, 162, 167; XII, 383, 395, 397, 399; XIII, 397, 408 f., 446; A.I of Aragon, the Battler, 110, 111, 112, 124, 136; II, 112, 129; III, 151, 152; IV, 153; V, the Magnanimous, 173, 177, 178, 197; A. de la Cerda, 140, 141; Infante A., called A. 'XII', 172, 174, 175
Algarve, 137
Algeciras (Cádiz), Muslim invasion at, 65; Almoravids land at, 108, 124; 141, 143; siege of, 143, 157; Conference of A., 412
Alghero (Sardinia), 153
Algiers, 222, 223, 224, 290, 341
Alhama (Granada), 192, 193
Alhambra (Granada), 124, 126; 159, 161, 173, 193, 194, 241, 242
Alhendín (Granada), 194
'Ali ibn Ḥammud, 90, 120
Aliaga, Fr., 294
Alicante, assigned to Aragon, 148; 322
Aljubarrota, battle of, 165
Almagro, Diego de, 259, 260
Almansa, battle of, 322
Almanzor, al-Manṣur, 87 f., 91, 97, 98, 119, 135
Almenara, Marquis of, 249; battle of A., 322

Almería, neolithic, 15, 22, 23, 24, 25 26; 42, 44, 48; attacked by Fatimids 86; taken by Alf. VII; 112, 133; 119 taifa of, 120; annexed by Granada 120, 121; 125; offered to Aragon, 141 193; bombarded by Germans, 439
Almizra, treaty of, 130
Almizaraque (Almería), 23, 24
almogáveres, 153
Almohads, 114, 115, 117, 125, 126, 128
Almoravids, 107, 108, 109, 112, 114, 123, 124
Alpujarras, 194, 241, 242, 243
Altamira (Santander), 18
Alvar Fáñez, 107
Alvarez del Vayo, Julio, 438
Alvaro Núñez de Lara, 118, 128
Amadeo of Savoy, 389, 391, 395
Amalaric, 55
Amaya (Burgos), 66, 69, 83
Ambrose, St., 49
Ameixial, battle of, 308
America, 195, 255
Amiens, 254; peace of, 347
Amirall, 405
Ana of Austria, dau. of Philip III, 289
anarchism, 398, 407; anarcho-syndicalism, 408; 410, 411, 412, 413, 416, 417, 422, 423, 425, 428, 430, 432, 437, 440
al-Andalus, Muslim Spain, 69, 70 f., 84 f.; traversed by Alfonso the Battler, 111; by Alfonso VII, 112; 118 f.
Andalusia, 21 f.; 'Tartessian', 28 f., 32 f.; Christianity in, 48; Muslim, 68 f., v. Córdoba, al-Andalus; ibn Ḥafṣun, 78; Christian control of, 107, 126 f.; trade of, 133; resettlement, 133, 134, 136, 137; Muslim revolt, 139; in civil wars, 147; frontiersmen, 142, 173, 175; in 16th c., 280; v. Cádiz; anarchism in, 407; agrarian reform in, 428, 429

INDEX 455

Anglo-Portuguese Alliance, 163 f.; 303, 306, 307, 337, 342, 345
Angoulême, Duke of, 367
Anjou, house of, Angevins; A. and Naples, 150, 151, 152, 177, 178, 197, 217, 225, 303
Annual, battle of, 419, 420
Antequera (Málaga), 24, 25, 160, 169 192
anti-clericalism, 372, 373, 374, 388, 389, 410, 413, 426
Anti-Comintern Pact, 440, 444
Antwerp, 240, 245, 252, 288
Apostolicals, 367, 368, 371, 375
Arabs, in Muslim conquest, 65, 66, 67, 68; 84; Almanzor and Arab nobility, 87, 90; suppression of junds, 119; A. taifas, 120
Aragon, county of, 81, 82; attached to Navarre, 91, 111, 112; kingdom of, 100, 101, 103, 104; A. and Saragossa, 110, 111, 112; expansion beyond the Ebro, 111, 129, 130; association with county of Barcelona, 112, 114, 129, 130; Greater Aragon, 129, 130, 137; intervention in Castile, 140 f.; A. and France, 145, 146; 147 f.; Trastámaras in, 169, 170 f., 176 f.; union with Castile, 176, 181, 183, 187, 188; Philip II and, 236, 246 f.; 283, 284; Juan José and, 310; loss of fueros, 323, 324
Aranda, Counts of, 311; 335, 338, 341, 342, 344
Aranjuez, 333, 338, 354; revolt of, 349, 350
Arcadius, 51
Archena (Murcia), 38
Arevaci, 28, 39
Argantonios, 30
Argar, El, 25, 26
Argentina, v. Buenos Aires, Plate
Argüelles, Agustín, 364, 376, 378

Arianism, Arians, 49, 51, 53, 55, 56, 57, 58
Arjona (Jaén), 130
Arlanzón, river, 83
Armada, Invincible, 252, 253
army, Visigothic, 60 f.; Muslim, v. junds, emiral, 72, 73, caliphal, 86, 87, 88, 119; royal, 167, 185; Bourbon reforms, 333, 339, 362; in 19th c., 362, 374, 375, 380, 386; Amadeo and, 391; 395, 404, 409, 415, 416, 417, 419, 420, 423, 427, 435, 443
Arriaga, cofradía of, 156
Arzila (Morocco), 90
Asdingians, 51, 52
asiento, 323, 326
Astepa, 33
Astorga (Leon), Roman, v. Asturica; Muslims enter, 66, 69; entered by Alf. I, 70; resettlement of, 93
Astures, 43, 69
Asturica, 42, 45
Asturias, 18; Romanized, 43; neo-Gothic, 69 f., 79 f.; 83, 147; rebellion in, 1934, 432, 433, 436, 439
Atahuallpa, 258, 259, 260
Atapuerca, battle of, 101
Athanagild, 55, 56, 57
Athens, Catalans in, 153
audiencia, 190, 324
Augsburg, 220; Interim of A., 227, 232, 234
Augustus, 43, 44
aula regia, 61
Aurelius, 79
Aureolus, 81
Aurignacians, 17
Austria, house of, v. Maximilian; Charles V's relations with, 215, 216, 221, 224, 228, 229; 285; Austrian party in Sp. court, 314, 315, 316, 317; v. Sp. succession, 326; 329, 330, 331, 332
Autrigones, 28, 81

Averroes, 125
Avila, Constitution of, 212
Avis, Master of, *v.* John I of Portugal
ayacuchos, 376
Azaila, 38
Azaña, Manuel, 425, 426, 427, 428, 429, 430, 432, 433, 434, 441
Azilians, 18
Aznar, Adm. J. B., 424
Aznar Galíndez, 82
Azores, 195, 246, 252
Aztecs, 219, 256 f.

BAAL, 34
Badajoz, 77, 103, 105, 106, 108, 120, 124, 359, 438
Badis, 121, 122
Baecula, Bailén, 37
Baetica, Roman Andalusia, 37; Augustus' division, 43; Caracalla's, 44; 45, 46; Vandals in, 52; Visigothic, 52, 53; Byzantine 55, 56; 57; *v.* al-Andalus, Andalusia
bagaudae, 53
Baghdad, 71
Bahia, 296, 299
Bailén, battle of, 354, 355
Bakunin, Mikhail Aleksandrovich, 407, 437
Balbus, L. C., 45
Balearic Islands, 13, 53; taifa of, 120; reconquest of, 126; War of Sp. Succession and, 322; Italy and, 438, 439, 440
Barbara of Braganza, 332, 335
Barbarossa, 221, 222
Barbastro, 111, 118
Barcelona, Visigothic, 52, 54; falls to Muslims, 65; to Franks, 72; 78, 81; attacked by Almanzor, 88; 96, 97, 99; association with Aragon, 104, 112; 118, 129; rise of city, 130, 134, 177; house of B., Ks. of Aragon, 148 f., 162; defies John II, 180, 181; 185; revolts against Olivares, 300, 301; occupied by French, 301, 302; reconquered, 306; taken by Vendôme, 315; in war of Sp. Succession, 322, 323; Bourbon reforms, 323; Espartero bombards, 376; anarchism in, 407, 408, 417; rebellion of, 1934, 432; Republican Govt. at, 440, fall of, 442
Baria, Vera (Almería), 37, 44
Barletta, 199
Bases de Manresa, 405
Basque Provinces, Basques, 27, 39, 43; independence of, 50; Leovigild and, 57; Muslims and, 67, 69; in Reconquest, 70, 79; B. and birth of Castile, 80; Navarrese, 81, 82; shipping in Reconquest, 131, 133; 156 f., 186; in America, 263; 327, 334, 340, 371, 374, 375, 395; and Republic, 429, 431, 432, 438, 439, 443
Baza, 193, 194
Beatrice of Swabia, 128
Beatriz of Portugal, 164, 165
Bedmar, Marquis of, 294
beehive hut, 23, 42
behetría, 156, 437
Belalcázar, Sebastián de, 261
Belgae, 27, 28
Belisarius, 55
bell-beaker, 24
Benaoján (Ronda), 19
Benedict XIII, 'Pope Luna', 155, 167, 176, 177; XIV, 335
Berenguela of Castile, 117, 118
Berenguer, Gen. Dámaso, 419, 423, 424
Berenguer Ramón, 99
Berbers, 46; in conquest of Sp., 64, 65, 66, 67; confederations, 68; rebellions of, 68, 70, 71; contingents, 86, 87, 89; sack of Córdoba, 90; taifas of, 119, 120; Sanhaja, Granada,

INDEX 457

Berbers—*cont.*
121, 122; garrisons in Granada, 141, 158, 159, 193; 412
Bergen-op-Zoom, 288
Berlepsch, Baroness, 315, 316
berracos, 40, 115
Berwick, 322
Besteiro, Julián, 441
Bethencourt, Jean de, 169
Bilbao, 281, 371, 372, 395, 439
Biscay, Vizcaya, 28, 157
Bizerta, 245
Black Prince, 146
Blake, Gen. Joaquín, 354, 359
Blanche of France, dau. of St. Louis, 139, 140; B. of Bourbon, 145; B. of Navarre, 158, 170, 173, 179
'Bloody Corpus', 300, 301
Blue Division, 446, 447
Blum, *v.* Flor
Boabdil, Abu 'Abdu'llah, 192, 193, 194
Bobastro, 78
Bolívar, Simon, 363
Bolivia (Upper Peru), 261, 262
Bologna, 165, 167, 219
Bonaparte, *v.* Napoleon; Joseph; Louis, K. of Holland, 349; Lucien, 347, 350
Boniface, VIII, 152
Boquique, 24
Borrell, 97
Bourbons, 319 f.
Bracara, Braga, 44; defeat of Suevi at, 53; 70, 109, 110
Braganza, house of, 301, 307, 337, 344
Bravo Murillo, Juan, 380
Brazil, 134, 196, 286, 296, 299, 337, 348
Breda, 296
Brihuega (Guadalajara), 322
Bronze Age, 25, 26
Brutus, Decius, 41
Buckingham, 297
Buenos Aires, 262, 340, 363

P*

Bureba, 101, 113
Burgos, 95, 136, 146, 147, 201, 279, 281, 322
Burgundy, *v.* Cluniac reform; Burgundian marriage, 109, 110; County of B., 200, 218, 222, 225; Duchy of B., 200; B. inheritance, 228, 229, 230; Philip II and, 233
Byng, Adm., 327, 335
Byzantium, Byzantines, conquer N. Africa, 55; in Sp., 55, 56, 57, 58; Córdoba and, 76; Aragon and, 150

CABALLEROS, 186, 274
Cabot, Sebastian, 262, 264
Cabrera, Ramón, 372, 379, 382, 386, 395
caciques, caciquismo, 396, 398, 404, 450
Cádiz, Phoenician settlement, 28 f., *v.* Gadir, Gades; sacked by Essex, 253, 288; American trade at, 264; Cecil's attack on, 297; 321, 330, 333, 347, 356, 357; cortes of, 358, 364
Caesar, 42
Caesar Augusta, Saragossa, 44
Calaf (Barcelona), 181
Calatanazor, 88
Calatayud (Saragossa), 111
Calatrava, 115; Order of C., 115, 189
Calderón, Rodrigo, 291, 292, 294, 295
Calatrava, José María, 374
caliphate, caliphs of Córdoba, 84 f.
Calomarde, Tadeo, 367, 369
Calvinism, in France, 233; in Netherlands, 238, 239, 240
Calvo Sotelo, José, 423, 435
camarilla, 361
Cambrai, league of, 201; peace of C., 219, 224
Cambó, Francisco, 411, 416, 417, 418, 433
Cambridge, Earl of, 164
Campi gothici, 54, 56, 60, 93

Campomanes, 338
Canalejas, José, 405, 413, 414
Canary Islands, rediscovery of, 169; 188, 195, 286
Cangas de Onís, 69
Cánovas del Castillo, Antonio, 395, 396, 397, 399, 400, 404
Cantabrian Mts., 15, 43, 69; Cantabria, Cantabrians, 28, 37, 43, 69, 70; C. War, 42
Cape Verde Islands, 196
captain(s)-general, 324, 362, 394, 423, 424
Caracalla, 44
Caracas, 363
Carlism, Carlists, 367, 370, 374, 379, 388, 389, 390, 391, 394, 395, 397 398, 409, 413, 414, 437, *v.* Carlos María Isidro, traditionalism
Carlos, Don, son of Philip II, 229, 231, 233, 236, 237; C. María Isidro, son of Charles IV, 368, 369, 370, 371, 374 *v.* Carlism
Carmona (Seville), 24, 71, 76, 131, 163
Caroline Islands, 400
Carpetani, 40
Carranza, Bartolomé de, 235
carreratge, 148
Cartagena, 'New Carthage', 32, 35, 37; taken by Vandals, 53; Byzantine C., 57; 333; canton of C., 393, 394; 437
Carteia, 65
Carthage, 30, 31 f., 37, 55, 221
Cart(h)aginensis, 44, 52, 57
Carvajal y Lancáster, José, 332, 335
Casas, Bartolomé de las, 265
Casa de Contratación, 264, 272
Casas Viejas, 429
Caspe (Saragossa), 176
Castaños, Gen., 354, 370
Castelar, Emilio, 385, 386, 388, 391, 392, 393, 394, 397, 398, 408

casticismo, 135
Castilblanco, 428
Castile, Castilla, formation of, 80, 81, 82; Roderic, Count of C., 83; C. and Almanzor, 88, 97, 98; Fernán González and, 92, 95; rise of, 92, 93, 95 f.; kingdom of C., 101 f.; rivalry of C. and Leon, 117; union with Leon, 118; C. language, 81, 134; C. society, 135, 137; expansion of, 136, 137; 'New' C., 136; towns of C., *v. fueros, cortes,* 143; C. and Basques, 156; C. in 15th c., 183, 185, 186, 187; great revolt in, 210 f.; 279, 280, 281, 282; Olivares and C., 298, 299; in War of Sp. Succession, 322; Bourbon C., 366
Castinus, 53
castros, 41
Catalans, Catalonia, 27; Roman, 45; Frankish, v. Barcelona, Gerona, 81; applied to greater county of Barcelona, q.v.; 114; barons of, 129; expedition to Majorca, 129; merchant colonies, 132, 148; C. and kingdom of Aragon, 148 f.; C. and Pyrenean frontier, 150; C. seapower, 151, 152; C. in Greece, 153; support of Pedro IV, 154, 155; v. Aragon; distrust of Ferdinand I, 177; conflict with John II, 180, 181, 183; Philip II and C., 251; 283, 284; Olivares and C., 300, 301; 'Bloody Corpus', 301; revolution of, 301, 302, 303; French invade, 315; and evacuate, 315; sides with Archduke Charles, 322; curtailment of autonomy, 323, 324; opposition to Espartero, 376, 405; C. and federalism, 392, 393; C. and protection, 376, 398; Lliga, 398, 406, 411; Catalanism, 405, 406; Solidaridad, 411; C. demands, 417; P. de Rivera and C., 420, 422; 423; automony

INDEX

Catalans, Catalonia—*cont.*
 of, 426, 427, 428, 429, 433, 440;
 Civil War and C., 440, 441; C.
 Grand Company, 153
Cateau-Cambrésis, 232, 254
catharists, 129
Catherine of Aragon, 218, 229; C. of
 Braganza, 307; C. of Lancaster, 165,
 168, 169, 190
Catholic League, 225; 253
Cato, 37
Cazalla, Dr Agustín, 235
Cazorla, treaty of, 114, 129
Cecil, Sir E., 297
CEDA (Confederación Española de
 Derechas Autónomas), 430, 431
Celtiberia, 28, 31, 35, 38, 39, 40, 41,
 84
Celts, 27, 28, 32, 41, 42, 43
Cempsi, 27
censos, 275
Cephissos, battle of, 153
Cerda, Infantes de la, 139, 140, 141,
 144, 147
Cerdagne, Cerdaña, 150, 197, 312
Cerignola, 199
Cerisolas, 224
Cervantes, 244
Cervera, Adm., 401
Ceuta, held by Theudis, 55; C. and
 the Muslim conquest, 64; seized by
 'Abdu'r-Raḥman III, 86; by Granadines, 141; by Portuguese, 195;
 passes to Sp., 286; 341
Chamberga, 310, 311, 312, 338
Chamber of Castile, 270
chancillería, 167, 190
Charlemagne, 71, 81, 219
Charles I of Sp., V. of the Empire, 200,
 202, 203, 207 f., 266 f., 232, 233;
 II of Sp., 306, 309 f.; III, 330, 332,
 336 f.; IV, 336, 343 f.; 'V', v. Carlos
 Ma. Isidro; 'VI', 378, 390; 'VII',
 390, 442, 443; Ch. II, the Bad, of

Navarre, 157; III, the Noble, 157,
 158, 170, 179; Ch. VIII, of France,
 182, 197, 198; Ch. I, of England,
 297, 303, 306; II, 307; Ch., Archduke, Emperor Ch. VI, 315, 316,
 321, 322, 323, 331; Ch. of Anjou,
 150, 151; Ch. Martel, 67; *v.* Viana,
 Prince of
Chile, 261, 363, 383
Choiseul, 336, 340
Church, early ch. in Sp. 47 f.; Visigothic, 56, 57, 58, 59; Sp. ch. and
 Islam, 66; Roman reform, 105 f.;
 Reformation, 234, 235; Sp. ch. in
 16th c., 275, 276, 277; in 18th c.,
 334, 335; ch. property, 373, 377;
 378, 381, 382, 404, 407
Churchill, Sir W., 447
Ciano, Galeazzo, 445
Cid, Rodrigo Díaz de Bivar, 84, 107,
 108, 124
Cierva, Juan de la, 411, 416, 417, 418,
 419, 424
Cipango, 197, 255
citânias, 41, 44
Ciudad Real, 13, 144
Ciudad Rodrigo, 163, 359
Clavijo, battle of, 83
Clement VII, 217, 218, 219, 225;
 Clementine League, 218; XIII, 338
Clovis, 55
Clunia, Coruña del Conde, 54
Cluny, 105, 106, 115
CNT (Confederación Nacional del
 Trabajo), 416, 418, 425, 448
Cobos, Francisco de los, 269, 271
Cochin China, 382
Coimbra, 88; sacked, 97; reconquered
 by Ferd. I, 103, 135; capital of
 Portugal, 134; cortes of C., 165
coinage, of Córdoba, 74, 75; of
 Leon, 116; of Castile, 166, 167;
 291, 292
Colombia, 259, 261, 363

Columbus, 195, 196, 197, 255, 263
Communist Party, communism, 436, 440
Companys, Lluís, 428, 432, 433, 434
compromisarios, 340, 366
comuneros, 211, 212, 213
Concell de Cent, 148, 323
Concordat, of 1751, 335; C. of 1851, 378, 379
Condé, 303, 306, 307
Conservative Liberals, 396, 406
Constance of Burgundy, 106, 109
Constance, Council of, 156
Constantine, 48, 49
Constantinople, 55, 153, 178, 223
Constituent Assembly of 1873, 392
Constitution, of Cádiz, of 1812, 358, 359, 360, 364, 365, 366, 374, 378; of 1837, 374, 375, 378; of 1845, 377, 378, 382; of 1876, 395, 396, 404, 420, 423, 424, 430; of 1931, 426, 427, 429, 430, 431, 433, 434
conventus, 44, 104
conversos, *v.* New Christians
Corbeil, treaty of, 150, 180
Córdoba, Luis de, 342
Córdoba, 55, 57; Muslim capital, 68, 71, 72; revolt in, 73; govt. of, 74, 75; mozarabs of, 77; caliphate of C., 84 f.; overthrow of, 90; republic 90; ascendancy over N. Sp., 94 f.; Alf. the Battler at, 111; Alf. VII at, 112; annexed by Seville, 120, 121; Christians reconquer, 128, 129; municipality of, 138; declares for Henry II, 147; 280
Corduba, Córdoba, 43, 44
Coria (Cáceres), 112
Coronel, María, 302
corregidor, 168, 189, 212, 268, 269, 278, 292, 323, 340
Corsica, Aragonese claim to, 152, 153; 177
Cortés, Hernán, 219, 224, 256, 257, 258

Cortes, functions of, 116; origins in Leon, 116; of Valladolid, 1282, 139; of 1295, 141; c. and regency, 142; c. and legal system, 144; unified c. of Castile and Leon, 148; of Toro, 1369, 163; of Valladolid, 1385, 166; of 1386-90, 167, 168; of Madrid, 174; c.-towns, 185, 186, 187; of Toledo, 1480, 189; suspended, 190; demands for, 207; of Valladolid, 1518, 209; Charles V and c., 210 f., 215, 219, 223; Philip II and c., 234, 235, 236; in 16th c. 277, 278; under Philip III, 292; Philip IV, 308, 319; Bourbons and c., 324, 344; representation in, 365, 366; of Cádiz, 358, 364; of 1834, 370, 371; Constituent C., 1869, 387, 388; 391, 404, 424; Constituent C., 1931, 426, 430; c. of 1933, 430, 431; 447; c. of Aragon, 117; General Cortes, 148, 236; of Egea, 1265, 149; of Saragossa, 1283, 1286, 151; 177, 183, 186; Philip II and c. of A., 236, 248; c. of Tarazona, 1592, 250, 283 f.; of Barbastro, 1626, 298; 324; c. of Catalonia, 117, 148; c. of Navarre, 324; c. of Valencia, 117, 148, 289; c. of Bayonne, 353, 358, 363; c. of Cádiz, 358, 359, 363
Corunna, La Coruña, 165
Costa Rica, 262
Council, royal, *v. curia*, 166, 189, 190, 267, 268, 269, 325; c. of Aragon, 270, 283; c. of Castile, 264, 270, 272, 324, 340, 355, 366, 367; c. of Finance, 271, 310, 313, 325; c. of the Indies, 264, 271, 272; c. of the Inquisition, 270, 271; Councils of the church, *v.* Constance, Pisa, Toledo, Trent, 216, 217, 220, 225
Covadonga, 69
Crato, Antonio, Prior of, 246, 253
Crépy, peace of, 224, 225

INDEX 461

Crete, 73, 76
Crô-Magnon, 16
Cromwell, 306
Croy, Guillaume de, Ld. of Chievres, 208
crusade, 108, 115, 118
cruzada, 236, 243, 272, 277
Cuba, 255, 330, 331, 337, 383, 393, 400, 401, 406
Cueva, Beltrán de la, 174
curatores, 47
curia, 116, 269
Cuzco, 258, 259, 260
Cyprian, St., 48
Cyprus, 244, 245

DAMASCUS, caliphate of, 67; separation of Sp. from, 70, 71
Damasus, Pope, 49
Daoiz and Velarde, 352
Daroca (Saragossa), 111
Dato, Eduardo, 414, 416, 417, 418
Decius, 48
defensor, 47, 61
Democrats, 381, 384, 387, 414
Denia (Alicante), 120, 214
Despacho Universal, 313, 320
Deza, Pedro de, 242, 243
Dias, Bartolomeu, 196
Díaz, Froilán, 317
Díaz de Bivar, R., *v.* Cid
Díaz de Montalvo, Alfonso, 189
Díaz de Solís, Juan, 262, 264
Diego Gelmírez, 110
Diego Peláez, 109
Di'n-Nun, banu, 120
Diocletian, 46, 47
diputados del común, 340
Directorate, 420
'Disaster', 1898, 394, 402, 425
diwan, 74
Dominicans, 273, 275, 276

Dominican Republic, *v.* Santo Domingo, 383
Domingo, Marcelino, 425, 426
Doria, Andrea, 219, 221
Douro, 54; evacuation of D. valley, 68, 70; reconquest of, 93
Drake, Sir F., 246, 252
Dunes, battle of the, 287
Dunkirk, 303, 307
Durango, 439
Dutch, *v.* Netherlands, Low Countries, 239, 251, 252, 286; peace with, 287, 288, 292, 293; renewal of war, 1621, 296, 297; 306

EBRO river, 43, 44, 45; Muslims and E. valley, 70; reconquest of, 111
Eburones, 27
Economic Societies, 334
Ecuador (Quito), 261
Edward III, 146; VI, 229
Egica, 62, 63
Egidio, Dr., 235
Egilona, 67
Egmont, Count of, 238, 239
Egypt, 84, 86
Eibar (Guipúzcoa), 439
Elcano, Juan Sebastián de, 256
Elche, Lady of, 38
Eleanor, dau. of Henry II of England, 113, 137
Elipandus, metropolitan of Toledo, 80
Elizabeth I of England, 246, 251, 252, 253, 286, 288; E. Farnese, Q. of Sp., 326, 327, 328, 329, 330, 332, 336; E. of Valois, 232
Elvas, 307
Elvira, Granada, 48, 49, 90, 119, 121; Council of E., 48
Emerita, Mérida, 44, 45
Empecinado, El, 359

emperor, title of, 83, 91, 101, 106, 113, 138
Encobert, El, 214
encomiendas, 264, 265
Eneco Arista, 82
England, *v.* William the Conqueror, Henry II; E. and Castile, 145 f., 163 f.; Charles V and E., 209, 224, 228, 229; E. and the Dutch, 239; E. and Portugal, 246, *v.* Anglo-Portuguese Alliance; *v.* Elizabeth I; James I; Commonwealth and Sp., 306, 307; Charles II, 307; E. and War of Sp. Succession, 321 f.; *v.* Gibraltar, 329; E. and Sp. America, 331, 336, 340, 341; E. and Sp. Marriages, 378, 379; E. and Moroccan question, 411, 412; Non-Intervention, 435, 436.
Ensenada, Zenon Somodevilla, Marquis of la, 332
Epila, battle of, 154, 183
Ermesinda, 69
Erwig, 62
Escobedo, Juan de, 247, 249
Escoiquiz, Canon, 346, 348, 350, 360
Escorial, El, 232, 279, 317
Espartero, Gen. Baldomero, Duke of la Victoria, 371, 372, 374, 375, 376, 377, 381, 388, 396
Espinosa, Diego de, 242, 270
Esquilache, *v.* Squillace
Eugene of Savoy, Prince, 321
Eulogius, 77
Euric, 54; code of 55, 57
exaltados, 364, 373, 377; progressists
Extremadura, 44, 115, 262

FADRIQUE, K. of Sicily, 152
FAI (Federación Anarquista Ibérica), 425
Falange, *v.* Phalanx
falcata, 40
Falkland Islands, 340

Family (Com-) Pact, 330, 332, 335, 336, 340, 344
Farinelli, 332
Fatimids, 84, 86
federalism, 387, 388, 392, 393, 428, 429, 432, 437
Félix of Urgel, 80
Ferdinand, I, first K. of Castile, 99, 100, 101, 103, 104, 121; II, of Leon, 113, 114, 115, 116, 117; III, St. F., of Leon and Castile, 117, 118, 126, 128, 130, 131, 132, 133, 137, 191; IV, 'el Emplazado', 140, 141, 159; V (II of Aragon), 163, 176, 179, 180, 181, 183 f.; VI, 332 f.; VII, 348, 349 f.; F. I of Aragon, 'of Antequera', 160, 168, 169, 170, 176; II, V of Sp.; F., K. of Portugal, 163, 164, 165; F., I of Naples, 178, 179, 198; II, 197, 198; F., Infante, Emperor F. I, 203, 215, 220, 221, 225, 227, 228, 229, 234; F., Cardinal-Infante, 299, 303
Fernán González, 92, 94, 95, 96
Fernández de Córdoba, Gonzalo, the Grand Captain, 198, 199, 201
Fernando de la Cerda, 139
Ferrer, Francisco, 412
Fez, 411, 414
Figueras, Estanislau, 391, 393
Five Kingdoms, 104, 132, 134
Flor, Roger de, 153
Floridablanca, José, Moñino, Count of, 338, 343, 344, 355
Fortún, 66, 77
France, relations with Aragon, 129, 132, 150; aids Infantes de la Cerda, 140, 141; alliance with Castile, 145, 146, 147, 163; F. and Navarre, 174; F. and Italy, 178, 197; F. and Catalonia, 180, 181; F. and Charles V, 209, 216, 217, 218, 219; Turkish alliance, 220, 221, 222 f.; peace of Cateau-Cambrésis, 232, 233; Philip

INDEX 463

France, relations with Aragon—*cont.*
II and F., 251, 252, 253, 254; marriage of Louis XIII to Ana of Austria, 289; French wars of 17th c., 299, 300, 306, 309, 312, 313, 314; F. and Sp. Succession, 316, 317, 318, 319, 320; F. and War of Sp. Succession, 321 f.; F. and Family Pacts, 330, 332; rivalry with England, 335, 340, 341; F. crisis and Sp., 344, 345; Napoleonic Wars, 346 f.; intervention against Sp. liberals, 367; F. and Quadruple Alliance, 371; F. and Sp. Marriages, 378, 379; Napoleon III, 383; F. and Morocco, 411, 414; F. and Sp. Civil War, 438
Franche-Comté, 200, 285, 309, 312, 313
Francis I of France, 202, 209, 216, 217, 218, 221, 222, 223, 224, 225, 227
Franciscan missions in Morocco, 131
Francisco de Asís, K.-consort, 379, 380; F. de Paula, Infante, 352, 378
Franco Bahamonde, Gen. Francisco, 436, 438, 440, 442, 445, 446, 447, 448, 449, 450
Franks, 46, 55, 56, 67, 70, 71, 78, 81, 82
Franqueza, Pedro, 291
Frederick of Prussia, 332
Free Companies, 146
freemasonry, 334, 361, 364
Fruela, 79
Fuenterrabía (Guipúzcoa), 217, 299
fueros, statute-law, charters, 'rights', of Castile, 138, 139, 140, 142, 144, 149, 189, 190, 211; f. of Aragon, 149, 236, 246, 248, 249, 311, 323, 324; f. of Basques, 156, 157, 299, 324, 340, 371, 375, 397, 437, 443; f. of Catalonia, 148, 298, 306, 323, 324; f. of Valencia, 324; F. Juzgo, 79, 138, 144, 211; f. real, 138, 144
Fuggers, 209
fusionism, 390, 397

GAETA, 178, 199
Gadir, Gades, Cádiz, 28, 30, 31, 32, 34, 44, 45
Galaici, Galacia v. Galicia
Galib, 85, 86, 87, 88, 98
Galicia, 'Celticness' of, 28; Roman, 41; province of, 44; Christianity in, 49, 50; Vandals and Suevi in, 52 f.; attached to Austurias, 70; attacked by Norsemen, 76; resettled, 79; cult of St. James, 80; recovers Tuy, 83; Ordoño, K. of Galicia, 92; troubles in, 96, 97; Vikings in, 97; kingdom of, 103, 104, 105; re-attached to Leon, 106, 109; supports Alf. VII, 110, 111; in resettlement of Andalusia, 133; absorption of mudejares, 134; royal law in, 138; loyalty to Pedro I, 146, 147, 163; unrepresented in cortes, 187, 210; in 16th c., 279, 322; autonomy, 429
Gallipoli, 153
Gama, Vasco da, 197
Gárcel, El, (Almeria), 22, 23
García, K. of Leon, 92; K. of Galicia, 103, 105, 106, 109; G. Sánchez, K. of Navarre, 94; G. the Tremulous, 98; G. Sánchez, 100, 101; G. Ramírez, K. of Aragon, 111, 112, 156; G. Fernández, Count of Castile, 93, 97, 98; G. Sánchez, 99; G. Jiménez, 107
García Prieto, Manuel, 416, 417, 419, 424
Gascones, Gascony, 82, 105, 114, 137, 157
Gattinara, Mercurino, 210, 215, 216, 217, 218, 219, 222
Gelves, Los, Jerba, 201, 243
General Cortes, of Aragon, *v.* cortes
General Privilege of Aragon, 151, 154
Generalife (Granada), 159
Generalitat, 180, 181, 300, 429, 432, 433, 434, 440

Genoa, Genoese, 112, 129, 132, 133, 143, 153, 169, 177, 178, 201, 216, 219, 221, 245
Germaine of Foix, 200
germania, 213, 214
Germans, Germany, 27, 28; 435, 440, 444, 445, 446, 447
Gerona, 71, 81, 180, 314, 315
Gerticos, 60
Ghent, 223
Gibraltar, Almohads and G., 125; won by Castile, 141; lost, 143, 159; reconquered, 192; taken by English, 322, 323, 326; 332, 335; siege of, 342; 399, 411, 444, 445, 446
Gil Robles, José Ma., 430, 431, 432, 433, 434, 450
Giral, José, 448, 449
Giralda (Seville), 131
Girón, Pedro, 212, 213
Giudice, Cardinal del, 325
glaciation, 14, 15, 20
Godoy, Manuel, 344, 345, 346, 347, 348, 349, 350
Goering, Gen. H., 444
Goletta, 221, 222
Golpejera, battle of, 105
Gomes da Silva, Rui, Prince of Eboli, 231, 237, 247
Gondomar, Count, 297
González Bravo, Luis, 381, 386, 390
Gonzalo, Count of Ribagorza and Sobrarbe, 111
Gor (Granada), 25
Goths, 49; *v.* Visigoths
Goya, 333, 343
Gracchus, T. Sempronius, 39
Granada, *v.* Elvira, 14; Byzantine, 57; Zirid (Sanhaja) kingdom of, 90, 108, 119, 120, 121, 122; under Almoravids, 124; under banu Hud, 124, 125; under Almohads, 125; seized by ibn Mardanish, 126;

Naṣrids of, 130, 131; abet Muslim revolt, 139; alliance with Marinids, 139, 143; aid Pedro I, 147; Naṣrid G., 158, 159, 160, 161; 168, 169; John II's campaign against G., 170, 173; Henry IV's campaign, 173; War of Granada, 191, 192, 193, 194; moriscos of, 240 f.; 280
Grand Alliance, 321, 322
grandes, grandees, 273, 286, 320, 323
Granja, La, 327; sergeants' revolt at, 374
Granvelle, Granvela, 220; 238, 269
Graus, 111
Gravelines, 232, 303
Gravesend, 164
Gravettians, 17
Great Schism, 155
Greece, Catalans in, 153
Greeks, 30, 31, 33, 38
greffa, 61
Gregory VII, 109; X, 139, 150; XVI, 379; G., Bishop of Elvira, 49
Grijalba, 256
Grimaldi, 337
Guadalajara, 439
Guadalete, battle of the, 65
Guadalquivir, 16, 24, 26, 30, 31, 32, 43, 44, 67, 76
Guadiana, 43, 45
Guadix (Granada), 25
Guatemala, 258, 261
Guesclin, Bertrand du, 146
guerrilleros, 357, 359, 362, 365, 371
guilds, 186, 211, 212, 213, 214, 215, 281
Guimarãis, 134
Guinea, 195
Guipúzcoa, 156, 274; G. Company, 330
Guise, Duke of, 251, 253
Guizot, F., 379
Gundared, 97
Guyenne, Duke of, 176

INDEX

HABUS, K. of Granada, 121
Hadrian, 45, 46
ḥajib, 74, 88, 119
al-Hakam I, 72, 73, 75; II, 86, 87
Hamilcar Barca, 31, 32
Hammudites, 90, 120
Hannibal, 31, 35, 39
d'Harcourt, Marquis, 302, 316, 320
Haro, Luis de, 302, 307, 308
Harrach, Count von, 315, 316
Hasdrubal, 31, 32, 35
Hemeroskopeion, Ifach, 31
Henry, I, of Castile, 118; II of Castile and Leon, Trastámara, 144, 145, 146, 147, 155, 162, 163, 164; 167; III, 157, 166, 167, 168, 169, 186, 190; IV, 171, 172, 173, 174, 175, 176, 180, 181, 185, 187, 190; Cardinal-K. of Portugal, 245; II, of France, 227, 232; III, 253; IV, 253, 254, 288; II of England, 113, 114; VIII, 209, 218, 229; H. of Burgundy, Count of Portugal, 109, 110; H. 'the Senator', Infante, 141; H., Duke of Seville, Infante, 379, 388; H., 'the Navigator', Infante of Portugal, 195; H., Infante, son of Ferd. I of Aragon, 170, 172, 173, 179; H., Duke of Lancaster, 145
Hercules, 34
hermandades, 140, 175, 185, 188, 189, 207, 212, 213
Hermenegild, 57
Hernández de Córdoba, 256
hidalgos, hidalguía, 209, 211, 212, 274
Higueruela, battle of the, 170
Hildebrand, 106, 109
Hisham I, 72; II, 86, 87, 88, 90, 120; III, 90
Hispalis, Seville, 44
Hispaniae, 37
Hispaniola, 196, 197, 255
'Hispanity', 444, 446
Hitler, Adolf, 439, 445, 446

Holland, *v.* Dutch, 240, 285, 312
Holy Junta, 212; H. League, 201, 202; 223
Honduras, 197, 261, 331, 336, 337, 341
Honorius, 51, 52
Hosius, 49
banu Hud, 112, 120, 124, 125, 128
Huesca, 111, 118
Huéscar, Duke of, 335
Huguenots, 253, 254, 299
Hurtado de Mendoza, Diego, 214; 227
Hydatius of Chaves, 53, 58

IACETANI, 37
Iberians, 26, 28, 37, 38, 39, 40
Ibiza, 130, 322
Idrisids, 85, 86
Ifriqiya, 86, 121, 133
Iglesias, Pablo, 407, 408, 412, 425
Ignatius of Loyola, St., 231, 276
Ilipa, Alcalá del Río, 37
Incas, 258, 259, 260
Independence, War of, the 'Peninsular War', 352 f.
Indo-Europeans, 27, 28, 30, 38, 40
Indortes, 31
infanzonía, 93
Ingunda, 57
Innocent III, 117
Inquisition, 190, 191, 234, 235, 236, 237; I. and the moriscos, 241, 242; I. and Aragon, 249, 250; Council of the I., 270, 271; 272, 273, 276, 317, 319, 325, 334, 339; suppression of, 355, 365
Irenaeus, St., 48
Isabella, I, 163, 172, 175, 176, 181, 183 f., 208; II, 368, 370, 374, 375, 376 f., I. of Bourbon, 289; I.-Clara-Eugenia, 287, 299
Isidore, St., 58, 59, 62, 77, 121
Istolatius, 31
Istúriz, 373, 374, 378

Italica, 45
Italy, Aragon and I., *v.* Naples; Franco-Sp. rivalry in, 197 f.; Charles V and I., 215 f., 228; 232, 233

JACA, 81, 82, 134, 149,
Jaén, 131, 139, 160, 173
Jamaica, 197, 306
James, St., 80; v. Santiago
James I of Aragon, 126, 129, 130, 139, 149, 150; II, 141, 151, 152, 153; I of England, 288, 297; II, 314; 'III', 327; 'III' of Sp., 413; 'Jaimists', Carlists, 414; J. of Majorca, 150, 151
Jenkins, Captain, 331
Jerez (Cádiz), 125, 139
Jerome, St., 49
Jesus, Society of, Jesuits, 238, 248, 273, 276, 334, 337, 338; reductions, 337, 341; 355, 373, 380, 387, 410, 427
Jews, 47, 48; Visigothic anti-semitism, 62, 63; in al-Andalus, 74, 75; of Granada, 119, 121, 122, 126; Andalusian, 136; tax-gatherers, 140, 144, 147; repression of Judaism, 167, 168, 169; Inquisition and J., 190, 191; expulsions, 191; Sp. J. and Inquisition, 234; 282
Jiménez de Cisneros, *v.* Ximénez
Jiménez de Quesada, Gonzalo, 261
Jiménez de Rada, Rodrigo, 117, 118
João das Regras, 165
Joan II, Q. of Navarre, 157; Joana of Portugal, 173, 174, 176; J. of Naples, 177
Jordana, Gen. Count, 443, 445, 447
John, Order of St., 111, 114, 115
John I, 164, 165, 166; II, 169, 170, 171, 172, 173; J. I of Portugal, 165; II, 196; IV, 301, 303; J. I of Aragon, 155; II, 158, 170, 173, 174, 176,

177, 178, 179, 180, 181, 182, 183; J. 'of Tarifa', 140, 141, 142; J. 'el Tuerto', 142; J. of Austria, son of Charles V, 237, 240, 243, 244, 245; J. of A., son of Philip IV, Juan José, 303, 307, 308, 309, 310, 311, 312, 313, 324; J. of Lancaster, 163, 164, 165; J. of Bíclaro, 58
josefinos, 362
Joseph Bonaparte, 350, 353 f., 363
Jovellanos, Melchor, 346, 355, 357
Jovinus, 52
Juan, Infante, 199, 214
Juan Manuel, Infante, 142; J. M. of Belmonte, 200, 207
Juana, dau. of Ferd. and Isabella, 'the Mad', 199, 200, 202, 207, 209, 212, 230, 237; J. Enríquez, Q. of Aragon, 173, 179, 180; J., dau. of Henry IV, 174, 175, 176, 187, 188
Julian, governor of Ceuta, 64
Julius II, Pope, 201; III, 227
junds, 68, 71, 119
Junot, Gen. A., 348, 354
juros, 233, 234, 274, 325
Justicia of Aragon, 150, 151, 154, 178, 247, 249, 250, 251
Justinian, 55, 58, 60, 167

KHALAF, 120
ibn al-Khaṭib, 159
Khayran, 120
Khindaswinth, 60, 62
Khintila, 59, 60
Kinsale, 288
'kingdoms' from taifas, 186
kura, 74

LABOUR, 404, 406, 407, 408, 415, 421, 422, 436
labradores, 186, 212, 213
Lamtunas, 123

INDEX 467

Landrécy, 224
Largo Caballero, Francisco, 425, 426, 433, 436, 438, 440
Lateran Council, 167
Law, royal, 137, 138, 143, 144, 145, 167, 189; L. of Jurisdictions, 409, 411; L. of Succession, 449
League of Nations, 421, 435
Leander, St., 57, 58
Leganés, Marquis of, 302
Legio, Leon, 44, 45, 47, 66
legists, 145, 166, 167
Leire, 82
Lens, 303
Leo IX, 105; X, 201, 216, 217, 277; XIII, 442
León, *v. Legio*; 48, 69; entered by Alf. I, 70; resettled, 83; destroyed by Almanzor, 88; kingdom of L., 91 f.; joined with Castile, 101, 106; separated, 103, 113; aspirations of, 113, 114; military Orders, 114, 115; cortes, 116; L. and Castile, 117; union of, 118, 132; society of L., 135
Leonor de Guzmán, 143, 144
Leopold I, of Austria, 315, 321; L. of Hohenzollern-Sigmaringen, 388
Leovigild, 57, 58
Lepanto, battle of, 224, 244, 252
Lérida, 118, 181, 302, 303, 440
Lerma, Duke of, 286 f.
Lerroux, Alejandro, 406, 411, 416, 425, 426, 430, 431, 432
Leyes de Estilo, 144
Leyva, Antonio de, 222
Liber iudiciorum, 60
Liberal Union, 381, 382, 383, 384, 386, 387, 388, 396
Libyans, 31, 32
Lima, 260, 364
Linhares, Count of, 300
Liria, 38
Lisbon, attacked by Suevi, 53; by Norsemen, 76; raided by Alf. II, 80; expedition against, 95, 97; conquest of, 115; capital of Portugal, 134, 163; falls to Alba, 246; Drake at, 246, 252; Restoration of Portuguese independence, 301; earthquake, 337
Liuva, 58
Llano Ponte, Canon, 353
Llantada, battle of, 105
Lliga, 398, 406, 411, 433
Loaysa, Cardinal, 220
Logroño, 83, 114, 354
Lope Díaz de Haro, 140
Louis the Pious, 81; IX, St. L., 139, 150; XI, 174, 180, 181, 188; XII, 198, 199; XIII, 289, 301, 302; XIV, 302, 307, 309, 312, 314, 315, 316, 317, 319, 320; XV, 327, 328, 340; XVI, 343, 344, 345; XVIII, 367; L.-Philippe, 371, 379
Low Countries, v. Netherlands, 200, 238
Lucena, 192
Lugo, 85
Luis, K. of Sp., 327, 328
Luisa-Carlota, Infanta, 369; L.-Fernanda, Infanta, Duchess of Montpensier, 378, 386; L.-Isabel of Orleans, 327, 328
Luna, Alvaro de, Constable of Castile, 170, 171, 172, 173, 185, 295; Pedro de L., v. Benedict XIII
Lusitania, Lusitanians, 40, 41, 44, 45, 48, 49; Alans in, 52; Visigoths in, 54; 58
Luther, Martin, 216, 217, 226; Lutheranism in Sp., 235; in Netherlands, 237, 238
Luxemburg, 224, 314

MACANAZ, 325, 326, 334
Maciá, Col., 422
McKinley, President W., 400, 401

468 INDEX

Madina az-Zahra', 85, 90
Madrid, 174; Francis I imprisoned at, 217; treaty of M., 218; capital of Sp., 232, 279, 322; riots of, 1766, 338; 342, 343; 'Dos de Mayo', 352, 353
Madrigal, 188
Magalhāis, Fernão de, Magellan, 255, 256
Magdalenians, 15, 17, 18, 19, 20
Magrib, Morocco, 68, 71, 86, 133, 159, 160
Mahdi, 125
Mainaké, 31
Maipú (Chile), battle of, 363
Majorca, 25; reconquest of, 129; 150, 151; incorporated into Aragon, 154; germania in, 214, 215
Majorianus, 53
Malaca, Málaga, 30, 45, 46
Málaga, taken by Sanhaja, 90, 119, 120, 121, 122; in War of Granada, 192, 193; 439
Malik ibn Anas, 72
Malta, siege of, 243
al-Ma'mun of Toledo, 105, 106
mancomunidades, 413, 417, 420
manifestacion, 247
Manfred of Sicily, 150
Manila, 337, 401
Manoel I, K. of Portugal, 217, 246
al-Manṣur, v. Almanzor
Mantua, Duke of, 293, 299; Duchess of, 300, 301
Manuel de Melo, Francisco, 303
Marañón, Gregorio, 425
Margaret of Parma, 233, 238; Margarita-Teresa, 315
María de Molina, 140, 141, 142; M.-Amalia of Saxony, 336; Ma.-Cristina of Naples, 368, 369, 370, 373, 374, 375, 376, 378, 381; Ma.-Cristina of Hapsburg-Lorraine, 397, 399, 408; Ma.-Luisa of Savoy, 320, 324; Ma.-Luisa of Orleans, 313, 314; Ma.-Luisa of Parma, 343, 344, 345, 346, 348; Ma.-Teresa, dau. of Philip IV, 303, 315, 318; Ma. I of Portugal, 341; II, 371; Ma. Teresa, Empress, 329, 332; Ma. de Padilla, 144, 145, 163
Mariana of Austria, 303, 307, 309, 310, 311, 312, 313, 314, 315
banu Marin, Marinids, 132, 139, 140, 143, 158, 159, 160, 162
Marineo Sículo, 277
Maroto, Gen. Rafael, 372, 374
Marrakesh, 114, 123, 125
ibn Mardanish, 126
Marseilles, 129, 217
Martin of Dume, St., 53, 56, 58
Martin, K. of Aragon, 155, 156; M. the Younger, 155, 156
Martí, José, 400
Martínez Campos, Gen. Arsenio, 393, 395, 400
Martínez de la Rosa, Francisco, 370, 372
ibn Marwan, 77
Mary Tudor, 229, 230, 232, 235; M., Q. of Scots, 251; M., sister of Charles V, 222
Masaniello, 303
Masséna, Gen. A., 357
Mastia, Mastieni, 32
Maura, Antonio, 408, 409, 411, 412, 416, 417, 418, 419; Miguel M., 425, 426, 427
Mauregato, 79
Mauretania, 46, 67, v. Morocco, Magrib
Maurice of Saxony, 226, 227
Maximilian I, Emperor, 198, 199, 200, 201, 202, 209, 210; II, 228, 229; M. of Mexico, 383
Mazarin, 306, 307
Mazarredo, Adm., 346, 347
Medinaceli, 39, 85, 87, 88, 95; Duke of M., 311, 313, 314

INDEX

Medina del Campo, 211, 212, 279
Medina Sidonia, Duke of, 301
Melilla, 86, 341, 418, 419
Mélito, Count of, 214
Melkart, 34
Méndez Núñez, Adm. Casto, 383
Mendizábal, Juan Alvarez, 373, 377
Mendoza, Cardinal, 187; Antonio de, 257; Pedro de, 262
Mérida, v. *Emerita*; conquered by Muslims, 65, 66; Berber revolts, 71; defies Córdoba, 72; Christians of, 77
meseta, 13, 14, 26, 27
Mesolithic, 20, 21
Mesta, 280
Metz, 224, 227
Mexico, 233, 256, 257, 258, 263, 265, 383, 447
Miaja, Gen. José, 441
Miguel da Paz, Infante, 199; Dom M., 371
Milan, Milanese, Duke of, 178; 198, 201, 202; Charles V and M., 216, 217, 218, 222, 224; Philip II and M., 224, 225; 233, 270, 285; link with Austria, 293; 313; loss of, 322, 323; 332; Edict of M., 48
Millares, Los, (Almería), 15, 16, 23, 24, 25, 42
Mina, 195
Minorca, 129; held by English, 322, 323, 326, 329, 332, 335, 341; lost, 342; 347
Miraflores, Marquis of, 384
moderados, 364, 374, 375, 376, 377, 380, 381, 389, 396, 397; v. Conservative Liberals
Mohács, battle of, 220
Mola, Gen. Emilio, 436, 438, 439, 442
Moluccas, 219, 256
Mondéjar, Marquises of, 241, 242, 243

Montemar, Duke of, 330
Montemolín, Count of, Charles 'VI', 378
Montero Ríos, Eugenio, 409, 410
Montes Claros, 308
Montezuma, 256, 257
Montferrat, 293, 299
Montiel, 147, 163
Montpellier, 150
Montpensier, Duke, Duchess of, 379, 386, 387, 388, 389, 399
Monzón, 283, 298, 302
Morella, 130
Moret, Segismundo, 409, 410, 413
Moriscos, Muslims treated as Christians, 240 f., 289 f.
Morocco, v. Magrib; 64; al-Andalus and M., 85; Almoravids, 107, 108, 123; Almohads, 114, 125; Ferd., III and M., 128, 131, 132, 137; Marinid M., 132 f.; trade of, 133, 140; last M. invasion of Sp., 143; M. and Naṣrid Granada, 158 f.; defeat of Sebastian in, 245; O'Donnell's campaign in, 382, 383; French expansion in, 399, 411; Sp. and M., 411, 412, 415, 418, 419, 420, 421, 444
Móstoles, alcalde of, 353
Moura, Cristóvão de, 246, 285, 286
Mozarabs, Christians living under Muslim rule, 72, 74, 76, 77, 93, 114, 124, 136; m. church, 77
Mudéjares, Muslims living under Christian rule, 134, 136, 137; Aragonese, 149; Navarrese, 157; 175, 185; Valencian, 213, 214; then, Moriscos
Muhammad, 64; M. I of Córdoba, 77, 83; II, 89; M. ibn al-Aḥmar, first Naṣrid K. of Granada, 130, 158; II, 140, 141, 158, 159; III, 141, 159; IV, 159; V, 160, 163; VI, 160; VII, 160, 170; VIII, 160; IX, 173

Muhlberg, battle of, 226
al-Mujahid, 120
Mulay Hasan, 173, 192, 193
Munda, Montilla, 42
municipia, 44; collapse of, 61
Muñoz, Fernando, Duke of Riánsares, 373
Munusa, 69
Murat, Gen. Joachim, 349, 350, 352, 353
Murcia, 67; opposes Almoravids, 112; assigned to Castile, 114; M. and taifas, 120, 122, 126, 128; capitulates to Castile, 130; removal of Mozarabs, 136; Muslim revolt in, 139; attacked by Granadines, 169; 174, 186
Muret, Battle of, 129, 150
al-Muṣhafi, 87
Musa ibn Nuṣair, 64, 65, 66
Mussolini, 421, 440, 445
al-Muʻtadid, 120, 121
al-Muʻtamid, 107, 108, 122, 123, 124
Mutarrif, 82
muwalladun, converts to Islam, 72, 78, 120, 135

NÁJERA, battle of, 146
Naples, Aragonese connection with, 150; conquest, 177, 178; Aragonese house of, 198; French attack on, 197; Ferd. V seizes, 198, 199; Charles V, 216; French claim, 218, 219, 221; Philip II, K. of, 270; Masaniello, 303; loss of, 323; returned to Charles (III), 330; passes to his brother, 336; French enter, 346
Napoleon, 346, 347, 348, 349, 350, 353 f.; III, 383, 388, 389
Narbonne, 55
Narváez, Pánfilo de, 257; Gen. Ramón, 374, 375, 376, 377, 379, 380, 382, 384, 385, 386, 391, 396, 407

Naṣr, 141, 159
Naṣrids, Ks. of Granada, 130, 131, 143, 159 f., 191, 192
National Guard, 372, 436; N. Socialism, 435, 443; N. Socialist Juntas, 442; N. Syndicalism, 445, 447, 448
Navarre, 27; Pompey in, 43; Charlemagne and, 71; growth of, 81, 82; v. Pamplona; county of, 82; attacked by ʻAbduʼr-Raḥman III, 85, 94; kingdom of, 91, 93, 94; invades Castile, 96, 99; house of, 91, 98, 99, 100, 101 f.; attached to Aragon, and separated, 111, 112, 156; seizes Rioja, 113; N. and France, 132, 157; mudéjares of, 134; Alf. X and N., 137; medieval N., 156, 157, 158; succession of, John II, 170, 173 f.; Castile and, 174; John II and, 178, 179; Ferd. V annexes, 202; French in, 213; 429
Navas de Tolosa, Las, 118, 126, 127, 129
Neanderthaloids, 16
Negrín, Juan, 438, 440, 441
Nelson, 347
Neolithic, 21, 22, 23
Nervii, 28
Netherlands, v. Low Countries, Dutch; 208, 215, 222, 223, 224, 225; attached to Sp., 228, 229, 230, 233, 234; religious question, 237; revolt of, 238, 239, 252; rule of Alb. and Isabella, 287, 296; 309, 310
New Carthage, Cartagena, 32, 35, 37
New Castile, 136
New Christians, 168, 190, 191, 234, 235, 273
New Plan, 324
New Spain, v. Mexico
Ney, 354
Nicaea, Council of, 49
Nicholas, IV, Pope, 152
Nile, battle of, 346

Nimwegen, peace of, 313, 315
Niño, Pero, 169
Nithard, Fr. Eberhard, 309, 310, 313
Non-Intervention, 435, 438, 439
Nordlingen, battle of, 299
Norsemen, 76
Noyon Conference, 439
Núñez de Balboa, Vasco, 255
Numantia, 39

OCILIS, Medinaceli, 39
O'Donnell, Gen. Leopoldo, 376, 380, 381, 382, 384, 385, 386, 390, 396, 407
Odysseia, 31
Ofalia, Count of, 374
Olavide, Pablo de, 339
Oliva, Abbot, 105
Olivares, 294 f.
Olmedo, 172, 175, 179
Olot, 13
Olózaga, Salustiano de, 377, 381, 384
Oporto, 41, 70
Oran, 201, 221, 286, 290, 322, 330, 341, 399, 445
Orders, Military, 126, 143, 173, 185, 189, 210, 213, 218, 272, 275, 280
Ordoño I, K. of Leon, 83; II, 94; III, 95, 97; IV, 'the Bad', 96
O'Reilly, Alexander, 339, 341
Orellana, 261, 262
Oretani, 32
Orihuela (Murcia), 67
Oropesa, Count of, 314, 315
Orry, Jean, 325, 326, 334
Ortega y Gasset, José, 425
Osca, Huesca, 42
Ostend, 287, 329
Ostrogoths, 55
Osuna, Dukes of, 294; 320
Otranto, 223
Oviedo, 79, 83, 353, 432

PACHECO, Juan, 172, 174, 175, 176
Pachs, Pedro, 214
Padilla, Juan de, 211, 212, 213
Palaces (Almería), 23
Palaeolithic, 16, 17
Palamós, 219, 315
palatium, 61
Pallantia, Palencia, 52
Pallars, Count of, 180, 181
Palma de Mallorca, 214, 215, 438
Palmela, 24
Palmerston, Ld., 371, 379
Palos, 196, 263
Pamplona (Navarre), founded by Pompey, 42; Visigothic, 54; Franks enter, 55; Muslims garrison, 70; Charlemagne and, 71; alliance with banu Qasi, 78; 81, 82; county of P., 82, 84, 94, 98; *v.* kingdom of Navarre; 173, 349
Panama, 255
Paraguay, 262
Parpalló (Valencia), 17
Pardo, pact of El, 397
parias, tribute, 103, 105, 106, 107
Paris, 200, 224; Spaniards enter, 253, 254; treaty of P., 1763, 337
Parma, Dukes of, 329, 346
pase foral, 156, 157
Paso Honroso, 171
Passau, 227
Patiño, José, 328, 329, 330, 332
Patriotic Union, 422, 423
Patrocinio, Sor, 379
Paul, St., 47; P. III, Pope, 222, 225, 227; IV, 230, 231, 232, 234, 273
Paulus Orosius, 54, 58
Pavia, battle of, 217; 224
Pavía, Gen. Manuel, 393, 394, 435
Pedro, K. of Castile; 144, 145, 146, 147, 155, 160; P. I of Aragon, 111; II, 129; III, 146, 150, 151; IV, the 'Ceremonious', 153, 154, 155, 177,

Pedro, K. of Castile—*cont.*
183; P. the regent, 142; P., Constable of Portugal, 181
Pelayo, 69, 79
Pelendones, 27, 28, 39
Peloponnese, 221
Peninsular War, War of Independence, 352 f.
Peñíscola (Castellón), 126, 155
Pérez, Antonio, 246, 247, 248, 249, 250; P. de Guzmán, 140
Peris, Vicente, 214
Pernambuco, 296
Perpignan, 182, 302, 345
Persia, 221, 286
Petronila, 112
Peru, 215, 233, 258 f., 265, 363, 383
Phalanx, Falange, 430, 442, 443, 444, 445, 447, 448, 449, 450
Phenobastuli, 32
Philip I, of Castile, 199, 200, 202, 207, 210; II, of Spain, 215, 224, 228, 229, 230 f., 267 f., 285; III, 285 f.; IV, 289, 294 f.; V. 319 f.; Ph. IV, of France, 140; Ph., regent, 142, 143
Philippa of Lancaster, Q. of Portugal, 165
Philippine Islands, 256, 286, 330, 337, 400, 401
Phocaeans, 30
Phoenicians, 28 f.
Pi y Margall, Francisco, 386, 392, 393
Pillars of Hercules, 13, 14, 131, 132, 162
Pisa, Council of, 155; Pisans, 133, 138, 153
Pisuerga, 99, 101
Pius V, 244, 277; IX, 379
Pizarro, Francisco, 259, 260; Gonzalo, 260, 261
Plata, Río de la, River Plate, 262, 363
Pliny, 33
Polybius, 31, 35
Pombal, 336, 337, 341

Pompaelo, Pamplona, 42
Pompey, 42, 43
Ponce de León, Juan, 255; Rodrigo, Marquis of Cádiz, 192
Portugal, Indo-European, 27, 28; Carthage and, 32; Lusitanian, 40 f.; Portus Cale, 41; *v.* Braga, Coimbra, Lisbon; county of, 109, 110; kingdom of, 104, 110, 113; recognized by Rome, 114; growth of, 134, 135; society of, 134, 137; Trastámaras and, 162 f.; Portuguese discoveries, 132, 195, 196; P. and succession of Isabella I, 188; annexed by Philip II, 245, 246; surrender of P. interests in east, 292; P. and Olivares, 297, 299, 300; Restoration, 301, 303, 306, 307; independence recognized, 310; P. and War of Sp. Succession, 321, 322, 323; Barbara of Braganza, 332; P. and Sacramento, 336, 337, 341, 342; 344, 345; Godoy's war in P., 347; Peninsular War, 348 f.; P. Republic, 418
Ponza, battle of, 178
Popular Front, 434, 436
Portela Valladares, M., 433
Portocarrero, Cardinal, 316, 317, 320
Potosí, 233
Pravia, 79
President of Castile, 270, 320
presidi, 285
Prieto, Indalecio, 425, 426, 438, 440
Prim y Prats, Gen. Juan, 376, 383, 385, 386, 388, 389, 392, 396, 405
Primo de Rivera, Gen. Fernando, 387; Gen. Miguel, 420, 421, 422, 423; José Antonio, 430, 442
primogènit, 176, 180, 181, 183
Principality, *v.* Catalonia
Priscillian, Priscillianists, 49, 50, 53
privileges of Aragon, 149, 150, 154
progressists, 373, 374, 375, 376, 377, 381, 384, 385, 387

INDEX 473

pronunciamientos, 260, 310, 396
Protestants, v. Reformation, Luther, Schmalkalde; 220, 225, 226, 227; in Sp., 235
Provence, 129, 150, 217, 222
Puerto Rico, 197, 342, 383, 400
Puig de Cebolla, 130
Pyrenees, 13, 14, 15, 26, 70; treaty of the P., 307

QADI, 74, 149
qa'id, 74
Qairwan, 71
banu Qasi, 77, 78, 82, 93, 94
Quadruple Alliance, 327; 371
Quiñones, Suero de, 171
Quiroga, Antonio, 364
Quito, 261

RAIMUNDO of Burgundy, Count of Galicia, 109, 110
Ramiro I of Leon, 80, 83; II, 92, 94, 95, 97; III, 96, 97; R. Sánchez I of Aragon, 100, 101, 111; II, 'the Monk', 111, 112
Ramón Berenguer II, Count of Barcelona, 122; IV, 112, V, 112, 129
Rastadt, peace of, 323
Ratisbon, treaty of, 314
Reccared, 58, 59
Recceswinth, 60, 61
Recopolis, 58
Reding, Theodore, 354
Reformation, 216, 217, 220, 225
Regency of Urgel, 366, 367, 368
regents, struggles of the, 141, 142
René of Provence, 178, 181
'renovationism', 416
repartimientos, 136; 264
republicanism, republicans, 385, 386, 387, 391, 392, 396, 397, 412, 414, 415, 416, 418, 423 f.

Requesens, Luis de, 240
residencia, 278
Restoration of Bourbons, 395, 396, 404, 415
Revolutionary Committee, 1930, 423, 424
Ribagorza, 81, 98, 99, 100, 111, 249
Richard of Cornwall, 138
Richelieu, 296, 297, 299, 300, 301, 302
Riego, Rafael, 364, 367
Riff Mts., 41, 86, 412, 418
Rijswick, 315
Rioja, 88, 94, 101, 113
Ríos, Fernando de los, 425
Ripoll, 105
Ripperdá, 328, 329
Rocroy, Battle of, 303
Rodezno, Count of, 442, 449
Roderic, 63, 65, 67, 69
Rodrigo, Count of Castile, 83
Rodríguez de Fonseca, Bishop, 264
Roger de Lauria, 151, 152
Romanones, Count, 413, 414, 417, 424
Rome, 31, 32; Roman Sp., 35 f.; Romanization, 37 f.; of Visigoths, 56, 57, 58; Islam and, R., 66; Santiago and, 80; R. and Sp. church, 105, 106; R. and 'empire', 113; papal delegates, 114, 129; use of canonical impediments, 117; intervention in S. France, 129; R. and Aragon, 111, 129, 150, 151, 152; Roman law, v. law, 167, 168; R. and Charles V, 216; Sack of R., 218; Charles V in R., 222; R. and Trent, 226, 227; Paul IV and Sp., 231, 232; Philip II and R., 234, 235, R. and Carlism, 379; *v*. church property, anticlericalism
Romero y Robledo, Francisco, 396
Roncesvalles, 71, 82
Ronda (Málaga), 78, 121, 141, 160, 193

474 INDEX

Ronquillo, Rodrigo, 211
Rooke, Sir George, 321
Roosevelt, F. D., 447
Rosendo, Bishop of Santiago, 97
rotativism, 396, 405, 408, 414, 418, 423
Roussillon, Rosellón, 150, 154, 155, 180, 181, 197, 199, 222, 224, 300, 302; annexed by France, 307, 312, 345
Royalist Volunteers, 367, 370
Rudolph of Hapsburg, 138, 199
Ruiz Zorrilla, Manuel, 390, 391, 397
Rumaikiya, 122, 124
Russia, 342, 417, 436, 438, 440, 445, 446

SACRALIAS, Zallaka (Badajoz), battle of, 108, 123
Sacramento colony, 337, 341
Sáez, Canon Victor, 367
Sa'd, 173
Sagasta, Práxedes M., 386, 390, 395, 397, 399, 400, 401, 402, 404, 405, 407, 408, 411
sagum, 40
Saguntum, 35, 38, 39
Sahagún, 106
Sahara, 15, 19, 20
St. Daniel's Night, 385
St.-Jean Pied-de-Port, 157
St. John, Order of, 111, 112, 114, 115
St. Quentin, 232
Salado, battle of the, 143, 159, 162
Salamanca, v. *Salmantica*, reconquered, 95; University of S., 167, 272, 279; battle of, 359
Salamanca, José, 380, 381
Salduba, Saragossa, 38
Salmantica, Salamanca, 44
Salmerón, Nicolás, 393, 397
Salvaterra, treaty of, 164
Samuel ben Negralla, 121, 122; S. Levi, 144

San Carlos, Duke of, 360
Sancho I of Leon, the Fat, 85, 95, 96, 98; II, of Castile, 103, 105, 107; III, 113; IV, 139, 140; S. Ramírez, I of Aragon, 111, 156; S. I Garcés, of Navarre, 91, 94; II, 88, 97, 98; III, the Great, 98, 99, 100, 101, 103, 104, 105, 111, 113, 156; IV, 'el de Peñalén', 156; S. Infante, son of Alf. VI, 109, 110; S. García, Count of Castile, 98, 99
'Sanchul', 88, 89, 119
Sanhaja, 86, 90, 119, 121, 122
San Juan de la Peña, 105, 106
San Julián de Pereiro, 115
Sanjurjo, Gen., 429, 431, 436, 442
San Luis, Count of, 380
San Martín, Gen. José, 364
San Miguel, Evaristo, 367
San Sebastián, 438; pact of, 423
Santa Coloma, 300, 301
Santa Cruz, A. de Bazán, Marquis of, 244, 246, 252
Santa Fe, 194
Santander, 17, 18
Santarem, treaty of, 163
Santiago de Compostela, cult of St. James, 80; sacked by Almanzor, 88, 98; S. and Rome, 105, 109, 110; cortes of S., 210; 279; S., Order of, 115, 117; Mastership of, 172, 174, 189
Santo Domingo, 196, 330, 345
Saragossa, Zaragoza, council at, 49; Visigoths enter, 54; besieged by Franks, 55; Muslim, 70; Charlemagne and, 71; defies Córdoba, 72; Muslim stronghold, 80; banu Qasi hold, 82; Castilian claim to, 83, 101, 103, 105, 107; Aragonese conquest of, 110, 111, 113, 114; taifa of, 120; capital of Aragon, 134, 148, 149, 185; opposition to Philip II, 247, 249; 322

INDEX

Sardinia, 152, 153, 155, 180, 322, 323, 327
Sauvage, Jean, 208, 209
Savoy, entered by France, 222; 293, 299; 323, 327; house of, 389, 390
Schmalkalde, League of, 220, 226
Schomberg, Marshal, 307, 310
Scipio, P. Cornelius, 35, 37
Sebastian, K. of Portugal, 237, 245, 246
Secunda, Shaqunda, 73
Security Council, 448, 449
Sedan, 389
Segadors, 300
Segovia, aqueduct at, 45; 186, 211, 279, 281
Segura, Cardinal, 426, 443
Selim I, 220; II, 244
Septum, Ceuta, 55
Septimania, 61, 67, 70, 81
Serrano, Gen. Francisco, 379, 385, 386, 387, 388, 389, 390, 391, 394, 395, 396; S. Súñer, Ramón, 443, 445, 446, 447
Sertorius, Q., 42, 45
Servet, Miguel, 234
'service', 116, 186, 208, 209, 215, 277
Seven Holy Men, 47
Seven Years War, 336, 337
Seville, Roman, 44; taken by Vandals, 53; by Byzantines, 55; by Visigoths, 56; by Muslims, 65; 67, 76; attached to Galicia, 103; tribute of, 106, 107; 'Abbadid S., 108, 120, 121, 122; falls to Almoravids, 124, 125; reconquest of, 130, 131; shipping of, 133, 147; resettlement of, 133, 134; court of Castile at, 133, 134, 143; massacre of Jews at, 168; S. and America, 263, 264; S. in Napoleonic Wars, 354; Treaty of S., 329
Sexi, Almuñécar, 30
Sforza, Ludovico, 198, 201; Francesco, 222

Sicily, refugees from, in Aragon, 150; the 'Vespers', 151; Aragonese claim to, 151, 152, 153; 155, 156, 177; crown offered to Charles of Navarre, 179; attached to crown of Aragon, 180; Ferd. V invades, 198; threatened by Turks, 221, 243; loss of S., 323, 327; entered by Charles (III), 330
Sierra Elvira, 170, 192; S. Morena, 19, 24, 26, 27, 31, 67, 339; S. Nevada, 15
Siete Partidas, 138, 142, 144
Silíceo, Cardinal Juan Martínez, 231, 273
Silingians, 51, 52
Silo, 79
Silva, Felipe da, 302
Silvela, Francisco, 406, 408
Silvestre, Gen. 418, 419
Simancas, 85, 88, 93, 95, 97
Singilis, Old Antequera, 46
Sintra, 354
Sisebut, 58, 59, 62
Sisnand, Visigothic K., 59; adviser to Ferd. I and Alf. VI, 107
'Slavs', 72, 87, 90, 119, 120
Sobrarbe, 81, 98, 99, 100, 111
socialism, 398, 407, 408, 412, 415, 422, 425, 426, 432, 436, 438, 440
Sokolli, 244
Solidaridad, 411
Solutréans, 17, 20
somatent, 180
Sorel, Georges, 408
Soria, 27, 28
Soult, Marshal N., 355, 356, 357, 359
Spanish language, 134; 'Sp. March', 70; Sp. Marriages, 378, 379; Sp. Succession, war of, 321 f., 352
Speyer, Diet of, 220
Spínola, 287, 296
Squillace, Marquis of, 336, 338, 340
Stanhope, Earl, 327, 328

Statute, Royal, 370, 377
Strabo, 13, 37, 42, 44
Strasbourg, 314
Subḥ, 86, 87
Suessiones, 27
Suevi, 51, 52, 53, 54, 56, 57
suffetes, 31, 35
Sulaiman, 89, 90; S. II, 220, 221, 223, 243
Supreme Junta, 354, 355, 356, 357, 358
Swinthila, 55, 59
Syrians, 45, 47, 68, 72

TAGUS, 45
Tahart, 86
Tahuantinsuyu, 258
taifas, 32, 101, 104, 107, 114, 119 f., 124, 125, 131
Talavera, Fr. Hernando de, 194
Talleyrand, 350, 352
Tamerlane, 169
Tamim, 122
Tangier, 64, 90, 123, 286, 383, 412, 421, 445, 447
Tanith, 34
Tarascon, treaty of, 152
Ṭarif ibn Mulluk, 64
Tarifa (Cádiz), 19, 64, 122, 139, 140, 141, 142, 159
Tariq ibn Ziyad, 64, 65, 66
Tarraco, Tarragona, 38, 44, 45
Tarraconensis, 44, 48, 52, 53, 55
Tarragona, 38, 44, 45, 72, 118
Tartessians, Tartessos, 16, 26, 27, 28 f., 68
Tavera, Cardinal, 267
Temple, Order of the, 111, 112, 114, 115
Tendilla, Count of, 194
Teresa, Countess of Portugal, 108, 109, 110
Termantia, 39

Tertullian, 48
Teruel, 129, 439, 440
Tetuán, 141, 169, 328, 382, 383, 418, 419
T(h)arshish, 30
Theobald of Navarre, 137, 157
Theodemir, 66
Theodoric, 53
Theodosius, 51, 92
Theudis, 55
tholoi, 23, 42
Thirty Years War, 293, 299, 306
tiraz, 75
Toledo, Visigothic capital, 56; falls to Muslims, 65; 68; defies Córdoba, 72, 73; 'day of the ditch', 73; 77; church of T., 79, 80; T. and reconquest, 83, 91, 103; conquest of, 106, 107; 110, 112, 113; taifa of, 120; annexation of, 119, 123, 124, 135; New Castile, 136, 137; T. in civil wars 1365-7, 146, 147; T. and comuneros, 209, 210, 211, 213; Charles V's capital, 279; Councils of T., 59, 62, 63; rite of T., 105
Toledo, Francisco de, 261; García de T., 201, 244
Topete, Adm. J. B., 387
Tordehumos, treaty of, 117
Tordesillas, 202, 207; treaty of T., 188, 196, 255
Toreno, Count, 373
Toro, 145, 163, 188
Toros de Guisando, 176
Torralba (Soria), 16
Tortosa (Tarragona), 120, 302, 440
Tota, Q. of Navarre, 85, 94, 95, 98
Tovar, Sancho de, 164
traditionalism, 367, 368, 390, 405, 442, 443, 449
Trafalgar, 347
'Tragic Week', 412, 416
Trajan, 45, 46
Trastámaras, 162 f.

INDEX 477

Trebbia, 332
Trent, Council of, 226, 227, 234, 238
Triana, 131
Tribunal of Tumults, 239, 240
tribute, *parias*, Christian to Córdoba, 94 f.; Muslim to Christians, 103, 105, 106, 107, 108, 116; of Granada, 130, 141, 143, 159, 173, 192
Trinidad, 197, 345
Tripoli, 224, 236
Trujillo (Cáceres), 128
Tudela (Navarre), held by banu Qasi, 82; reconquest of, 111; 118; League of T., 174
ibn Tufayl, 125
Tujibids, 84, 94
Tulga, 60
Tungri, 28
Tunis, Tunisia, 64, 132, 151, 221, 245
Turdetani, 31, 33
Turks, 153, 178; T. and the Empire, 220, 221; T. and the Mediterranean, 221, 222; land in Italy, 223; Philip II and T., 236; T. and Granada, 243, 244; sea-war with, 244
Turones, 27
Tuy (Pontevedra), 83
Tyre, 30
Tyrone, Earl of, 288

UCEDA, Duke of, 287, 294, 295
Uclés, battle of, 109, 124
UGT (Unión General de Trabajadores), 416, 425, 449
Ultrapuertos, 157
Umaiyads, 70, 71 f., 75, 84 f.
'Umar ibn Ḥafṣun, 78, 83, 84
Unamuno, Miguel de, 425
Union of Aragon, 151, 154
United provinces, *v.* Netherlands, Dutch, 288, 292, 293, 295, 296, 306
United States of America, 342, 400, 401, 406, 446

Universal suffrage, 397, 398, 404, 408
'Uqba ibn Nafi', 64
Urci (Almería), 16
Urgel, Llanos de, 27, 81; Count of U., 176, 177, 181
Urraca, dau. of Ferd. I, 103, 105, 106; dau. of Alf. VI, 108, 109, 110, 111
Ursins, Mme. des, 320, 325, 326
Utica, 28, 30
Utrecht, peace of, 323, 327, 331

VACA DE CASTRO, 260
Vaccei, 28, 35, 39, 40, 52, 54
Valdivia, Pedro de, 261
Valtelline, 293, 295, 296, 299
Valençay, 359, 360
Valencia, Hermenegild imprisoned at, 57; Ferd. I besieges, 103; Cid and V., 84, 107, 108; 124; rises against Almoravids, 112; assigned to Aragon, 114, 129; 119; taifa of, 120, 126; reconquest of, 126, 130; 'kingdom' of, 135; 149; demands *justicia*, 154; colonial society, 183; Charles V and V., 209; *germania*, 213, 214; moriscos of, 240; Lerma and V., 286, 287, 289; expulsion of moriscos, 289, 290; Olivares and V., 298; V. in Napoleonic Wars, 353, 359; Ferd. VII at, 360; seat of Republican Govt., 438, 440, 441
Valenzuela, Fernando de, 311, 312
validos, 144, 295
Valladolid, 139, 141, 165, 279
Válor, Fernando de, 242
Valtelline, 293, 295, 296, 299
Vandals, 49, 51, 52, 53
Vascones, 71, 78, 81, 82
Vasto, Marquis del, 224
Vaucelles, peace of, 232
Vázquez de Mella, 415, 418
Vega, battle of the, 142, 159

Velasco, 82
Velegienses, 28
Vellido Dolfos, 106
Vélez, Marquis of los, 242, 243, 247; 293, 294, 303
Vendôme, 315, 325
Venezuela, 261, 330, 363
Venice, Catalan alliance with, 153; Ferd. V and, 198, 199, 201; V. and Holy League, 223; 244; 293; conspiracy of V., 293, 294
Vergara, Convention of, 372, 375
Verginius, 393, 394, 400
Vermudo II, of Leon, 88, 97, 98; III, 99, 101
Vernon, Adm., 331
Verona, Congress of, 367
Versailles, treaty of, 1763, 342
Vespucci, Amerigo, 197, 264
Vettones, 40, 42
Viana, Charles, Prince of, 158, 174, 179, 180
Vicálvaro, 380
Vienna, 220, 221; treaty of, 330
Vikings, 97
Villa Real *v.* Ciudad Real
Villacampo, Gen., 395, 396
Villalar, 213
Villena, Enrique de, 171; marquisate of V., 170, 172; Marquis of V., 333
Viriatus, 41
Viseu, 70
Visigoths, 51 f.; fall of V. state, 64 f.
Vitoria (Alava), founded, 57; 359
Vives, Luis, 219
Vizcaya, *v.* Biscay

WAD-RAS, 383
Waldseemuller, 197
Walia, 52
Wall, Richard, 335, 337
Wamba, 61, 62

Wellington, 354, 356, 359
West India Company, Dutch, 296
Westphalia, peace of, 306
Weyler, Gen. 400, 408, 423
William the Conqueror, 109; III, 314, 316; W. III of Prussia, 389; W. of Orange, 238, 239, 240, 252
Winchelsea, 164
Witeric, 58
Witiza, 62, 63, 65, 69
wool, 186, 280, 281, 282

XIMENA, 92, 94
Ximénez de Cisneros, 194, 200, 203, 207, 208, 209, 275

YAHYA IBN ḤAKAM, 76
Yuste, 230
Yusuf ibn Tashfin, 108, 123, 124; Y. I of Granada, 159; III, 160

ZACCARIA, Benedetto, 133
Zafadola, 112
az-Zagal, 192, 193, 194
Zahara, 192
Zallaka, battle of, 108, 123, 124, 126
zalmedina, 149
Zambrano, Marquis of, 369
Zamora, 85, 88, 93, 96, 97, 106, 163, 188
Zanata, 68, 86, 120
Zawi ibn Ziri, 90, 119, 121
Zea Bermúdez, Francisco, 367, 369, 370
Ziryab, 75
Zorrilla, *v.* Ruiz Zorrilla
Zumalacarregui, Gen. Tomás, 371
Zuhayr, 120, 121
Zúñiga, Juan de, 231; Baltasar de Z., 294

For Product Safety Concerns and Information please contact our EU representative GPSR@taylorandfrancis.com
Taylor & Francis Verlag GmbH, Kaufingerstraße 24, 80331 München, Germany

www.ingramcontent.com/pod-product-compliance
Lightning Source LLC
Chambersburg PA
CBHW071432300426
44114CB00013B/1409